THE NATURE AND THEORY OF CRIME

FIRST EDITION

Edited by John M. Stogner
University of North Carolina—Charlotte

Bassim Hamadeh, CEO and Publisher

Michael Simpson, Vice President of Acquisitions

Jamie Giganti, Senior Managing Editor

Jess Busch, Senior Graphic Designer

Amy Stone, Field Acquisitions Editor

Mirasol Enriquez, Senior Project Editor

Luiz Ferreira, Senior Licensing Specialist

Allie Kiekhofer and Claire Yee, Interior Designers

www.cognella.com   800-200-3908

CONTENTS

1 | Introduction to the Nature and Theory of Crime   1
JOHN M. STOGNER

2 | Deterrence and Delinquency   11
JOHN P. HOFFMAN

3 | The Rational Choice Perspective   25
DEREK B. CORNISH AND RONALD V. CLARKE

4 | Routine Activity Theory   49
LAWRENCE E. COHEN AND MARCUS FELSON

5 | Situational Crime Prevention   63
RONALD V. CLARKE

6 | Biological Positivism   81
ROGER HOPKINS BURKE

7 | The Future of Biosocial Criminology: Beyond Scholars' Professional Ideology   97
JOHN PAUL WRIGHT AND FRANCIS T. CULLEN

8 | A Theory of Differential Association   115
EDWIN H. SUTHERLAND AND DONALD R. CRESSEY

9 | Nothing Is as Practical as a Good Theory   121
RONALD L. AKERS

10 | Hirschi's Social Bond Theory   141
NOEL S. BOST

11 | Self-Control Theory   153
TRAVIS HIRSCHI AND MICHAEL R. GOTTFREDSON

12 | Durkheim, Anomie and Strain   169
TIM NEWBURN

13 | Labelling Theories   189
ROGER HOPKINS BURKE

14 | Crime, Shame, and Reintegration   203
JOHN BRAITHWAITE

15 | The Influence of Neighborhoods on Crime   213
ZACHARY R. HAYES

16 | Decent and Street Families   225
ELIJAH ANDERSON

17 | Adolescence and Crime: Continuity and Change   239
MICHAEL L. BENSON

18 | Feminist Perspectives in Criminology   267
CLAIRE M. RENZETTI

19 | Radical and Critical Criminology   279
TIM NEWBURN

CHAPTER ONE

Introduction to the Nature and Theory of Crime

JOHN M. STOGNER, PHD

Welcome to the first edition of *The Nature and Theory of Crime*! Whether your course is titled "Criminology," "Criminal Behavior," "Foundations of Criminology," "Criminological Theory," or "The Nature and Theory of Crime," you will likely find this text an excellent resource as you explore one of the most fascinating areas within the field of criminology and criminal justice. Many students find this course to be among their favorites, and many faculty members, myself included, enjoy teaching and discussing this material more than any other topic. That is not to say that learning, understanding, and evaluating criminological theories is an easy process. You will be challenged as the course forces you think in abstract terms, focus on population variation as opposed to individual cases, and consider practical ways to implement idealized policy recommendations. You will be exposed to new terminology, the importance of careful empirical evaluation, and alternate ways of thinking about deviant behavior. The journey will be worth the work. At the end of the course, you should find that you have a better understanding of the world and the work that you will be doing in a few short years. That being said, don't be surprised if at the end of the course you have as many questions as answers. Criminological theories have by no means reached the end of their evolution. Hopefully, you will not only be asking the right questions, but also help to answer them, as you begin your career in criminology and criminal justice.

What Is Criminological Theory?

In our field, *theory* is a broad term. It encompasses several aspects of social life, regulation development, deviant behavior, and law enforcement. At one point, the field grouped all of these topics under the umbrella of criminology. Sutherland and his contemporaries would have included each of these topics into the same course and discussion 75 years ago. However, today we typically choose to separate the study of law breaking from the study of lawmaking and law enforcement. *Criminology*, or *criminological theory*, focuses on the understanding and explanation of deviant behavior. Put another way, it focuses on violations of normative behaviors and the law. It is not the study of why certain laws are in place. That important topic is more appropriately labeled *theory of law*. Similarly, the understanding of why the police enforce only certain laws (or do so inconsistently), why the courts function as they do, and why penalties are enforced all fall under the label of *criminal justice theory*.

It is imperative moving forward to have a solid understanding of what constitutes a theory. *Theory* can be defined as an interconnected set of propositions about the relationships between constructs. A theory should also specify under which circumstances those propositions apply. Theory can be envisioned as a logical way of understanding one outcome or a set of outcomes (in this case, deviant behavior or crime). Theories typically discuss antecedents of a certain behavior and the way in which they promote, facilitate, or allow that behavior. They are a series of arguments, founded in past research, that connect what are perceived to be cause and effect. Theories may be thought of as generalizations about how certain events or conditions are typically connected. In the end, criminological theories are generalized explanations of crime and deviance.

The goal of criminological theory is not the explanation of individual cases. The theories described in the following pages should not be utilized in an attempt to trace the processes that led John Wayne Gacy to kill a number of young men in the 1970s or why John Allen Muhammad became the "DC Sniper" in 2002. Whatever explanations are developed for these tragic behaviors are idiographic. *Idiographic explanations* are those that seek to understand what specific events led to another specific event. They explain individual occurrences. This individually focused and autobiographical approach is more suited for courses on profiling offenders. Criminological theories, in contrast, are nomothetic. *Nomothetic explanations* are those that explain patterns within a population. They describe how variation in one phenomenon leads to variation in another. Put another way, nomothetic explanations in criminology detail how certain traits, events, or experiences are generally, but not always, associated with deviant behavior.

Thus, the main goal of criminological theory is to explain *variation* in a behavior within a population. Theories attempt to explain what has generally led people to behave differently from one another. When evaluating a theory, academics often refer to explained variation. As a statistical term, *explained variance* refers to the proportion of dispersion that is accounted for in a mathematical model. A high explained variance (i.e., closer to one) indicates that the model is successful in explaining/predicting the outcome (crime in this case), whereas scores closer to zero indicate the opposite. *Explained variation* is the wording typically used to represent this concept when not specifically discussing a single mathematical model (although some use the terms interchangeably). It is the goal of criminologists to maximize the explained variation of their theory, but it is unreasonable to expect that any social theory will explain all of the variation of a behavior. Criminologists strive to understand as much as possible about what makes us different from one another, but, given the complexities of social life, a perfect theory that explains all of a population's behaviors is out of reach. It is better for us to think about the explained variation of a theory relative to that of other theories. The question should not be whether a theory explains all of the variation in a behavior, but whether it explains more variation than another theory or a previous iteration of that same theory.

A second goal of criminological theory is to predict rates and variation in future occurrences. Criminologists typically strive to understand variation in the recent past, but do so largely in an effort to prepare better predictions of both future individual-level variation in an outcome and population-level changes in the rates of that behavior. These goals can alternatively be thought of as the quests to understand which traits or experiences make certain behaviors more likely in the future and to predict how the population as a whole will change over time. A well-designed criminological theory should be able to anticipate changes in community and national crime rates.

Another goal of criminological theory is to summarize the current knowledge base related to deviant behavior and crime. Each year, hundreds of books are published on the topic of criminology and thousands of articles are published in scientific journals. Even the most gifted criminologist cannot read and retain that amount of information. Theories help to draw large clusters of those works into a manageable form. They utilize the relevant information to develop a viewpoint that is based on the majority of the related studies. They take the details (individual academic articles) and use that to paint the big picture (a theory). Of course, there are countless ways to combine these individual studies, just as there are countless ways that the same basic colors can be applied to a canvas. Throughout the course, you will use a series of criteria (discussed in the next section) to determine which theories are the "masterpieces" and which are more suited for hanging on a refrigerator.

The final, and perhaps most important, goal of criminological theory is to inform policy. Even the most empirically supported theory is rendered useless if its tenets fail to reach the individuals that design and reform policy. Criminological theorists have the goal of understanding behavior, but they are also motivated to better understand what may be done to change it. Many students initially have a negative perception of theory because they view it as distinct and unrelated to their planned futures. They fail to see its utility. However, it is imperative to avoid this type of kneejerk reaction. As a later reading will claim, "nothing is as practical as a good theory." Some theoretical perspectives and condensed summaries of a theory may not explicitly lay out the practical applications of that theory, but rest assured that each is related to practice in some way. They may only be briefly mentioned, as the theorists choose to focus on refining a theory before calling for policy changes, but each certainly suggests changes that should be made within our society. As a practitioner, you should always consider policy and program changes in the light of established theory. Those that are based on unsubstantiated or unsupported theories should be avoided, whereas those connected to leading theoretical perspectives merit attention.

Before moving forward, it is critical to ensure that you avoid a common assumption held among those new to criminology: (with the exception of some outdated theories long discarded by the field) *criminological theories are not deterministic*. Each theory describes constructs, traits, or events linked to deviant behavior or crime, but none posit that these connections are absolute. They do not argue that every individual that possesses certain risk factors will commit numerous criminal acts, only that deviance is more common among those that possess them. Criminology accepts that individuals have free will. Even those whose life circumstances most promote delinquency may choose not to engage in a life of crime. However, it is readily apparent that our ability to make choices is limited by social setting and that traits and conditions influence our decisions.

Criminologists take a view that is labeled soft determinism (sometimes *indeterminism* or *bounded free will*). *Soft determinism* is the view that behaviors are neither the deterministic result of social setting nor the expression of unadulterated free will. Individuals are assumed to make choices, but those choices are constrained and influenced by a number of factors. Our theories can have empirical success in that they can identify factors generally linked to deviance, but only explain a portion of variation due to individuals having free will. For this reason, speaking in absolute terms is inappropriate in the study of criminological theory. Criminologists do not argue that individuals with certain traits or exposed to certain environments will engage in delinquency. Instead, they discuss risk factors that are associated with a greater likelihood of delinquency and protective factors associated with a lesser likelihood of deviance. The use of "more likely" and "less likely" is appropriate when discussing theoretical concepts related to deviance.

What Makes a Good Theory?

As part of this course, you will be tasked with evaluating the theories that are presented within the text and in lectures. It is not enough to be able to recite the theoretical propositions of a work—you must be able to critically evaluate each theory. This not only helps you better understand the theories included in this work, but it also exposes you to some of the greater challenges within criminology and prepares you for assessing theoretical advances in the field after you graduate. The following characteristics should not be thought of as a score sheet where a theory simply needs to meet the majority of benchmarks. A theory that fulfills all but one criterion still may be a weak contribution to the field. A truly satisfactory and useful theory meets each of these criteria.

First, a good theory must be parsimonious. Outside of academia, parsimony serves as a synonym of frugality. However, in this context *parsimony* means simple, condensed, refined, and as straightforward as possible. Scientists often speak of approaches that maximize parsimony. They mean that it is preferable to choose the simplest option that adequately reaches the goal. Any theory can be improved by incorporating countless caveats, assumptions, and minor propositions, but doing so may weaken its practical utility. After all, if the goal is to influence policy, a theory must be accessible to those designing and voting on policy. Theories can be complex; however, they must be as direct and straightforward as possible to be considered parsimonious. Explanations of tenets, advice on measurement, and refined issues may be discussed in intricate detail, but the core propositions of a theory should be brief, clear, and accessible. It may help you to think of parsimony this way: can you explain the key issues within the theory to your grandmother or some other relative who does not work in the criminal justice field in a half hour? If you cannot, the theory may not be adequately parsimonious.

Second, a theory must be *abstract* and be able to be described in abstract form. As mentioned earlier, criminological theories are nomothetic. They focus on connecting variation between constructs more generally in the population and are not tied to individual cases. A strong theory has to be able to be discussed in this way. Theories should not be based on a handful of individual cases; the use of stories and individual profiles in criminology should be limited or nonexistent. It is often more challenging to think about concepts and traits than individuals, but there is utility in divorcing thought from case studies. Doing so provides a better understanding of our outcomes of interest and reinforces that criminological theories utilize soft determinism.

A strong theory must also have *breadth*. Theories specific to one crime may have utility for that behavior, but, by definition, they are specific only to one crime. Similarly, theories that only explain variation in a portion of the population (e.g., teenage Hispanic males) can only be used to inform policies that affect that demographic. Therefore, criminologists strive to develop theories that are effective in explaining variation in multiple types of offenses for large portions of the population. They speak of "general" theories that can be extended to all crime types in all populations. Rather than focusing on specific behaviors, criminologists develop theories to explain the propensity to violate regulations, laws, and social norms. References to crime, delinquency, and/or deviance more generally do not necessarily refer to specific banned acts, but to violations of the codes in the area in which those people live. After all, some behaviors are legal in portions of the world and banned in others. There is even variation within the same country (you may have noted that policies related to marijuana are very different in Colorado as compared to the Carolinas). Thus, most theories are developed to explain the propensity to violate rules and regulations in general and not specific crime types. However, this is not to say that a developed theory will explain all forms of deviance equally well. Several of the theories covered in this text offer more to our understanding of one illicit behavior (e.g., violence) than others (e.g., drug use).

Fourth, a good theory is one that is *logically sound*. To be considered logically sound, a theory must be developed in a rational manner and each proposition tied to the others. The arguments contained within must connect with one another in a consistent manner. This trait may seem to be an obvious need for a theory—and one that is expected to the point that this trait could be omitted from the list. However, it is critical to acknowledge that skilled authors may distract readers from key flaws in their reasoning or portions of their theory that are not supported by data by discussing in greater detail those portions that are substantiated. Keep in mind that we often make mental connections that should not be made. For example, after reading a criminological work that theoretically establishes that Condition A leads to Condition B and that Condition C leads to Condition D, a reader may infer that variation in Condition A should explain variation in Condition D. This is inaccurate because no connection between Condition B and Condition C was ever established. Although this is easy to spot when only a handful of undefined terms are used, it may be challenging to spot logical errors within lengthy theoretical arguments. To be logically sound, a theoretical work has to use proper logic and be *internally consistent* and *nontautological*. Internally consistent simply means that no portion of the work should contradict another portion of the work. A *tautology* is an argument that uses circular reasoning. Therefore, a theory is nontautological if it does not use circular logic. Once again, this may seem simple to avoid, but you will find hidden tautologies in several major works that will be discussed in the course. You should also apply the criteria of being logically sound to theorists' critiques of other theories. These criticisms are often wrought with inconsistencies, false assumptions, and errors in reasoning. One common form this takes is the *straw man argument* in which an author describes a simplified or weaker version of a theory and critiques that rather than attacking the full version of the theory. You have likely seen this flawed form of argument used (often successfully) in American political debates.

Next, the components of a good criminological theory should be *quantifiable*. A trait, event, or construct is quantifiable if it can be measured with an adequate degree of accuracy. Measurement is one of the most challenging aspects of the social sciences. The topics of interest in our field are much more difficult to consistently measure than those in the traditional sciences. There are very few instances where we can simply use a scale, thermometer, or laboratory test. Instead, social observations and self-reports have to be used to measure concepts such as state anger, internalization of the street code, and expectations of differential reinforcement. Fortunately, psychology and other fields often offer insight into how to best measure certain factors. However, there is often disagreement as to how a factor should be measured. Often different techniques will provide distinct results. Whereas two calibrated scales will give near identical weights for an object, two distinct social science measures of the same concept may not match consistently. Most theoretical constructs in criminology are quantifiable, but how accurately they are measured is another question. Those with unquantifiable factors (e.g., repressed memories) should be discarded and care taken to measure concepts as accurately as possible otherwise.

Sixth, a good theory is *falsifiable*. This means that there is potential for a well-designed and reasonable study to provide evidence that the propositions of the theory are not accurate. It must be possible to disprove a theory. Whether using experimental designs, social observations, or self-report data, there should be the potential for two outcomes: results consistent with the theory and results inconsistent with the theory. That is, empirical research must have the potential to yield negative results and not only positive and neutral results. Some theories may be set up in a way that a significant empirical test would support the theory while a nonsignificant result could be interpreted as failure to find support rather than an indication of lack of support. This type of theory and test should be avoided.

Seventh, a good theory should be *empirically supported*. This means that the components of the theory are quantifiable, the theory is falsifiable, *and* research studies indicate that the propositions within the theory are consistent with available data. Not only is the theory testable, but it has been tested and those tests suggest that it does explain some of the variation in crime and delinquency. As noted earlier, it is unreasonable to expect a theory to explain all of the variation in an outcome. At a minimum, the theory should be explaining a significant amount of variation; however, the empirical validity of a theory is often not compared to this low standard but viewed in relative comparison to other criminological theories. Rather than examining whether a theory helps to explain deviant behavior, we often consider whether a theory helps explain deviant behavior better than alternative theories. This may be unclear for some time after initial publication of a theory as measures must be refined and the scientific method stresses replication—multiple studies are required to indicate support for theoretical propositions.

Finally, a theory must have sound *policy applications*. A theory should have utility outside of the ivory tower of academia. It must do more than explain—it must offer insight as to how we should reform policy to better avoid the negative impact of crime. A theory's policy implications should also be ethical, feasible, and practical. It must offer advice on how to improve social conditions and reduce crime in a way that is consistent with the U.S. Constitution and notions of personal freedoms. Some historic theories extoled and implied recommendations for policy reform inconsistent with the rights of individuals. Modern theories avoid major ethical concerns by focusing on applications that are designed for at-risk individuals rather than punitive towards certain groups. Feasibility and practicality are also challenging given that the programs most likely to be effective are often those most likely to be costly. Most programs in existence today, whether targeting those at-risk, the population as a whole, or former offenders, have some tie to theory. This may not be directly stated, but a link is present—the bigger issue is that many policies are based on theories that fail to receive adequate empirical support. It is unreasonable to expect policy to work when it is based on an inaccurate theoretical perspective. You should keep in mind that failure of a program is not necessarily an indication that the theory is inaccurate. The implementation of the program may have been problematic or the intervention failed to affect the concepts on which the theory focuses.

Therefore, policy assessment involves much more than measuring recidivism and crime rates; it must include measurement of the theoretical concepts it was intended to affect.

To summarize, the best theories and those we should use as a basis for future criminological theorization and policy reform are those that (1) are parsimonious, (2) are abstract, (3) have breadth, (4) are logically sound, (5) are quantifiable, (6) are falsifiable, (7) are empirically supported, and (8) have ethical and feasible policy applications. As you read each section and later review your notes from class, you should use these criteria to assess each theory. Look below the surface—a theory may have hidden issues. It may be described in a way that is logically sound, but quantified in a way that is tautological. It may appear falsifiable on the surface, but the use of vague terminology may prevent it from being disproved. It may only have utility for one crime or one population. Examining these criteria will also help you remember a theory and think about how it might be improved.

Facts a Criminological Theory Ought to Fit

Another way of assessing a criminological theory is to determine whether it "fits" with what we do know about crime and delinquency. Much is still debated in the field of criminology; in fact, there is more about which criminologists disagree than agree. However, there are some "facts" that are generally agreed upon. If a criminological theory is to be accurate it should be consistent with these issues. This is not to say that each concept has to be explicitly included in theories or that any of them must be considered causal. A theory should simply match or fit with these pieces of established knowledge. That means that crime may either be affected by, affect, or be spuriously correlated with the issues presented within the list. A theory that proposes no association between crime and these issues (e.g., contends that marital status is unrelated to crime) or a relationship in the opposite direction (e.g., proposes a theory that would suggest females engage in crime more often than males) should be avoided. John Braithwaite first presented a list of 13 "facts" in his 1989 book *Crime, Shame, and Reintegration* (you will read a portion of this work in Chapter 14). The last two have been added to update Braithwaite's list:

1. Crime is committed disproportionally by males.
2. Crime follows an age–crime curve; 15 to 25 year olds are overly responsible for crime.
3. Crime is committed disproportionally by unmarried people.
4. Crime is committed disproportionally by people in urban areas.
5. Crime is committed disproportionally in areas with high residential mobility.
6. Adolescents attached to their school commit fewer crimes.
7. Adolescents with high educational and occupational aspirations commit fewer crimes.
8. Adolescents who do poorly in school commit more crimes.
9. Adolescents attached to their parents commit fewer crimes.
10. Adolescents who associate with deviant peers commit more crimes.
11. Those who strongly believe in following the law commit fewer crimes.
12. Crime is committed disproportionally by those at the bottom of the socioeconomic class structure.
13. Crime rates (at the time of his book, with the exception of Japan) have increased since World War II.
14. Crime rates, and specifically violent crime rates, began to fall in the mid-1990s.
15. Antisocial behavior is associated with biological risk factors in certain environments.

Macro- and Micro-Level Theories

Criminological theories typically explore the sources of individual variation or the sources of variation between groups. The former type focuses on determining what factors influence individuals within a population to behave differently from one another. Theories that fit this description focus on individual traits and experiences. These theories are considered *micro-level theories*. Conversely, *macro-level theories* of crime offer insight into why different groups commit crime at a different rate (or different crimes) than other groups. Macro-level theories may explore what features of American society have led it to have higher crime rates than other developed countries or why certain groups offend more frequently than others. These theories focus on community, structural, and cultural factors that are hypothesized to influence the crime rate within that population. Do note that the distinction between micro and macro is not absolute. A theory can cross levels and explain differences both between cultures and between individuals. Theories that do this, such as social structure–social learning, may be referred to as *macro/micro-level theories*. Some theorists use the term *meso-level theories* when referring to group-level theories that are at a more intermediate level. They use this term to characterize theories that may offer assistance in explaining variations in crime rates at any level between individual (micro) and cultural (macro). For example, neighborhood- and community-level explanations of crime may be considered meso level.

The level of analysis of a theory is critically important for theory evaluations. Although each level focuses on the same basic outcomes, crime and delinquency, the way in which these outcomes should be measured is tied to the level of the theory. Evaluations of theories focused at individual variation must use individual-level data. To assess an individual-level theory (self-control theory or social learning, for example), a researcher must collect data on individuals' offending histories, personal traits, and experiences. They may use self-report data, official data (arrest reports), or observational data, but the offenses committed by individuals must be known. In contrast, macro- and meso-level theories (such as institutional anomie theory) are focused on national- and community-level variation, and as such should utilize overall crime rates at those levels. Often researchers will collect data from individuals and aggregate it to create a community-level rate of offending, but the outcome is still community-level rates of crime. This must be done to ensure that the evaluation of a theory is consistent with the assumptions and propositions of that theory.

Most social scientists accept that individuals who behave one way in a certain situation may not behave the same way in a vastly different environment. Put another way, the behavior of a group/community is different from the sum of the way individuals would have acted in isolation. Our focus, crime, may not be an aberrant behavior so much as a somewhat normal reaction of individuals in an abnormal situation. Therefore, we should not make inferences about an individual based on theory and research describing the group he or she falls within. Academics describe the *ecological fallacy* as the false assumption that inferences about an individual can be made based on group-level data. In truth, if we only study group-level processes, we only know information at the group level. For example, community-level studies indicate that crime is higher in areas where people move often, but this information cannot be extended to claim that an individual within that type of community is more likely to be deviant. A related error is tied to the *reductionist fallacy* whereby an individual draws conclusions about group-level processes solely from information about individuals that comprise those groups.

Thinking about Theories

As you begin to read this text and explore criminological works elsewhere, you may begin to feel overwhelmed by the sheer number of theories, many of which have distinct variants and have changed over time. You may find it easiest to first think of theories in terms of their general perspective. A criminological *perspective* can be considered a "school of thought" or a cluster of distinct theories that have a similar basis and begin with a similar set of assumptions about the social world and individual behavior. Thinking about the broader perspective first and then the details that separate each theory from one another will help you understand where the theory fits within the broader field and will reduce the amount of rote memorization. When considering the control perspective, recognize that each of those works argues that their focus is on what prevents individuals from engaging in delinquency rather than what encourages it. When considering any theory within the learning perspective, realize that they do not view crime as innate, but rather learned.

This text first introduces you to the classical perspective (or classical school) that stresses that crime is related to rational hedonistic decision-making processes. This perspective was the first to provide a testable theory of crime and replaced what may be labeled the demonic perspective. That perspective, which attributed harmful behavior to the influence of the devil and other evil forces, has not been seriously considered for well over 200 years, and is therefore excluded from this volume. The text then introduces the biological/biosocial perspective, which attributes behavior solely to biological variation (outdated biological theories) or biological variation interacting with the environment (modern biosocial criminology). Theoretical readings with the learning perspective section will then argue that crime is learned through interactions with others. The control perspective follows, and the included theories offer insight as to why the majority of us do not engage in severe forms of delinquency. The anomie/strain perspective section discusses the pressures and stressors that influence crime. Then, the labeling perspective readings consider how the way in which society classifies individuals influences their behavior. The work concludes by exploring neighborhood/community influences, the feminist perspective, the radical/critical perspective, and epidemiological criminology.

As you read each work within this text consider whether the theoretical propositions are well argued and supported by logic and common sense. Keep in mind, however, that this is only the first step in evaluating a theory. Look for issues with breadth, consider whether portions of the theory may be tautological, and gauge the ways in which the theoretical constructs are measured. Ask not only whether a theory makes sense, but also whether it is supported by the data. Consistently refer to this chapter so that you consider how each theory may meet or fall short of fulfilling each of the aforementioned criteria. Never consider a theory to be a finished product—use your evaluation to think about how it is likely to evolve in the future. Better yet, think creatively and consider how each theory could be improved.

DISCUSSION QUESTIONS

By John M. Stogner

1. Note the distinction between nomothetic and idiographic explanations of behavior as well as the broader goals of criminological theories. Given that information, is it appropriate to use case studies when presenting, critiquing, and empirically evaluating a criminological theory?

2. The chapter describes one goal of criminological theories being to maximize the explained variation in deviant behaviors within a particular population. Without reading ahead, consider what percentage of the differences between members of a population that a theory should explain before it is considered reputable enough to base policy changes upon.

3. If a theory is able to account for the majority of the variation in a behavior (say 60%), should constructs from that theory be considered as legitimate legal excuses in criminal trials? Should they be considered mitigating factors that reduce culpability? Why or why not?

4. The chapter presents a number of characteristics of a good theory. Which of these characteristics is most important? Should any additional characteristics be added?

5. Which do you believe has more utility for the criminal justice system: a strong macro-level theory or a strong micro-level theory? Justify your answer.

CHAPTER TWO

Deterrence and Delinquency

JOHN P. HOFFMAN

STUDENT INTRODUCTION
By John M. Stogner

Our study of criminological theories starts with the first fully developed and testable theory of crime and delinquency. Cesare Beccaria, an Italian philosopher, jurist, economist, and criminologist, provided the theoretical framework for what is now referred to as *deterrence theory* in his highly influential 1764 work *On Crimes and Punishments*. Beccaria can therefore be considered both the founder of the classical school and criminological theory more generally; however, it seems that his overarching goal was systematic reform rather than the establishment of a new field of study. Beccaria challenged the use of torture and the death penalty, called for procedural reforms, and offered guidance for a more effective criminal justice system. In doing so, he provided several rational and testable hypotheses about crime.

Beccaria's works and discussions often stressed free will and rationality, so it is not unsurprising that these concepts found their way into his criminological arguments. He contended that people are not under the control of supernatural forces but instead make their own decisions—decisions driven by the desire to maximize pleasure and to minimize discomfort. He argued that people act in their own self-interest and are willing to harm others if doing so is likely to improve their own lives. He reasoned that criminal behavior is deterred if the punishment for committing such an act is considered more painful than the pleasures gained from it. As you will note in Hoffman's writing, Beccaria stressed that a punishment for an offense must be appropriately *severe*, *swift*, and *certain* to be an effective deterrent. His arguments assume that individuals perform rational calculations when considering a crime and avoid that crime if punishment is severe, swift, and certain. Beccaria further stresses that the law and the punishment for violating it must be well-known for policies to have any deterrent effect.

Beccaria's work has been quite influential. It could even be said that Beccaria was a greater influence on the development of the U.S. criminal justice system than the country's own founding fathers. They championed his ideas and drew from his work when designing the American system of law and punishment. As you read, you will likely feel familiarity with Beccaria's ideology and suggestions. This perspective may also be partially attributed to Jeremy Bentham, an Englishman who authored *A Fragment on Government* in 1776, and has been advanced by countless theorists in the last 250 years. As you read, make sure to take note of the characteristics of punishment hypothesized to be most effective, the distinction between general and specific deterrence, and the frequent ineffectiveness of deterrence-based policies.

DETERRENCE AND DELINQUENCY
By John P. Hoffman

This chapter is concerned with one of the oldest theories of crime and delinquency: deterrence theory. A key assumption of this theory is that people, both young and old, make decisions about how to behave based on a rational calculation of its risks and rewards. This may sound simple, but deterrence involves a much more complex set of circumstances than one might think. Consider two U.S. Supreme Court decisions regarding the death penalty for those who commit capital crimes as juveniles—*Stanford v. Kentucky* (1989) and *Roper v. Simmons* (2005). The facts in *Stanford* and *Roper* are quite similar. An[1] adolescent committed a murder, showed little or no remorse, there were aggravating circumstances (such as robbery, sexual assault, or kidnapping), and the trial court sentenced the convicted adolescent to death.

Prior to *Roper* the leading death penalty case for juveniles was the *Stanford* case, decided just 16 years earlier. The court in *Stanford* held that the execution of an offender convicted of a capital crime, who was either 16 or 17 at the time of the offense, is allowed by the U.S. Constitution. Although *Stanford* was a controversial decision, it was the law of the land long enough for 19 juvenile offenders to be convicted and executed for capital crimes (Amnesty International USA, 2005).

One of the arguments raised by the defense in the *Stanford* case was that the death penalty for juveniles "fails to serve the legitimate goal of penology...it fails to deter because juveniles, possessing less developed cognitive skills than adults, are less likely to fear death." The Supreme Court rejected this argument, claiming "as the socio-scientific data suggests...it is not demonstrable that no 16-year-old is adequately responsible or significantly deterred. It is rational, even if mistaken, to think the contrary." Therefore, the Supreme Court in 1989 suggested that if the threat of death deterred even one 16-year-old from committing a capital offense, then a legitimate societal goal is achieved.

In the *Roper* case the U.S. Supreme Court, by a vote of five to four, broke with precedent and determined that the execution of juvenile offenders who committed capital crimes was unconstitutional. A particularly important part of its decision stated:

> [a]s for deterrence, *it is unclear* whether the death penalty has a significant or even measurable deterrent effect on juveniles...[T]he absence of evidence of a deterrent effect is of special concern because the same characteristics that render juveniles less culpable than adults suggest as well that juveniles will be less susceptible to deterrence. In particular,... "[t]he likelihood that the teenage offender has made the kind of cost—benefit analysis that attaches any weight to the possibility of execution is so remote as to be virtually nonexistent." To the extent the juvenile death penalty might have a residual deterrent effect, it is worth noting that the punishment of life imprisonment without the possibility of parole is itself a severe sanction, in particular for a young person (*Roper v. Simmons*, 2005, pp.17–18).

The reasoning of the Supreme Court in the *Roper* case was different from in the *Stanford* decision on the issue of deterrence and how it might affect adolescent decision-making. So which strategy is correct? Can juveniles be deterred from crime or, because of their status as juveniles, is deterrence largely ineffective?

The U.S. legal system relies mainly on the idea that people are rational decision makers. If people are to obey the law, then there must be punishments that outweigh the rewards for breaking the law. This type of thinking also lies at the heart of contemporary theories of rational choice and deterrence, although we shall learn that there are other aspects as well. However, what is meant by deterrence, and what is deterrence theory? Furthermore, how could the *Stanford* court readily accept the role of deterrence in juvenile capital cases, whereas the *Roper* court clearly doubted that deterrence is effective for juveniles who commit murder?

To address these questions, as well as related theoretical issues, this chapter outlines the basic arguments of deterrence theory. We begin with a discussion of the origins of deterrence theory. We then discuss some of the major complexities of deterrence theory, especially how punishment—a core component of the theory—is presumably most effective when it is swift, certain, and severe. We also describe the various forms of deterrence that are thought to affect decision-making among juvenile offenders. A key part of this chapter involves assessing the research on the effectiveness of deterrence: Does it prevent or minimize delinquent behavior? We conclude by evaluating the promises, problems, and policy implications of deterrence theory.

The Evolution of Ideas About Deterrence and Delinquency

The starting point for an introduction to deterrence theory is a short book published in 1764 by the Italian philosopher Cesare Beccaria entitled *On Crimes and Punishment*. His work helped lay the groundwork for deterrence theory as a crime control strategy. At the time of its publication the system of justice was quite different from today. Importantly, there was not a separate juvenile justice system, nor was there a distinct notion of juvenile delinquency that was separate from the concept of a *criminal*. Therefore, Beccaria's work applied to the criminal offender in general, with little regard for the age of the offender.

Over time, as the concept of a separate period of life known as adolescence was recognized, a distinction between juvenile and adult offenders emerged. Moreover, during the late nineteenth century, one of the first formally defined juvenile courts appeared in Chicago. From this Chicago court, the idea of a juvenile justice system, separate and distinct from the adult criminal justice system, spread across the country and today remains an integral part of the justice system in the United States. Since the inception of the juvenile court there remains an unresolved debate over deterrence as a crime control strategy for delinquent behavior, however. Even though deterrence theory continues to be the basis for much of the adult criminal justice system, those who organize and study the juvenile system have remained skeptical about its place in evaluating juvenile offenders. In fact, much of the historical emphasis in the juvenile justice arena has been on treatment and rehabilitation rather than on deterrence through punishment.

The Foundations of Deterrence Theory

The Rational Person

Beccaria saw as the heart of deterrence theory the assumption of a "rational person" who makes choices and reaches decisions based upon a calculation of risk and reward, punishment and pleasure. It is the game that gamblers play on a regular basis: How much risk is involved? How much is the potential reward? If the rewards outweigh the risks, then the person is likely to choose to behave in a certain way. A more general area of research that addresses these issues involves *rational choice theory* (Matsueda et al., 2006).[2]

Clearly, deterrence theory is strongly grounded in choice, and the choice is considered rational and reasonable to the decision maker based upon all available information at the time, or what some economists call the *information set*. The fundamental premise of deterrence theory is that we all choose; that the choices are rational based upon our interpretation of pleasure and pain generated by the situation we are confronted with and the information available to us; and that the decisions are ours to make. Consistent with accepted principles of the criminal and juvenile law, because actors have decided to commit acts they are blameworthy or culpable and deserve punishment.

However, theorists have also noted that the way people judge the costs and benefits of their behaviors is affected by their past experiences and the experiences of others. Suppose that a young person has been caught in the past for trying to shoplift. This may change her calculation of future chances of getting caught shoplifting. Now, suppose she has successfully shoplifted 10 times in the past week. This may create a sense that there is little risk to shoplifting. Similarly, if her two best friends have shoplifted without getting caught, then they may encourage her that the risks are low and the rewards are high. In general, this means that one's judgment of the rewards and risks of delinquent behavior can change over time and is affected by experiences and by one's peers (Matsueda et al., 2006).

Deterrence and Punishment

According to deterrence theory the way to prevent future delinquent acts is to adjust the risk (pain) of the act so it outweighs its rewards (pleasure). Generally, deterrence theory has focused on punishment as a way to adjust risk. As the risk of punishment increases to surpass the reward of committing the act, a rational individual will choose not to violate the law. It is through this mechanism of deterrence that delinquency is prevented. In brief, a person is deterred from committing the offense because the risks ("I'll get caught and punished") outweigh the rewards ("I'll get money"; "I'll get back at an enemy").

However, what is meant by the term *punishment*? According to the philosopher Hugo Bedau:

> Punishment under law is *the authorized imposition of deprivations—of freedom or privacy or other goods to which the person otherwise has a right, or the imposition of special burdens—because the person has been found guilty of some criminal violation, typically (though not invariably) involving harm to the innocent* (Bedau, 2003, italics in original).

Observe the careful use of the terms *deprivations* and *special burdens* rather than *pain*. In addition, punishment must be for a violation of rules, it must be directed at a specific offender or offenders, it must be intentionally administered by someone other than the offender, and it must be unwanted on the part of the offender (Newman, 1985). However, for punishment to occur, not only should it satisfy these criteria, but also, according to Beccaria and other scholars, it must have three qualities to be effective as a deterrent: swiftness, certainty, and severity.

Swiftness (celerity)

Swiftness, or celerity, of punishment involves how closely the punishment follows the offense, with more immediate punishments thought to have a greater deterrent effect. Beccaria (1985 [1764], p.55) argued for the promptness of punishment: "The more promptly and the more closely punishment follows upon the commission of a crime the more just and useful it will be." He also contended:

> I have said the promptness of punishment is more useful because when the length of time that passes between the punishment and the misdeed is less, so much the stronger and more lasting in the human mind is the association of these two ideas, crime and punishment (Beccaria, 1985 [1764], p.56).

Certainty

Certainty considers the likelihood of apprehension or the likelihood that punishment attaches for an act. Here, Beccaria argued (1985 [1764], p.58):

> One of the greatest curbs on crimes is not the cruelty of punishments, but their infallibility...the certainty of a punishment will always make a stronger impression than the fear of another which is more terrible but combined with the hope of impunity.

Moreover, certainty of apprehension and punishment is more important than either swiftness or severity (see Nagin and Pogarsky, 2001). The wrongdoer must expect punishment for the behavior.

Severity

Beccaria argued that for punishment to be an effective deterrent it must also be severe. However, when considering this final component of effective punishment, he was careful to argue that by severity he did not mean that summary executions for minor violations are an effective deterrent. Rather, by severity Beccaria meant that the punishment must be proportionate to the harm done to society by the offense:

> the purpose can only be to prevent the criminal from inflicting new injuries on its citizens and to deter others from similar acts. Always keeping due proportions, such punishments and such method of inflicting them ought to be chosen, therefore, which will make the strongest and most lasting impression on the minds of men, and inflict the least torment on the body of the criminal. For punishment to attain its end, the evil which it inflicts has only to exceed the advantage derivable from the crime...[A]ll beyond this is superfluous and for that reason tyrannical (Beccaria 1985 [1764], pp.42–43).

The end result of deterrence theory is a model that looks roughly like the depiction in Figure 2.1. As portrayed in the diagram, deterrence theory suggests that all that is necessary to prevent delinquency is punishment that is swift, certain, and severe. If these qualities are in place, especially certainty, then delinquency will be held in check.

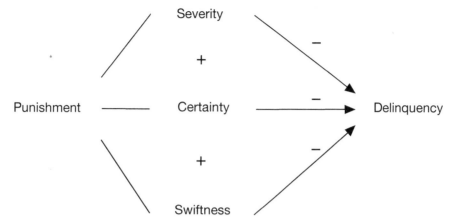

FIGURE 2.1 The basic deterrence model.

How to Think About Deterrence

It is important to realize that deterrence is rather complex. In particular, there are different ways of thinking about deterrence, different methods to determine whether deterrence works, and important questions about whether or not juveniles can be deterred from delinquent behavior in the same way that adults can be deterred from criminal behavior.

What are Some Types of Deterrence?

General deterrence

There are several different ways to categorize *deterrence*. First, there is a distinction between *general* and *specific* deterrence. General deterrence occurs when adolescents contemplating wrongdoing opt not to engage in delinquency because they have seen the consequences of the delinquent act for offenders who have been caught. Suppose that Bryan contemplates breaking into a car to steal a sound-system.

However, during this period of contemplation, the local police department announces a crackdown on theft from vehicles, introduces a no-plea policy for those arrested and charged with larceny from a motor vehicle, and recounts a story of an adolescent recently arrested for such an offense. Bryan, upon hearing the announcement, decides to abandon his crime plan; in the language of deterrence theory Bryan has been generally deterred and a crime has been prevented.

Specific deterrence

Specific deterrence focuses not on preventing delinquent acts in general, but rather on preventing another act from being committed by a particular adolescent. It is targeted at those individuals already involved in delinquency; the objective of specific deterrence is to punish the offender with certainty, severity, and swiftness so that the likelihood of future acts is significantly reduced. Therefore, deterrence theory can be targeted at the general population or it can be targeted at specific offenders. The sentencing structure in New York State, for example, allows for increasing sanctions for repeat offenders even if the offense does not change or the harm done does not increase. Suppose, for example, that Susan is caught in a "buy and bust" operation on the street. She sold a small quantity of crack-cocaine to an undercover operator. This is her first felony arrest so she pleads guilty and receives probation as punishment. A few months later she is caught by police a second time in virtually the same way. However, this time Susan receives a sentence to a secure juvenile institution. Why the increase in severity of the sanction if the act committed and the harm done is identical for both offenses? According to specific deterrence, increasing the sanction the second time is reasonable because obviously the pain of probation was not sufficient to outweigh the pleasure3 derived from selling crack-cocaine. Therefore, it is necessary to increase the punishment in an attempt to deter future drug-dealing behaviors. If, after the period of incarceration, Susan does not go back to selling cocaine then we assume that she has been specifically deterred from such behavior. On the other hand, what if Susan shifts from selling crack-cocaine to marijuana or to shoplifting? Has she been deterred?

Absolute and restrictive deterrence

Another issue involves the notion of absolute versus restrictive deterrence (Nagin and Paternoster, 1991). In general, it is safe to argue that selling crack-cocaine is a more serious crime than selling marijuana. Suppose that, after a second conviction, Susan shifts away from selling crack-cocaine and instead sells marijuana, which is far less profitable, but far less serious in terms of the presumed "harm" it does to society. Some argue that deterrence has failed in this case as Susan is still involved in street-level drug sales, but others argue that deterrence has succeeded because she no longer sells crack-cocaine.

Absolute deterrence focuses on an "all or nothing" proposition, and only if Susan completely stops selling drugs is deterrence theory supported. Those who embrace, though, the idea of restrictive deterrence would probably celebrate Susan's shift in behavior from a more serious to a less serious offense. If it were not for the punishment for selling crack-cocaine, Susan would continue to sell a dangerous drug. Therefore, Susan has been deterred. Rather than absolute, the deterrence has been restrictive.

Does this example illustrate a success or a failure for deterrence theory? There are no simple answers to this question since people can reasonably disagree on which is preferable, although most would probably choose absolute deterrence as the most desirable goal.

Objective and subjective deterrence

Yet another complexity is whether the risk of punishment in terms of certainty, severity, and swiftness should be objective (what it is in reality) or subjective (what the individual perceives it to be). Much of the research on deterrence theory during the mid-twentieth century focused on objective deterrence (Nagin [1998] provides a review of this research); however, most contemporary research considers what people perceive as risky versus what is actually risky. For example, what is more risky in terms of likelihood of death: flying in an airplane to Miami or driving a car to Miami? Actually, driving is far more dangerous (objective risk), but many people perceive flying to be more dangerous (subjective risk). So, when we consider risk of punishment from the justice system should we consider what juveniles perceive the risk of punishment to be, what the actual risk of punishment is, or both? Similarly, there are different views of what is pleasurable or rewarding.

Research on Deterrence and Delinquency

Three research strategies have been implemented to ascertain the effects of deterrence on adolescents. The first strategy focuses on research that uses pre-test → intervention → post-test studies. In this type of study there is a preintervention assessment of juvenile delinquency, an intervention, and then a post-intervention assessment to ascertain what proportion of study subjects has stopped offending and was presumably deterred. The second strategy is to assess whether or not deterrence works for adolescents the same way it is supposed to work for adults. This strategy considers the effects, if any, of subjective deterrence on a sample of adolescents to see if their perceptions of risk predict their involvement in delinquency. In these studies, deterrence theory is thought to be supported if, for example, a high perceived risk of apprehension is accompanied by less delinquent behavior. The final strategy is to compare juvenile justice and criminal justice processing. The criminal justice system is generally considered more punitive than the juvenile justice system; thus, if deterrence operates as expected one would see a substantial drop-off in delinquent behavior as the jurisdiction shifts from juvenile to criminal (general deterrence) and, among those enmeshed in the system, one would expect to see lower rates of repeat offending for those in the criminal justice system than those who remain in the juvenile justice system (Levitt, 1998).

Pre-test → Intervention → Post-test

Although there are several examples of this type of research, we highlight only two studies: *Scared Straight!* and the *Pulling Levers Program. Scared Straight!* was a program that began in New Jersey and became quite popular. Many jurisdictions around the United States and in other nations implemented *Scared Straight!* programs with the goal of deterring petty juvenile offenders from a life of crime. There are several good websites with *Scared Straight!*-like themes, and there are also several documentaries based on the original *Scared Straight!* program at Rahway State Prison (now called East Jersey State Prison).

The *Scared Straight!* program takes "at-risk" adolescents who have had contact with the juvenile justice system and sends them on a "field trip" to a maximum security prison to meet with a group of inmates doing 25 years to life for violent crimes. During their "field trip" the adolescents are processed into the prison by gruff guards, walk through the cell blocks where they are taunted by inmates behind bars, and spend time with a group of "lifers." The lifers tell them about life on the inside; they swear, they yell, they intimidate. The developers of *Scared Straight!* envisioned a program so forceful, so compelling, and so frightening that the young offenders would be deterred from subsequent offending. Several documentaries about the program claimed that it was an unqualified success. The most recent, *Scared Straight! 20 Years Later* (1999), revisits the original participants in the 1978 documentary to see how they are doing. All are living conventional lives, with the exception of a few who developed into serious, chronic offenders. Based upon these accounts, it is difficult to believe that *Scared Straight!* is anything but an impressive success that needs to be widely implemented.

However, Finckenauer (1982; Finckenauer and Gavin, 1999) and Petrosino and colleagues (2000) have argued that scientific evidence does not support the claim that *Scared Straight!* is an effective program. In an exhaustive review of research addressing these programs, Petrosino and colleagues (2000) discovered that not only did it appear that *Scared Straight!* had not deterred subsequent involvement in delinquency and crime, but the results from several studies indicated that groups exposed to the "lifers" had higher offending rates and were involved in more severe offenses after the program than groups of young people that had not gone through the program. These researchers concluded that, even when intentions are noble, programs may have unintended consequences and may do more harm than good.

The second pre-test → intervention → post-test program is referred to as *Pulling Levers* (Braga et al., 2001). This program began in response to the substantial number of homicides committed by juveniles in Boston, MA. Kennedy and colleagues (1996) discovered that most of the juvenile homicides were located in specific areas of Boston and many, though not all, juvenile homicide victims and offenders were gang members. A large inter-agency working group considered these findings and began to think about strategies to decrease juvenile homicides. The working group believed that they would not "be able to prevent gang violence unless gang members believe that unpleasant consequences will follow on violence and gun use, and [that they] choose to change their behavior" (Kennedy et al., 1996, p.166). So, the group devised a strategy of zero-tolerance toward youth gang violence. The basic message was something like this:

- We know that you are a gang member and we are watching you and all of your peers.
- If there is a homicide or a shooting that is attributable to one of your gang members we will come down hard on the gang as a whole and not just the shooter.
- Therefore, if one of your members is responsible for a shooting we will crack down in your area of operation. We will make arrests for minor transgressions. We will conduct home searches of probationers and parolees; we will revoke any probationer or parolee in violation of his conditions of release. We will prosecute those arrested on gun and drug charges in federal courts and we will push for maximum penalties. We will disrupt the street-level drug trade, any outstanding warrants will be executed, and everyone in the gang will be punished for the "bad" behavior of one.
- These actions will be swift, certain, and severe.

The message was sent to the gangs and then the working group waited for the next juvenile homicides to occur. One occurred in 1996 and a gang known as the Intervale Posse was apparently responsible. The crackdown began and 20 Intervale members were arrested after an exhaustive nine-month investigation. Ten of the members were prosecuted under federal law, which tends to be more punitive than state law. The working group then sent out another message: "Who's next?" Between 1991 and 1995 the city of Boston experienced about 44 youth homicides per year; after implementation of this deterrence project the number of youth homicides dropped to 15 in 1996. A comparison of youth homicide victimization rates across the major U.S. cities indicated that Boston's reduction was "significantly larger than those in most other American cities at the time" (Braga et al., 2001, p.219).

So how can these discrepant findings between *Scared Straight!* and *Pulling Levers* be understood? Does deterrence directed at certain youth work successfully as indicated in *Pulling Levers* or does deterrence have minimal impact and perhaps even increase the risk of subsequent offending as found in the evaluations of *Scared Straight!*? The answer is not clear and may involve the groups that were targeted and the degree to which the programs were implemented.

Perceptual Deterrence Among Adolescents

A second approach to studying whether deterrence affects delinquent behavior looks at what adolescents perceive the risk of punishment to be and then looks at their delinquent behaviors. If deterrence plays a role in controlling adolescent behavior then one would expect that those adolescents who perceive punishment to be most certain, most swift, and most severe are also least involved in delinquency. Unfortunately, even though there have been dozens of studies of perceptual deterrence (Pratt et al., 2007), few have used adolescent samples.

Nonetheless, in an important study, Nagin and Paternoster (1991) considered whether perceptual deterrence is an effective mechanism among adolescents. They used survey responses from about 1,100 high school students who were followed over a three year period: tenth, eleventh, and twelfth grades. During each year, the students were asked about their delinquency and their perceived certainty of arrest for theft. The basic model examined in the study is depicted in Figure 2.2.

Nagin and Paternoster (1991) also measured delinquency in two different ways: *prevalence* and *incidence*. The prevalence measure assessed whether or not youths committed any offense in the past year, which was used to judge the presence of an absolute deterrence effect. The incidence measure considered the number of times each student engaged in delinquency in the past year, and therefore was used to ascertain if there is a restrictive deterrent effect.[4] They therefore considered whether perceived risk of arrest at time 1 is an absolute or restrictive deterrent to delinquency at time 2. Their results indicated that those youths who reported greater perceived certainty of arrest were less involved overall and reduced their offending, thus indicating both an absolute and a restrictive deterrent effect.

More recent studies have attempted to elaborate the role of perceptual deterrence among adolescents by examining factors that might affect these perceptions. Using a large sample of adolescents from across the United States, Pogarsky and colleagues (2005) found, contrary to deterrence theory, that getting arrested did not influence perceptions of certainty and prior offending did not decrease the perceived risks of delinquency. Those who had delinquent friends perceived less certainty than others of getting caught for violating the law. However, those adolescents who had been involved in delinquency *and* reported more moral inhibitions about offending tended to perceive higher risks of future delinquent behavior.

In a similar study, Matsueda and colleagues (2006) determined that adolescents who had been involved in delinquency, but had rarely been questioned or arrested by the police, tended to judge that their risk of getting caught for future offenses is low. On the other hand, those who had been questioned or arrested

FIGURE 2.2 Perceived risk and deterrence (based on Nagin and Paternoster, 1991, p.567).

more frequently were highly likely to think they would get caught for future offending. Over time, youths who judged that they would likely be caught for delinquent acts were substantially less likely to commit delinquent acts. However, perceptual deterrence is not a simple matter of how likely the risks of offending appear to be, but is also affected by beliefs about whether or not delinquent behavior is wrong and whether delinquency enhances a youth's status, and with whom one associates (see also Matthews and Agnew, 2008). In other words, there are many aspects to the perceived risks and rewards of delinquent behavior. Moreover, perceived risks of getting caught are consistently affected by previous experiences. This suggests that evaluations of the risks and rewards of delinquent behavior can change because of previous experiences with rule-breaking and apprehension.

Although these studies suggest that perceived certainty of punishment can deter adolescents in some situations, it remains unclear if this is also the case for severity and swiftness of punishment. A large and sophisticated review of deterrence studies indicated that severity is, at best, only weakly associated with subsequent offending (Pratt et al., 2007). Moreover, a study of college students that compared the three aspects of punishment determined that certainty is the most influential element (Nagin and Pogarsky, 2001). It is important to consider whether or not adolescents are even aware of the particular punishment that may result from their delinquent behavior, however. For deterrence to be effective, presumably there must be knowledge of the specific risks involved in misbehaviors. Yet many youths, especially those who are short-sighted and do not consider the consequences of their actions (see the discussion of impulsivity in Chapter 3 and self-control in Chapter 8), may not be aware of the official sanctions for their behaviors. Thus, as discussed later in the chapter, we may need to change our assumptions about rational decision-making when considering adolescents.

Juvenile Justice Processing and Deterrence

The third strategy used to assess deterrence among adolescents considers whether the justice system itself acts as a deterrent to delinquent behavior. Several studies using this strategy address the effects of *juvenile waiver* (see Redding [2003] for a review of these studies). Juvenile waiver involves the transfer of juvenile offenders from the juvenile to the adult court system. In the two Supreme Court decisions mentioned at the outset of this chapter the defendants were processed through the criminal court rather than the juvenile court; they were treated as adults rather than juveniles. In serious felony cases where the defendant is a juvenile most states have a mechanism in place whereby the juvenile court waives jurisdiction and the defendant is processed through the criminal court. This waiver to criminal court is driven, in part, by deterrence theory. The deterrence argument for waiver is that the juvenile system does not have a sufficiently certain process and it does not have amply severe sanctions to effectively deter some of the most serious juvenile offenders. Therefore, processing serious juvenile offenders through the criminal justice system should be a greater deterrent than processing them through the juvenile justice system.

Fagan (1996) explored whether adolescents processed in criminal court are less likely to reoffend (are more deterred) than those processed in juvenile court. He identified a sample of 15 and 16 year olds in New York and New Jersey who were charged with either robbery or burglary. The New York State offenders were processed through criminal court whereas the New Jersey offenders were processed through juvenile court. In considering certainty Fagan compared the proportion of those found guilty in New York with the proportion of those found guilty in New Jersey. If deterrence is more likely to be present in the criminal rather than the juvenile system one would anticipate higher conviction rates in criminal court. Interestingly, Fagan found higher convictions rates in criminal court than juvenile court for robbery but not burglary. He also determined that those convicted in criminal court for robbery or burglary are far more likely to be incarcerated than those adjudicated in juvenile court. Therefore, for robbery offenses the criminal justice system appears more certain and more severe, and for burglary the criminal justice system appears only more severe than the juvenile justice system. It stands to reason, then, that youths processed through the adult system should have lower reoffending rates. This was not the case. Those processed through criminal court on robbery charges were *more likely* to be re-arrested and re-incarcerated than those processed through the juvenile system—the exact opposite of what deterrence theory anticipates. Furthermore, no differences in reoffending or reincarceration were found among those adolescents charged with burglary.

Based on Fagan's (1996) study, it is easy to reach the conclusion that increases in certainty and severity, above and beyond that already present in the juvenile justice system, do not act to further deter subsequent behavior. In fact, in the case of those charged with robbery, increases in certainty and severity may intensify rather than deter the behavior. This is one of the arguments made by labeling theorists (see Chapter 9). Nonetheless, Fagan's study did not address swiftness of punishment, a key component of theories of deterrence.

In contrast, Levitt (1998, p.1159) determined that "harsher punishments for juveniles (within the juvenile justice system) are strongly associated with lower rates of juvenile offending." He reached this conclusion after comparing the proportion of juveniles in custody with the juvenile crime rate over time and across jurisdictions. As juvenile custody rates increase, juvenile crime rates decrease. Levitt (1998) took the analysis one step further and looked at age groups over time to see if as adolescents become adults in the eyes of the law their criminal involvement decreases. He found that jurisdictions that have the most severe criminal sanctions relative to juvenile sanctions see significant reductions in crime as groups of adolescents move into adulthood. However, in jurisdictions where criminal justice sanctions are more lenient relative to juvenile justice sanctions, the transition from adolescence to adulthood results in more rather than less crime. Implied by Levitt's research is that relative severity of sanctions in the juvenile justice system, followed by sanctions that are at least as severe in the criminal justice system, maximizes the overall deterrent effect, at least in the short term. Similar results have been found when researchers have examined arrest rather than custody: When the rate of arrests for violent crimes increases, the number of juvenile offenses such as drug dealing and assault tend to decrease, thus suggesting a general deterrent effect (Mocan and Rees, 2005).

Thus, there is mixed evidence from studies that compare the deterrent effect of the juvenile justice and criminal justice systems. Perceived certainty of punishment may operate consistently as a perceptual deterrent, although it is also affected by several factors. However, the effects of objective certainty and severity are less consistent. Yet there remains a fundamental issue that deterrence theorists must address: Can the assumption of the rational actor be applied to juvenile offenders? The next section highlights two broad lines of research that directly examine this issue: research on adolescent brain development and functioning, and adolescent decision-making in a psychosocial context.

The promises and limitations of deterrence theory

The evidence discussed thus far suggests that perceived certainty of apprehension and punishment appears to decrease subsequent involvement in delinquency. Jurisdictions with more severe penalties for adults relative to adolescents may also provide a general deterrent effect. However, recent research calls into question the overall usefulness of deterrence theory for adolescents.

At the start of this chapter we discussed two Supreme Court decisions that reached opposite conclusions about the role of deterrence among adolescents. When thinking about the applicability of deterrence for adolescents the issue of culpability or responsibility based on an argument of diminished capacity comes to the forefront. Recall that for punishment to operate as a deterrent the person being targeted for punishment must be deserving of punishment. If the person does not deserve punishment then not only is it unjust, it is also unlikely to deter. Moreover, deterrence theory assumes that people are aware of the consequences and risks of their behaviors. This raises an important distinction between *deterrence* and *deterrability*. Deterrability refers to a potential offender's ability to perform the rational calculations that are part of the deterrence process (Jacobs, 2010; Pogarsky, 2002). However, some offenders may not have the capacity for full-blown calculations of risks and rewards.

DISCUSSION QUESTIONS
By John M. Stogner

1. Deterrence theory assumes that crime is committed after a rational decision-making process. Do you believe that offenders assess the risk (notably the certainty, severity, and celerity of punishment) before acting? How accurate are they likely to be in their assessments?

2. Is punishment an effective social tool if it only has a specific deterrent effect? Which is more important: general or specific deterrence? Do your answers to the preceding questions create ethical concerns?

3. Over 200 years after Becarria's work, Stafford and Warr would challenge that "it is possible that punishment avoidance does more to encourage crime than punishment does to discourage it." Discuss what this means in the context of deterrence theory.

4. Has the America system of justice effectively instituted Beccaria's ideas? What modifications may be necessary to develop a system more congruent with his vision?

5. How does deterrence theory relate to the separate adult and juvenile criminal justice systems? Would Becarria argue for similar punishments or different reactions?

CHAPTER THREE

The Rational Choice Perspective

DEREK B. CORNISH AND RONALD V. CLARKE

STUDENT INTRODUCTION
By John M. Stogner

Ronald Clarke and Derek Cornish developed a new theory in the mid-1980s that was built upon the same foundation as Beccaria's work. Much like Beccaria, they believe that people are generally rational actors and are hedonistic—they seek to maximize pleasure and minimize pain and discomfort. Whereas Beccaria was primarily concerned with the pain/discomfort side of the issue, Clarke and Cornish devote attention to the rewards of criminal activity as well. In simplest terms, deterrence theory focused almost exclusively on the costs of crime while Clarke and Cornish's rational choice theory considers both the costs and benefits.

This is clearly not the only distinction between the theories. Clarke and Cornish challenge the idea that individuals are fully rational and capable of accurately considering the costs of crime. Instead, they describe people as being bounded or limited in their rationality. They suggest that people act upon assumptions, misinformation, and miscalculations. They note that decisions may be hurried and judgments impaired by external forces. Clarke and Cornish also describe *informal costs* in addition to the formal sanctions imposed by the government that were the focus of Beccaria's work. Informal sanctions might include shame, guilt, and loss of a relation's respect. Many have argued that these informal sanctions do more to deter crime than the threat of formal sanctions.

Rational choice theory is often simplified into a version that simply states that crime occurs when an individual believes the benefits of that crime outweigh the likely costs. However, Clarke and Cornish's work is far more intricate. As you read, pay careful attention to the six core arguments of rational choice theory, consider the utility of evaluating criminal involvement and criminal events separately, and deliberate on the use of crime scripts in a field primarily concerned with nomothetic explanations of behavior.

THE RATIONAL CHOICE PERSPECTIVE
By Derek B. Cornish and Ronald V. Clarke

Introduction

Asked why he robbed banks, Willie Sutton is said to have replied, 'Because that's where the money is' (Cocheo 1997). His wisecrack was later elevated into a rule-of-thumb—Sutton's Law—to guide physicians when making diagnoses: 'Go first for the most likely explanation.' Curiously there seems to be no equivalent Sutton's Law in criminology, where one might most expect to find one.

Maybe, though, by responding to a question about motivation with an answer about target selection, Willie Sutton has a message for the discipline. By turning a question about motivation into an answer about criminal decision-making, the wisecrack pinpoints the disconnect between traditional criminological theory—preoccupied with the development of criminality and the supposed roots of crime- and a newer crime science, more concerned with the practical business of understanding how to prevent crime here and now. If there were to be a Sutton's Law for crime science, it might run along the following lines: 'If you want to develop practical ways of preventing criminal activity, go for the obvious: pay less attention to theorising about criminal motivation, and more attention to finding out about how crimes happen.'

The rational choice perspective provides just one such theory for practice. Instead of viewing criminal behaviour as the outcome of stable criminal motivations, it views the desires, preferences and motives of offenders and potential offenders as similar to those of the rest of us, and as in continual interaction with contemporary opportunities and constraints to produce, reinforce and sometimes reduce criminal behaviours. At its core are the concepts of choice and decision-making, present-centredness, and the centrality of the crime event to continued criminal activity—success in offending driving the development of criminal lifestyles, and failure leading to reduction and change in criminal activity, or to desistance.

Background and History

The rational choice perspective was one outcome of a general shift of focus in British criminology that took place during the 1970s (Clarke and Cornish 1983). In the 1960s criminal behaviour was believed to be primarily the result of long-standing criminal predispositions and psychopathologies that caused individuals to offend. Research efforts were therefore heavily invested in programmes to prevent the development of criminality, viewed as a complex of attitudes, personality traits, and dispositions to offend. Criminality, it was thought, could be changed through appropriate treatments, and these changes once made would then persist.

When evaluations of existing programmes failed to find convincing evidence of their effectiveness, it called into question this prevailing medico-psychological model of the causation of offending. Many of these programmes, including the ones we studied (Cornish and Clarke 1975), often removed offenders from their natural environments, treated them in residential institutions, and reinserted them with varying degrees of support into their post-treatment environments. Once released, relapse was commonplace, but one of the puzzling features of the failure of rehabilitation to bring about lasting change was the fact that offenders were clearly affected by their treatment environments during their stay. Whether because of the rewards and punishments handed out by staff or as a result of other features of the treatment environment, such as the opportunities it offered to misbehave, institutional regimes varied in the effects they had on the behaviour of their inmates during treatment.

One positive by-product of the failure of the rehabilitative ideal, then, was the realisation that even if the effects of treatment were not permanent—that is, not generally maintained in the post-treatment environment—the treatment environments themselves seemed to have an influence on behaviour while the offender was exposed to them. Sinclair's (1971) study of probation hostels, for example, indicated that hostels varied in their failure rates—that is, proportions of boys leaving prematurely as the result of absconding or other misbehaviour—while Clarke and Martin's (1975) study of absconding from residential schools for delinquent children showed widely differing rates. Taken together these studies provided striking evidence of the effects of the immediate environment on inmates' behaviour.

Although offering little support to medico-psychological models of rehabilitation, such findings pointed to the influence of the current environment on behaviour. The resulting 'environmental/learning theory' explanation that was developed (Clarke and Martin 1975; Cornish and Clarke 1975) had four main elements (Clarke and Cornish 1983: 37):

1. While an individual's emotional inheritance and upbringing play some part in delinquency, the major determinants are those provided by the current environment.

2. The current environment provides the cues and stimuli for delinquency, as well as the reinforcements. Thus, a temporary mood of unhappiness, anxiety or euphoria, resulting from recent crises or events, may place someone in a state of emotional readiness to commit an initial delinquent act. Whether in fact he or she does so will depend to a large extent on opportunity and the example of others. Once committed, a delinquent act, like any other behaviour, will become part of the individual's behavioural repertoire. Thereafter, reinforcement as well as opportunity becomes salient to its maintenance.

3. Since delinquent acts are learned in particular environments, they will only be repeated under closely similar conditions. Consistencies in behaviour over time are therefore dependent on consistencies in environments.

4. Delinquent acts of different kinds do not serve equivalent functions for the actor; each is acquired and maintained by situational variables specific to it, and it alone. This is not to deny, however, that some individuals, by virtue of their particular circumstances, may learn a range of delinquent behaviours.

The environmental/learning theory was specifically designed to explain the shortcomings of the medico-psychological model and redirect future efforts. Though rudimentary, the theory seemed to point to important influences on criminal behaviour that had been neglected, revealing it as being much more malleable, and dependent on environmental contingencies than had previously been supposed. As such, the theory provided an initial way of thinking about how the immediate environment influenced the likelihood of offending, and how it might be manipulated in order to prevent or reduce crime (see Clarke, Chapter 10, this volume).

Even so, the theory suffered from its use of concepts drawn from radical behaviourism, a theoretical orientation which was rapidly losing traction within psychology because of its reluctance to investigate cognitive aspects of behaviour. The rapid growth of situational crime prevention practice demanded a revised explanatory framework within which both developments in situational crime prevention and the criticisms which it was already attracting could be properly examined. Situational crime prevention was already beginning to use the language of choice and decision-making, and a simple choice model had been developed (Clarke 1980) as an opening move to counter the common criticism that situational measures would merely—and inevitably—lead to displacement. This was the notion that, stopped from committing a particular offence, the offender would simply displace the offending by choosing another time or place, a different target, a different modus operandi, or a different form of crime (Reppetto 1974). The adoption of the language of choice and decision-making allowed a more nuanced discussion of the circumstances under which displacement might or might not be expected to occur.

The transition from a radical behaviourist to a rational choice perspective was also mandated by practical considerations. The language of intentionality and choice is the discourse of the criminal justice system and of everyday life. Getting inside the offender's head to look at his or her decision-making was a far cry from the black box approach adopted by radical behaviourism. But the move to a new conceptual framework was needed to handle the burgeoning research on offenders' perceptions and decision-making that was taking place in the early 1980s (Bennett and Wright 1984; Maguire and Bennett 1982; Walsh 1980), especially given its relevance to situational crime prevention.

By this time the choice model was on its way to becoming a rational choice one (Clarke and Cornish 1983: 50). A study of gambling provided support for this development. Traditionally, psychiatrists had depicted much gambling as pathologically motivated, while economists and decision theorists had often found gamblers' choices to be apparently irrational in financial terms when measured against outcomes. Viewed in the light of gamblers' real-life motives, needs and options, however, gambling emerged as both more complex and more rational than suspected, especially given the circumstances under which gambling took place and given the difficulty of making decisions under conditions of uncertainty, using partial and sometimes deliberately misleading information (Cornish 1978).

A survey of the criminological literature of the time (Clarke and Cornish 1985: 149) described 'the convergence of interest among a variety of academic disciplines—the sociology of deviance, criminology, economics, and cognitive psychology—upon a conception of crime as the outcome of rational choices' on the part of offenders. This view was further developed in a volume that assembled original papers from researchers working, broadly speaking, within a rational choice perspective (Cornish and Clarke 1986). The picture that emerged was one of offenders as reasoning criminals, using cues present in potential crime settings to guide their decisions about whether (or not) to commit particular crimes and, if so, how to commit them.

Core Concepts of the Rational Choice Perspective

The rational choice perspective is a heuristic device or conceptual tool rather than a conventional criminological theory. (We will return to this important point later.) Its purpose has always been to offer a way of looking at offending that is both present-centred and recognises the influence of the environment on behaviour. This environment is both the environment of everyday life—lifestyle and its motives, needs and inducements—and the more particular environment of instrumental action to achieve particular goals. As currently conceptualised the rational choice perspective consists of six core concepts and four decision-making models embodying them.

- Criminal behaviour is purposive.
- Criminal behaviour is rational.
- Criminal decision-making is crime-specific.
- Criminal choices fall into two broad groups: 'involvement' and 'event' decisions.
- There are separate stages of involvement.
- Criminal events unfold in a sequence of stages and decisions.

Criminal Behaviour is Purposive

When trying to make sense of human behaviour, we seem to make use of a rather simple theory of action. People have needs and desires, and beliefs about how these can be fulfilled. Guided by these beliefs, they take actions to achieve their particular goals. This relationship between desires, beliefs and actions gives behaviour its purposive character, and we go about making behaviour intelligible to ourselves by trying to establish the purposes of actions and by identifying the nature of desires and beliefs that fuel and guide them.

When it comes to crime, however, we often lose sight of the instrumental nature of much action. Media reports of crime—particularly of violent crimes against persons, animals, and property—are replete with descriptions of offending as senseless, incomprehensible, irrational or thuggish when applied to offences as diverse as joyriding, domestic violence, assault, rape, football hooliganism and vandalism. While these may rightly reflect our horror and outrage, the emotions they arouse do little to help us understand and prevent criminal behaviour. The rational choice perspective takes the view that crimes are purposive and deliberate acts, committed with the intention of benefiting the offender. The benefits of offending include satisfying the usual human motives, such as desires for sexual gratification, excitement, autonomy, admiration, revenge, control, reduction of tension, material goods and so on. Money, of course, can buy many of these satisfactions—sex, drugs, freedom from control by others—so it becomes a convenient and important goal of offending in its own right.

Criminal Behaviour is Rational

In daily life we assume most of the time that people's actions are not only purposive and intelligible, but also rational: that, given their motives and goals, individuals will try to select the best available means to achieve them. This presumption of rationality underpins explanations of human action. As Herrnstein (1990: 356) has commented, it 'comes close to serving as the fundamental principle of the behavioral sciences. No other well articulated theory of behavior commands so large a following in so wide a range of disciplines.' Karl Popper also emphasised the advantages of using the presumption of rationality as an essential methodological principle (Knepper 2007).

Presuming rationality is not, however, the same as presuming perfect rationality. It is here that the rational choice perspective departs from the normative models of rational choice found in modern economics and decision theory. Instead, the perspective offers a more nuanced view of rationality in practice, borrowing from Herbert Simon (1990) the notion of a more limited or bounded rationality. This recognises that in the real world action often has to be taken on the basis of decisions made under less than perfect circumstances. Offending is inherently a risky business, and the possible costs and benefits are difficult to estimate in advance. To these uncertainties are added time pressures, and differences in skill and experience on the part of individual offenders in interpreting what information there is. Under these conditions, which are far from perfect, and despite offenders' best efforts, decisions are likely to produce 'satisficing'—that is, satisfactory and sufficient—outcomes rather than optimal ones most of the time.

The presumptions of purposiveness and (bounded) rationality put criminal behaviour on the same footing as any other human activity. Of course, offenders vary in their skills, experience and intelligence, sometimes make mistakes, act rashly, fail to consider all sides of a problem, ignore or downplay risks, or act while under the influence of drugs and alcohol. But these departures from rationality hardly make offenders more fallible than anyone else. And criminal decision-making is by its very nature likely to be prone to error because of the constraints under which it often has to operate.

Criminal Decision-Making is Crime-Specific

Crime is often treated as though it were one unitary phenomenon, rather than a set of rather diverse behaviours. There is a place for generalising about crime—aggregate crime rates, for example, can be used as indicators of societal malaise- and all crime by definition involves law-breaking. But treating crime as a unitary phenomenon often leads to the development of simple theories to explain crime and simple policies to combat it. Practical crime-control efforts are forced to be less ambitious and better focused. When called upon to do something about crime, distinctions start to be made in terms of type, degree and consequences within the general category of crime. What people want is to be protected from particular types of crime events. At the local level, getting tough on crime is shorthand for dealing with a shopping list of specific criminal activities that people want stopped.

In fact, offenders don't commit crime, but carry out specific crimes, each of which has its own particular motives, purposes and benefits. Rape may gratify sexual need and desires for dominance, control and humiliation; burglary may satisfy a need for cash or goods, but also a desire for 'sneaky thrills' (Katz 1988). In other words, specific offences bring particular benefits to offenders and are committed with specific motives in mind. Because crimes differ from one another, the factors weighed by offenders, and the variables influencing their decision-making, will also differ greatly with the nature of the offence. This is especially noticeable when considering the choices and decisions made when committing the crime itself. The circumstances surrounding the passing of a dud cheque—the nature of the risks, efforts and rewards, the activities undertaken and the locations within which they take place—are very different from those surrounding the planning and committing of a terrorist event.

This means that even the ostensibly finer distinctions among crimes, made by lawyers and statisticians—such as violent crime, computer fraud or sex offending—may be too broad to use as a basis for understanding criminal decision-making. This is because they may still include many differently motivated offences, committed by a wide range of offenders, using a variety of methods with varying degrees of skill. Even offences that seem to cluster into natural groupings—car thefts, for example—will be found to differ in important ways according to the purposes for which they are committed and the ways they are carried out. Therefore, it is always important to distinguish the choices and decisions made in relation to joyriding from those related to vehicle theft for temporary transport, for parts, or for selling on to various markets. How crime-specific one needs to become will ultimately be a pragmatic decision, based upon the purpose at hand. While it may be important for theory to draw finer distinctions, for practical crime prevention purposes the stop-rule might well be the extent to which this would improve the prospects for designing more successful interventions.

The need to be crime-specific does not ignore the fact that many offenders are generalists, in the sense that they may commit a wide range of crimes over the course of their careers. Indeed, in order to support a criminal lifestyle an experienced offender may be engaging in many different crimes over the same period—from illegal parking and receiving stolen property to burglary, social security fraud, mugging drunks and aggravated assault—all to support and facilitate the different aspects of his or her life. But each of these crimes has its own purposes and its own methods of crime-commission at which the offender can hope to become more proficient over time, and out of which certain ones may become preferred solutions to particular needs.

Distinguishing Criminal Involvement from Crime Event Decisions

The decisions that offenders and potential offenders make can be divided into two broad categories: involvement decisions and event decisions. Event decisions are crime-centred and concentrate upon crime-commission; as mentioned previously, they are crime-specific, and concern choices and decisions made when preparing for, carrying out and concluding the commission of a particular type of crime. Although the timescales of these decisions may differ for various types of crime, they are only as long as is necessary to complete these activities. The factors considered by offenders are also limited, being concerned primarily with the immediate tasks at hand, such as selecting a potential robbery victim, or choosing a safe location for a rape. Involvement decisions, on the other hand, concern the offender's criminal career, and include decisions about initial involvement (initiation), continued involvement (habituation) and desistance. Because of this they extend over longer timescales and, while they incorporate decisions about, and reactions to, offending, they are also concerned with a wider range of variables.

Involvement decisions, like event ones, are crime-specific, and must be studied separately for different crimes. Contemplating whether or not to get involved in a terrorist attack on a subway train is clearly very different from thinking about whether or not to fiddle one's tax returns, in terms of the relative complexities of the undertakings, the risks involved, the skills required, the alternatives to the crime in question, the moral considerations involved, and the costs of discovery. Similar considerations apply to decisions about continuation and desistance from particular crimes. One form of crime (a parking violation, for example) may play a relatively marginal role in sustaining a life of crime, while another (such as drug-dealing) may be economically vital. And the centrality of a crime, such as paedophilia, to other aspects of a person's life is likely to give decisions about continuation and desistance a special significance.

Distinguishing the Separate Stages of Criminal Involvement

Separating an offender's involvement in a particular form of crime into the three broad stages of initiation, habituation and desistance serves to emphasise the fact that at each stage different sets of variables influence the offender's decisions. For example, decisions about getting involved for the first time in that form of crime might be influenced by prior experience of having committed other kinds of crime, and by a range of background factors, such as personality and upbringing, and current circumstances, such as the individual's lifestyle and the needs and motives it generates, together with the opportunities and inducements available to the potential offender.

On the other hand, decisions to continue offending or to desist will be most powerfully affected by the criminal's success or failure in continuing to carry out the chosen crime, and by their impact on his or her lifestyle. Nor in real life are the transitions from initiation to desistance likely to be inevitable, smooth or sequential, since changes of pace and lulls in offending may also be affected by extraneous factors, such as ill health, marriage, divorce, death of a family member and other life events and crises.

In practice, too, an offender may be involved to varying degrees in a number of different forms of crime. In such cases, he or she will be making many different choices and decisions simultaneously, and existing experience at committing one form of crime may influence decisions about committing others. Decisions about desistance provide good examples of these issues. Lack of success at committing a particular type of crime—say, auto theft—may lead to a reduction in its frequency or even to desistance. But, if the offender is experienced and skilled at that form of offending, it may also lead to displacement. Thus, an offender may be able to continue committing the same type of offence, albeit at different times of day, at different locations, or towards different targets. Alternatively, especially if the offender has a wide repertoire of offending skills, he or she may turn to other methods—as from simple car theft to key theft (Copes and Cherbonneau 2006) or car-jacking—some of which may involve innovation. Finally, some offenders may turn to totally different forms of crime, especially where these share some of the important characteristics of previously preferred ones.

Multi-Stage Decision-Making During the Crime Event

Identifying the *modus operandi* used by an offender in furtherance of a particular crime has long been recognised as an important aspect of both crime detection and crime prevention, but attention has often been confined to decision-making in relation to the central stages of a crime event, without equivalent attention to its opening and closing stages. But even beginning middle-and-end conceptualisations of the process are too simple to capture the dynamic unfolding of criminal events, and the detailed requirements of the crime in terms of the resources and actions needed during each of its stages.

Empirical research during the 1980s and 1990s began to provide some of the necessary detail. Walsh's (1980) study of residential burglary, for example, drew attention to how offenders made use of local criminal knowledge networks when looking around for opportunities to burgle; and Rossmo's (2000) studies of serial murder have indicated just how complex are the demands of successful offending in terms of choice of locations for different stages of the crime event.

The Decision-Making Models

We developed a set of simple flow diagrams to illustrate the decision processes for the three stages of criminal involvement, and for the criminal event. In the choice of crime to be modelled in the diagrams, we were guided by both theoretical and practical considerations: we wanted to be as crime-specific as existing knowledge allowed, but also to select an offence that was sufficiently common and serious to justify special preventive efforts. For these reasons we chose burglary as a volume crime over which there was considerable concern, and in relation to which considerable empirical research had been generated. In terms of crime-specificity, we chose suburban burglary, rather than residential burglary or simply burglary because we believed that burglaries committed in suburbs were quite different from those committed in the city centre. This belief was subsequently confirmed by Poyner and Webb (1991) who found that inner-city burglaries tended to be committed by offenders on foot who were looking for cash and jewellery, whereas those in the suburbs were committed by offenders who used cars and targeted electronic goods. Differences in the methods used to gain access were also found. Because there is restricted access to the side and rear of older town houses in England, entry was often gained through the front door or a front window. In the suburbs, however, burglars were as likely to enter from the back or side of the house as the front.

Initiation

Figure 3.1 illustrates the factors influencing the initial decision to become involved in suburban burglary. Box 1 lists various psychological and sociological background factors traditionally thought to influence the values, attitudes and personality traits that dispose people to commit crime. In terms of the rational choice perspective these factors are viewed as having more of an orienting function. On the one hand, they contribute to ongoing processes of learning and experience (Box 2) that influence the individual's perceptions and judgements about the attractiveness and viability of criminal activity. On the other hand the background factors also influence the individual's material conditions and the particular problems and opportunities to which they will be exposed. Thus, Box 3 deals with the offender 's current life circumstances, such as his or her friends, employment, housing, marital status, aspects of lifestyle, and so on. These help to shape an individual's current needs and motives (Box 4), as well as current opportunities for meeting these needs, and the inducements that may trigger or increase them (Box 5). The other boxes indicate how these needs are translated by the offender, based on his or her accumulated experience and learning, through a process of identifying and evaluating alternative courses of action (Boxes 6 and 7) into a readiness to become involved in this form of crime (Box 8). During this stage, background factors have their greatest influence, since they shape both the nature of the individual's accumulated learning and experience, and his or her current life circumstances.

Habituation

During habituation (Figure 3.2), background factors play less of a part in decisions. Instead, the dominant roles are exercised by contemporary ones: by the rewards of crime and by consequent changes in the offender 's circumstances, such the acquisition of new friends, increased professionalism, and changes in lifestyle and associated values.

Desistance

At the stage of desistance (Figure 3.3), background factors have ceased to play any significant part in decision-making. Rather, it is lack of success in bringing crimes to satisfactory completion (including brushes with the law) and increasing reluctance to take risks, together with further changes in current life

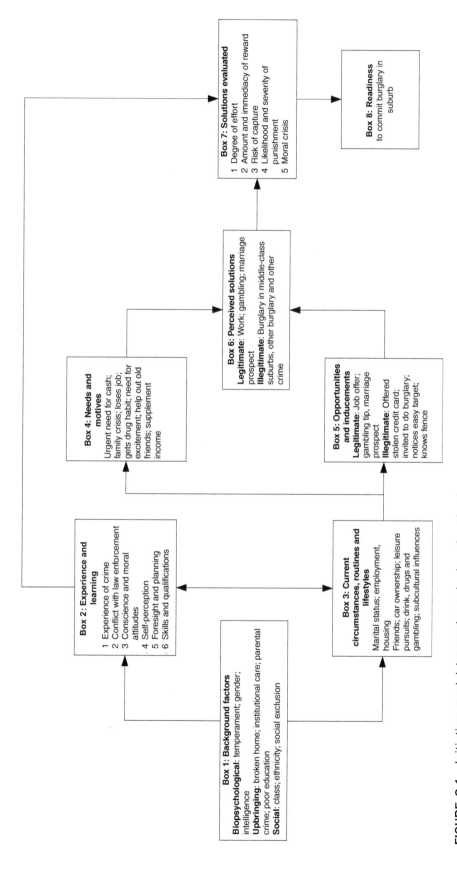

FIGURE 3.1 Initiation model (example: suburban burglary)
(*Source: adapted from Clarke and Cornish 1985*)

circumstances (such as marriage and increasing family responsibilities) that play the important roles in decisions to desist.

The Crime Event

For an experienced offender, decision-making in relation to the crime event (Figure 3.4) will tend to concentrate solely on those situational factors that hinder or advance instrumental action in fulfilment of the criminal goal. Since questions of needs and motives, moral scruples and readiness have already been addressed, they are unlikely to intrude into the decision-making process at this point unless the offender is inexperienced, or the action has been disrupted in some way—perhaps by unanticipated opposition or additional criminal opportunities that require a change of plan. But although the source of the variables considered during crime-commission may narrow, the decisionmaking process is not a simple one.

Crime Scripts

In Figure 3.4, attention is focused on just two of the steps involved—the selection of area and target house—but as mentioned earlier offenders are presented with a much more complex sequence of decisions. To assist analysis of this process, Cornish (1994) subsequently proposed the concept of crime scripts, which are step-by-step accounts of the procedures used by offenders to commit particular crimes. Crime scripts are designed to help identify every stage of the crime-commission process, the decisions and actions that must be taken at each stage, and the resources—such as criminal cast, props and suitable locations—required for effective action at each step. By providing a template that outlines the necessary steps involved in any kind of successful offending, crime scripts can reveal the rationality in even ostensibly 'senseless' crimes, and the complexities of even simple ones.

One such possible sequence is briefly sketched out in Figure 3.5's crime script for suburban burglary. Notice that the stages of the crime script are relatively uniform across crimes, while their contents—the cast, props, locations and actions—are specific to the crime being described.

A need for cash, a chance meeting between burglars, or a hot tip about a suitable target may start the crime event. Preparations may include assembling tools for a break-in, and the theft of a vehicle for the trip to the suburban development. The next steps involve entering the neighbourhood, adopting a plausible reason for being there, and selecting a house to enter—ideally, one for which the promise of reward is high, and the effort and risks of breaking in are low. Getting into the house, systematically searching for, and rapidly choosing the goods to steal follow this stage. The goods must then be carried out to the van or car without being seen by neighbours or passers-by. Afterwards, they may have to be stored in some safe location while buyers are found. Finally, they must be delivered to the buyers in exchange for cash. Where they occur, the 'further stages' referred to in Figure 3.5 often constitute crime scripts of their own.

Such crime scripts range from comparatively simple sequences to more complex ones where many participants, locations and actions may be involved, and within which a number of crime scripts may be merged—as where vehicles and guns are stolen for a robbery, witnesses injured or killed, and the spoils are afterwards marketed (see, for example, the script for professional auto theft, or 'ringing': Cornish and Clarke 2002). The crime scripts themselves are subject to further development as new empirical data

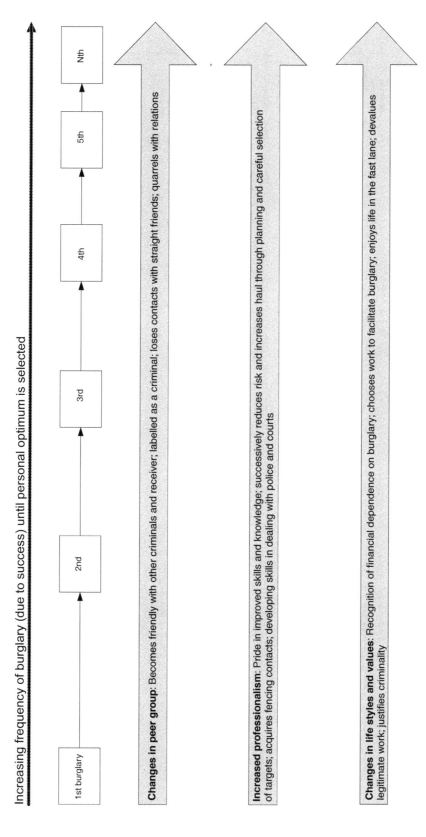

FIGURE 3.2 Habituation model (example: suburban burglary)

(*Source: adapted from Clarke and Cornish 1985*)

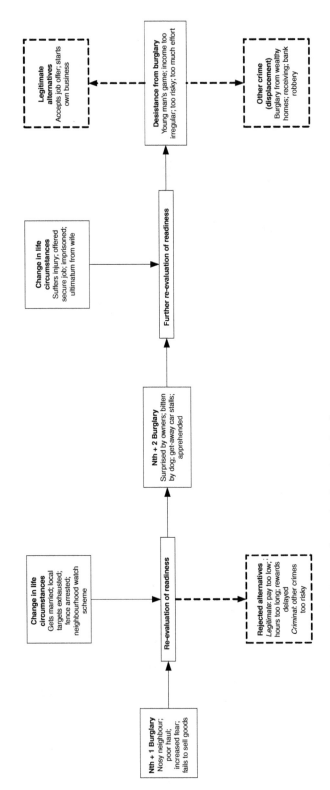

FIGURE 3.3 Desistance model (example: suburban burglary)
(*Source: adapted from Clarke and Cornish 1985*)

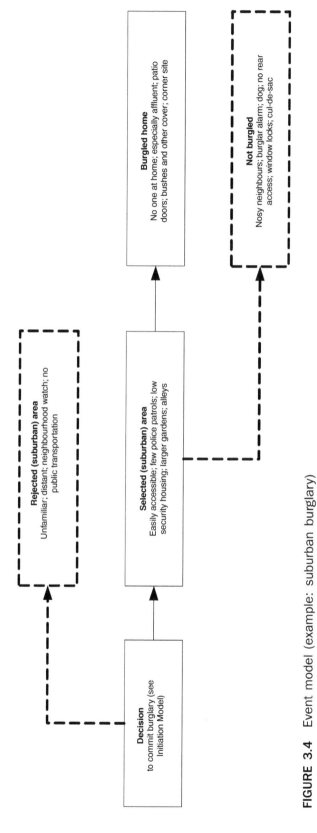

FIGURE 3.4 Event model (example: suburban burglary)
(*Source: adapted from Clarke and Cornish 1985*)

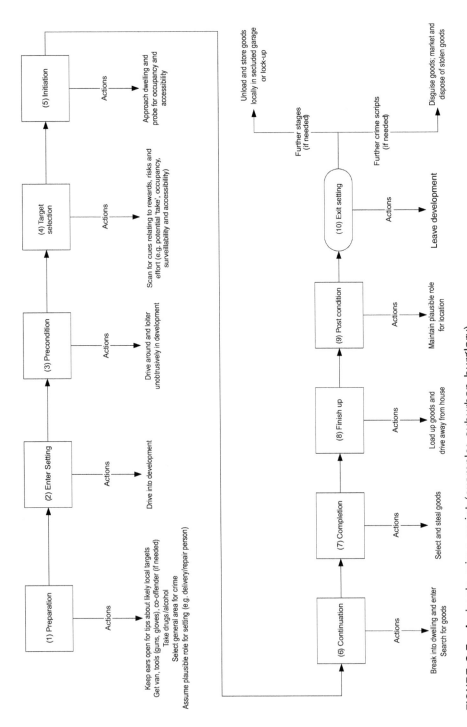

FIGURE 3.5 A simple crime script (example: suburban burglary)
(*Source: adapted from Cornish and Clarke 2006*)

come to light. For example, Nee and Meenaghan (2006) have recently provided new data on methods of search used by burglars within targeted houses; and, in the context of auto theft, Cherbonneau and Copes (2006) have described in detail some of the strategies used by offenders to avoid detection ('hiding in the open') while driving a stolen vehicle. As well as making important contributions to our understanding of specific crime scripts involving auto theft, such research also suggests the need to pay more attention to analogous strategies used by offenders to establish and maintain plausible roles before, during and after the commission of other types of crime.

The concept of crime scripts has helped to provide further evidence of the importance of offender decision-making, its pervasive presence in criminal activity and its rational, purposeful nature. It also provides a detailed understanding of the crime-commission process—from the analysis of body switching, which involves the switching of vehicle identity numbers from crashed but legitimate vehicles to the bodies of stolen ones (Tremblay *et al.* 2001), to the hunting process of serial sex offenders (Beauregard *et al.* 2007), or the *modus operandi* of adolescent sex offenders (Leclerc and Tremblay 2007). The use of script analysis can be particularly illuminating when used in relation to complex crimes, such as terrorism (see, for example, the elaborate script developed by Clarke and Newman (2006) for suicide bombing).

Misperceptions and Criticisms

Partly because of its perceived association with economics, and partly because it does not fit in with conventional views about what constitutes a criminological theory, the rational choice perspective has faced a range of misunderstandings, misperceptions and criticisms. Many arise from misunderstandings about, or objections to, its metatheoretical assumptions and practical goals. Psychologists often criticise it for not paying sufficient attention to the development and importance of criminal motivation, and to the merits of early prevention. Sociologists tend to criticise it for failing to contextualise offending and its meaning(s) within the rich tapestry of offenders' lives and lifestyles, and for being too policy-oriented—that is, too concerned with preventing crime. These differences in preoccupations, theoretical goals and orientations towards practice exist and have to be recognised. Some of the most common ones are briefly noted here.

Offenders Act Rationally Less Often Than is Claimed

As was noted earlier, because of the conditions under which they make them, the decisions made by offenders tend to evidence limited rather than perfect rationality. Since they may very well be doing the best they can in the circumstances, however, it is generally conceded that this is enough to qualify their behaviour as rational. A review of research on property offenders, such as auto thieves, burglars and robbers, for example, concluded that there was considerable support for this conclusion (Gibbons 1994). Many times, however, offenders are reported as acting without much forethought—failing to do much planning, acting impulsively, ignoring consequences and making mistakes. They are also reported as offending under the influence of drugs or drink, or as having been spurred on to act recklessly by their peers (see, for example Wright *et al.* 2006).

It is often difficult to determine how widespread or significant are these alleged departures from the norm of bounded rationality, and the extent to which they should be allowed to qualify the general picture. Since abandoning the view that offenders act rationally can lead to a subtle re-pathologisation—or, just as dangerous, a romanticisation—of their behaviour and a reopening of the debate over the extent to which delinquents and criminals are different from the rest of us, this is a serious step for social scientists to take. Before doing so, it might be wise to ask the following questions:

- Are the respondents a representative sample of those committing the offence in question, or are they those who have been particularly unsuccessful at offending?
- Do they have reasons for concealing evidence of prudential behaviour? Are they, for example, trying to assert spontaneity, daring and carelessness of consequences as a way of impressing their peers or questioners?
- Is evidence of deliberate heedlessness of consequences necessarily evidence of irrationality?
- Is lack of evidence of planning, evidence of lack of planning? Could the lack of evidence be explained by a failure on the part of the researcher to seek it in the details of how such crimes are carried out?
- Is an apparent lack of overt planning on the part of experienced offenders evidence of irrationality? Or does it denote routinisation of much of the crime script in question?
- Is evidence of thrill or pleasure seeking in offending, or offending to support a partying lifestyle, evidence of irrationality?

Issues such as these are difficult to resolve since they turn not only on the quality of the empirical data but also on questions of the definition of rationality, the correct identification of motives and purposes, the truthfulness of respondents, the knowledge and expertise of researchers in relation to what is going on, and the extent to which they buy into the presumption of rationality as a necessary discipline when theorising in the social sciences.

Ironically, since so much effort has been expended over it, the whole debate is only of tangential importance to the rational choice perspective itself. This is because its interest is not so much in the extent to which offenders are, in fact, rational actors as in the more relevant question for situational crime prevention of whether reliable information about how particular crimes are successfully committed can be gleaned and reconstructed from offenders' accounts of their criminal activities. If this can be done, then there is a good chance that situational measures can be designed on the basis of this information—and, indeed, from information relating to failures and attempts—to successfully prevent or disrupt the crime events in question. It scarcely needs adding that measures designed to prevent or disrupt purposeful, rational action will be even more likely to prevent or disrupt purposeful action that falls short of this degree of rationality. Indeed, actions that do not conform to the logic of the situation will tend to fail of their own accord.

Some Crimes are Not Rational

Predatory property crimes, organised crime and white-collar crimes are generally perceived as rational, instrumental activities with commonplace, easily understood motives and clear material objectives. Crimes involving sex and violence, on the other hand, raise issues in all these areas. Consistent with the desire to distance ourselves from these offenders, there is often a reluctance to explore the motives in question, or to view any means associated with their fulfilment as rational and instrumental. This is particularly the case in relation to violent offending where, despite (or perhaps because of) most people's experiences in schoolyard and workplace, the notion that violence could be an attractive instrumental option for achieving valued goals is an uncomfortable one.

This reluctance appears to stem from three sources. The first is the belief that only economically motivated crimes should be considered rational. This view is patently absurd since it rules out from consideration a whole swathe of criminal activity fuelled by common human desires and motives (Clarke and Cornish 2001: 33, Table 1)—for example, to assert dominance or control, to avenge an insult, to hurt or frighten someone, to prove toughness and bravery, to have fun, to gain status and admiration and so on. The second source of reluctance arises when the process of correctly identifying a motive is replaced by one of labelling it—for example, as senseless, inconceivable, inhuman and so on. Since the motive cannot be contemplated, the observer is absolved from the business of judging whether either the motive is intelligible or the means taken to secure its fulfilment are rational. The third reason for reluctance is similar, and arises from the failure to make distinctions between means, ends and motives. In the case of serial sexual murder, for example, if certain elements of the crime seem pathological e.g. the motive itself and the use of disproportionate or even frenzied violence to complete the crime—then the whole crime-commission process may be dismissed as irrational, even when there is considerable evidence of planning, target selection, disposal of evidence and other attempts to avoid discovery.

Judging the rationality of a particular criminal action can only be done after the motive has been properly identified: a 'senseless' mugging may become viewed as intelligible or even rational once its motive has been correctly determined. This having been done, the rationality of the methods used can then in turn be assessed. To take another example, the issue of lack of overt planning is still cited by many researchers as evidence of irrational decisionmaking, despite the well-attested fact that, especially during habituation—the stage of involvement during which crime scripts are likely to be most well developed—experienced offenders may routinise many aspects of their decision-making. These useful rules of thumb might include adopting standing decisions to offend, going equipped with weapons as a routine self-protective precaution by those living a criminal lifestyle, as well as a routine preparation for offending if the circumstances arise, and using pattern planning. As Sommers and Baskin put it:

> As the circumstances of the women's lives changed, it became less and less likely that they actively considered alternatives to committing crimes. Decisions concerning the execution of violent crimes became routine or 'patterned,' relying largely on their ability to recognize and seize situational opportunities. (Sommers and Baskin 1993: 157)

Lack of attention to the details of crime-commission and to the multi-tasking nature of offenders' lifestyles may often be responsible for researchers' failures to see rational decision-making where it is present. Nevertheless, given that, to our mind, the best and most persuasive evidence for the rationality of offending comes from the many ethnographic studies of particular crimes, how is it that their authors regularly come to conclusions about the rationality of offenders' decision-making that are so much at variance with our own, especially when their data would appear to conform so closely to all the assumptions of the rational choice perspective? The issues discussed above go some way to explaining this, but ultimately they may well reflect the mutual tensions inevitable in a field of interdisciplinary studies such as that of criminology, where conceptual frameworks collide and disciplinary preoccupations and missions vary. Radically divergent views on the relative importance of explaining as opposed to controlling crime, on criminal justice policy matters, and on the status and value of policy-oriented theory and practice may all reduce mutual respect and the inclination to cooperate (see Clarke 2004). Some of these issues are explored briefly below.

Conclusion

The core concepts of the rational choice perspective outlined above are a set of working assumptions, and the perspective itself is more a set of sensitising concepts than a conventional criminological theory. Its main purpose is to provide a heuristic device for analysing the conditions leading to the occurrence of crime events: fruitfulness rather than empirical truth is therefore its primary objective. Treating offending 'as if' it is rational involves viewing offenders as reasoning criminals. This in turn suggests the utility of a decision-making approach, and of the development of decision-making models which explore further the implications of the rationality presumption in the context of criminal involvement and crime-commission. Such models provide a framework within which to synthesise the results of ethnographic research on offending, and a perspective by means of which new research directions can be identified. In particular, by providing a way of identifying some of the conditions under which crimes occur, novel ways of preventing or disrupting criminal activity can be developed.

As we have made clear, the rational choice perspective was conceived primarily to assist the development of situational prevention, but it has also made some other, specific contributions to criminology. Thus, it has been able to provide plausible explanations, backed by empirical data, for phenomena such as repeat victimisation (Farrell *et al.* 1995), the preferences of thieves for particular types of products (Clarke 1999), and the dramatic fall in the suicide rate following the substitution of natural gas for coal gas in the UK (Clarke and Mayhew 1988).

More generally, the rational choice perspective itself and allied approaches such as crime pattern analysis have gradually extended their analyses of criminal behaviour from property crimes such as burglary and auto theft into the area of so-called expressive offending, such as opioid addiction (Bennett 1986), serial murder (Rossmo 2000) and child sexual abuse (Wortley and Smallbone 2006)—all crimes often cited as being inaccessible to a rational choice analysis because of their allegedly irrational, impulsive or pathologically motivated aspects.

The rational choice perspective is still very much a work in progress—a theory that is good enough for the present rather than simply 'good enough'. As a theory for practice it has always tended, once its initial assumptions were in place, to be reactive rather than proactive, growing alongside the development of situational crime prevention and developing as the result of the need to better understand criminological phenomena: the role of displacement, the details of the crime-commission process and the different aspects of criminal decision-making. Growth and change is also occurring in response to critiques of its minimalist view of the offender (Wortley 2001; Cornish and Clarke 2003; Ekblom 2007). The recognition that crime prevention practice has implicitly assumed the existence not only of the sociopathic predator, but also of offenders with less determination and moral scruples, has led to progressively greater recognition of the roles of excuses, and situational pressures and provocations in decisions to offend. We hope that this openness to new ideas and concepts will be maintained in the future.

References

Beauregard, E., Proulx, J., Rossmo, K., Leclerc, B. and Allaire, J.-F. (2007) 'Script Analysis of the Hunting Process of Serial Sex Offenders', *Criminal Justice and Behavior*, 34: 1069–84.

Bennett, T. (1986) 'A Decision-making Approach to Opioid Addiction', in D.B. Cornish and R.V. Clarke (eds) *The Reasoning Criminal: Rational Choice Perspectives on Offending*. New York: Springer-Verlag.

Bennett, T. and Wright, R. (1984) *Burglars on Burglary: Prevention and the Offender*. Aldershot, UK: Gower.

Cherbonneau, M. and Copes, H. (2006) ' "Drive it Like You Stole it": Auto Theft and the Illusion of Normalcy', *British Journal of Criminology*, 46: 193–211.

Clarke, R.V. (1980) ' "Situational" Crime Prevention: Theory and Practice', *British Journal of Criminology* 20: 136–47.

Clarke, R.V. (1999) *Hot Products: Understanding, Anticipating and Reducing Demand for Stolen Goods*, Police Research Series, Paper 112. London: Home Office.

Clarke, R.V. (2004) 'Technology, Criminology and Crime Science', *European Journal on Criminal Policy and Research*, 10: 55–63.

Clarke, R.V. and Cornish, D.B. (1983) 'Editorial Introduction', in R.V. Clarke and D.B. Cornish (eds) *Crime Control in Britain*. Albany, NY: State University of New York Press.

Clarke, R.V. and Cornish, D.B. (1985) 'Modeling Offenders' Decisions: A Framework for Research and Policy', in M. Tonry and N. Morris (eds) *Crime and Justice: An Annual Review of Research*, *Vol. 6*. Chicago, IL: University of Chicago Press.

Clarke, R.V. and Cornish, D.B. (2001) 'Rational Choice', in R. Paternoster and R. Bachman (eds) *Explaining Criminals and Crime: Essays in Contemporary Criminological Theory*. Los Angeles, CA: Roxbury.

Clarke, R.V. and Martin, D.N. (1975) 'A Study of Absconding and its Implications for the Residential Treatment of Delinquents' in J. Tizard, I.A. Sinclair and R.V. Clarke (eds) *Varieties of Residential Experience*. London: Routledge and Kegan Paul.

Clarke, R.V. and Mayhew, P. (1988) 'The British Gas Suicide Story and its Criminological Implications', in M. Tonry and N. Morris (eds) *Crime and Justice: An Annual Review of Research*, *Vol. 10*. Chicago, IL: University of Chicago Press.

Clarke, R.V. and Newman, G.R. (2006) *Outsmarting the Terrorists*. Westport, CT: Praeger Security International.

Clarke, R.V. and Weisburd, D. (1994) 'Diffusion of Crime Control Benefits: Observations on the Reverse of Displacement', in R.V. Clarke (ed.) *Crime Prevention Studies, Vol. 2*. Monsey, NY: Criminal Justice Press.

Cocheo, S. (1997) 'The Bank Robber, the Quote and the Final Irony', *ABA Banking Journal*, Vol. 89, March (www .banking.com/aba/profile_0397.htm).

Copes, H. and Cherbonneau, M. (2006) 'The Key to Auto Theft: Emerging Methods of Auto Theft from the Offenders' Perspective', *British Journal of Criminology*, 46: 917–34.

Cornish, D.B. (1978) *Gambling: A Review of the Literature and Its Implications for Policy and Research*, Home Office Research Studies 42. London: HMSO.

Cornish, D.B. (1994) 'The Procedural Analysis of Offending, and its Relevance for Situational Prevention', in R.V. Clarke (ed.) *Crime Prevention Studies*, Volume 3. Monsey, NY: Criminal Justice Press.

Cornish, D.B. and Clarke, R.V. (1975) *Residential Treatment and its Effects on Delinquency*, Home Office Research Studies 32. London: HMSO.

Cornish, D.B. and Clarke, R.V. (eds) (1986) *The Reasoning Criminal: Rational Choice Perspectives on Offending*. New York, NY: Springer-Verlag.

Cornish, D.B. and Clarke, R.V. (1987) 'Understanding Crime Displacement: An Application of Rational Choice Theory', *Criminology* 25(4): 933–47.

Cornish, D.B. and Clarke, R.V. (2002) 'Analyzing Organized Crimes', in A.R. Piquero and S.G. Tibbetts (eds) *Rational Choice and Criminal Behavior: Recent Research and Future Challenges*. New York: Routledge.

Cornish, D.B. and Clarke, R.V. Clarke (2003) 'Opportunities, Precipitators and Criminal Decisions: A Reply to Wortley's Critique of Situational Crime Prevention', in M.J. Smith and D.B. Cornish (eds) *Theory for Practice in Situational Crime Prevention. Crime Prevention Studies, Vol. 16*. Monsey, NY: Criminal Justice Press.

Cornish, D.B. and Clarke, R.V. (2006) 'The Rational Choice Perspective', in S. Henry and M.M. Lanier (eds) *The Essential Criminology Reader*. Boulder, CO: Westview Press.

Ekblom, P. (1995) 'Less Crime, by Design', *Annals of the American Academy of Political and Social Science*, 539: 114–29.

Ekblom, P. (2007) 'Making Offenders Richer ', in G. Farrell, K. Bowers, S. Johnson and M. Townsley (eds) *Imagination for Crime Prevention: Essays in Honour of Ken Pease. Crime Prevention Studies, Vol. 21*. Monsey, NY: Criminal Justice Press.

Farrell, G., Phillips, C. and Pease, K. (1995) 'Like Taking Candy. Why Does Repeat Victimization Occur?', *British Journal of Criminology*, 35: 384–99.

Gibbons, D. (1994) *Talking About Crime and Criminals: Problems and Issues in Theory Development in Criminology*. Englewood Cliffs, NJ: Prentice-Hall.

Herrnstein, R.J. (1990) 'Rational Choice Theory: Necessary but not Sufficient', *American Psychologist*, 45(3): 356–67.

Hesseling, R.B.P. (1994) 'Displacement: A Review of the Empirical Literature', in R.V. Clarke (ed.) *Crime Prevention Studies, Volume 3*. Monsey, NY: Criminal Justice Press.

John Jay College (2007) 'On the Edge: Transgression and the Dangerous Other. A Celebratory Exploration of Intellectual and Artistic Transgression'. Conference, 9–10 August, New York City. (www.jjay.cuny.edu /ontheedge/ OnTheEdgeConferenceProgram.pdf).

Katz, J. (1988) *Seductions of Crime*. New York: Basic Books.

Knepper, P. (2007) 'Situational Logic in Social Science Inquiry: From Economics to Criminology', *Review of Austrian Economics* 20(1): 25–41 (www.springerlink.com/ content/a761072678017n83/fulltext.pdf).

Laub, J.H. and Sampson, R.J. (2003) *Shared Beginnings, Divergent Lives: Delinquent Boys to Age 70*. Cambridge, MA: Harvard University Press.

Leclerc, B. and Tremblay, P. (2007) 'Strategic Behavior in Adolescent Sexual Offenses Against Children: Linking Modus Operandi to Sexual Behaviors', *Sexual Abuse: A Journal of Research and Treatment*, 19: 23–41.

Maguire, M. and Bennett, T. (1982) *Burglary in a Dwelling*. London: Heinemann.

Matza, D. (1964) *Delinquency and Drift*. New York: Wiley.

Nee, C. and Meenaghan, A. (2006) 'Expert Decision Making in Burglars', *British Journal of Criminology*, 46: 935–49.

Poyner, B. and Webb, B. (1991) *Crime Free Housing.* Oxford: Butterworth Architecture. Reppetto, T.A. (1974) *Residential Crime.* Cambridge, MA: Ballinger.

Rossmo, D.K. (2000) *Geographic Profiling.* Boca Raton, FL: CRC Press.

Simon, H.A. (1990) 'Invariants of Human Behavior ', *Annual Review of Psychology,* 41: 1–19.

Sinclair, I.A.C. (1971) *Hostels for Probationers.* Home Office Research Studies No. 6. London: HMSO.

Smith, M.J., Clarke, R.V. and Pease, K. (2002) 'Anticipatory Benefits in Crime Prevention', in N. Tilley (ed.) *Analysis for Crime Prevention. Crime Prevention Studies, Vol. 13.* Monsey, NY: Criminal Justice Press.

Sommers, I. and Baskin, D.R. (1993) 'The Situational Context of Violent Female Offending', *Journal of Research in Crime and Delinquency,* 30(2): 136–62.

Tremblay, P., Talon, B. and Hurley, D. (2001) 'Body Switching and Related Adaptations in the Resale of Stolen Vehicles: Script Elaborations and Aggregate Crime Learning Curves', *British Journal of Criminology,* 41: 561–79.

Tunnell, K.D. (1992) *Choosing Crime: The Criminal Calculus of Property Offenders.* Chicago, IL: Nelson-Hall.

Walsh, D.P. (1980) *Break-Ins: Burglary from Private Houses.* London: Constable.

Weisburd, D., Wyckoff, L.A., Ready, J., Eck, J.E., Hinkle, J.C. and Gajewski, F. (2006) 'Does Crime Just Move Around the Corner? A Controlled Study of Spatial Displacement and Diffusion of Crime Control Benefits', *Criminology,* 44(3): 549–92.

Wortley, R. (2001) 'A Classification of Techniques for Controlling Situational Precipitators of Crime', *Security Journal* 14: 63–82.

Wortley, R. and S. Smallbone (eds) (2006) *Situational Prevention of Child Sexual Abuse. Crime Prevention Studies, Vol. 19.* Cullompton, UK: Willan Publishing.

Wright, R., Brookman, F. and Bennett, T. (2006) 'The Foreground Dynamics of Street Robbery in Britain', *British Journal of Criminology,* 46: 1–15.

DISCUSSION QUESTIONS

By John M. Stogner

1. Is there utility in a theory based on rationality that admits that perfect rationality is rare? Given the admission of imperfect rationality, should we attribute deviance to rational decisions following an analysis that favors crime or errors in rationality?

2. How does substance use affect the theoretical propositions of rational choice theory? A large number of crimes are committed under the influence of alcohol or other drug—does this strengthen or weaken your assessment of the theory?

3. What is the utility of evaluating the criminal involvement and criminal event models separately?

4. Is criminal behavior as purposive as Clarke and Cornish suggest?

5. Without reading ahead, what guidance does rational choice theory offer for policymakers? Police officers? Correctional officials?

CHAPTER FOUR

Routine Activity Theory

LAWRENCE E. COHEN AND MARCUS FELSON

STUDENT INTRODUCTION
By John M. Stogner

The majority of criminological theories begin with a focus on potential offenders, examining individual disposition or decision making; however, Lawrence Cohen and Marcus Felson took a very different approach when developing their routine activities theory. Their theory does note the existence of people motivated and willing to violate the law, but many of its propositions relate more to changes in law-abiding behaviors than to changes in deviant motivation. Simply put, Cohen and Felson asked whether changes in routine law-abiding behaviors may have influenced growing crime rates more than changes in criminal disposition. In 1979, they noted that crime in the United States had been increasing since World War II despite the fact that social conditions were improving. They suggested that this growth in crime rates may be linked to the average (noncriminal) citizen's behaviors changing over time rather than factors specific to offenders.

Cohen and Felson identify three conditions that necessarily have to converge in time and space for a crime to occur. First, there must be an individual willing to engage in deviance—what Cohen and Felson label a *motivated offender*. Second, a target must be perceived as suitable; a *suitable target* is one that is valued and accessible. Third, there needs to be a *lack of appropriate guardians* against deviance.

Cohen and Felson did not imply that this guardianship was limited to formal agents (police)—ordinary citizens frequently act as potential guardians due to their potential to intervene or report a violation. Their work does not imply that each convergence of a motivated offender with a suitable target when guardians are absent will result in a crime. Instead, it contends that crime rates are related to the frequency of these conditions converging. When these conditions converge in time and space more frequently, crime increases.

As you read, attempt to develop an understanding for Cohen and Felson's definition for each of the three prerequisites for a crime to occur. You should also attempt to evaluate their arguments about changes in routine activities between the 1940s and 1970s while also considering how their theory relates to changes in crime rates between the work's publication (in 1979) and today. Remember that crime rates continued to increase in the United States through the mid-1990s but are no longer following that trajectory. Ask yourself whether our routine activities changed in the 1990s in some way that altered the frequency of the three conditions converging. Finally, as you read contemplate how each of the three prerequisite conditions is best quantified.

ROUTINE ACTIVITY THEORY
By Lawrence E. Cohen and Marcus Felson

We argue that structural changes in routine activity patterns can influence crime rates by affecting the convergence in space and time of the three minimal elements of direct-contact predatory violations: (I) motivated offenders, (2) suitable targets, and (3) the absence of capable guardians against a violation. We further argue that the lack of any one of these elements is sufficient to prevent the successful completion of a direct-contact predatory crime, and that the convergence in time and space of suitable targets and the absence of capable guardians may even lead to large increases in crime rates without necessarily requiring any increase in the structural conditions that motivate individuals to engage in crime. That is, if the proportion of motivated offenders or even suitable targets were to remain stable in a community, changes in routine activities could nonetheless alter the likelihood of their convergence in space and time, thereby creating more opportunities for crimes to occur. Control therefore becomes critical. If controls through routine activities were to decrease, illegal predatory activities could then be likely to increase....

Unlike many criminological inquiries, we do not examine why individuals or groups are inclined criminally, but rather we take criminal inclination as given and examine the manner in which the spatiotemporal organization of social activities helps people to translate their criminal inclinations into action. Criminal violations are treated here as routine activities which share many attributes of, and are interdependent with, other routine activities....

The Minimal Elements of Direct-Contact Predatory Violations

As we previously stated, despite their great diversity, direct-contact predatory violations share some important requirements which facilitate analysis of their structure. Each successfully completed violation minimally requires an *offender* with both criminal inclinations and the ability to carry out those inclinations, a person or object providing a *suitable target* for the offender, and *absence of guardians* capable of preventing violations. We emphasize that the lack of any one of these elements normally is sufficient to prevent such violations from occurring. Though guardianship is implicit in everyday life, it usually is marked by the absence of violations, hence it is easy to overlook. While police action is analyzed widely, guardianship by ordinary citizens of one another and property as they go about routine activities may be one of the most neglected elements in sociological research on crime, especially since it links seemingly unrelated social roles and relationships to the occurrence or absence of illegal acts.

The conjunction of these minimal elements can be used to assess how social structure may affect the tempo of each type of violation. That is, the probability that a violation will occur at any specific time and place might be taken as a function of the convergence of likely offenders and suitable targets in the absence of capable guardians. Through consideration of how trends and fluctuations in social conditions affect the frequency of this convergence of criminogenic circumstances, an explanation of temporal trends in crime rates can be constructed . . . .

The Ecological Nature of Illegal Acts

Since illegal activities must feed upon other activities, the spatial and temporal structure of routine legal activities should play an important role in determining the location, type and quantity of illegal acts occurring in a given community or society. Moreover, one can analyze how the structure of community organization as well as the level of technology in a society provide the circumstances under which crime can thrive. For example, technology and organization affect the capacity of persons with criminal inclinations to overcome their targets, as well as affecting the ability of guardians to contend with potential offenders by using whatever protective tools, weapons and skills they have at their disposal. Many technological advances designed for legitimate purposes—including the automobile, small power tools, hunting weapons, highways, telephones, etc.—may enable offenders to carry out their own work more effectively or may assist people in protecting their own or someone else's person or property.

Not only do routine legitimate activities often provide the wherewithal to commit offenses or to guard against others who do so, but they also provide offenders with suitable targets. Target suitability is likely to reflect such things as value (i.e., the material or symbolic desirability of a personal or property target for offenders), physical visibility, access, and the inertia of a target against illegal treatment by offenders (including the weight, size, and attached or locked features of property inhibiting its illegal removal and the physical capacity of personal victims to resist attackers with or without weapons). Routine production activities probably affect the suitability of consumer goods for illegal removal by determining their value and weight. Daily activities may affect the location of property and personal targets in visible and accessible places at particular times. These activities also may cause people to have on hand objects that can be used as weapons for criminal acts or self-protection or to be preoccupied with tasks which reduce their capacity to discourage or resist offenders.

While little is known about conditions that affect the convergence of potential offenders, targets and guardians, this is a potentially rich source of propositions about crime rates. For example, daily work activities separate many people from those they trust and the property they value. Routine activities also bring together at various times of day or night persons of different background, sometimes in the presence of facilities, tools or weapons which influence the commission or avoidance of illegal acts. Hence, the timing of work, schooling and leisure may be of central importance for explaining crime rates . . . .

Microlevel Assumptions of the Routine Activity Approach

The theoretical approach taken here specifies that crime rate trends in the post-World War II United States are related to patterns of what we have called routine activities. We define these as any recurrent and prevalent activities which provide for basic population and individual needs, whatever their biological or cultural origins. Thus routine activities would include formalized work, as well as the provision of standard food, shelter, sexual outlet, leisure, social interaction, learning and childrearing. These activities may go well beyond the minimal levels needed to prevent a population's extinction, so long as their prevalence and recurrence makes them a part of everyday life.

Routine activities may occur (1) at home, (2) in jobs away from home, and (3) in other activities away from home. The latter may involve primarily household members or others. We shall argue that, since World War II, the United States has experienced a major shift of routine activities away from the first category into the remaining ones, especially those nonhousehold activities involving nonhousehold members. In particular, we shall argue that this shift in the structure of routine activities increases the probability that motivated offenders will converge in space and time with suitable targets in the absence of capable guardians, hence contributing to significant increases in the points in the direct contact predatory crime rates over these years.

If the routine activity approach is valid, then we should expect to find evidence for a number of empirical relationships regarding the nature and distribution of predatory violations. For example, we would expect

		Rape	Robbery	Assault	Personal Larceny with Contact	Total
A.* PLACE OF RESIDENCE	In or near home	63	129	572	75	839
	Elsewhere	119	584	1,897	1,010	3,610
B. VICTIM-OFFENDER RELATIONSHIP	(Lone Offender)					
	Relative	7	13	158	5	183
	Well Known	23	30	333	30	416
	Casual Acquaintance	11	26	308	25	370
	Don't Know/Sight Only	106	227	888	616	1,837
	(Multiple Offender)					
	Any Known	10***	68	252	43	373
	All Strangers	25***	349	530	366	1,270
C.* NUMBER OF VICTIMS	One	179	647	2,116	1,062	4,004
	Two	3	47	257	19	326
	Three	0	13	53	3	9
	Four Plus	0	6	43	1	50
D.** LOCATION AND RELATIONSHIP (sole offender only)	Home, Stranger	61	147	345	103	654
	Home, Nonstranger	45	74	620	22	761
	Street, Stranger	1,370	7,743	15,684	7,802	32,460
	Street, Nonstranger	179	735	5,777	496	7,167
	Elsewhere, Stranger	129	513	1,934	2,455	4,988
	Elsewhere, Nonstranger	47	155	1,544	99	1,874

Table 4.1. Incident-Specific Risk Rates for Rape, Robbery, Assault and Personal larceny with Contact, United States, 1974

*Calculated from Handelang et al., 1977: Tables 3.16, 3.18, 3.27, 3.28. Rates are per 100,000 persons ages 12 and over.

**See fn. 6 for source. Rates are per billion person-hours in stated locations.

***Based on white date only due to lack of suitable sample size for nonwhites as victims of rape with multiple

routine activities performed within or near the home and among family or other primary groups to entail lower risk of criminal victimization because they enhance guardianship capabilities. We should also expect that routine daily activities affect the location of property and personal targets in visible and accessible places at particular times, thereby influencing their risk of victimization. Furthermore, by determining their size and weight and in some cases their value, routine production activities should affect the suitability of consumer goods for illegal removal. Finally, if the routine activity approach is useful for explaining the paradox presented earlier, we should find that the circulation of people and property, the size and weight of consumer items etc., will parallel changes in crime rate trends for the post-World War II United States.

The veracity of the routine activity approach can be assessed by analyses of both microlevel and macrolevel interdependencies of human activities. While consistency at the former level may appear noncontroversial, or even obvious, one nonetheless needs to show that the approach does not contradict existing data before proceeding to investigate the latter level.

Empirical Assessment

Circumstances and Location of Offenses

The routine activity approach specifies that household and family activities entail lower risk of criminal victimization than nonhousehold-nonfamily activities, despite the problems in measuring the former.

National estimates from large-scale government victimization surveys in 1973 and 1974 support this generalization (see methodological information in Hindelang et al., 1976: Appendix 6). Table 5.1 presents several incident-victimization rates per 100,000 population ages 12 and older. Clearly, the rates in Panels A and B are far lower at or near home than elsewhere and far lower among relatives than others. The data indicate that risk of victimization varies directly with social distance between offender and victim. Panel C of this table indicates, furthermore, that risk of lone victimization far exceeds the risk of victimization for groups. These relationships are strengthened by considering time budget evidence that, on the average, Americans spend 16.26 hours per day at home, 1.38 hours on streets, in parks, etc., and 6.36 hours in other places (Szalai, 1972:795). Panel D of Table 34.1 presents our estimates of victimization per billion person-hours spent in such locations. For example, personal larceny rates (with contact) are 350 times higher at the hands of strangers in streets than at the hands of nonstrangers at home. Separate computations from 1973 victimization data (USDJ, 1976: Table 48) indicate that there were two motor vehicle thefts per million vehicle-hours parked at or near home, 55 per million vehicle-hours in streets, parks, playgrounds, school grounds or parking lots, and 12 per million vehicle-hours elsewhere. While the direction of these relationships is not surprising, their magnitudes should be noted. It appears that risk of criminal victimization varies dramatically among the circumstances and locations in which people place themselves and their property.

Target Suitability

Another assumption of the routine activity approach is that target suitability influences the occurrence of direct-contact predatory violations. Though we lack data to disaggregate all major components of target suitability (i.e., value, visibility, accessibility and inertia), together they imply that expensive and movable durables, such as vehicles and electronic appliances, have the highest risk of illegal removal.

As a specific case in point, we compared the 1975 composition of stolen property reported in the Uniform Crime Report (FBI, 1976: Tables 26-7) with national data on personal consumer expenditures for goods (CEA, 1976: Tables 13-16) and to appliance industry estimates of the value of shipments the same year (*Merchandising Week*, 1976). We calculated that $26.44 in motor vehicles and parts were stolen for each $100 of these goods consumed in 1975, while $6.81 worth of electronic appliances were stolen per $100 consumed. Though these estimates are subject to error in citizen and police estimation, what is important here is their size relative to other rates. For example, only 8¢ worth of nondurables and 12¢ worth of furniture and nonelectronic household durables were stolen per $100 of each category consumed, the motor vehicle risk being, respectively, 330 and 220 times as great. Though we lack data on the "stocks" of goods subject to risk, these "flow" data clearly support our assumption that vehicles and electronic appliances are greatly overrepresented in thefts.

The 1976 Buying Guide issue of *Consumer Reports* (1975) indicates why electronic appliances are an excellent retail value for a thief. For example, a Panasonic car tape player is worth $30 per lb., and a Phillips phonograph cartridge is valued at over $5,000 per lb., while large appliances such as refrigerators and washing machines are only worth $1 to $3 per lb. Not surprisingly, burglary data for the District of Columbia in 1969 (Scarr, 1972: Table 9) indicate that home entertainment items alone constituted nearly four times as many stolen items as clothing, food, drugs, liquor, and tobacco combined and nearly eight times as many stolen items as office supplies and equipment. In addition, 69 percent of national thefts classified in 1975 (FBI, 1976: Tables 1, 26) involve automobiles, their parts or accessories, and thefts from automobiles or thefts of bicycles. Yet radio and television sets plus electronic components and accessories totaled only 0.10 percent of the total truckload tonnage terminated in 1973 by intercity motor carriers, while passenger cars, motor vehicle parts and accessories, motorcycles, bicycles, and their parts, totaled only 5.5 percent of the 410 million truckload tons terminated (ICC, 1974). Clearly, portable and movable durables are reported stolen in great disproportion to their share of the value and weight of goods circulating in the United States.

Family Activities and Crime Rates

One would expect that persons living in single-adult households and those employed outside the home are less obligated to confine their time to family activities within households. From a routine activity perspective, these persons and their households should have higher rates of predatory criminal victimization. We also expect that adolescents and young adults who are perhaps more likely to engage in peer group activities rather than family activities will have higher rates of criminal victimization. Finally, married persons should have lower rates than others… . We note that victimization rates appear to be related inversely to age and are lower for persons in "less active" statuses (e.g., keeping house, unable to work, retired) and persons in intact marriages. A notable exception is… where persons unable to work appear more likely to be victimized by rape, robbery and personal larceny with contact than are other "inactive persons." Unemployed persons also have unusually high rates of victimization. However, these rates are consistent with the routine activity approach offered here: the high rates of victimization suffered by the unemployed may reflect their residential proximity to high concentrations of potential offenders as well as their age and racial composition, while handicapped persons have high risk of personal victimization because they are less able to resist motivated offenders. Nonetheless, persons who keep house have noticeably lower rates of victimization than those who are employed, unemployed, in school or in the armed forces. . . .

Burglary and robbery victimization rates are about twice as high for persons living in single-adult households as for other persons in each age group examined. Other victimization data (USDJ, 1976: Table 21) indicate that, while household victimization rates tend to vary directly with household size, larger households have lower rates per person. For example, the total household victimization rates (including burglary, household larceny, and motor vehicle theft) per households were 168 for single-person households and 326 for households containing six or more persons. Hence, six people distributed over six single-person households experience an average of 1,008 household victimizations, more than three times as many as one six-person household. Moreover, age of household head has a strong relationship to a household's victimization rate for these crimes. For households headed by persons under 20, the motor vehicle theft rate is nine times as high, and the burglary and household larceny rates four times as high as those for households headed by persons 65 and over (USDJ, 1976: Table 9).

While the data presented in this section were not collected originally for the purpose of testing the routine activity approach, our efforts to rework them for these purposes have proven fruitful. The routine activity approach is consistent with the data examined and, in addition, helps to accommodate within a rather simple and coherent analytical framework certain findings which, though not necessarily new, might otherwise be attributed only "descriptive" significance. In the next section, we examine macrosocial trends as they relate to trends in crime rates.

Changing Trends in Routine Activity Structure and Parallel Trends in Crime Rates

The main thesis presented here is that the dramatic increase in the reported crime rates in the U.S. since 1960 is linked to changes in the routine activity structure of American society and to a corresponding increase in target suitability and decrease in guardian presence. If such a thesis has validity, then we should be able to identify these social trends and show how they relate to predatory criminal victimization rates.

Trends in Human Activity Patterns

The decade 1960-1970 experienced noteworthy trends in the activities of the American population. For example, the percent of the population consisting of female college students increased 118 percent (USBC, 1975: Table 225). Married female labor force participant rates increased 31 percent (USBC, 1975: Table 563), while the percent of the population living as primary individuals increased by 34 percent (USBC,

1975: Table 51; see also Kobrin, 1976). We gain some further insight into changing routine activity patterns by comparing hourly data for 1960 and 1971 on households unattended by persons ages 14 or over when U.S. census interviewers first called.... These data suggest that the proportion of households unattended at 8 A.M. increased by almost half between 1960 and 1971. One also finds increases in rates of out-of-town travel, which provides greater opportunity for both daytime and nighttime burglary of residences. Between 1960 and 1970, there was a 72 percent increase in state and national park visits per capita (USBC, 1975), an 144 percent increase in the percent of plant workers eligible for three weeks vacation (BLS, 1975: Table 116), and an 184 percent increase in overseas travellers per population (USBC, 1975: Table 366). The National Travel Survey, conducted as part of the U.S. Census Bureau's Census of Transportation, confirms the general trends, tallying an 81 percent increase in the number of vacations taken by Americans from 1967 to 1972, a five-year period (USBC, 1973a: Introduction).

The dispersion of activities away from households appears to be a major recent social change. Although this decade also experienced an important 31 percent increase in the percent of the population ages 15-24, age structure change was only one of many social trends occurring during the period, especially trends in the circulation of people and property in American society.

The importance of the changing activity structure is underscored by taking a brief look at demographic changes between the years 1970 and 1975, a period of continuing crime rate increments. Most of the recent changes in age structure relevant to crime rates already had occurred by 1970; indeed, the proportion of the population ages 15-24 increased by only 6 percent between 1970 and 1975, compared with a 15 percent increase during the five years 1965 to 1970. On the other hand, major changes in the structure of routine activities continued during these years. For example, in only five years, the estimated proportion of the population consisting of husband-present, married women in the labor force households increased by 11 percent, while the estimated number of non-husband-wife households per 100,000 population increased from 9,150 to 11,420, a 25 percent increase (USBC, 1976: Tables 50, 276; USBC, 1970-1975). At the same time, the percent of population enrolled in higher education increased 16 percent between 1970 and 1975.

Related Property Trends and Their Relation to Human Activity Patterns

Many of the activity trends mentioned above normally involve significant investments in durable goods. For example, the dispersion of population across relatively more households (especially nonhusband-wife households) enlarges the market for durable goods such as television sets and automobiles. Women participating in the labor force and both men and women enrolled in college provide a market for automobiles. Both work and travel often involve the purchase of major movable or portable durables and their use away from home.

Considerable data are available which indicate that sales of consumer goods changed dramatically between 1960 and 1970 (as did their size and weight), hence providing more suitable property available for theft. For example, during this decade, constant-dollar personal consumer expenditures in the United States for motor vehicles and parts increased by 71 percent, while constant-dollar expenditures for other durables increased by 105 percent (calculated from CEA, 1976: Table B-16). In addition, electronic household appliances and small household shipments increased from 56.2 to 119.7 million units

(*Electrical Merchandising Week,* 1964; *Merchandising Week,* 1973). During the same decade, appliance imports increased in value by 681 percent (USBC, 1975: Table 1368).

This same period appears to have spawned a revolution in small durable product design which further feeds the opportunity for crime to occur. Relevant data from the 1960 and 1970 Sears catalogs on the weight of many consumer durable goods were examined. Sears is the nations largest retailer and its policy of purchasing and relabeling standard manufactured goods makes its catalogs a good source of data on widely merchandised consumer goods. The lightest television listed for sale in 1960 weighed 38 lbs., compared with 15 lbs. for 1970. Thus, the lightest televisions were $2^1/_2$ times as heavy in 1960 as 1970. Similar trends are observed for dozens of other goods listed in the Sears catalog. Data from Consumer *Reports Buying Guide,* published in December of 1959 and 1969, show similar changes for radios, record players, slide projectors, tape recorders, televisions, toasters and many other goods. Hence, major declines in weight between 1960 and 1970 were quite significant for these and other goods, which suggests that the consumer goods market may be producing many more targets suitable for theft. In general, one finds rapid growth in property suitable for illegal removal and in household and individual exposure to attack during the years 1960-1975.

Related Trends in Business Establishments

Of course, as households and individuals increased their ownership of small durables, businesses also increased the value of the merchandise which they transport and sell as well as the money involved in these transactions. Yet the Census of Business conducted in 1958, 1963, 1967, and 1972 indicate that the number of wholesale, retail, service, and public warehouse establishments (including establishments owned by large organizations) was a nearly constant ratio of one for every 16 persons in the United States. Since more goods and money were distributed over a relatively fixed number of business establishments, the tempo of business activity per establishment apparently was increasing. At the same time, the percent of the population employed as sales clerks or salesmen in retail trade declined from 1.48 percent to 1.27 percent between 1960 and 1970, a 14.7 percent decline (USBC, 1975: Table 589).

Though both business and personal property increased, the changing pace of activities appears to have exposed the latter to greater relative risk of attack, whether at home or elsewhere, due to the dispersion of goods among many more households, while concentrating goods in business establishments. However, merchandise in retail establishments with heavy volume and few employees to guard it probably is exposed to major increments in risk of illegal removal than is most other business property.

Composition of Crime Trends

If these changes in the circulation of people and property are in fact related to crime trends, the *composition* of the latter should reflect this. We expect relatively greater increases in personal and household victimization as compared with most business victimizations, while shoplifting should increase more rapidly than other types of thefts from businesses. We expect personal offenses at the hands of strangers to manifest greater increases than such offenses at the hands of nonstrangers. Finally, residential burglary rates should increase more in daytime than nighttime.

The available time series on the composition of offenses confirm these expectations. For example, Table 39.1 shows that commercial burglaries declined from 60 percent to 36 percent of the total, while daytime residential burglaries increased from 16 percent to 33 percent. Unlike the other crimes against business, shoplifting increased its share. Though we lack trend data on the circumstances of other violent offenses, murder data confirm our expectations. Between 1963 and 1975, felon-type murders increased from 17 percent to 32 percent of the total. Compared with a 47 percent increase in the rate of relative killings in this period, we calculated a 294 percent increase in the murder rate at the hands of known or suspected felon types.

Thus the trends in the composition of recorded crime rates appear to be highly consistent with the activity structure trends noted earlier. In the next section we apply the routine activity approach in order to model crime rate trends and social change in the post-World War II United States.

The Relationship of the Household Activity Ratio to Five Annual Official Index Crime Rates in the United States, 1947–1974

In this section, we test the hypothesis that aggregate official crime rate trends in the United States vary directly over time with the dispersion of activities away from family and household. The limitations of annual time series data do not allow construction of direct measures of changes in hourly activity patterns, or quantities, qualities and movements of exact stocks of household durable goods, but the Current Population Survey does provide related time series on labor force and household structure. From these data, we calculate annually (beginning in 1947) a household activity ratio by adding the number of married, husband-present female labor force participants (source: BLS, 1975: Table 5) to the number of non-husband-wife households (source: USBC, 1947-1976), dividing this sum by the total number of households in the U.S. (source: USBC, 1947-1976). This calculation provides an estimate of the proportion of American households in year t expected to be most highly exposed to risk of personal and property victimization due to the dispersion of their activities away from family and household and/ or their likelihood of owning extra sets of durables subject to high risk of attack. Hence, the household activity ratio should vary directly with official index crime rates.

Our empirical goal in this section is to test this relationship, with controls for those variables which other researches have linked empirically to crime rate trends in the United States. Since various researches have found such trends to increase with the proportion of the population in teen and young adult years (Fox, 1976; Land and Felson, 1976; Sagi and Wellford, 1968; Weliford, 1973), we include the population ages 15-24 per 100,000 resident population in year t as our first control variable (source: USBC, various years). Others (e.g., Brenner, 1976a; 1976b) have found unemployment rates to vary directly with official crime rates over time, although this relationship elsewhere has been shown to be empirically questionable (see Mansfield et al., 1974: 463; Cohen and Felson, 1979). Thus, as our second control variable, we take the standard annual unemployment rate (per 100 persons ages 16 and over) as a measure of the business cycle (source: BLS, 1975).

Four of the five crime rates that we utilize here (forcible rape, aggravated assault, robbery and burglary) are taken from FBI estimates of offenses per U.S. population (as revised and reported in OMB, 1973)....

For our homicide indicator we employ the homicide mortality rate taken from the vital statistics data collected by the Bureau of the Census (various years). . . .

Findings

Our time-series analysis for the years 1947-1974 consistently revealed positive and statistically significant relationships between the household activity ratio and each official crime rate change. . . .

Discussion

In our judgment many conventional theories of crime (the adequacy of which usually is evaluated by cross-sectional data, or no data at all) have difficulty accounting for the annual changes in crime rate trends in the post-World War II United States. These theories may prove useful in explaining crime trends during other periods, within specific communities, or in particular subgroups of the population. Longitudinal aggregate data for the United States, however, indicate that the trends for many of the presumed causal variables in these theoretical structures are in a direction opposite to those hypothesized to be the causes of crime. For example, during the decade 1960-1970, the percent of the population below the low-income level declined 44 percent and the unemployment rate declined 186 percent. Central city population as a share of the whole population declined slightly, while the percent of foreign stock declined 0.1 percent, etc. (see USBC, 1975: 654, 19, 39).

On the other hand, the convergence in time and space of three elements (motivated offenders, suitable targets, and the absence of capable guardians) appears useful for understanding crime rate trends. The lack of any of these elements is sufficient to prevent the occurrence of a successful directcontact predatory crime. The convergence in time and space of suitable targets and the absence of capable guardians can lead to large increases in crime rates without any increase or change in the structural conditions that motivate individuals to engage in crime. Presumably, had the social indicators of the variables hypothesized to be the causes of crime in conventional theories changed in the direction of favoring increased crime in the post-World War II United States, the increases in crime rates likely would have been even more staggering than those which were observed. In any event, it is our belief that criminologists have underemphasized the importance of the convergence of suitable targets and the absence of capable guardians in explaining recent increases in the crime rate. Furthermore, the effects of the convergence in time and space of these elements may be multiplicative rather than additive. That is, their convergence by a fixed percentage may produce increases in crime rates far greater than that fixed percentage, demonstrating how some relatively modest social trends can contribute to some relatively large changes in crime rate trends. . . .

Without denying the importance of factors motivating offenders to engage in crime, we have focused specific attention upon violations themselves and the prerequisites for their occurrence. However, the routine activity approach might in the future be applied to the analysis of offenders and their inclinations as well. For example, the structure of primary group activity may affect the likelihood that cultural transmission or social control of criminal inclinations will occur, while the structure of the community may affect the tempo of criminogenic peer group activity. We also may expect that circumstances favorable for carrying out violations contribute to criminal inclinations in the long run by rewarding these inclinations.

We further suggest that the routine activity framework may prove useful in explaining why the criminal justice system, the community and the family have appeared so ineffective in exerting social control since 1960. Substantial increases in the opportunity to carry out predatory violations may have undermined society's mechanisms for social control. For example, it may be difficult for institutions seeking to increase the certainty, celerity and severity of punishment to compete with structural changes resulting in vast increases in the certainty, celerity and value of rewards to be gained from illegal predatory acts.

It is ironic that the very factors which increase the opportunity to enjoy the benefits of life' also may increase the opportunity for predatory violations. For example, automobiles provide freedom of movement to offenders as well as average citizens and offer vulnerable targets for theft. College enrollment, female labor force participation, urbanization, suburbanization, vacations, and new electronic durables provide various opportunities to escape the confines of the household while they increase the risk of predatory victimization. Indeed, the opportunity for predatory crime appears to be enmeshed in the opportunity structure for legitimate activities to such an extent that it might be very difficult to root out substantial amounts of crime without modifying much of our way of life. Rather than assuming that predatory crime is simply an indicator of social breakdown, one might take it as a by product of freedom and prosperity as they manifest themselves in the routine activities of everyday life.

DISCUSSION QUESTIONS

By John M. Stogner

1. Is it possible that reductions in crime due to situational crime prevention efforts are temporary? Do potential offenders likely adapt and crime rates return to their previous levels?
2. Are situational crime prevention efforts ethical? Should governmental funds be spent on issues that affect crime and other outcomes (poverty, health, etc.) rather than just one outcome?
3. Is the distinction between situational crime prevention and crime prevention through environmental design (CPTED) a meaningful one?
4. What examples of situational crime prevention or CPTED programs have you seen in your neighborhood, city, and school? Do you think these were effective?
5. Some situational crime prevention–based environmental changes are noticeable and obviously intended to reduce crime (e.g., cameras). In other situations, it may not be as obvious that the changes were implemented to reduce crime (e.g., changes to traffic patterns, removal of shrubbery, etc.). How do you think this affects their efficacy?

CHAPTER FIVE

Situational Crime Prevention

RONALD V. CLARKE

STUDENT INTRODUCTION
By John M. Stogner

One of the subsequent chapter authors argues "nothing is as practical as a good theory"; unfortunately, many criminology students find theory classes challenging because they have difficulty seeing this practicality. This is partially the fault of criminologists; theorists and classroom instructors often focus heavily on the "why" in criminology and less on the "so what." Your course began with a theory recommending clear and reasonable policies. Deterrence theory plainly suggests that crime can be reduced by publicizing the law while setting appropriately severe penalties that are both swift and certain. Unfortunately, the propositions of deterrence

theory generally lack empirical support—meaning deterrence-based policy reforms are unlikely to have a significant impact on crime rates. You have since read the works of two pair of theorists (Clarke and Cornish; Cohen and Felson) whose theories may be more challenging to relate to practice. The "so what" may not be as accessible in their works. For this reason, Chapter 5 presents a discussion of situational crime prevention.

Situational crime prevention should not be thought of as a theory—it is a programmatic means of reducing crime based on two well-developed criminological theories. Although routine activities and rational choice offer distinct explanations of crime, their recommendations are similar. Both suggest that policymakers should act to reduce opportunities, situational temptations, and provocations to commit crime. These theories assume that crime will be lessened by environmental modifications that make crime less appealing. They highlight the impact of modifying situations rather than individuals' dispositions. Situational crime prevention is a way that the insight from these theories is put into practice. The theories attempt to explain crime while situational crime prevention utilizes that understanding of criminal behavior to alter the rate of crime in the future. Put another way, situational crime prevention is the action, whereas the theories justify that action.

As you read this chapter, take note of the recommendations and examples. You should also take time to think about how each of these is consistent with both theoretical frameworks. The material within this chapter should strengthen your understanding and, perhaps, your appreciation of both theories. You should also consider the inadequacies and limitations of situational crime prevention and the two theories. Unfortunately, some later theories and chapters will fall short of implicitly discussing the practical applications of theory. In these circumstances, reflect on how those theories can connect with policy in the same way that routine activities theory supports situational crime prevention programs.

SITUATIONAL CRIME PREVENTION
By Ronald V. Clarke

Situational crime prevention is a highly practical and effective means of reducing specific crime problems. Essentially, it seeks to alter the situational determinants of crime so as to make crime less likely to happen. It is often criticised for being a simplistic, atheoretical approach to crime prevention, but it has a sound basis in the theories of environmental criminology. It is also criticised for not preventing crime, but simply 'displacing' it, that is, moving crime somewhere else or changing its form. However, the criticism is overstated and this chapter shows that many dramatic reductions in crime can be credited to situational prevention. But first the chapter lays out the theory behind situational prevention.

Theoretical Background

As said, situational prevention is rooted in the theories of environmental criminology discussed in this book—routine activity theory, the rational choice perspective, crime pattern theory— and more recently it has made use of social and environmental psychological theory. This chapter does not discuss these theories in detail, but rather sets out some of their underlying assumptions that are particularly important for situational prevention.

Crime Results from the Interaction of Motivation and Situation

Most criminological theories try only to explain why some people become delinquent or criminal. Whether biological, psychological or sociological in approach, these theories are 'dispositional' because they are seeking to explain a general disposition or propensity to commit crime. But crime is an act, not merely a propensity, and it can only be explained in terms of the interaction between the disposition (sometimes also called 'criminal motivation') and the situation that provides the opportunity for crime to occur.

In early discussions of situational prevention opportunity was used synonymously with situation. However, later discussions recognise that situations provide more than just 'opportunities' for crime; they also provide temptations, inducements and provocations (Wortley 2001) and this recognition has enhanced the scope of situational prevention. Even so, it is convenient to use the term 'opportunity' to refer to the broader roles of situational factors and this chapter adopts this convention.

Crime is Always a Choice

The interaction between motivation and situation that results in crime is mediated through decisions made by individual offenders. Every time someone commits a crime, they have made a decision to do so As Taylor, Walton and Young (1973) pointed out many years ago, nobody is compelled to commit crime. Thus, discrimination and disadvantage do not propel robbers through the doors of the bank; rather, robbers *choose* to rob banks because they want money, and they want large amounts of it.

In fact, people commit crimes because they judge this will bring them some benefit. The benefit is not always financial, but it might be excitement, sex, power, intoxication, revenge, recognition, loyalty, love—indeed, anything that people want. Whether they choose to commit crime depends on a rough calculation of the chances of obtaining the reward and the risks of failure—arrest, punishment, a physical beating, humiliation, etc. Their choices may be made under emotional pressure or when intoxicated. They might also be split-second, foolhardy, ill-informed or ill-advised—but they are choices nonetheless.

If people choose to commit crime, it follows that even those who are more disposed to crime will choose to avoid it when the circumstances are unfavourable. Creating unfavourable circumstances is the objective of situational crime prevention.

Opportunity Plays a Powerful Role in Crime

Even when traditional, dispositional theorists have granted some role to opportunity, they have assumed that opportunity is subsidiary to motivation. In their view motivation is the first and most important thing to explain. Environmental criminology, on the other hand, while recognising the importance of motivation gives equal importance to opportunity in explaining crime. Some environmental criminologists, including the author of this chapter, go much further and make important claims, including the following:

- Opportunity plays a part in every form of crime, even carefully planned crimes such as bank robbery and terrorism.
- Opportunity is an important *cause* of crime.
- Criminally disposed individuals will commit a greater numbers of crimes if they encounter more criminal opportunities.
- Regularly encountering such opportunities could lead these individuals to seek even more opportunities.
- Individuals without pre-existing dispositions can be drawn into criminal behaviour by a proliferation of criminal opportunities.
- Generally law-abiding individuals can be drawn into committing specific forms of crime if they regularly encounter easy opportunities for these crimes.
- The more opportunities for crime that exist, the more crime there will be.
- Reducing opportunities for specific forms of crime will reduce the overall amount of crime.

Proof exists for only the first and last of these claims (see Clarke 2005), but they are all generally consistent with environmental criminology, and together they make the case for situational prevention.

Principles of Situational Prevention

More than making the case for situational prevention, the theory discussed above helps in framing the principles that should guide situational prevention projects. The overriding principle is, of course, that preventive measures should try to change the 'near ', situational causes of crime, rather than the 'distant' dispositional causes. Changing near causes is more likely to succeed in reducing crime because the link between cause and effect is more direct. It will also achieve a more immediate effect on crime than will trying to change 'distant' causes such as upbringing or psychological disadvantage. Changing distant causes can only bring crime prevention benefits in the future, whereas reducing opportunities can result in immediate reductions in crime.

Even if they accept these points, dispositional theorists will often claim that situational prevention is not enough; that crime can only be truly prevented if the 'root' causes are also removed. However, not every cause of a crime must be removed for prevention to succeed; it is often enough to remove one small but key ingredient of opportunity. Dispositional theorists find this difficult to accept because they believe disposition is much more important in causation than opportunity. Even if this were true, however, there is no necessary connection between the power of an explanatory variable and its importance for prevention. For example, we might all concede that lack of parental love is an important cause of delinquency, but as James Q. Wilson (1976) pointed out, nobody knows how to make parents more loving. If parental love cannot be manipulated through policy it has no importance for prevention.

Another slightly different argument is sometimes put forward by dispositional theorists to cast doubt on situational prevention and to make the case for changing dispositions. It is that the causes of crime must be fully understood before it can be prevented. This is claimed in countless research proposals for funds to study the causes of delinquency, but it is not true. For example, if traffic engineers want to stop speeding on a stretch of road, they do not need to mount detailed studies of the causes of speeding. All they need do is introduce speed bumps and, as long as they do this carefully with full awareness of other nearby routes that drivers might take instead, speeding will be reduced. This may seem a trivial example, but the same point can be made about some measures that were introduced in the United States in the 1980s to reduce random homicides. These measures consisted of tamper-proof packaging for all medicines and foods in response to an outbreak of deaths resulting from the purchase of painkillers laced with cyanide. The perpetrators of the crimes were not caught and their motivation was never revealed. But a straightforward opportunity-blocking measure eliminated future occurrences (see Clarke and Newman 2005).

With this brief digression on the relationship between causes and preventive measures, we can now turn to principles of situational prevention.

Focus on Very Specific Categories of Crime

A situational prevention project will succeed only when it is focused on a specific category of crime, such as juvenile joyriding, rather than some broader category of crime such as 'juvenile delinquency' or 'car thefts'. This is because the situational determinants of any specific category of crime are quite different from those of another one, even one that seems similar. It may also be committed for different motives, by different offenders with quite different resources and skills.

These points can be illustrated by research on residential burglary undertaken by Poyner and Webb (1991) in one British city. They showed that burglaries committed in the suburbs were quite different from those committed in the city centre. City-centre burglaries were committed by offenders on foot who were looking for cash and jewellery. Because most of the housing was built in terraces they could only get in through the front door or a front window. The suburban burglars, on the other hand, used cars and were targeting electronic goods such as videocassette players and TVs. They were more likely to enter through the back windows than through the front. They needed cars to get to the suburbs and to transport the stolen goods. The cars had to be parked near to the house, but not so close as to attract attention. The layout of housing in the newer suburbs allowed these conditions to be met, and Poyner and Webb's preventive suggestions included better surveillance of parking places, improved security at the back of houses and a crackdown on fencing of stolen goods. To prevent inner-city burglaries, on the other hand, they suggested improving security and surveillance at the front of the house. As for disrupting the market for stolen goods, this approach had more relevance to the suburban burglaries, targeted on electronic goods, than to the inner-city burglaries that targeted cash and jewellery.

Understand How the Crime is Committed

We have just seen that Poyner and Webb could make useful preventive suggestions when they understood *how* the burglaries were committed and what goods were being sought. Notice that they did not spend time researching *why* the burglars wanted to steal goods. It was enough to know that there were some individuals out there with the motivation to steal things from other people's homes.

This brings us to an important distinction between *motivation* and *motive*. Motivation is a longer-term disposition, in this case a criminal motivation. Motive is a much more immediate driver of behaviour and is a much more tangible concept. The motive for both sets of Poyner and Webb's burglars was financial, but in the case of the city burglars, it was to get small, easy rewards in the form of cash or jewellery. The suburban burglars, on the other hand, were looking for greater rewards by stealing electronic goods even though this involved more work in fencing the goods after they had been stolen. In general, it is helpful for situational prevention to understand the *motives* for particular forms of crime even if it can often ignore the roots of motivation.

In seeking to understand how a specific form of crime is done, it is important to adopt the offender 's perspective—seeing the task from the offender's point of view. Sometimes interviews with offenders to ask them about their methods can be helpful, as long as these concentrate on *modus operandi* and do not stray into more general questions such as about the offender's background (Decker 2005). When this cannot be done, an alternative is to 'think thief' (Ekblom 1995). This means putting oneself in the shoes of the offender and trying to think through in detail the decisions that he or she must make to complete the crime. This process reveals another important fact for prevention—committing a crime is not a simple matter of merely snatching a bag or pocketing goods in a store. Rather, it consists of a linked series of steps, each of which involves decisions by the offender (Cornish 1994). To take the shoplifting example, the offender has to decide which store to hit, which goods to steal, how to take them without being seen, how to conceal them, how to escape from the store without being caught, how to sell them (Sutton 2004), what price to ask, who to sell them to and how to make sure that the goods will not be traced back to the offender. For some crimes, of course—take the example of theft of cars for export—the process is much longer and more complicated. The important point is that understanding how a crime is committed helps in finding points of intervention to make the crime more difficult, risky or less rewarding. And the more detailed the understanding of the process, the richer and more diverse will be the possibilities for intervening.

Use an Action-Research Model

Situational prevention belongs to a 'family' of similar preventive approaches deriving from environmental criminology, including design against crime (DAC, see Ekblom, Chapter 11, this volume) and crime prevention through environmental design (CPTED, see Cozens, Chapter 9, this volume). The main difference between situational prevention and these two approaches is that situational prevention seeks to eliminate *existing* problems, whereas DAC and CPTED seek to eliminate *anticipated* problems in new designs on the basis of past experience with similar designs. In fact, the problem-solving methodology of situational prevention is shared by another preventive approach called problem-oriented policing (see Scott *et al.*, Chapter 12, this volume). In both cases, the problem-solving methodology is a form of 'action research' in which the problem is studied, hypotheses about the main determinants are developed, a range of solutions are identified and studied, the chosen measures are put into place, and the results are then evaluated.

Consider a Variety of Solutions

Later in this chapter the final stage of the action research model is discussed—evaluation of situational prevention. This section concentrates on the preventive solutions. As mentioned, a detailed understanding of the sequential steps involved in committing the crime will yield many possible points of intervention. Generally speaking, a situational prevention project is more effective when it adopts a package of measures, each of which is directed to a particular point of the process of committing the crime. Thus, Poyner and Webb's recommendations to stop suburban burglaries were directed at different points in the process of completing these crimes—better surveillance of places where burglars might park their cars, improved security at the back of houses to stop them breaking in, and a crackdown on local fencing operations to make selling the stolen goods more difficult.

To assist the process of selecting solutions, situational prevention researchers have described and classified the many different ways that exist to reduce crime opportunities. The latest example is shown in Table 4.1. This classification shows 25 opportunity-reducing techniques grouped under five main headings: increase the effort, increase the risks, reduce the rewards, reduce provocations and remove excuses. The first three of these derive from the rational choice perspective (see Cornish and Clarke,); reducing provocations derives from social and environmental psychological theory (Wortley 2001, and Chapter 3, this volume); and removing excuses derives from Matza's and from Bandura's ideas about the facilitating role in crime of justifications made by offenders for their behaviour (Clarke and Homel 1997).

This discussion of solutions needs to conclude with a harsh fact: situational prevention might be easier to undertake than longer-term efforts to alter dispositions, but it can still be very difficult to implement (Knutsson and Clarke 2006). This is especially the case when situational prevention needs coordinated action among different agencies to be implemented, takes a long time and requires a series of steps, is implemented by staff with little understanding of the problem or the solutions, and lacks either the support of top administrators or a 'champion' to push things forward. Difficulties also occur when the solutions are implemented by an agency that is in turmoil or is poorly resourced and that gains little direct benefit from the work.

Increase the effort	Increase the risks	Reduce the rewards	Reduce provocations	Remove excuses
1. Target harden • Steering column locks and ignition immobilisers • Anti-robbery screens • Tamper-proof packaging	**6. Extend guardianship** • Go out in group at night • Leave signs of occupancy • Carry cell phone	**11. Conceal targets** • Off-street parking • Gender-neutral phone directories • Unmarked armoured trucks	**16. Reduce frustrations and stress** • Efficient lines • Polite service • Expanded seating • Soothing music/muted lights	**21. Set rules** • Rental agreements • Harassment codes • Hotel registration
2. Control access to facilities • Entry phones • Electronic card access • Baggage screening	**7. Assist natural surveillance** • Improved street lighting • Defensible space design • Support whistleblowers	**12. Remove targets** • Removable car radio • Women's shelters • Pre-paid cards for pay phones	**17. Avoid disputes** • Separate seating for rival soccer fans • Reduce crowding in bars • Fixed cab fares	**22. Post instructions** • 'No Parking' • 'Private Property' • 'Extinguish camp fires'
3. Screen exits • Ticket needed for exit • Export documents • Electronic merchandise tags	**8. Reduce anonymity** • Taxi driver IDs • 'How's my driving?' decals • School uniforms	**13. Identify property** • Property marking • Vehicle licensing and parts marking • Cattle branding	**18. Reduce temptation and arousal** • Controls on violent pornography • Enforce good behaviour on soccer field • Prohibit racial slurs	**23. Alert conscience** • Roadside speed display boards • Signatures for customs declarations • 'Shoplifting is stealing'
4. Deflect offenders • Street closures • Separate bathrooms for women • Disperse pubs	**9. Use place managers** • CCTV for double-deck buses • Two clerks for convenience stores • Reward vigilance	**14. Disrupt markets** • Monitor pawn shops • Controls on classified ads • License street vendors	**19. Neutralise peer pressure** • 'Idiots drink and drive' • 'It's OK to say No' • Disperse troublemakers at school	**24. Assist compliance** • Easy library checkout • Public lavatories • Litter receptacles
5. Control tools/weapons 'Smart guns' • Restrict spray paint sales to juveniles • Toughened beer glasses	**10. Strengthen formal surveillance** • Red light cameras • Burglar alarms • Security guards	**15. Deny benefits** • Ink merchandise tags • Graffiti cleaning • Disabling stolen cell phones	**20. Discourage imitation** • Rapid repair of vandalism • V-chips in TVs • Censor details of modus operandi	**25. Control drugs and alcohol** • Breathalysers in bars • Server intervention programmes • Alcohol-free events

Table 5.1. Twenty-five techniques of situational prevention

(*Source*: Clarke and Eck 2003; Cornish and Clarke 2003)

Hope and Murphy's (1983) description of a vandalism prevention project undertaken in eleven schools in a British city gives a flavour of these difficulties. The project was not considered a success because the recommendations were only fully implemented in two of the schools; in six schools one or more recommendations failed to materialise; and in the remaining three schools none were put in place. This was partly due to strike action by local government employees during the implementation phase and to the turmoil resulting from a reorganisation of the schools following a decline in pupil numbers. But there were also some more specific reasons, as follows:

- It was recommended that vulnerable windows in some schools should be replaced with poly-carbonate glazing or toughened glass, but not a single pane of either type was installed. It turned out that polycarbonate could prevent escape in the event of a fire and it might give off toxic fumes. Toughened glass had to be cut to size before it was toughened, but the panes came in too many sizes to store a few of each size in readiness. It would also have taken too long to supply a pane to order.

- The municipal agency charged with moving a playground in one school to a less vulnerable area and replacing it with flowerbeds got no further than providing an estimate for the work. The relocation work was then contracted to a private builder, but due to a misunderstanding only half the proposed area was resurfaced. At the end of the project, vandalism was unchanged, there were no flowers, and the school had acquired a useless, narrow strip of concrete.

- Recommendations that were the sole responsibility of the school system's maintenance depart-ment were all implemented; however, none of those involving coordination with other departments or agencies ever materialised. For example, two schools developed a plan for encouraging people who lived nearby to report anything suspicious to the police that occurred after hours. This plan required cooperation between the police, the school system administrators, and the staff of the schools. All liked the idea, but no one would take the lead.

- At one badly affected school it was decided to mount a security patrol in the holidays staffed by school maintenance workers. This was immediately successful in reducing vandalism and was extended beyond school holidays to evenings and weekends. Other schools demanded the same protection and more maintenance workers wanted the additional overtime payments. Ultimately the costs became too high and the project was scrapped.

The effectiveness of situational prevention

Many, many case studies using the principles of situational prevention have been published since the concept was first described more than 25 years ago (Clarke 1980). Smith *et al.* (2002) identified 142 situational prevention case studies at 211 sites, most of which involve common property offences of burglary, car theft and vandalism, but which also cover fraud, robbery, street prostitution, drug-dealing, and violent assaults (Homel *et al.* 1997). More recently, situational prevention has applied to child sexual abuse (Wortley and Smallbone 2006), crime and misconduct in prisons (Wortley 2002), internet frauds (Newman and Clarke 2003) and terrorism (Clarke and Newman 2006).

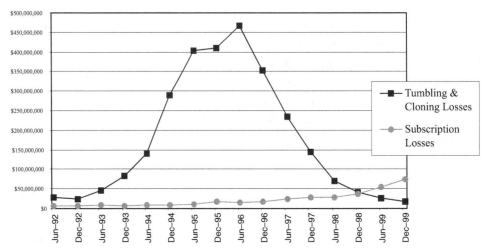

FIGURE 5.1 Semi-annual fraud dollar losses, United States, June 1992–December 1999
(Source: Clarke et al. 2001)

Reductions in the specific crimes addressed have generally been achieved and sometimes the reductions have been dramatic. To take two examples, a plague of bus robberies in New York and eighteen other US cities in the early 1970s was largely eliminated by the introduction of exact fares systems coupled with the installation of drop safes in buses (Chaiken *et al.* 1974; Stanford Research Institute 1970). This form of 'target removal' meant that there was no longer any point in attempting to rob the driver. More recently, US cellphone companies largely wiped out cloning by the introduction of five new anti-cloning technologies (Clarke *et al.* 2001); at its height, this problem had been costing the companies about $800 million per year in fraudulent phone calls (see Figure 4.1).

Probably no other form of crime control can claim this record of evaluated successes, but some critics continue to dispute the evidence. They continue to focus on failures, such as the school vandalism project discussed above, and they argue that situational prevention has been evaluated using only weak research designs; that the reductions claimed are negated by displacement (i.e. the offenders shift their attention to other places, times and targets, use different methods or commit different crimes); that situational prevention results in escalation (i.e. offenders resort to more harmful methods to gain their ends); and that even if displacement does not occur immediately, the criminal population adapts in the long run to reduced opportunities by discovering new ways to commit crime.

Displacement

The most persistent of these criticisms concerns displacement. Because of dispositional assumptions, critics seem to assume that there is a drive to commit crime that cannot be thwarted. But crime is very rarely a compulsion and the displacement thesis is overstated. It may be credible for some crimes, but certainly not for all. Thus, it is highly unlikely that motorists prevented from speeding on a particular stretch of road would seek out another road, somewhere else, on which to speed, or that the shoppers, prevented from stealing at their local supermarket by new security measures, would begin to shop at some more distant store where they could continue to shoplift. Even less likely is that they would turn to mugging senior citizens because shoplifting is easier to rationalise and much less risky than mugging. In fact, almost by definition, any instance of escalation is more costly for offenders. Some of them may be prepared to make more difficult rationalisations or run additional risks, but they will be a minority.

Developments in theory have further undermined claims about the inevitability of displacement and the risks of escalation. If opportunity increases the amount of crime, and crime can result from a variety of situational precipitators, there is every reason to believe that reducing these opportunities and inducements will result in real reductions in crime. In fact, this is the message of the empirical research. Three separate reviews of the evidence on displacement found that it can occur, but it is not inevitable. In the most recent review, Hesseling (1994) found no evidence of displacement in 22 of the 55 studies he examined; in the remaining 33 studies, he found some evidence of displacement, but in no case was there as much crime displaced as prevented.

Much the same would probably be found if his review were repeated today, when many more studies of displacement have been reported. For example, little displacement seems to have occurred to 'subscriber' fraud, the second largest category of cellphone fraud, when cloning was largely eliminated in the United States (see the lower line in Figure 4.1). Subscriber frauds involve the use of a false name and address to obtain cellphone service. They would be difficult to reproduce on a wide scale and would therefore not be attractive to organised groups. Cloned phones, on the other hand, were 'mass produced' by offenders who had learned how to acquire hundreds of legitimate phone numbers and programme them into stolen phones.

We have no way of knowing whether the offenders stopped from cloning turned to other forms of fraud not involving cellphones, but it is possible that many of them were not exclusively dependent on crime for a living. It might have been a sideline for them, or merely a way of making money for a time. When cloning was closed down, they might have had to make do with reduced income—like we all must do from time to time—or they might have turned their energies to legitimate ways of making money. Such positive outcomes from the application of situational prevention become conceivable once freed from dispositional assumptions about crime.

Diffusion of Benefits and Anticipatory Benefits

Another positive outcome of situational prevention is 'diffusion of benefits'. Sometimes described as the reverse of displacement, the term refers to the fact that situational prevention can often bring about reductions in crime beyond the immediate focus of the measures introduced (Clarke and Weisburd 1994). This greatly enhances the practical appeal of situational prevention, especially as the phenomenon is quite general, as shown by the following examples:

- Security added to houses that had been repeatedly burgled in Kirkholt reduced burglaries for the whole of the estate, not just for those houses given additional protection (Pease 1991).
- When 'red light' cameras were installed at some traffic lights in Strathclyde, Scotland, not only did fewer people 'run the lights' at these locations, but also at other traffic lights nearby (Scottish Central Research Unit 1995).
- CCTV cameras installed to monitor car parks at the University of Surrey reduced car crime as much in one not covered by the cameras as in the three that were covered (Poyner 1991).

- When a New Jersey discount electronic retailer introduced a regime of daily counting of valuable merchandise in the warehouse, employee thefts of these items plummeted—but thefts also plummeted of items not repeatedly counted (Masuda 1992).

The explanation for these results seems to be that potential offenders often know that new prevention measures have been introduced, but they may be unsure of their precise scope. They may believe the measures are more widespread than they really are, and that the *effort* needed to commit crime, or the *risks* incurred, have been increased for a wider range of places, times or targets than in fact is the case.

The benefits of diffusion are likely to decay when offenders discover that the risks and effort of committing crime have not increased as much as they had thought. Thus, in a smaller city than Strathclyde, with more local traffic, people might quickly have learned exactly which junctions had red light cameras and the diffusion of benefits might have been short-lived. This means that ways will have to be found of keeping offenders guessing about the precise levels of threat, or quite how much extra effort is needed if they are to continue with crime.

Just as offenders often overestimate the reach of situational prevention, they often believe that prevention measures have been brought into force before they actually have been. This is what is meant by the 'anticipatory benefits' of prevention. Smith *et al.* (2002) found evidence of anticipatory benefits in perhaps as many as 40 per cent of situational prevention projects. Apart from using publicity, little is known about how to deliberately enhance these benefits, but they certainly provide 'added value' to situational prevention.

Adaptation

The concept of criminal adaptation further complicates evaluation of situational prevention. It refers to the process through which offender *populations* discover new crime vulnerabilities after preventive measures have been in place for a while. It is a longer-term process than displacement, which refers to the ways in which *individual* offenders seek to circumvent measures put in place to stop them.

One clear example of adaptation concerns baggage and passenger screening measures introduced in the early 1970s to curb hijackings of airliners between the United States and Cuba. These measures, together with an agreement between the countries to treat hijackers as criminals, quickly eliminated the hijackings (see Table 4.2). Other countries soon adopted the screening measures and hijackings outside the Americas also declined (bear in mind that the table shows actual numbers of hijackings, not rates, and during this period there was a huge increase in the number of airliners and flights). Despite some claims to the contrary, there was no real evidence of any displacement (see Clarke and Newman 2006); in particular, as Table 10.2 shows, there was no increase in sabotage bombings of airlines. However, the screening measures were premised on the assumption that hijackers were not intent on suicide and, anyway, the authorities became increasingly lax over time. This allowed the 9/11 hijackers to find loopholes in the security and seize the airliners. Their attack is a clear example of adaptation to preventive measures. It is not displacement because the 9/11 hijackers were completely different from the offenders (those operating in the 1970s between the United States and Cuba) who made the original introduction of the screening measures necessary.

Period	Number of Years	Average hijackings per year US	Average hijackings per year non-US	Average bombings per year worldwide
1961–1967	7	1.6	3.0	1.0
1968	1	20.0	15.0	1.0
1969–1970	2	30.5	58.0	4.5
1971–1972	2	27.0	33.0	4.5
1973–1985	13	9.4	22.7	2.2
1986–1989	4	2.8	9.0	2.0
1990–2000	11	0.3	18.5	0.3
2001–2003	3	1.3	5.7	0.0
1961–2003	43	6.7	17.9	1.6

Table 5.2. Numbers of airliner hijackings and sabotage bombings, 1961–2003*

*Including attempts

(Source: Clarke and Newman 2006)

Social and Ethical Issues

When first proposed, critics condemned situational prevention for promoting 'big brother' social controls and a 'fortress society'. Since then it has been criticised for 'blaming the victim', for restricting personal freedoms, for 'piecemeal social engineering' (see Tilley 2004 for a discussion), for serving the interests of the powerful, for promoting a selfish exclusionary society and for diverting government attention from the root causes of crime. These criticisms have rarely been spelled out in any detail, though some are discussed in Von Hirsch *et al.* (2000). Answers can be given to each one of them (for example, see Table 4.3 for summaries), but leaving aside their substance, there are two reasons why the criticisms are misconceived.

First, many of the criticisms are addressed to the *practice* of situational prevention, not its *principles*. Many times opportunity-reducing measures are put into place without the careful analysis and evaluation required by situational prevention. For example, a government might decide for largely political reasons that CCTV should be installed in public places. This can result in it being placed where it offends people's notions of privacy or where it may not be needed, so that there is little effect on crime. Such failures cannot be used to criticise the concept of situational prevention, only the way it has been implemented. Another example is that, in its early days, situational prevention was criticised for being focused only on crimes committed by the 'working class', not by the middle classes ('crime in the streets, not in the suites'). There was some truth to this, partly because situational prevention was developed by government criminologists in the UK's Home Office, who were trying to deliver practical crime reduction ideas in a society deeply disturbed by levels of burglary, car theft and vandalism. Twenty-five years later, as more criminologists have become interested in the concept, situational prevention has been applied to a broader range of offences—including frauds, child sexual abuse and drunk driving—committed by people from all walks of life.

Second, the criticisms generally neglect a fundamental point about the action-research *process* of situational prevention—it requires a careful assessment of possible solutions before they are implemented.

	Criticism	Rebuttal
1	It is simplistic and atheoretical	It is based on three crime theories: routine activity, crime pattern and rational choice. It also draws on social psychology.
2	It is ineffective; it displaces crime and often makes it worse	Many dozens of case studies show that it can reduce crime, usually with little displacement.
3	It diverts government attention from the root causes of crime	It achieves immediate results and allows time for finding longer-term solutions to crime.
4	It is a conservative, managerial approach to the crime problem	It promises no more than it can deliver. It requires that solutions be economic and socially acceptable.
5	It promotes a selfish, exclusionary society	It provides as much protection to the poor as to the rich. Thus, one of the first applications of situational prevention principles was in public housing (Newman 1972).
6	It promotes Big Brother and restricts personal freedoms	The democratic process protects society from these dangers. People are willing to endure inconvenience and small infringements of liberty when these protect them from crime
7	It blames the victim	It empowers victims by providing information about crime risks and how to avoid them.

Table 5.3. Seven criticisms of situational crime prevention–and rebuttals
(*Source:* Clarke 2005)

As explained above, many different solutions can be found for a specific problem of crime and disorder if it is analysed in enough detail. These solutions need to be carefully assessed for their cost and benefits. In all cases, the assessment must go beyond financial considerations and must include a variety of social and ethical costs—intrusiveness, inconvenience, unfairness, discrimination, etc. Even if the assessment is informal, as it usually must be, this stage should never be skipped. Because there are always many different ways to reduce opportunities, there is no necessity to adopt a particular solution if it is found unacceptable in certain respects.

Conclusion

From the start, criminologists have generally shown little interest in situational prevention, for reasons that are not difficult to understand. Apart from the fundamental disagreement about causal theory, situational prevention does little to promote the welfarist, social reform agendas of most criminologists. It also offends many of their attitudes, which include suspicion of governmental authority, distaste for business, fear of corporate power, distrust of wealth and sympathy for the criminal underdog. Moreover, many criminologists are uncomfortable with situational prevention's crime control agenda. They see their role as being simply to understand and explain crime, leaving others to draw out the policy implications.

In their view, situational prevention threatens to turn criminology into a technical discourse more in tune with the police and the security industry than with academia.

Some commentators believe that situational prevention is the fastest growing form of crime control worldwide and it might seem that the lack of criminological interest has not harmed situational prevention. On the other hand, if criminologists had laid claim to situational prevention they could take credit for its successes. If more of them had taken an interest in the concept, there would now be an even more solid record of success covering a wider set of crimes. The underlying theories might have been developed more fully and the failures of dispositional explanations might have been exposed sooner (see Weisburd and Piquero, in press). The scientific understanding of crime would also have been enriched by incorporating the wealth of findings about situational determinants. Finally, many more young criminologists would have been launched on rewarding crime control careers, contributing to society and helping to improve the lives of ordinary people, while at the same time bypassing the serious problems of criminal justice sanctioning.

References

Chaiken, J. M., Lawless, M.W., Stevenson and K.A. (1974) *The Impact of Police Activity on Crime: Robberies on the New York City Subway System*, Report No. R-1424-N.Y.C. Santa Monica, CA: Rand Corporation.

Clarke, R. V. (1980) 'Situational Crime Prevention: Theory and Practice', *British Journal of Criminology*, 20: 136–47.

Clarke, R. V. (2005) 'Seven Misconceptions of Situational Crime Prevention', in N. Tilley (ed.) *Handbook of Crime Prevention and Community Safety*. Cullompton, UK: Willan Publishing.

Clarke, R. V. and Eck, J. (2003) *Become a Problem-solving Crime Analyst: In 55 Small Steps*. London: Jill Dando Institute of Crime Science, UCL (accessible at www.popcenter.org).

Clarke, R. V. and Eck, J. (2005) *Crime Analysis for Problem Solvers in 60 Small Steps*. Washington, DC: US Department of Justice Office of Community Oriented Policing Services (accessible at www.popcenter.org).

Clarke, R. V. and Homel, R. (1997) 'A Revised Classification of Situational Crime Prevention Techniques', in S. P. Lab (ed.) *Crime Prevention at a Crossroads*. Cincinnati, OH: Anderson.

Clarke, R. V. and Newman, G. (eds) (2005) *Designing Out Crime from Products and Systems. Crime Prevention Studies, Vol. 18*. Monsey, NY: Criminal Justice Press (accessible at www.popcenter.org).

Clarke, R. V. and Newman, G. (2006) *Outsmarting the Terrorists*. Westport, CT: Praeger Security International.

Clarke, R. V. and Weisburd, D. (1994) 'Diffusion of Crime Control Benefits: Observations on the Reverse of Displacement', in R.V. Clarke (ed.) *Crime Prevention Studies, Vol. 2*. Monsey, NY: Criminal Justice Press.

Clarke, R. V., Kemper, R. and Wyckoff, L. (2001) 'Controlling Cell Phone Fraud in the US: Lessons for the UK "Foresight" Prevention Initiative', *Security Journal*, 14: 7–22.

Cornish, D. B. (1994) 'The Procedural Analysis of Offending, and its Relevance for Situational Prevention', in R.V. Clarke (ed.) *Crime Prevention Studies, Vol. 3*. Monsey, NY: Criminal Justice Press.

Cornish, D. B. and Clarke, R.V. (2003) 'Opportunities, Precipitators and Criminal Decisions', in M.J. Smith and D.B. Cornish (eds) *Crime Prevention Studies, Vol. 16*. Monsey, NY: Criminal Justice Press (accessible at www. popcenter.org).

Decker, S. H. *Using Offender Interviews to Inform Police Problem Solving. Problem-Oriented Guides for Police,* Problem Solving Tools Series, No. 3. Washington, DC: US Department of Justice. Office of Community Oriented Policing Services (accessible at www.popcenter.org).

Eck, J., Clarke, R.V. and Guerette, R. (2007) 'Risky Facilities: Crime Concentrations in Homogeneous Sets of Establishments and Facilities', in G. Farrell, K. Bowers, S. Johnson and M. Townsley (eds.) *Imagination for Crime Prevention. Crime Prevention Studies, Vol 21.* Monsey, NY: Criminal Justice Press (accessible at www.popcenter. org).

Ekblom, P. (1995) 'Less Crime, by Design', *Annals of the American Academy of Political and Social Science,* 539: 114–29.

Hesseling, R.B.P. (1994) 'Displacement: A Review of the Empirical Literature', in R.V. Clarke (ed.) *Crime Prevention Studies, Vol. 3.* Monsey, NY: Criminal Justice Press.

Homel, R., Hauritz, M., McIlwain, G., Wortley, R. and Carvolth, R. (1997) 'Preventing Drunkenness and Violence around Nightclubs in a Tourist Resort', in R.V. Clarke (ed.) *Situational Crime Prevention: Successful Case Studies,* 2nd edn. Albany, NY: Harrow and Heston.

Hope, T. and Murphy, D. (1983) 'Problems of Implementing Crime Prevention: The Experience of a Demonstration Project', *The Howard Journal,* 22: 38–50.

Knutsson, J. and Clarke, R.V. (eds) (2006) *Putting Theory to Work. Crime Prevention Studies, Vol 20.* Monsey, NY: Criminal Justice Press (accessible at www.popcenter. org).

Masuda, B. (1992) 'Displacement vs. Diffusion of Benefits and the Reduction of Inventory Losses in a Retail Environment', *Security Journal,* 3: 131–6.

Newman, G.R. and Clarke, R.V. (2003) *Superhighway Robbery: Preventing E-commerce Crime.* Cullompton, UK: Willan Publishing.

Newman, O. (1972) *Defensible Space: Crime Prevention Through Urban Design.* New York: Macmillan.

Pease, K. (1991) 'The Kirkholt Project: Preventing Burglary on a British Public Housing Estate', *Security Journal,* 2: 73–7.

Poyner, B. (1988) 'Video Cameras and Bus Vandalism', *Journal of Security Administration* 11: 44–51.

Poyner, B. (1991) 'Situational Prevention in Two Car Parks', *Security Journal,* 2: 96–101.

Poyner, B. and Webb, B. (1991) *Crime Free Housing.* Oxford, UK: Butterworth Architect.

Scottish Central Research Unit (1995) *Running the Red: An Evaluation of the Strathclyde Police Red Light Camera Initiative.* Edinburgh: The Scottish Office.

Smith, M.J., Clarke, R.V. and Pease, K. (2002) 'Anticipatory Benefits in Crime Prevention', in N. Tilley (ed.) *Analysis for Crime Prevention. Crime Prevention Studies, Vol. 13.* Monsey, NY: Criminal Justice Press (accessible at www.popcenter.org).

Stanford Research Institute (1970). *Reduction of Robbery and Assault of Bus Drivers. Vol. III, Technological and Operational Methods.* Stanford, CA: Stanford Research Institute.

Sutton, M. (2004) 'Tackling the Roots of Theft: Reducing Tolerance Toward Stolen Goods Markets', in R. Hopkins Burke (ed.) *Hard Cop, Soft Cop.* Cullompton, UK: Willan Publishing.

Taylor, I., Walton, P. and Young, J. (1973) *The New Criminology.* London: Routledge and Kegan Paul.

Tilley, N. (2004) 'Karl Popper: A Philosopher for Ronald Clarke's Situational Crime Prevention', *Israeli Studies in Criminology,* 8: 39–56.

Von Hirsch, A., Garland, D. and Wakefield, A. (eds) (2000) *Ethical and Social Issues in Situational Crime Prevention.* Oxford: Hart Publications.

Weisburd, D. and Piquero, A.R. (in press) 'Taking Stock of How Well Criminologists Explain Crime: A Review of Published Studies', *Crime and Justice*. Chicago: University of Chicago Press.

Wilson, J. Q. (1975). *Thinking about Crime*. New York: Basic Books.

Wortley, R. (2001) 'A Classification of Techniques for Controlling Situational Precipitators of Crime', *Security Journal*, 14: 63–82.

Wortley, R. (2002) *Situational Prison Control: Crime Prevention in Correctional Institutions*. Cambridge: Cambridge University Press.

Wortley, R. and Smallbone, S. (2006) *Situational Prevention of Child Sexual Abuse. Crime Prevention Studies, Vol. 19*. Monsey, NY: Criminal Justice Press (accessible at www. popcenter.org).

DISCUSSION QUESTIONS
By John M. Stogner

1. Describe how routine activities theory might account for crime trends since its publication. Can it account for patterns in offending/victimization between 1979 and today as well as it does for those trends between World War II and the 1970s?

2. Consider your daily activities and compare them to those of your parents, and then grandparents, when they were your age. Do these distinctions account for differences in risk of crime/victimization?

3. How can we know how many motivated offenders exist (or the degree of their motivation) when crime only occurs in circumstances where motivation overlaps with an unguarded target?

4. Does routine activities theory adequately explain demographic (gender, age, race, etc.) disparities in victimization? How so?

5. Does routine activities theory adequately account for the victim—offender overlap (the finding that offenders are more likely to be/have been victimized than nonoffenders)?

CHAPTER SIX

Biological Positivism

ROGER HOPKINS BURKE

STUDENT INTRODUCTION
By John M. Stogner

Many of the claims of Italian physician and professor Cesare Lombroso may seem bizarre, racist, and ethically inappropriate to a modern reader; however, Lombroso was a pioneer within the field, and his works represent a significant contribution to the study of criminal behavior. His perspective and theory were flawed, yet he inspired the field to consider a broader array of influences on behavior and demonstrated that the scientific method could be applied to the study of crime. In fact, his arguments that criminological theories should be evaluated through physical and social observation and his use of the scientific method likely represent his greatest contribution

to the field. Alternatively, the way he evaluated his ideas has been more important than the ideas themselves. Lombroso was meticulous in his measurements and detailed in his findings. His initial work on the subject, *L'Uomo Delinquente* (*The Criminal Man*, 1876), contains numerous tables summarizing his data collection efforts. Hand-sketched diagrams depict the bone structure of those in his study. Lombroso provided a (flawed) example of how criminological theories should be assessed.

Drawing on the work of Darwin, perhaps misinterpreting *On the Origin of Species*, Lombroso initially claimed that criminals were biologically different from the rest of society. He believed them to be biologically inferior *atavists*, evolutionary throwbacks more similar to our ancestral species. He claimed these atavists were not adequately evolved or equipped to succeed in modern society, and as a result relied on their more primitive nature. According to Lombroso, atavists were born criminals who could not be deterred. As such, he did not appear to believe that modifying the certainty or severity of punishment would impact their behavior. In his works, Lombroso argued that atavists could be identified by their body structure and physical features—he described a number of traits or stigmata that indicated atavism, ranging from ear size to palmar creases. Lombroso's following works indicate that he later believed that environmental factors also played a role in the etiology of deviant behavior. He would eventually create an offender typology that included criminal types influenced by biology and the environment to differing degrees.

As you read the chapter, try to imagine how Lombroso's work may have been viewed in the late 1800s. Take note of his ideas and those of his contemporaries, particularly Ferri and Garofalo, considering how they may have reached conclusions we now know to be inaccurate. Examine the potential utility of twin, family, and adoption studies, noting that the works discussed in the chapter are not as statistically rigorous as modern biosocial criminology research. You should also carefully consider the policy implications of each work, whether explicit or implied, and consider their morality. It may be best to consider older biological theories in the field as outdated precursors rather than as defensible theories. As such, consider how these theories likely impacted the acceptance of later, better informed biosocial research.

BIOLOGICAL POSITIVISM
By Roger Hopkins Burke

T he foundations of the biological variant of the predestined actor model of crime and criminal behaviour — or biological positivism—can be located primarily in the work of Cesare Lombroso, Enrico Ferri and Raffaele Garofalo. These early and highly influential biological criminologists—or the Italian School as they are usually collectively known—argued that criminology should focus primarily on the scientific study of criminals and criminal behaviour. Both their methodology—and clearly some of their findings—might seem highly simplistic and even laughable by the standards of today but they nevertheless established an enduring scientific tradition which has become increasingly sophisticated over the years and at the time of writing is enjoying something of an explanatory renaissance.

Early Biological Theories

Cesare Lombroso (1836–1909) was both a psychiatrist at the University of Turin and a physician employed in the Italian penal system. In 1875 he published his most famous work *L'Uomo Delinquente* (*On Criminal Man*) and the primary—and most significant—theme in this early work is that criminals represent a physical type distinct from non-criminals. Said to represent a form of degeneracy apparent in physical characteristics suggestive of earlier forms of evolution, criminals are *atavistic*, throwbacks to earlier forms of evolutionary life. Ears of unusual size, sloping foreheads, excessively long arms, receding chins and twisted noses are indicative signs of criminality. Although essentially a biological positivist, we should nevertheless note that in the later editions of his work, Lombroso came increasingly to pay attention to environmental factors such as climate, poverty, immigration and urbanisation.

Lombroso now classified criminals in four main categories. First, *born criminals* are simply those who can be distinguished by their physical atavistic characteristics. Second, *insane criminals* are those including idiots, imbeciles, paranoiacs, epileptics and alcoholics. Third, *occasional criminals* or *criminaloids* are those who commit crimes in response to opportunities when these might be available—as identified by rational actor theorists—but importantly in contrast to that alternative tradition have innate traits that predispose them to commit criminal behaviour. Fourth, *criminals of passion* are those motivated to commit crime because of anger, love or honour.

Lombroso made little reference to female offenders and considered their criminality to be predominantly restricted to prostitution and abortion, and observed that a man was invariably responsible for instigating their involvement in these crimes. This stereotypical view—that women engage in prostitution because of their sexual nature—nevertheless totally disregarded the obvious motivation of economic necessity, and was to remain an enduring and influential explanation of female criminal behaviour until very recently and is discussed in more detail in Chapters 8 and 11.

Lombroso undoubtedly used primitive methodology based on very limited data and a very simplistic use of statistics. Moreover, he did not have a general theory of crime that would enable him to organise his data in any meaningful way (Taylor, Walton and Young, 1973). Criminals were simply those who had broken the law and the problem thus appeared deceptively straightforward. All one needed to do was locate the differences between people that produce variances in their tendencies to violate the law.

Early biological proponents of the predestined actor model fundamentally assumed that offenders differ in some way from non-offenders. They then problematically observed that offenders appeared to differ among themselves and committed different types of crime. Moreover, offenders who committed the same type of crime appeared alike in terms of important characteristics. The solution to this problem was to subdivide the criminal population into types—each of which would be internally comparable with respect to the causes of crime—and different from other types on the same dimensions.

Most today consider the approach of Lombroso to have been simplistic and naïve but we should observe that he did make three important contributions to the development of modern criminological theory. First, he directed the study of crime away from the armchair theorising that had characterised the early proponents of the rational actor model towards the scientific study of the criminal. Second, although his methodology was rather primitive, he demonstrated the importance of examining clinical and historical records. Third, and most significantly, he recognised the need for multi-factor explanations of crime that include not only hereditary, but social, cultural and economic factors. These latter important factors were also emphasised by his successors in the early biological tradition Enrico Ferri and Raffaele Garofalo.

Enrico Ferri (1856–1929) was thus not simply a biological positivist but significantly argued that criminal behaviour could be explained by studying the interaction of a range of factors: *physical factors* such as race, geography and temperature; *individual factors* such as age, sex and psychological variables; and *social factors* such as population, religion and culture (Ferri, 1895). He rather radically proposed that crime could be controlled by improving the social conditions of the poor and to that end advocated the provision of subsidised housing, birth control and public recreation facilities and it was a vision that fitted well with the socialist views of Ferri. In the 1920s he was invited to write a new penal code for Mussolini's Fascist state, but his positivistic approach was rejected for being too much of a departure from rational actor model legal reasoning. Sellin (1973) observes that Ferri was attracted to Fascism because it offered a reaffirmation of the authority of the state over the excessive individualism that he had always rejected.

Raffaele Garofalo (1852–1934) was both an academic and a practising lawyer remembered for his doctrine of 'natural crimes' where he argued that because society is a 'natural body', crimes are offences 'against the law of nature'. Criminal behaviour is therefore unnatural. The 'rules of nature' are the rules of right conduct revealed to human beings through their powers of reasoning. For Garofalo, the proper rules of conduct come from thinking about what rules should be allowed or prohibited and he identified acts that he argued no society could refuse to recognise as criminal and, consequently, repress by punishment.

Garofalo argued that these *natural crimes* violated two basic human sentiments which are found among people of all ages, namely the sentiments of *probity* and *pity*. Pity is the sentiment of revulsion against the voluntary infliction of suffering on others, while probity refers to respect for the property rights of others. Garofalo argued that these sentiments are basic moral sensibilities that appear in the more advanced forms of civilised society and proposed that some members of society may have a higher than average sense of morality because they are superior members of the group. True criminals, on the other hand, lack properly developed altruistic sentiments and have psychic or moral anomalies that can be inherited.

Garofalo identified four criminal categories, each one distinct from the others because of deficiencies in the basic sentiments of pity and probity. The first category, *murderers* are totally lacking in both pity and probity and will kill and steal whenever the opportunity arises. Lesser criminals are however more difficult to identify and this category is subdivided on the basis of whether criminals lack sentiments of either pity or probity. Thus, the second category, *violent criminals* lack pity and can be influenced by environmental factors such as the consumption of alcohol, or the fact that criminality is endemic to their particular population. The third category, *thieves* suffer from a lack of probity, a condition that might be more the product of social factors than is the case for criminals in the other categories. His fourth category contains *sexual criminals*, some of whom will be classified among the violent criminals because they lack pity. Others require a separate category because their actions stem from a low level of moral energy rather than a lack of pity.

The penological implications of the respective theories of Lombroso and Garofalo are substantially different. Lombroso had wanted to provide treatment for—and change—deviants so that they could be reintegrated back into society. Garofalo reasoned that criminal behaviour demonstrated a failure to live by the basic human sentiments necessary for the survival of society. Criminals should therefore be eliminated in order to secure that survival. Life imprisonment or overseas transportation was proposed for lesser criminals.

Significantly, both Garofalo and Ferri were prepared to sacrifice basic human rights to the opinion of 'scientific experts' whose decisions would take no account of the opinions of either the person on whom they were passing judgement or the wider general public. Their work was thus acceptable to the Mussolini regime in Italy, because it provided scientific legitimisation to ideas of racial purity, national strength and authoritarian leadership (Vold, 1958). It will be seen in the following sections that later biological explanations of crime and criminal behaviour became—and indeed have *become*—increasingly more sophisticated. The logical conclusions that can be reached from the implications of the tradition established by Garofalo and Ferri nevertheless remain the same. If an incurable criminal type exists and can be identified then the logical solution is surely to isolate and remove such individuals permanently from society. Some would indeed suggest that this process of isolation take place before the individual has the opportunity to offend. The notion of treatment should not be automatically assumed to be a soft option to the punishment intervention advocated by proponents of the rational actor model. The term treatment can have much more sinister connotations with serious civil rights implications. We should thus perhaps be grateful that the latter apparently more sophisticated biological variants of the predestined actor model remain inherently problematic.

Inherited Criminal Characteristics

An idea arose at the end of the nineteenth century that criminality is inherited in the same way as physical characteristics and evidence to support this supposition has subsequently been obtained from three sources: (i) criminal family studies; (ii) twin studies and (iii) adopted children studies.

Criminal Family Studies

Criminal family studies have their origins in the work of Dugdale (1877) who traced 709 members of the Juke family and found that the great majority were either criminals or paupers. Goddard (1914) subsequently traced 480 members of the Kallikak family and found that a large number of them had been criminals. Interestingly, while both researchers had observed social as well as inherited criminal characteristics as causes of crime, both emphasised the link between criminality and 'feeblemindedness'. Indeed, following the invention of intelligence tests (IQ tests) by Alfred Binet in 1905, inherited feeble-mindedness was commonly proposed as a principal cause of crime, although it was to go out of fashion for some considerable time from the 1920s onwards.

Goring (1913) reported a fairly sophisticated study of 3,000 prisoners, with a history of long and frequent sentences, and a control group of apparently non-criminals. The prisoners were found to be inferior to the control group in terms of physical size and mental ability while strong associations between the criminality of the children and their parents and between brothers were found. Moreover, it was found that children who were separated from their parents at an early age, because the latter were imprisoned, were as likely, or more likely, to become criminals compared with other children not separated in this way. Thus, contact with a criminal parent did not seem a significant factor associated with criminal conduct. Goring thus claimed that the primary source of criminal behaviour is inherited characteristics rather than environmental factors.

Three principal weaknesses can be identified in Goring's study. First, there is a failure to measure satisfactorily the influence of environmental effects on criminal behaviour. Second, a comparison of stealing and sex offences is based on the assumption that parental contagion is restricted entirely to techniques of crimes and fails to consider the possibility that the transmission of values is more important. Third, the study was restricted to male criminals, although the ratio of 102 brothers to six sisters imprisoned is mentioned. It would seem logical that if criminality is inherited females should be affected to a similar extent as males unless it is a sex-linked condition. Twin and adoption studies have attempted to provide a more sophisticated examination of the relationship between criminality and heredity (Sutherland and Cressey, 1978).

Twin Studies

There are clear genetic differences between identical (monozygotic) twins and fraternal (dizygotic) twins. Identical twins occur when a single fertilised egg produces two embryos. They are thus genetically identical. Fraternal twins are the outcome of two different eggs being fertilised at the same time and they are as genetically different as children born after separate pregnancies. It is obvious that differences in the behaviour of identical twins cannot be explained by different inherited characteristics but, on the other hand, various studies have proposed that similarities in their conduct can be explained by shared heredity.

Lange (1930) examined a group of 30 men, comprising 13 identical twins and 17 fraternal twins, all of who had a prison record and found that in 77 per cent of cases for the identical twins, the other brother had such a record. However, for the fraternal twins, only 12 per cent of the second twins had a prison record. This percentaged relationship is referred to as a criminal concordance. Two hundred pairs of ordinary brothers—near to each other in age—were also compared. Where one brother had a criminal record, the same applied to the other brother in only 8 per cent of cases. Lange thus concluded that heredity plays a major part in the causation of criminal behaviour.

Christiansen (1968) examined official registers to discover how many of 6,000 pairs of twins born in Denmark between 1881 and 1910 had acquired a criminal record and found that in the 67 pairs of identical male twins—where at least one brother had a criminal record—the criminal concordance was 35.8 per cent. There were 114 pairs of fraternal male twins where at least one brother was a convicted criminal, but the criminal concordance was only 12.3 per cent. The criminal concordance was found to be higher for both categories where more serious offences had been committed.

A problem with twin studies is a lack of clarity about the sort of characteristics that are supposed to be passed on and this is important, as variations might reveal themselves in quite different forms of behaviour (Trasler, 1967). For example, some pairs of twins in Lange's study had committed very different types of offences from each other and it could well be the case that a predisposition to offend is inherited but the actual form of offending is determined by other factors.

Christiansen did not however claim that inherited characteristics were the only—or for that matter the dominant—factor that led to the higher concordance for identical twins. He was of the opinion that twin studies could increase our understanding of the interaction between the environment and biological traits and, in fact, he used variations in concordance rates in urban and rural areas to suggest that environmental factors might play a greater part in an urban setting. It is, nevertheless, a central criticism of such studies that they cannot accurately assess the balance between the effects of inherited characteristics and those of the environment. Twins are more likely than ordinary siblings to share similar experiences in relation to family and peers and it is possible that such similarities will be greater in the cases of identical twins.

Dalgard and Kringlen (1976) studied 139 pairs of male twins where at least one brother had a criminal conviction and concordances of 25.8 per cent and 14.9 per cent were found for identical and fraternal twins, respectively. However, when the researchers controlled for mutual closeness, no appreciable difference in concordance rates was found between the types of twins and they thus concluded that hereditary factors were not significant in explaining crime. However, Cloninger and Gottesman (1987) reviewed the same data and reached a very different conclusion observing that if Dalgard and Kringlen had been correct, then the environmental effects would cause psychologically close identical twins to act the same as each other, and psychologically distant identical twins to act differently. This did not happen.

A more recent twin study supports both inherited characteristics and environmental explanations of criminality. Rowe and Rogers (1989) collected data from self-report questionnaires involving 308 sets of twins in the Ohio State school system in the USA and concluded that inherited characteristics partly determine the similarity of behaviour of same-sex and identical twins. They nevertheless recognised that interaction between siblings could cause initially discordant siblings to become concordant in their levels of offending. Moreover, as twins are brought up together as a general rule, it becomes virtually impossible to reach any firm conclusion as to the role of inherited characteristics alone (Rowe, 1990). Studies of adopted children have sought to overcome that inherent methodological problem.

Adopted Children Studies

In the case of adopted children—where contact with a criminal parent has obviously been limited—any association between criminal behaviour can be attributed to inherited characteristics with a greater degree of certainty. Hutchings and Mednick (1977) carried out a study of male adoptees born in Copenhagen between 1927 and 1941 and found that 48 per cent of young males with a criminal record and 37.7 per cent with a record of minor offences had a birth father with a criminal record. Among young males without a criminal record, 31.1 per cent had a birth father with such a record. The study discovered that an adoptee was more likely to have a record where both the birth and adoptive father had previous convictions.

In a further comparison, 143 of the adoptees with criminal records were matched with a control group containing the same number of adoptees without convictions. Among the sample group, 49 per cent were found to have criminal birth fathers, 18 per cent had criminal birth mothers and 23 per cent had criminal adoptive fathers. Among the control group 28 per cent were found to have criminal birth fathers, 7 per cent had criminal birth mothers and 9.8 per cent had criminal adoptive fathers. On the basis of these findings a very strong link between inherited characteristics and criminal behaviour was proposed.

The research was later replicated in a wider study that encompassed all nonfamilial adoptions in Denmark between 1924 and 1947 (Mednick *et al.*, 1984). A similar though slightly less strong correlation between birth parents and their adoptee children was found and again the most significant results were when both birth and adoptive parents were criminal. The researchers concluded that there was an inherited characteristic element that was transmitted from the criminal parents to their children that increased the likelihood of the children becoming involved in criminal behaviour. It is nevertheless important to note that adoption agencies try to place children in homes situated in similar environments to those from which they came and it remains a possibility that it is upbringing not inherited characteristics that cause criminal behaviour. On the other hand, some people may be genetically endowed with characteristics that render them more likely to 'succumb to crime' (Hutchings and Mednick, 1977: 140). Exactly what these inherited crime inducing characteristics might actually be is not really considered.

Criminal Body Types

A further category of the biological variant of the predestined actor model has its foundations directly in the Lombrosian tradition of concentrating on body type. Kretschmer (1964, originally 1921) identified four criminal body types: first, *asthenics* are lean and narrowly built, flat-chested and skinny with their ribs easily counted; second, *athletics* have broad shoulders, deep chests, flat stomachs and powerful legs; third, *pyknics* are of medium build with an inclination to be rotund with rounded shoulders, broad faces and short stubby hands; and fourth, *mixed types* are those which are unclassifiable. Kretschmer argued that the asthenic and athletic builds are associated with schizophrenic personalities, while pyknics are manic-depressives.

Hooton (1939) conducted a detailed analysis of the measurements of more than 17,000 criminals and non-criminals and concluded that the former are organically inferior to other people, that low foreheads indicate inferiority, and that 'a depressed physical and social environment determines Negro and Negroid delinquency to a much greater extent than it does in the case of Whites' (Hooton, 1939, Vol.1: 329). Hooton was not surprisingly widely condemned for the racist overtones of his work and his failure to recognise that the prisoners he studied represented only those who had been caught, convicted or imprisoned. Moreover, his control group appeared to be representative of no known population of humanity.

Sheldon (1949) produced the first modern systematic linking of body traits with criminal behaviour but was at the same time highly influenced by his predecessors in this tradition. He significantly shifted attention from adults to offending male youths, studying 200 between 15 and 21 years of age in an attempt to link physique to temperament, intelligence and offending behaviour, classifying the physiques of the boys by measuring the degree to which they possessed a combination of three different body components. First, *endomorphs* tended to be soft, fat people; second, *mesomorphs* were of muscular and athletic build; and third, *ectomorphs* had a skinny, flat and fragile physique. Sheldon concluded that most offenders tended towards mesomorphy and because the youths came from parents who were offenders, the factors that produce criminal behaviour are inherited.

Glueck and Glueck (1950) conducted a comparative study of offenders and non-offenders and gave considerable support to the work of Sheldon, finding that, as a group, offenders tended to have narrower faces, wider chests, larger and broader waists and bigger forearms than non-offenders. Approximately 60 per cent of the offenders were found to be predominantly mesomorphic but the researchers—like their predecessors—failed to establish whether this group were offenders because of their build and disposition, or because their physique and dispositions are socially conceived to be associated with offending. Or indeed whether a third set of factors associated with poverty and deprivation, affected both their body build and offending behaviour.

Body type theories can be criticised for ignoring different aspects of the interaction between the physical characteristics of the person and their social circumstances. People from poorer backgrounds will tend to have a poorer diet and thus be small in stature while young people in manual occupations are likely to acquire an athletic build. The over-representation of such people among convicted criminals may thus be explained by a variety of sociocultural—rather than biological—factors.

Gibbons (1970) argues that the high proportion of mesomorphy among offenders is due to a process of social selection and the nature of their activities is such that deviants will be drawn from the more athletic members of that age group. Cortes and Gatti (1972), in contrast, propose that such arguments falsely accuse biological explanations of criminal behaviour of being more determinist than they actually are. They propose that as physical factors are essential to the social selection process, human behaviour has both biological and social causes.

Hartl, Monnelly and Elderkin (1982) conducted a thirty year follow-up of Sheldon's research subjects and found that the criminal group still showed significant signs of mesomorphy but, on the other hand, the highly influential longitudinal Cambridge Study in Delinquent Development found no evidence that offenders were in any way physically different from non-offenders (West, 1982). There thus remains much ambiguity in the findings from body-type research although researchers continue to pursue this approach with Raine *et al.* (2000) finding that three-year-old children (boys or girls)—who were just half an inch taller than their peers—had a greater than average chance of becoming classroom bullies with the ambitious suggestion that they would go on to be violent criminals.

Biochemical Theories

Biochemical explanations of criminal behaviour are similar to the altered biological state theories discussed in the following section. The difference lies in the fact that biochemical explanations involve substances—or chemical processes—already present in the body while altered state explanations involves the introduction of outside agents. In this section we will consider sexual hormones, blood sugar levels, and adrenaline sensitivity.

Sexual Hormones

Glands such as the pituitary, adrenals, gonads, pancreas and thyroid produce hormones. They control—and are themselves controlled by—certain anatomical features that affect the thresholds for various types of responses and have extensive feedback loops with the central nervous system. Schlapp and Smith (1928) first suggested a causal relationship between hormones and criminal behaviour arguing that either an excess or underproduction of hormones by the ductless glands could lead to emotional disturbance followed by criminal behaviour.

It has long been recognised that male animals—of most species—are more aggressive than females and this has been linked to the male sex hormone, testosterone (Rose *et al.*, 1974; Keverne, Meller and Eberhart, 1982). The relationship between sex hormones and human behaviour does appear more complex even though testosterone has been linked with aggressive crime such as murder and rape. However, it does seem that in most men testosterone levels do not significantly affect levels of aggression (Persky, Smith and Basu, 1971; Scarmella and Brown, 1978). Studies of violent male prisoners suggest that testosterone levels have had an effect on aggressive behaviour. However, these results were not as strong as had been expected from the studies of animals (Kreuz and Rose, 1972; Ehrenkranz, Bliss and Sheard, 1974).

Problematically, these studies of humans have not differentiated between different forms of aggression, although later studies sought to address this issue. Olwens (1987) thus conducted a study of young men with no marked criminal record and found a clear link between testosterone and both verbal and physical aggression with a further distinction between provoked and unprovoked aggressive behaviour: provoked aggressive behaviour tended to be more verbal than physical and was in response to unfair or threatening behaviour by another person; unprovoked aggressive behaviour, in contrast, was violent, destructive and involved activities such as starting fights and making provocative comments. The relationship between testosterone and unprovoked violence was nevertheless found to be indirect and would depend on other factors such as how irritable the particular individual was. Schalling (1987) discovered that high testosterone levels in young males were associated with verbal aggression but not with actual physical aggression which suggests a concern to protect status by the use of threats. Low testosterone level boys would tend not to protect their position, preferring to remain silent. Neither study suggests a direct link between testosterone and aggression, but in a provocative situation those with the highest levels of testosterone were found more likely to resort to violence.

Ellis and Crontz (1990) note that testosterone levels peak during puberty and the early 20s and this correlates with the highest crime rates. It is a finding that they claim provides persuasive evidence for a biological explanation of criminal behaviour and argue that it explains both aggressive and property crime observing that sociological researchers have failed to explain why it is that this distribution exists across all societies and cultures. There is nevertheless no evidence of a causal relationship between criminal behaviour and the level of testosterone. The link may be more tenuous with testosterone merely providing the environment necessary for aggressive behaviour to take place.

McBurnett *et al.* (2000) propose that violent behaviour in male children may be associated with low saliva levels of the stress hormone cortisol finding those with low concentration were three times more likely to show indications of aggression.

Blood Sugar Levels

Hypoglycaemia or low blood sugar levels—sometimes related to diabetes mellitus—may result in irritable, aggressive reactions, and may culminate in sexual offences, assaults, and motiveless murder (see Shah and Roth, 1974). Shoenthaler (1982) conducted experiments where it was discovered that by lowering the daily sucrose intake of young offenders held in detention it was possible to reduce the level of their antisocial behaviour. A discussion of the effects of under-nutrition on the central nervous system and thus on aggression can be found in Smart (1981). Virkkunen (1987) has linked hypoglycaemia with other activities often defined as antisocial such as truancy, low verbal IQ, tattooing and stealing from home during childhood and alcohol abuse. If alcohol is drunk regularly and in large quantities, the ethanol produced can induce hypoglycaemia and increase aggression.

Clapham (1989) cites the case of a man who stabbed his wife to death and attempted suicide but was acquitted of murder. The man had been on a strict diet for two months preceding the fatal incident—losing three stone in weight—and had been starved of all sugar, bread, potatoes and fried food. On the fateful morning he had consumed two glasses of whisky and was found immediately after the killing to be suffering from amnesia. Blood tests were conducted in prison several weeks later and he was found to be still suffering from reactive hypoglycaemia. The jury accepted the expert medical opinion that the man had been reduced to an automaton and could not be held responsible for his actions.

Adrenaline Sensitivity

The relationship between adrenaline and aggressive behaviour is a similar area of study to that involving testosterone with each involving the relationship between a hormonal level and aggressive antisocial behaviour. Schachter (cited in Shah and Roth, 1974) thus found that injections of adrenaline made no difference to the behaviour of normal prisoners but a great difference to psychopaths; while, Hare (1982) found that when threatened with pain, criminals exhibit fewer signs of stress than other people. Mednick *et al.* (1982) discovered that not only do certain—particularly violent—criminals take stronger stimuli to arouse them, but once they are in a stressed state they recover more slowly to their normal levels than do non-criminals. Eysenck (1959) had offered a logical explanation for this relationship some years previously. An individual with low stress levels is easily bored, becomes quickly disinterested in things and craves exciting experiences. Thus, for such individuals normal stressful situations are not disturbing, they are exciting and enjoyable, something to be savoured and sought after.

Baldwin (1990) suggests that the link between age and crime rates can be partially explained by considering arousal rates observing that children can quickly become used to stimuli that had previously excited them and thus seek ever more thrilling inputs. The stimulus received from criminal type activities does nevertheless decline with age, as does the level of physical fitness, strength and agility required to perform many such activities. Baldwin interestingly explains both the learning of criminal behaviour and its subsequent decline in terms of stimuli in the environment which does then pose the question as to whether the production of adrenaline is biologically or socially dictated.

Treating the Offender

Central to the biological variant of the predestined actor model of crime and criminal behaviour is the perception that criminality arises from some physical disorder within the individual offender and it is argued that by following a course of treatment, individuals can be cured of the predisposing condition that causes their criminality. We will now briefly consider three forms of individualised treatment: surgical intervention, chemotherapy and electrocontrol.

Surgical intervention often means pre-frontal leucotomy, a technique that severs the connection between the frontal lobes and the thalamus. It causes some degree of character change—mainly a reduced anxiety level—and has been used with some success to treat the paranoid and paraphrenic types of schizophrenia, but has now been largely replaced by neuroleptic drugs. It has also been used on 'sexually motivated' and 'spontaneously violent' criminals. Castration has been used on sex offenders in Denmark and the USA with indecisive results. Stürup in Denmark claimed 'acceptable' results with sex offenders, but Mueller (1972 cited in Menard and Morse, 1984) tells of a rapist in California who—following castration—turned from rape to child molesting and murder.

Chemotherapy involves the use of drugs in treatment programmes and also for control purposes. Some drugs are used for the treatment of specific behaviour patterns, for example, antabuse has been used in the treatment of alcoholics, cyclozocine for heroin addicts (both are blocking agents), benperidol (cyproterone acetate), an anti-libidinal drug, and stilboestrol (a female hormone) for sex offenders.

Benperidol and stilboestrol constitute 'chemical castration' and their use on prisoners in the UK and USA instigated widespread intense debate. Proponents insist that these chemicals can only be ethically used on people who freely offer their services as volunteers but there is considerable doubt as to whether one can ever find 'free volunteers' in prison. These drugs also have unpleasant side effects, for example, stilboestrol causes atrophy of the genitals, female breast development, nausea, feminisation, obesity and serious psychiatric disorders.

Some drugs are used exclusively for control purposes. Mace and CS gas are routinely used for riot control. Sedatives and tranquillisers are frequently used to keep potential troublesome prisoners calm. In nineteenth century prisons opium was used for this purpose and in the contemporary UK, Valium, Librium and Largactil are generally used. In the USA a heavy tranquilliser (prolixin) is used which reduces hostility, anxiety, agitation and hyperactivity but often produces a zombie-like effect. It has some other unpleasant side effects which according to the manufacturers include automatic reactions, blurred vision, bladder paralysis, glaucoma, faecal impaction, techychardia, liver damage, skin disorders and death. It is extensively used in prisons for the sole purpose of keeping troublemakers quiet.

Electro-control is still a little futuristic since the research programme is still ongoing in the USA with the idea being to plant a telemetric device on—or in—the prisoner. This will transmit data about the physical state of the subject to a central computer programmed to assess from the information the mental state of the subject. If the indications are that he or she is about to commit an offence an impulse is sent to a receiver planted in the brain that has the potential to cause pain, paralysis or even death. These devices could enable a *dangerous* offender to be safely released from prison. The two main obstacles to the implementation of such schemes have been the limited range of the equipment and ethical concerns raised by civil liberty groups.

Conclusions

Each of the attempts to explain crime and criminal behaviour discussed in this chapter follow directly in the biological predestined actor model tradition established by Lombroso. Each theory has sought explanations in the measurable, organic part of individuals, their bodies and their brains and it is certainly impossible to deny that some of these studies really do explain the criminality of a tiny minority of offenders. Closer investigation of individual cases nevertheless demonstrates that social and environmental factors have been equally important. Indeed, it is important to note that most of the researchers—from Lombroso onwards—came to increasingly recognise that reality.

The early biological positivists had proposed that discoveries about the natural world—and natural laws—would find a counterpart within human behaviour. The criminological emphasis of this approach has thus been on the scientist as the detached objective neutral observer who has the task of identifying natural laws that regulate criminal behaviour. Once these natural laws have been discovered, a reduction in offending behaviour is seen as possible by the use of treatment programmes aimed at ameliorating or eliminating the causes of that behaviour. It has also been proposed that investigations should be extended into the lives of individuals who are deemed to be 'at risk' of offending in order that treatment might be instigated and many offences be prevented before they occur. In short, criminal behaviour is perceived to be a sickness—an inherently problematic analysis—that has led to treatments that are intrusive, in some cases unethical, and on occasion with horrendous wider implications.

The early biological positivists replaced the rational calculating individual of the rational actor model with an organism subject to the forces of biological heredity and impulsive behaviour beyond conscious control. From this same source, however, came Social Darwinism, a mode of thought based on the notion that *The Origins of the Species* offered a new evolutionary and scientific basis for the social sciences as well as for biology. It was an idea highly compatible with interests in the wider world and was soon used to give 'scientific' legitimacy to an old idea, namely that the capacity for rational judgement, moral behaviour and, above all, business success was not equally distributed among the various races and divisions of humanity.

Quite prominent figures of late-nineteenth-century social science began to argue that Africans, Indians, the 'negroes' of North America, paupers, criminals and even women had inherited smaller brains and a reduced capacity for rational thought and moral conduct than everyone else. Such ideas were particularly appealing in the USA, which was experiencing an influx of immigrants of diverse ethnic background and where people were particularly ready to equate the biological processes of natural selection with the competition of an unrestricted market. In both Britain and the USA programmes of selective breeding were proposed to encourage progress or to prevent civilisation from degenerating (Jones, 1980). It was a view that was to remain popular into the early decades of the twentieth century and which was to obtain support from the 'science' of *eugenics* and its supporters who were concerned with 'improving' the genetic selection of the human race. The biological variant of the predestined actor model of crime and criminal behaviour was highly compatible with this viewpoint. Goring (1913) was convinced that criminality was passed down through inherited genes and in order to reduce crime, recommended that people with such characteristics should not be allowed to reproduce. The more recent and rigorous research in search of the 'criminal gene' has rather similar implications.

In 1994 a new Centre for Social, Genetic and Development Psychiatry was opened at the Maudsley Hospital in south London to examine what role genetic structure plays in determining patterns of behaviour, including crime (Muncie, 1999). The following year a major conference was held behind closed doors to discuss the possibility of isolating a criminal gene—the basis of which rested on the study of twins and adoptees (Ciba Foundation, 1996). Moreover, one of the best-selling social science books of the 1990s, *The Bell Curve* (Herrnstein and Murray, 1994) claimed that black people and Latinos are over-represented among the ranks of the poor in the USA because they are less intelligent. The suggestion is that inherited genes mainly determine IQ and that people with low intelligence are more likely to commit crime because they lack foresight and are unable to distinguish right from wrong. Muncie (1999) observes that such theories continue to be attractive—at least to some—because they seem to provide scientific evidence that clearly differentiates us from 'them', an out group we feel legitimately entitled to target, outlaw and in the final instance, eradicate. It is an argument that Einstadter and Henry (1995) note to be characteristic of totalitarian regimes whether they are Nazi Germany, the former USSR, and by extension to the more recent forced therapy programmes in the USA.

Morrison (1995) observes that the Holocaust—the systematic extermination of over six million people by Nazi Germany during the Second World War—was undoubtedly the crime of the twentieth century, yet it had provided such a great problem for criminology that it had not previously been mentioned in any textbook. For he observes the essential question to be whether the Holocaust is at odds with modernity or simply the logical consequence of a project of which we might note the biological variant of the predestined actor model of crime and criminal behaviour to simply be a component. There is certainly strong available evidence to support the latter proposition. The Jewish social theorist Hannah Arendt argues that the Holocaust destroyed the semblance of any belief that evil must be motivated by evil and conducted by evil people. She observes that, 'the sad truth of the matter is that most evil is done by people who never made up their mind to be either good or bad' (Arendt, 1964: 438). Morrison (1995: 203) observes that this horrendous and unsurpassable crime can only be explained by 'the weakness of individual judgement in the face of reason, in the face of the claims of organisation, in the face of claims of the normal, in the face of claims for progress…'.

The outcome was to destroy our belief in the right of experts—whether they are scientists, social engineers or managerial politicians—to think for us unquestioned. It was suddenly no longer possible to take the notion of modernist civilisation for granted or to accept an unilinear image of social progress in human affairs. The biological variant of the predestined actor model had led to the plausibility of ideas such as sterilisation, genetic selection and even death for the biologically untreatable. Such work was now unpalatable for many in the context of the mid-twentieth century experience of mass systematic extermination in death camps of outsider groups whether based on their ethnicity (in the case of the Jews, Slavs and Gypsies), their sexuality (in the case of homosexuals), their health (in the case of the disabled and seriously ill) or their behaviour (in the case of whole categories of criminals).

In more recent years there has been a sustained campaign to rehabilitate biological theories with the recognition that physical and social environment factors are more closely linked. There remains however serious ethical implications surrounding possible treatment regimes

Note

1. The following website provides a very extensive list of people past and present who it is said have beenor are on the autistic disorder spectrum: http://www. geocities.comIrichardg_uk/ famousac. html.

DISCUSSION QUESTIONS
By John M. Stogner

1. What factors led Lombroso to his conclusions? Why did he believe that criminals were evolutionarily inferior and easily identified by physical traits?
2. What policies would Lombroso and his contemporaries support? How did they believe that crime was best prevented/managed?
3. If Lombroso was meticulous in his measurements, how could he come to the conclusion that his theory was accurate?
4. What are some potential issues with the conclusions drawn from twin and adoption studies like those described in the chapter?
5. If you were to compare the physical traits and hormone levels of people incarcerated in the United States today with those of a representative sample from the general population, what differences would you likely see? Would these be meaningful in our quest to understand criminal behavior?

CHAPTER SEVEN

The Future of Biosocial Criminology: Beyond Scholars' Professional Ideology

JOHN PAUL WRIGHT[1] AND FRANCIS T. CULLEN[1]

STUDENT INTRODUCTION
By John M. Stogner

The problematic policy recommendations of nineteenth- and early twentieth-century biological criminology, along with the associated flawed studies, eventually created a bias in the field against theories that contained biological elements. The leading theories of the latter half of the twentieth century all ignored the potential for biology to be related to criminal disposition. In the following chapter, John Wright and Francis Cullen explore the motivation behind this exclusion and the general dearth of biological research in criminology prior to the last two decades. They highlight the reticence of the field to incorporate biology into theory and to consider new methodologies. The unwillingness to fully reconsider biology as an influence on crime may have actually led to a situation where fields other than criminology were leading advancement in the study of deviance. Matthew Robinson perhaps summarized the situation best in 2004: "The biological sciences have made more progress in advancing our understanding about crime and behavior in the past 10 years than sociology has made in the past 50 years."

Wright and Cullen do not present a summary of a theory. In fact, biosocial criminology is a perspective without a unifying theory (biological criminology may be used to encompass older,

[1] University of Cincinnati, Cincinnati, OH, USA

largely deterministic theories, whereas biosocial criminology is used to represent modern research concluding that both biology and the environment influence behavior). Biosocial criminology works generally support the idea that deviance is partially influenced by genetic factors. That is, they suggest and statistically demonstrate that a large portion of the variation in deviance can be attributed to heredity. Similarly, the majority of biosocial criminologists argue that biological factors condition the relationship between environmental factors on crime. Put another way, they believe that the relationship between social influences and crime is partially contingent on genetics—that biology and the environment interact with one another rather than operating independently. Similarly, many works suggest that impediments to biological and cognitive development, whether the result of trauma, exposure to toxins, malnutrition, social isolation, or other factors, can increase the propensity to engage in violence. Given that the perspective is still in its infancy, it is not possible for a single chapter to summarize the state of theory in biosocial criminology; those looking for a detailed account of theoretical ideas rooted in biosocial research may want to read *The Nurture Versus Biosocial Debate in Criminology*, published in 2014.

Wright and Cullen's work does offer insight into how the perspective is likely to evolve in the future. As you read, take note of their vision for the field and consider how a modified outlook may yield criminological theories more inclusive of biological influence. You should attempt to understand the challenges faced by those proposing, advancing, and evaluating biosocial arguments and become familiar with factors that may prejudice you and others against such works. Biosocial criminology is one of the most dynamic areas in the field—an area ripe for new theories. Closed-mindedness should not impede progress in our understanding of deviant behavior or willingness to explore new issues. Remain unbiased as you read the chapter, consider Wright and Cullen's points, and attempt to understand why other perspectives may lack a full picture of deviance due to the exclusion of biology.

THE FUTURE OF BIOSOCIAL CRIMINOLOGY: BEYOND SCHOLARS' PROFESSIONAL IDEOLOGY

By John Paul Wright and Francis T. Cullen

Keywords

Biosocial, genetics, biology, crime, criminology

By now the story has been told so often that it is a mere script in criminological discourse. The script is repeated, almost instinctively, by critics of biological theorizing in the social sciences and remains printed in virtually every course text in criminology (for an exception see Brown, Esbensen, & Geis, 2010; Wright & Miller, 1998;). In short, the script goes something like this: Biological theorizing is a "dangerous" idea because it created Nazism, was used to justify racism and sexism, and led to the eugenics movement in the United States (Pinker, 2003; Rafter, 2008). With this script in hand, the professional ideology of criminology has worked to almost eliminate biological theorizing from the field. For example, empirical studies show that biological theorizing is rarely taught at PhD granting criminology/criminal justice programs, that almost no biologically informed dissertations are completed each year, and that few biological studies have been published by mainstream criminology journals (Wright et al., 2008).

As Hunt (1999) and others have so readily documented, the repression of science is not new. "Old style" scientific repression, where a church or government restricts scientific investigation, is a common historical theme, and occasionally emerges in American society (DeLisi, Beaver, Vaughn, & Wright, 2009). Confronting us today is what Hunt (1999) refers to as the "New style" of scientific repression. This form of repression is internal to academic disciplines in that it restricts scientific inquiry by imposing rigid ideological boundaries about certain topics and it requires scholars to self-censor their own work (Gottfredson, 1994). Of course, when science is repressed, either directly through the State or indirectly through threat of disciplinary excommunication, knowledge suffers. Moreover, science itself takes on an entirely political meaning—one that advocates for certain causes and for specific groups and one that marshals resources when those causes or groups are subject to criticism. Berger (2002) echoed these sentiments when, speaking to his fellow sociologists, he stated that " the ideologues who have been in the ascendancy for the last thirty years have deformed science into an instrument of agitation and propaganda...invariably for causes on the left of the ideological spectrum" (p. 29). In criminology, the script equating biological theorizing to aversive governmental interventions represents more than a simple but questionable account of the history of biological criminology, it represents an ideological boundary that has been used to exclude a large body of science from the field.

Yet there is evidence that the tide may be turning and that the old ideological boundaries are beginning to collapse. Today there is a growing interest in biological theorizing on crime and understanding of the biological and genetic factors related to crime producing individual traits. This interest has created a new criminology—one that merges biological theorizing with more traditional social investigations. Known as *biosocial criminology*, this new paradigm stands in the forefront of theoretical and empirical advancement in criminology. If carried out fully, biosocial criminology has the potential to create a fundamental

John Paul Wright and Francis T. Cullen, "The Future of Biosocial Criminology: Beyond Scholars' Professional Ideology," *Journal of Contemporary Criminal Justice*, vol. 28, no. 3, pp. 237-253. Copyright © 2012 by SAGE Publications. Reprinted with permission.

paradigm shift in the field—a shift, we believe, that will advance criminology as a science and will lead to a more complete understanding of the biological and social factors related to pathological behavior.

Although the potential for this shift remains to be fully realized, we are also sensitive to the roadblocks and landmines that could deter continued expansion of the biosocial paradigm. Indeed, there remains an ingrained resistance to biological theorizing in criminology—a resistance that is based largely in ideology and not on scientific merits (see Walby & Carrier, 2010 a & b, for an excellent illustration of a purely ideological critique of biosocial criminology). The ideological resistance, we argue, comes not simply from the role that biological thinking played in lending credence to Nazism, racism, or eugenics in a previous historical era. Rather, today's continuing antagonism can be tied more closely to the fact that biological theorizing confronts many sacred values in the social sciences generally and in criminology specifically.

In the following pages, we thus document the fundamental role of ideology in criminology, how ideology worked to exclude a broad base of scientific findings from the field, and how a biosocial criminology can simultaneously reduce ideological influences and elevate the role of science in the field. We conclude that biosocial criminology offers scientific consilience (Wilson, 1998) and will, ultimately, lead to new insights into human violence and even to more humane ways of managing criminal behavior.

Before embarking on this journey, we want to state what should be obvious but often is not understood. In advocating that criminologists take seriously a biosocial perspective, we are not some latter-day Lombrosians embracing a crude form of biological determinism. In fact, as with any scientific findings and theorizing, biosocial knowledge should be subjected to organized skepticism, a core norm of science (Merton, 1973). Rather, our view is simply as follows: The precise connection of biological factors to criminal conduct is not a matter of ideology but of objective reality. This connection can only be unpacked through careful study. Whether one wishes biology to be robustly implicated in crime or to have no role whatsoever is really beside the point. What matters is what, in reality, the relationship is revealed to be through rigorous scholarship.

Related, we do not deny—as critics have shown—that biological thinking has been put to ill use, especially in supporting coercive policies targeted at poor and minority peoples (Cullen, 2011). We can make the trite but still true rejoinder that many of these same critics do not condemn Marxist thinking, despite its role in legitimizing authoritarian regimes with awful human rights records. The point, of course, is that scientific ideas about the human condition—whether biological or Marxist—can be distorted to justify many untoward policies and practices. The responsibility for inhumanity ultimately lies with those who practice it. To use these bad acts to try to stifle scientific inquiry does not make the world a better place but an inauthentic one in which intellectual fear curtails what we are willing to study and know. Science must lead to truth—to the obligation to "tell it like it is." If someone then attempts to use this knowledge in disquieting ways, as moral citizens, we must all stand up against policies and practices that are needlessly harmful. But we cannot let the tail (potential consequences) wag the dog (what we are willing to study). We will return to this point—the policy implications of a biosocial perspective—closer to the end of this article.

The Depth of Ideology in Criminology

Criminologists have carefully documented how ideology influences a range of lay views on the causes of crime (Gabbidon & Boisvert, 2012), on the criminal justice system (Flannigan & Longmire, 1996), and on support for correctional policies (Cullen, Vose, Johnson, & Unnever, 2007). The consistent pattern found in these studies is that ideology matters—that is, ideology shapes, molds, and influences world views that, in turn, influence views on crime and justice. Perhaps, however, this is to be expected by a lay audience. After all, the general public largely does not consult academic journals, has no formal scholarly training, and tends to rely on the media and personal experience for information about crime. In part owing to the influence of ideology on lay viewpoints, criminologists often classify public perceptions of crime as "misinformed" or as "naive."

The implicit assumption, however, is that lay views differ from expert views—for no other reason than expert views are thought to have developed out of prolonged, objective, research. As several studies have revealed, however, this assumption is incorrect for at least two reasons: First, criminologists, the data tell us, are also frequently beholden to political ideology. In a series of studies dating back two decades, Walsh, Ellis, and their colleagues have carefully documented the pervasive influence of ideology in criminology and how ideology strongly predicts "expert" views on the causes of crime. So strong is the influence of ideology in criminology that Walsh and Ellis (2004) labeled it the "Achilles Heel" of criminology. Results from their studies, for example, have consistently found that amongst criminologists, self-identified political orientation predicts, almost perfectly, criminologists' views on the causes of crime. Liberals, they found, uniformly favored theories that locate the causes of crime in an unfair economic system, in social inequality, and in racism. Conversely, conservatives tended to favor theories that locate the causes of crime in individual traits or in dysfunctional family processes (Cooper, Ellis, & Walsh, 2008; Cooper, Walsh, & Ellis, 2010; Ellis & Hoffman, 1990; Walsh & Ellis, 2004). Neither group, these studies point out, favors biological explanations.

Rather remarkably, parallel results were found in a survey of Philadelphia, Pennsylvania residents by Gabbidon and Boisvert (2012). Gabbidon and Boisvert presented respondents with 37 statements designed to reveal support for various criminological theories. They found that self-reported political orientation corresponded to lay views on the causes of crime—in a fashion very similar to the results presented by Cooper, Ellis, and Walsh (2008). "Conservatives were significantly more supportive than moderates and liberals of classical theory, biological theory, psychological theory, and social control theory," they report, whereas "Liberals were significantly more supportive of critical theory than moderates and conservatives" (Gabbidon & Boisvert, 2012, p. 53). Moreover, similar to Cooper et al. (2010), they also found that biological explanations for crime received the lowest endorsements overall, with a majority of conservatives, moderates, and liberals rating biological explanations as the least potent cause of crime. That "expert" and "lay" views are so similar points to the overarching power of ideology in understanding crime—especially amongst criminologists.

Second, criminologists are not the only group of scholars influenced by political ideology. Virtually every study ever completed on the political orientation of university faculty has found that liberal ideology is the dominant ideology on campuses across the United States; in fact, in many academic fields, it is virtually the only ideology (Klein, Stern, & Western, 2005; Lipset, 1994). For example, in a study of 1,471 professors from 927 universities, Gross and Simmons (2007) found that in major research institutions—institutions that produce most of the research on crime—less than 4% of faculty classified themselves as "conservative." Moreover, in a study of political party affiliation, Klein and Stern (2006) found that the average Democrat to Republican ratio amongst all surveyed faculty was 15:1; the lowest ratio was found in economics (3:1), whereas the highest ratios were found in anthropology (30:1) and sociology (28:1). The ideological sentiments of sociologists are especially important to criminology, if for no other reason than criminology evolved out of sociology and many criminologists have been trained as sociologists. Furthermore, it is instructive that Klein and Stern (2006) also found that political ideology was a robust predictor of support for a range of traditionally liberal government interventions, such as advocacy for gun control and limitations on the free-market.

Political ideology thus shapes not only the views of the general public but also the views of scholars, especially social scientists (Horowitz, 1994). Indeed, there is reason to believe that much of what passes for social science, including criminology, is the extension of an ideologically informed worldview. This worldview, we argue, has excluded biology from the study of crime for reasons that have little to do with the normal narrative presented by critics. To be sure, the past role of biological thinking in justifying oppressive measures is not inconsequential. But most of these outrageous acts occurred 50 to 100 years ago and would hardly seem possible in 21st-century America (e.g., a call for eugenics would not find a receptive audience, including among biosocial criminologists). Instead, we suspect that the persisting antagonism to biology occurs because this approach violates many deeply held personal and professional convictions. That is, using biology to explain human conduct, including crime, is inconsistent with scholars' ideological allegiance to what Haidt (2011) describes as "sacred values."

The Tribal Moral Community and the Rejection of Biology

At the 2011 meeting of the Society for Personality and Social Psychology, Jonathan Haidt queried the audience of over 1,000 psychologists to divulge their political orientation. With slightly more than 1,000 people in attendance, only 3 publically admitted to being politically conservative. Haidt estimated the ratio of liberals to conservatives in the audience to be about 266:1. This, he said, was statistically impossible. What was more important than the lopsided ratio, according to Haidt, was the culture those raw numbers represented. According to Haidt, the field of social psychology has evolved into a tribal moral community (TMC).

In any TMC, argued Haidt, there are sacred values—that is, values that *bind and blind* members to a specific way of thinking. These values produce conformity because the majority believes in the values and because any violation of the values results in strong moral condemnation. Members of the TMC will, stated Haidt, claim the mantle of science "Until the moment that it threatens a sacred value." When that happens, members of the TMC will *ditch or distort* science to enforce the sacred value. Haidt listed five sacred values that function to limit scholarly discourse and to stigmatize violators: Race differences, sex differences, blaming the victim, stereotype accuracy, and what he termed *nativism*.

Again referring to Haidt, the social sciences underwent a transformation in the 1960s. Scholars in the social sciences became enamored with civil rights, racism, feminism, the antiwar movement, and Marxism (see also Lipset, 1994). They imported these values into their fields and established strong moral boundaries by creating vertical moral hierarchies. At the top of this moral hierarchy was a belief in what we label as *pure egalitarianism*. Pure egalitarianism reflects two-pronged belief system endemic in liberal academic thinking: First, pure egalitarianism is a value based judgment—not a science based judgment—that all individuals are essentially equal. There is an embrace of the incontrovertible assumption that there are no preexisting, meaningful differences between individuals or groups in their traits, propensities, or behaviors. In many ways, a belief in pure egalitarianism is similar to "blank slate" views on individuals (Pinker, 2003); however, the pure egalitarian viewpoint highlights the elevated moral sentiment that enshrines this core sacred value. The second prong of the pure egalitarian viewpoint is the related idea that if differences exist, they must be produced by factors external to the individual. In this way, differences between racial groups, between sexes, or between economic classes must be explained without referring to individual traits or behaviors, which would be synonymous with blaming the victim.

Although the roots of the rejection of biological theorizing date back before the 1960s, especially with the work of Sutherland (1947), biological theorizing became a polarizing, career ending, issue from the late 1960s onward. It did so, we argue, because biological theorizing violates not just one of Haidt's sacred values, but *all of them*. Biological theorizing, for example, focuses on the nature of individual genetic and biological variation; it focuses on genetic differences between races and sexes; it argues that evolution has shaped our mental, physical, and behavioral capacities; it recognizes that human beings have evolved senses (some refer to these as instincts), but above all, it points out that pure egalitarianism is a social fiction. Human beings vary in almost every trait and some of this variation is caused by difference in genes.

The perceived threat to sacred academic values materialized with sometimes vicious and sometimes career ending results. Indeed, contemporary academic history is littered with examples where honest scholars have been publically sanctioned, their lives threatened, or their careers terminated for violating sacred values.

- The eminent scholar Arthur Jenson, whose work on human intelligence still shapes the field, had his life threatened and required a bodyguard when on campus after he questioned the ability of government programs to equalize the intelligence of children.
- Linda Gottfredson, a psychologist who challenged affirmative action, saw her bid for promotion undermined and witnessed her university ban her from receiving research funds from a funding agency (http://www.udel.edu/educ/ gottfredson/reprints/2009interview.pdf).
- James Watson, who codiscovered the famous double-helix of DNA, was removed from his research duties at the lab he founded for linking race to intelligence.
- Larry Summers, at the time president of Harvard University, created a firestorm when he suggested the possibility that women are underrepresented in top science programs because they are dissimilar to men in certain mental abilities.
- More pertinent to criminology, James Q. Wilson (1975) was lambasted for his book Thinking About Crime, where he challenged the core criminological belief in "root causes" of crime, and again when he published with Richard Herrnstein (1985) Crime and Human Nature. Indeed, the criminological reaction to Crime and Human Nature was decidedly hostile.
- Richard Herrnstein and Charles Murray's (1994) The Bell Curve, which generated accusations of racism and resulted in the American Psychological Association issuing a formal statement about human intelligence.
- Finally, we note the difference in criminological reaction to Gottfredson and Hirschi's (1990) A General Theory of Crime, which focuses on an individual trait, and Sampson and Laub's (1993)

Crime in the Making, which emphasizes traditional social environmental causes. Gottfredson and Hirschi's work generated tremendous ideological hostility (Geis, 2000), even though it has been largely empirically confirmed (Pratt & Cullen, 2000), whereas Sampson and Laub's work has been devoid of criticism and has won every major award in the field.

The role of ideology in criminology, and in the social sciences more broadly, has strongly shaped research agendas and research findings. It has prevented research from being conducted, prevented ideas from being explored and even discussed, and it has sterilized most criminological theories. Even Gottfredson and Hirschi's (1990) theory on self-control finds no room for genetic or biological functioning—which is contrary to evidence that self-control is strongly genetic (Beaver, Wright, & DeLisi, 2007; Friedman et al., 2008; Wright & Beaver, 2005). From our viewpoint, the "sacred values" of criminology impeded the legitimate study of the role of biology, not because the study of biological linkages to human conduct inevitably leads to harsh or brutal government interventions, as critics propose, but because biological thinking and biologically based empirical findings directly confront the professional ideology of criminologists. As Haidt (2011) notes, when a field holds sacred values it cannot be said to be a "reality-based community."

Shifting Context and New Possibilities

Despite the almost total exclusion of biology from criminology, a few criminologists undertook research in the area. Anthony Walsh, Lee Ellis, Nicole Rafter, David Rowe, Adrian Raine, and Diana Fishbein produced important scholarly writings of enduring value. Yet because their work was overtly biological in its orientation, it failed to gain traction with the majority of criminologists. Even today, antagonism toward biological thinking remains high—as we have stated.

Still, the ideological damn preventing the development of biosocial perspectives is weakening and has sprung some leaks. The reality that humans are biological creatures who vary in biological traits is becoming too obvious to ignore. As this special issue shows, more and more criminologists are being attracted to the biological paradigm. Collectively, they have helped not only to rejuvenate biological research into crime but, to a degree, have made discussions about the role of biology in antisocial behavior respectable (Beaver et al., 2009; Boisvert, & Wright, 2008; Boutwell & Beaver, 2008; DeLisi, Beaver, Vaughn, & Wright, 2009; Vaske, Makarios, Boisvert, Beaver, & Wright, 2009; Vaughn, DeLisi, Beaver, & Wright, 2009).

Why has this occurred? Although other considerations likely are relevant, we will cite four factors that have created a context more conducive to the development of biosocial criminology. First, although somewhat implicitly, biology moved into mainstream criminology with the publication of Moffitt's (1993) seminal article on lifecourse-persistent and adolescence-limited offenders. She introduced a new type of biology—what we would term a "sanitized biology." By sanitized, we mean that she set forth biosocial theory of antisocial conduct without explicitly claiming to do so. In such a palatable form, criminologists embraced a biosocial theory without realizing they had done so.

Thus, Moffitt helped to draw attention to biological processes without alienating criminologists in two ways: First, she snuck in biological criminology into the field by attributing biological deficits to external social sources, such as exposure to environmentally based teratogens (e.g., mothers taking drugs). This linked aspects of the social environment to biological functioning. Second, she used the language of "neuropsychological deficits" to describe brain dysfunction rather than the more tainted language of biological pathology or heritability. We suspect this was appealing to criminologists because it unwittingly disarmed them from their traditional distrust of biological theorizing. But let us make no mistake about Moffitt's work: It is fundamentally a biosocial theory because it links a biological deficit to environmental reactions that then ensnare a child in a pathway of antisocial cumulative continuity. The wealth of research on her theory, especially on the neuropsychological deficits (e.g., measured through mothers' smoking in pregnancy), made inquiry into biological factors more acceptable.

Second, criminology does not exist in a vacuum. The biological revolution is widespread and has swept across many fields of study. Importantly, advances in behavioral genetics and brain imaging have created the technology to move beyond the crude biology of Lombroso into a 21st century biology that is highly sophisticated. The linkage of advances in biology to the possibility of curing previously incurable diseases has displayed how biological thinking can produce social good. The potential to apply these new ideas and technology to criminology is thus an exciting development.

Third, we are now in the second decade of the 21st century and not in the 1960s. As the social context changes, so too do ideas about crime (Lilly, Cullen, & Ball, 2011). The professional ideology of criminologists has not vanished—indeed, it is powerful in many ways—but its hegemony becomes less complete (Cullen & Gendreau, 2001). Criminologists are now increasingly trained in separate criminology/criminal justice programs and are drawn from a variety of disciplines with diverse assumptions about human nature (e.g., economics). As time marches onward, the 1960s is increasingly distant, and thus the number of scholars with ties to that era is declining rapidly. As such, the ideological space to explore new ideas may be increasing.

Fourth, as Kuhn (1970) has shown, scientific paradigms emerge and flourish if they are able to provide a plethora of new "puzzles" that can be solved and thus result in publications (see also Cole, 1975). The biosocial paradigm meets this criterion. Thus, even in the face of antagonistic reviewers, biosocial research is fresh and is capable of challenging or specifying assumed social causes of crime. Accordingly, it is able to offer rich opportunities for publication. If nothing else, self-interest might lead increasing numbers of younger, if not older, criminologists into the biosocial paradigm. In this context, we turn next to the issue of the nature and potential importance of biosocial criminology.

What Is Biosocial Criminology?

Biosocial criminology is more a paradigm than a theory. By this we mean that biosocial criminology encompasses a broad range of biologically informed perspectives, research methods, and statistical tools. It brings the research skills of a diverse array of scholars under one general umbrella to understand how biological processes matter in the etiology of antisocial and criminal behavior, how these processes shape and are shaped by environmental features, and how individuals develop over the life-course. Because biosocial criminology draws on research findings and methodologies from a broad array of fields, it seeks consilience rather than retaining allegiance to disciplinary boundaries. Put simply, biosocial criminology is inherently multidisciplinary and integrative, and it prioritizes discovery over reifying disciplinary traditions.

There are three broad components to biosocial criminology: biological variation, ontogeny, and interaction. First, biological variation is an evolutionary product. Due to varying selection pressures over evolutionary history human beings have acquired a range of traits that vary, sometimes substantially, between individuals, between groups of individuals, and between the sexes. Genetic variation is a key concept in Darwinian evolution. Biosocial criminologists are interested in genetic variation and tend to focus on traits related to crime and antisocial behavior to understand how much variance in a specific trait can be attributed to genetic and environmental sources. Insights from behavioral genetics have proven invaluable in this regard and show, quite consistently, that antisocial behavior is modestly to highly heritable (Mason & Frick, 1994), that unique environmental experiences are also important, but that shared environmental influences have little to no influence (Rutter, 2006).

Meta-analytic analyses of heritability studies, for example, show that antisocial behavior is roughly 50% heritable, whereas specific studies find that antisocial behavior can range from 40 to 85% heritable (Arseneault et al., 2003). Traits related to crime, moreover, have also been found to be modestly to highly heritable. Behavioral genetic studies on self-control and other executive functions often reveal substantial levels of heritability, ranging from 80 to 100% (Friedman et al., 2008). More recently, behavioral genetic studies have investigated *callous/unemotional traits*, or traits that appear to distinguish particularly violent offenders from nonviolent offenders. These studies also find substantial heritability in these traits (Viding, Blair, Moffitt, & Plomin, 2005). However, "genetic influences are strongest," note Mofffit, Ross, and Raine (2011, p. 60) in a recent review of biological factors related to crime, for offenders who have a "criminal career that begins at an early age and is persistent, severe, and involves callous unemotional symptoms, such as a lack of remorse."

Second, ontogeny reflects the origins and life-course development of an individual organism. Biosocial criminologists are concerned with ontogenic development because much human development is preprogramed and emerges in a somewhat orderly and predictive fashion, sometimes with only limited environmental input. Ontogenic development also encompasses important developmental shifts as individual's age, as individual's acquire physical strength, mobility, verbal communication, and as individuals begin to interact on their immediate environment. Much ontogenic development appears to be closely linked to continued maturation of the brain and central nervous system throughout the life-course.

One of the key differences between modern humans and all other animals, for example, is that humans acquired the ability to communicate orally. Humans appear to be *hard wired* for language acquisition, which occurs on a well-known timetable. Delays in language acquisition and deficits in expressive and receptive vocabulary have been consistently linked to aggressive behavior (Dionne, Boivin, Tremblay, Laplante, & Perusse, 2003) and to problems in self-regulation (Beaver, DeLisi, Vaughn, Wright, & Boutwell, 2008). Delays in normative developmental sequences provide researchers with opportunities to better understand how developmental dysfunction is linked to the onset of problem behaviors, but, more importantly, this information also provides targets for treatment and intervention.

Third, and finally, much human development occurs in interaction with others across varying social contexts. Interactions between humans set the stage for social learning but, as research tells us, humans are not simply passive observers in their own lives. From infancy, humans begin to operate on their immediate social environment—that is, their traits, behaviors, and propensities emerge and interact with the behaviors and personalities of others. Biosocial criminology focuses attention on the interpersonal relationships of individuals because relationships bring together in one setting sometimes potent environmental factors and preexisting genetic propensities. Studies that examine how genes correlate and interact with environmental variables have proven insightful, if not invaluable, because they show (a) that environmental exposure to certain risk factors is not always random but is instead produced by individual genetic propensities, (b) that genes frequently condition the effects of environmental risk factors, and (c) that many environmental variables appear to also be genetically influenced (Reiss, Neiderhiser, Hetherington, & Plomin, 2000; Rutter, 2008).

It is nonetheless worth emphasizing that biosocial criminology includes a strong focus on environmental factors related to crime. Critics of biology appear to fear that biological findings will somehow squeeze out environmental influences or that a focus on biology will inevitably lead to biological reductionism. The research evidence shows, however, that this premise is entirely wrong. Biosocial studies help to better specify not only which environmental risk factors are important, but also why specific children, for example, are harmed by specific environmental risk factors although other children, exposed to the same risk factors, remain resilient. This level of specificity has never been achieved before in criminology.

Although working within these three broad areas—biological variation, ontogenic development, and social interactions—biosocial criminologists draw on a range of research methodologies. Behavioral genetic analyses are conducted on genetically informed samples using complex statistical methods; candidate gene studies rely on genotyping technology; physiological studies, such as skin conductivity tests, rely on medical technology; and brain imaging studies rely on highly advanced neuroscientific technology. Each technology brings with it a different type of insight and a host of complex measurement issues. Obviously, given the complexity and costs associated with these technologies, biosocial criminologists often have to collaborate with other scholars or, more efficiently, they simply draw on the work of other disciplines. To be able to understand at a level sufficient to conduct academic research, the nuances of these methodologies require a different type of criminological training. Biosocial criminologists need to be versed in traditional theories of crime, but they also need to be well versed in human development, molecular genetics, Darwinian evolution, evolutionary psychology, neuroscience, behavioral genetics, and physiology. This is a tall order.

The Power of the Biological Revolution and the Future of Criminology

Biosocial criminology has emerged as a powerful way of organizing scientific findings into a broader, biologically informed criminology. The paradigm appears to be gaining momentum: More biologically informed studies of crime have been published in traditional criminology journals; more books on the topic have been published in the past few years than ever before; more students have been trained in the area; and more conference panels have been produced at major academic conferences. More importantly, at least from our perspective, scholars have learned that discussing biology in the context of crime does not automatically lead to career death or to disciplinary banishment. In a fortunate turn of events, even traditional sociologists have started to incorporate biological principles and variables into their studies. For example, Ronald Simons, a highly respected sociological criminologist and his colleagues (Simons et al., 2011) recently published a biologically informed study in the *American Sociological Review*—the top journal in sociology. We believe this reflects the power of the biological revolution, which is not to be found in the technologies that people so frequently point to in awe, but in the power it possess to inform a broad domain of scientific disciplines—even the social sciences (DeLisi, Wright, Vaughn, & Beaver, 2009).

For biosocial criminology to expand, however, criminology will have to change. First, most PhD granting programs in criminology place a heavy emphasis on criminological theory. PhD students are forced to understand the minutia of theories, many of which many are useless to our understanding of crime, in favor of understanding empirical findings from a diverse range of fields. Criminology is a multidisciplinary field, yet most of the training students receive is based only in sociology. For students to become biosocial criminologists, however, they need training in fields outside of traditional criminology. Although traditional criminology has much to offer, biosocial criminologists require more than an understanding of four social bonds.

Second, as we have hopefully made clear, the subjugation of science to disciplinary "sacred values" should be abandoned. Criminology touches on politically difficult subjects, such as the intersection of race, behavior, and justice. Too frequently, however, discussions of these subjects are couched in ways designed to recognize and to protect the field's sacred values. If criminology is to advance as a science, it must abandon its political sensitivities in favor of an emphasis on the sometimes politically inconvenient findings that emerge from science. Biosocial criminology obviously threatens the sacred values of the discipline, but it can replace those values with others—such as scientific honesty, scientific objectivity, and scientific discourse unencumbered by political considerations.

Although biosocial criminology offers much to the study of crime and criminals, it remains to be seen if it will continue to expand and to be more broadly accepted. We believe the field is presented with at least three choices: First, criminology can do nothing. It can simply relegate biosocial criminology to yet another theoretical perspective, much like it has with dozens of other perspectives. We, of course, believe this would be a mistake as the empirical evidence emerging out of biosocial criminology is consistent, insightful, useful, and sometimes even remarkable.

Second, and more importantly, criminology can choose to reinforce its sacred values and continue to try to isolate biosocial criminology as a fringe movement. As we have pointed out, biosocial criminology is multidisciplinary and emphasizes science over ideology. This conflicts with powerful disciplinary views that see criminology as a singular discipline, or as a mere extension of sociology. This also conflicts with views that see the social sciences as places for social advocacy or that want to transform the field into a "public criminology" where "science" is used to advance the scriptures of "social justice" (Deflem, 2005). Indeed, the academic forces that would silence biosocial criminology appear to be on the move. In a recent article, Walby and Carrier (2010b) take aim at biosocial criminology and biosocial criminologists. In the subcultural language of the postmodern community, Walby and Carrier (2010b) equate the work of modern biosocial criminologist to a mere focus on "bios," or body parts, and to "bodily economies." Accordingly, their

> approach treats the bodily economies of 'criminal man' as cultural artifacts visualized, captured, constructed, and analyzed by criminologists. The concept 'bodily economies' refers to a nonessentialized notion of the body, one that is always in flux. Here, it is mobilized to focus on the ways in which

criminologists have isolated and visualized particular parts, layers and sections of the body, and granted these elements of human bodily economies causal powers in claims about past, actual and future behavior of 'criminal man.' (p. 262)

Of course, we strongly disagree with the characterizations of biosocial criminology made by Walby and Carrier (2010b), but that is not the point. Instead, Walby and Carrier offer a view of criminology that is in competition with ours. Their view, held to varying degrees by a diverse set of criminologists, is directly opposed to science. It substitutes sophistication in language for clarity of thought, replaces theoretical insights with ideological subterfuge, and it elevates political considerations over empirical substance. Whereas Walby and Carrier (2010b) refer to biosocial criminology as a "nightmare," we believe just the opposite is true: The rejection of science is the antipathy of reasoned scholarship.

We also wish to return to a point made earlier in this article, which further rejects the notion that biological knowledge is a nightmare fraught with inherently dangerous consequences. We are persuaded that rigorous science—including biosocial criminology—is integral to the more effective and humane treatment of offenders and those on an antisocial pathway into crime (Cullen, 2005; Farrington & Welsh, 2007). Critics often commit the fallacy of "genetic fatalism," which is to assume that a biological or biosocial cause of crime consigns a person to a life in crime (see Alpert & Beckwith, 1993). In large part, this is why these critics believe that biological thinking is dangerous; if offenders cannot be changed, then the only option is incapacitation or some other repressive intervention. In reality, however, the behavioral effects of biological factors are not immutable—any more than poor eyesight cannot be altered through eyeglasses. Such effects can be addressed through medication and through a range of treatment modalities (e.g., cognitive-behavioral programs). And once understood, they can be prevented through a range of early interventions, such as the nurse-home visitation program that seeks to help pregnant at risk mothers engage in healthy practices that spare their children neuropsychological deficits (Olds, 2007). What is misguided, then, is to allow ideology—however well intentioned—to blind us to the objective causes of waywardness and, in turn, to stop us from developing interventions targeted to reverse the effects of biosocial risk factors.

Third, criminology can join the 21st century, it can embrace contemporary scientific technologies and methodologies, and it can usher in a criminology that substantively advances our understanding of serious, chronic, criminal behavior. Elevating a biosocial criminology will attach our field to other, more technically advanced, disciplines. It will elevate the status of our field with funding agencies, such as the National Institute of Health and the National Institute of Mental Health. Moreover, as noted, it will advance the cause of science and could, ultimately, lead to better insights about how social processes damage and harm those most at risk. Elevating biosocial criminology will also open criminology up to the study of the complete life-course, from infancy through adulthood, instead of retaining our focus on adolescence. It can push criminologists to abandon their obsessive focus on theory in favor of empirical discoveries that have real policy and treatment ramifications.

In the end, a vibrant, evolving, increasingly sophisticated biosocial criminology has the capacity to destroy the ideological walls that surround criminology's sacred values. These walls may be starting to crumble, but only time will tell if they fall. It is our hope that readers of this special issue will see the value of a biosocial criminology and will, eventually, help to destroy the sacred values that "bind and blind" criminology.

Declaration of Conflicting Interests

The authors declared no potential conflicts of interest with respect to the research, authorship, and/or publication of this article.

Funding

The authors received no financial support for the research, authorship, and/or publication of this article.

References

Alper, J. S., & Beckwith, J. (1993). Genetic fatalism and social policy: The implications of behavior genetic research. *Yale Journal of Biology and Medicine, 66,* 511–526.

Arseneault, L., Moffitt, T. E., Caspi, A., Taylor, A., Rijsdijk, F. V., Jaffee, S. R., & Measelle, J. R. (2003). Strong genetic effects on cross-situational antisocial behaviour among 5-year-old children according to mothers, teachers, examiner-observers, and twins' self-reports. *Journal of Child Psychology and Psychiatry, 44,* 832–848.

Beaver, K. M. (2009). *Biosocial criminology: A primer.* Dubuque, IA: Kendall/Hunt.

Beaver, K. M., DeLisi, M., Vaughn, M. G., Wright, J. P., & Boutwell, B. B. (2008). The relationship between self-control and language: Evidence of a shared etiological pathway. *Criminology, 46,* 939–970.

Beaver, K. M., Eagle Schutt, J., Boutwell, B. B., Ratchford, M., Roberts, K., & Barnes, J. C. (2009). Genetic and environmental influences on levels of self-control and delinquent peer affiliation: Results from a longitudinal sample of adolescent twins. *Criminal Justice and Behavior, 36,* 41–60.

Beaver, K. M., Wright, J. P., & DeLisi, M. (2007). Self-control as an executive function: Reformulating Gottfredson and Hirschi's parental socialization thesis. *Criminal Justice and Behavior, 34,* 1345–1361.

Berger, P. (2002). Whatever happened to sociology? *First Things, 126,* 27–29.

Boisvert, D., & Wright, J. P. (2008). Nonshared environmental influences on sibling differences in externalizing problem behavior. *Criminal Justice and Behavior, 35,* 863–878.

Boutwell, B. B., & Beaver, K. M. (2008). A biosocial explanation of delinquency abstention. *Criminal Behavior and Mental Health, 18,* 59–74.

Brown, S., Esbensen, F., & Geis, G. (2010). *Criminology: Explaining crime and it's context* (7th ed.). Cincinnati, OH: Anderson.

Cole, S. (1975). The growth of scientific knowledge: Theories of deviance as a case study. In L. A. Coser (Ed.), *The idea of social structure: Papers in honor of R. K. Merton* (pp. 175–200). New York, NY: Harcourt Brace Jovanovich.

Cooper, J., Ellis, L., & Walsh, A. (2008). 'Criminologists' opinions about the causes and theories of crime: A follow-up. *The Criminologist, 33,* 23.

Cooper, J., Walsh, A., & Ellis, L. (2010). Is criminology moving towards a paradigm shift? Evidence from a survey of the American Society of Criminology. *Journal of Criminal Justice Education, 21,* 332.

Cullen, F. T. (2005). The twelve people who saved rehabilitation: How the science of criminology made a difference—The American Society of Criminology 2004 presidential address. *Criminology, 43,* 1–42.

Cullen, F. T. (2011). Beyond adolescence-limited criminology: Choosing our future—The American Society of Criminology 2010 Sutherland address. *Criminology, 49*, 287–330.

Cullen, F. T., & Gendreau, P. (2001). From nothing works to what works: Changing professional ideology in the 21st century. *Prison Journal, 81*, 313–338.

Cullen, F. T., Vose, B. A., Johnson, C. L., & Unnever, J. D. (2007). Public support for early intervention: Is child saving a 'habit of the heart'? *Victims and Offenders, 2*, 109–124.

Deflem, M. (2005). Public sociology, hot dogs, apple pie, and chevrolet. *Journal of Professional and Public Sociology, 1*(1), 1.

DeLisi, M., Beaver, K. M., Vaughn, M. G., & Wright, J. P. (2009). All in the family: Gene x environment interaction between DRD2 and criminal father is associated with five antisocial phenotypes. *Criminal Justice and Behavior, 36*, 1187–1197.

DeLisi, M., Wright, J. P., Vaughn, M. G., & Beaver, K. M. (2009). Copernican criminology. *The Criminologist, 34*(1), 14–16.

Dionne, G., Boivin, M., Tremblay, R., Laplante, D., & Perusse, D. (2003). Physical aggression and expressive vocabulary in 19-month-old twins. *Developmental Psychology, 39*, 261.

Ellis, L., & Hoffman, H. (1990). Views of contemporary criminologists on causes and theories of crime. In L. Ellis & H. Hoffman (Eds.), *Crime in biosocial, moral, and social contexts* (pp. 50–58). New York, NY: Praeger.

Farrington, D. P., & Welsh, B. C. (2007). *Saving children from a life in crime: Early risk factors and effective interventions.* New York, NY: Oxford University Press.

Flannigan, T., & Longmire, D. (Eds.). (1996). *Americans view crime and justice: A national public opinion survey.* Thousand Oaks, CA: SAGE.

Friedman, N. P., Miyake, A., Young, S. E., DeFries, J. C., Corley, R. P., & Hewitt, J. K. (2008). Individual differences in executive functions are almost entirely genetic in origin. *Journal of Experimental Psychology: General, 137*, 201–225.

Gabbidon, S., & Boisvert, D. (2012). Public opinion on crime causation: An exploratory study of Philadelphia area residents. *Journal of Criminal Justice, 40*, 50–59.

Geis, G. (2000). On the absence of self-control as the basis for a general theory of crime: A critique. *Theoretical Criminology, 4*, 35–53.

Gottfredson, L. S. (1994). Egalitarian fiction and collective fraud. *Society, 31*(3), 53–59.

Gottfredson, M. R., & Hirschi, T. (1990). *A general theory of crime.* Palo Alto, CA: Stanford University Press.

Gross, N., & Simmons, S. (2007). *The social and political views of American professors.* Unpublished manuscript. Available online at http://www.studentsforacademicfreedom.org/news/1893/

Haidt, J. (2012). *The righteous mind: Why good people are divided by politics and religion.* New York, NY: Pantheon Books.

Herrnstein, R. J., & Murray, C. (1994). *The bell curve: Intelligence and class structure in American life.* New York, NY: Free Press.

Horowtiz, I. L. (1994). *The decomposition of sociology.* New York, NY: Oxford University Press.

Hunt, M. (1999). *The new know-nothings: The political foes of the scientific study of human nature.* New Brunswick, NJ: Transaction Publishing.

Klein, D., & Stern, C. (2006). Sociology and classical liberalism. *The Independent Review, XI*(1), 37.

Klein, D., Stern, C., & Western, A. (2005). *Political diversity in six disciplines.* New York, NY: Springer.

Kuhn, T. S. (1970). *The structure of scientific revolutions* (2nd ed.). Chicago, IL: University of Chicago Press.

Lilly, J. R., Cullen, F. T., & Ball, R. A. (2011). *Criminological theory: Context and consequences* (4th ed.). Thousand Oaks, CA: SAGE.

Lipset, S. M. (1994). The state of American sociology. *Sociological Forum, 9,* 199.

Mason, D. A., & Frick, P. J. (1994). The heritability of antisocial behavior: A meta-analysis of twin and adoption studies. *Journal of Psychopathology and Behavioral Assessment, 16,* 301–323.

Merton, R. K. (1973). *The sociology of science: Theoretical and empirical investigations.* In Norman K. Storer (Ed.). Chicago, IL: University of Chicago Press.

Moffitt, T. E. (1993). Adolescence-limited and life-course-persistent antisocial behavior: A developmental taxonomy. *Psychological Review, 100,* 674–701.

Olds, D. L. (2007). Preventing crime with prenatal and infancy support of parents: The nursefamily partnership. *Victims and Offenders, 2,* 205–225.

Pinker, S. (2003). *The blank slate: The modern denial of human nature.* New York, NY: Penguin.

Pratt, T. C., & Cullen, F. T. (2000). The empirical status of Gottfredson and Hirschi's general theory of crime: A meta-analysis. *Criminology, 38,* 931–964.

Rafter, N. (2008). *The criminal brain: Understanding biological theories of crime.* New York, NY: New York University Press.

Reiss, D., Neiderhiser, N. M., Hetherington, E. M., & Plomin, R. (2000). *The relationship code: Deciphering the genetic and social influences on adolescent development.* Cambridge, MA: Cambridge University Press.

Rutter, M. (2006). *Genes and behavior: Nature-nurture interplay explained.* Malden, MA: Blackwell.

Rutter, M. (2008). *Genes and behavior: Nature-nurture interplay explained.* Oxford, UK: Blackwell.

Sampson, R. J., & Laub, J. H. (1993). *Crime in the making: Pathways and turning points through life.* Cambridge, MA: Harvard University Press.

Simons, R. L., Lei, M. K., Beach, S., Brody, G. H., Phillbert, R. A., & Gibbons, F. X. (2011). Social environmental variation, plasticity genes, and aggression: Evidence for the differential susceptibility hypothesis. *American Sociological Review 76,* 833–912.

Sutherland, E. (1947). *Principals of criminology* (4th ed.). Philadelphia, PA: Lippincott.

Vaske, J., Makarios, M., Boisvert, D., Beaver, K. M., & Wright, J. P. (2009). The interaction of DRD2 and violent victimization on depression: An analysis by gender and race. *Journal of Affective Disorders, 112*(1–3), 120–125.

Vaughn, M. G., DeLisi, M., Beaver, K. M., & Wright, J. P. (2009). DAT1 and 5HTT are associated with pathological criminal behavior in a nationally representative sample of youth. *Criminal Justice and Behavior, 36,* 1103–1114.

Viding, E., Blair, R. J. R., Moffitt, T. E., & Plomin, R. (2005). Evidence for substantial genetic risk for psychopathy in 7-year-olds. *Journal of Child Psychology and Psychiatry, 46,* 592–597.

Walby, K., & Carrier, N. (2010a). Dreaming of biosocial criminology? Political blindness, ontologization of crime and other criminological nightmares. *American Society of Criminology,* San Francisco, CA.

Walby, K., & Carrier, N. (2010b). The rise of biosocial criminology: Capturing observable bodily economies of 'criminal man.'. *Criminology and Criminal Justice, 10,* 261.

Walsh, A., & Ellis, L. (2004). Ideology: Criminology's Achilles' heel. *Quarterly Journal of Ideology, 27,* 1–25.

Wilson, E. O. (1998). *Consilience: The unity of knowledge.* New York, NY: Knopf.

Wilson, J. Q. (1975). *Thinking about crime.* New York, NY: Basic Books.

Wilson, J. Q., & Herrnstein, R. (1985). *Crime and human nature: The definitive study of the causes of crime.* New York, NY: Simon & Schuster.

Wright, J. P., & Beaver, K., M. (2005). Do parents matter in creating self-control in their children? A genetically informed test of Gottfredson and Hirschi's theory of low self-control. *Criminology, 43,* 1169–1202.

Wright, J. P., Beaver, K. M., DeLisi, M., & Vaughn, M. G. (2008). Evidence of negligible parenting influences on self-control, delinquent peers, and delinquency in a sample of twins. *Justice Quarterly, 25,* 544–569.

Wright, J. P., Beaver, K. M., DeLisi, M., Vaughn, M., Boisvert, D., & Vaske, J. (2008). Lombroso's legacy: The miseducation of criminologists. *Journal of Criminal Justice Education, 19,* 325.

Wright, R. A., & Miller, J. M. (1998). Taboo until today? The coverage of biological arguments in criminology textbooks, 1961 to 1970 and 1987 to 1996. *Journal of Criminal Justice, 26*(1), 1–19.

DISCUSSION QUESTIONS
By John M. Stogner

1. Do you believe that "tribal morality" or indirect scientific repression aimed against biological criminology impeded advancement in our understanding of deviance?

2. Behavioral genetic studies suggest that half of the variation in antisocial behavior can be attributed to heredity. If this is accurate, how can any theory exclude genetic influence?

3. Use your library resources to find a landmark study: "Role of Genotype in the Cycle of Violence in Maltreated Children." How did this work advance our understanding of violence, and why has it been so influential?

4. Would the understanding that genetic factors are linked to increased criminal propensity lessen the culpability of offenders who possessed those genetic factors?

5. If laws change over time, is it reasonable to base a theory on factors that do not (e.g., genes)? Why or why not?

CHAPTER EIGHT

A Theory of Differential Association

EDWIN H. SUTHERLAND AND DONALD R. CRESSEY

STUDENT INTRODUCTION
By John M. Stogner

This short chapter provides a glimpse of one of the most discussed and respected theories in criminology. A University of Chicago graduate credited with initiating the study of white-collar crime, Edwin Sutherland introduced "a theory of differential association" in 1939. His work did not tie deviant behavior to biological variation or deficiencies in the certainty and severity of punishment. He similarly believed that offending was affected by more sociological factors than class and poverty. In short, he argued that deviance and criminal behavior were learned. He believed that being exposed to individuals engaging in delinquency strongly impacted an individual's own likelihood of offending. Succinctly, according to Sutherland, criminal behavior is not innate, but learned through communication and interactions with others. He argued that individuals commit delinquent acts when the balance of *definitions* favors doing so—we become delinquent when we have an excess of definitions favorable to violation of the law.

As you read Sutherland's work, consider how it might have appealed to those who rejected the connection between biology and deviance. Think about what this theory would mean for policy and what types of programs would be supported by Sutherland's arguments. As you read his nine propositions, question whether each is logical and well-defined. Pay careful attention to Sutherland's wording and assess whether any of the terms he introduces are unnecessarily vague. Evaluate whether the theory could be presented in a more parsimonious form, and, finally, ask yourself whether his work is likely to explain both lower-class crime and his specialty, white-collar crime.

A THEORY OF DIFFERENTIAL ASSOCIATION

By Edwin H. Sutherland and Donald R. Cressey

Before Sutherland developed his theory, crime was usually explained in terms of multiple factors—like social class, broken homes, age, race, urban or rural location, and mental disorder. Sutherland developed his theory of differential association in an effort to explain why these various factors were related to crime. In doing so, he hoped to organize and integrate the research on crime up to that point, as well as to guide future research.

Sutherland's theory is stated in the form of nine propositions. He argues that criminal behavior is learned by interacting with others, especially intimate others. Criminals learn both the techniques of committing crime and the definitions favorable to crime from these others. The sixth proposition, which forms the heart of the theory, states that "a person becomes delinquent because of an excess of definitions favorable to law violation over definitions unfavorable to violation of law." According to Sutherland, factors such as social class, race, and broken homes influence crime because they affect the likelihood that individuals will associate with others who present definitions favorable to crime.

Sutherland's theory has had a tremendous influence on crime research and it remains one of the dominant theories of crime. Studies on the causes of crime routinely attempt to determine whether individuals are associating with delinquent or criminal others. Although one can learn definitions favorable to crime from law-abiding individuals, one is most likely to learn such definitions from delinquent friends or criminal family members. These studies typically find that association with delinquent others is the best predictor of crime, and that these delinquent others partly influence crime by leading the individual to adopt beliefs conducive to crime (see Agnew, 2000; Akers, 1998; Akers and Sellers, 2004; Warr, 2001 for summaries of such studies).

Sutherland's theory has also inspired much additional theorizing in criminology. Theorists have attempted to better describe the nature of those definitions favorable to violation of the law. They have attempted to better describe the processes by which we learn criminal behavior from others. And they have drawn on Sutherland in an effort to explain group differences in crime rates. Sutherland's theory of differential association, then, is one of the enduring classics in criminology (for excellent discussions of the current state of differential association theory, see Matsueda, 1988, and Warr, 2001).

The following statement refers to the process by which a particular person comes to engage in criminal behavior:

1. *Criminal behavior is learned.* Negatively, this means that criminal behavior is not inherited, as such; also, the person who is not already trained in crime does not invent criminal behavior, just as a person does not make mechanical inventions unless he has had training in mechanics.

2. *Criminal behavior is learned in interaction with other persons in a process of communication.* This communication is verbal in many respects but includes also "the communication of gestures."

3. *The principal part of the learning of criminal behavior occurs within intimate personal groups.* Negatively, this means that the impersonal agencies of communication, such as movies and newspapers, play a relatively unimportant part in the genesis of criminal behavior.

4. *When criminal behavior is learned, the learning includes (a) techniques of committing the crime, which are sometimes very complicated, sometimes very simple; (b) the specific direction of motives, drives, rationalizations, and attitudes.*

5. *The specific direction of motives and drives is learned from definitions of the legal codes as favorable or unfavorable.* In some societies an individual is surrounded by persons who invariably define the

legal codes as rules to be observed, while in others he is surrounded by persons whose definitions are favorable to the violation of the legal codes. In our American society these definitions are almost always mixed, with the consequence that we have culture conflict in relation to the legal codes.

6. *A person becomes delinquent because of an excess of definitions favorable to violation of law over definitions unfavorable to violation of law.* This is the principle of differential association. It refers to both criminal and anti-criminal associations and has to do with counteracting forces. When persons become criminal, they do so because of contacts with criminal patterns and also because of isolation from anti-criminal patterns. Any person inevitably assimilates the surrounding culture unless other patterns are in conflict; a Southerner does not pronounce "r" because other Southerners do not pronounce "r." Negatively, this proposition of differential association means that associations which are neutral so far as crime is concerned have little or no effect on the genesis of criminal behavior. Much of the experience of a person is neutral in this sense, e.g., learning to brush one's teeth. This behavior has no negative or positive effect on criminal behavior except as it may be related to associations which are concerned with the legal codes. This neutral behavior is important especially as an occupier of the time of a child so that he is not in contact with criminal behavior during the time he is so engaged in the neutral behavior.

7. *Differential associations may vary in frequency, duration, priority, and intensity.* This means that associations with criminal behavior and also associations with anticriminal behavior vary in those respects. "Frequency" and "duration" as modalities of associations are obvious and need no explanation. "Priority" is assumed to be important in the sense that lawful behavior developed in early childhood may persist throughout life, and also that delinquent behavior developed in early childhood may persist throughout life. This tendency, however, has not been adequately demonstrated, and priority seems to be important principally through its selective influence. "Intensity" is not precisely defined but it has to do with such things as the prestige of the source of a criminal or anti-criminal pattern and with emotional reactions related to the associations. In a precise description of the criminal behavior of a person these modalities would be stated in quantitative form and a mathematical ratio be reached. A formula in this sense has not been developed, and the development of such a formula would be extremely difficult.

8. *The process of learning criminal behavior by association with criminal and anticriminal patterns involves all of the mechanisms that are involved in any other learning.* Negatively, this means that the learning of criminal behavior is not restricted to the process of imitation. A person who is seduced, for instance, learns criminal behavior by association, but this process would not ordinarily be described as imitation.

9. *While criminal behavior is an expression of general needs and values, it is not explained by those general needs and values since non-criminal behavior is an expression of the same needs and values.* Thieves generally steal in order to secure money, but likewise honest laborers work in order to secure money. The attempts by many scholars to explain criminal behavior by general drives and values, such as the happiness principle, striving for social status, the money motive, or frustration, have been and must continue to be futile since they explain lawful behavior as completely as they explain criminal behavior. They are similar to respiration, which is necessary for any behavior but which does not differentiate criminal from non-criminal behavior.

It is not necessary, at this level of explanation, to explain why a person has the associations which he has; this certainly involves a complex of many things. In an area where the delinquency rate is high, a boy who is sociable, gregarious, active, and athletic is very likely to come in contact with the other boys in the neighborhood, learn delinquent behavior from them, and become a gangster; in the same neighborhood the psychopathic boy who is isolated, introverted, and inert may remain at home, not become acquainted with the other boys in the neighborhood, and not become delinquent. In another situation, the sociable, athletic, aggressive boy may become a member of a scout troop and not become involved in delinquent behavior. The person's associations are determined in a general context of social organization. A child is ordinarily reared in a family; the place of residence of the family is determined largely by family income; and the delinquency rate is in many respects related to the rental value of the houses. Many other aspects of social organization affect the kinds of associations a person has.

The preceding explanation of criminal behavior purports to explain the criminal and non-criminal behavior of individual persons. As indicated earlier, it is possible to state sociological theories of criminal behavior which explain the criminality of a community, nation, or other group. The problem, when thus stated, is to account for variations in crime rates and involves a comparison of the crime rates of various groups or the crime rates of a particular group at different times. The explanation of a crime rate must be consistent with the explanation of the criminal behavior of the person, since the crime rate is a summary statement of the number of persons in the group who commit crimes and the frequency with which they commit crimes. One of the best explanations of crime rates from this point of view is that a high crime rate is due to social disorganization. The term "social disorganization" is not entirely satisfactory and it seems preferable to substitute for it the term "differential social organization." The postulate on which this theory is based, regardless of the name, is that crime is rooted in the social organization and is an expression of that social organization. A group may be organized for criminal behavior or organized against criminal behavior. Most communities are organized both for criminal and anti-criminal behavior and in that sense the crime rate is an expression of the differential group organization. Differential group organization as an explanation of variations in crime rates is consistent with the differential association theory of the processes by which persons become criminals.

REFERENCES

Agnew, Robert. 2000. "Sources of Criminality: Strain and Subcultural Theories." In Joseph F. Sheley (ed.), *Criminology: A Contemporary Handbook*, 3rd edition, pp. 349–371. Belmont, CA: Wadsworth.

Akers, Ronald L. 1998. *Social Learning and Social Structure: A General Theory of Crime and Deviance*. Boston: Northeastern University Press.

Akers, Ronald L. and Christine S. Sellers. 2004. *Criminological Theories: Introduction and Evaluation*, 4th edition. Los Angeles: Roxbury Publishing.

Matsueda, Ross L. 1988. "The Current State of Differential Association Theory." *Crime and Delinquency* 34: 277–306.

Warr, Mark. 2001. "The Social Origins of Crime: Edwin Sutherland and the Theory of Differential Association." In Raymond Paternoster and Ronet Bachman (ed.), *Explaining Criminals and Crime*, pp. 182–191. Los Angeles: Roxbury Publishing.

DISCUSSION QUESTIONS
By John M. Stogner

1. Is Sutherland's concept of *definitions* adequately described? Given his description, is it possible to fully comprehend what he intended the term to encompass? How can definitions be measured?

2. In his seventh proposition, Sutherland describes the modalities of association. Readers typically accept that associations that are greater in duration, frequency, and intensity are more influential than others; however, there is debate regarding priority. Why would Sutherland consider priority an important modality rather than recency? Do earlier friends have a greater influence than present ones on our present behaviors and definitions?

3. Is Sutherland's theory incomplete in that it does not explore or explain the process of learning and instead simply claims that criminal behavior is learned in the same way as other behaviors?

4. Does Sutherland's work imply that for a crime to occur that a person has to believe that the action is appropriate?

5. If Sutherland were writing today, how would he likely view the potential influence on delinquency of social media and other "virtual peers"?

CHAPTER NINE

Nothing Is as Practical as a Good Theory

Social Learning and the Treatment and Prevention of Delinquency

RONALD L. AKERS

STUDENT INTRODUCTION

By John M. Stogner

Working with Robert Burgess, Ronald L. Akers developed "a differential association-reinforcement theory" in 1966. His work drew from both Sutherland and leading behavioral psychologists. His efforts eventually led to the formation of what is referred to as *social learning theory*. Akers's social learning theory is a broader explanation of deviant behavior and appears to correct some of the limitations of differential association theory. Akers argues that his theory does not refute Sutherland's work, but rather builds upon and enhances it. It retains the principles of differential association theory, intertwining them with operant and respondent conditioning. Akers's theory is currently one of the most researched and empirically supported explanations of deviance. When evaluated alongside other theories, learning variables typically emerge as those most strongly associated with deviance. While critics have challenged that this support is inflated by measurement problems or spuriousness, social learning theory continues to be a leading criminological theory.

Akers's theory is more parsimonious than Sutherland's, as he relies on four core constructs rather than nine propositions. Akers links variation in deviance to differences in *differential association*, *definitions*, *imitation*, and *differential reinforcement*.

Differential reinforcement refers to the balance of anticipated rewards and costs tied to an action. Akers argues that deviant behaviors are likely when individuals expect the rewards for engaging in that behavior to exceed the costs. He notes that anticipated costs and rewards are linked to the degree to which that behavior has been rewarded (or punished) in the past and whether an individual has seen others rewarded/punished for that same behavior. Given his description of the construct, it may be better labeled *differential expectations of reinforcement* rather than *differential reinforcement*. In addition, Akers often differentiates between social and nonsocial reinforcement, suggesting that it may be best to divide this construct into two components.

Akers has recently expanded upon social learning theory and created what he refers to as the "social structure-social learning model (SSSL)." This newer theory attempts to also explain why other, broader issues correlate with crime in addition to learning variables. He suggests that structural factors are related to crime because they impact social learning constructs. Put another way, social learning variables are hypothesized to mediate the relationship between variables such as race, gender, and anomie and deviance. He describes four categories of structural variables: *differential social organization, differential location in the social structure, theoretically defined structural variables*, and *differential social location within groups*. Given the scope of the SSSL model, it is not unsurprising that it has yet to be fully tested; however, works evaluating portions of the model typically provide significant support for Akers's SSSL hypotheses.

As you read this chapter, consider the differences between Akers's views and those of Sutherland. Apply the criteria for a good theory (from Chapter 1) to Akers's arguments and assess the overall utility of his work. Question whether rational choice theory was a unique contribution to the field given that Akers published his work, with a focus on differential reinforcement, 20 years earlier. Finally, allow this chapter to remind you that a good theory is only useful if it helps us develop better policy and programs. Social learning is an empirically supported theory that has successfully impacted programming; however, Akers also demonstrates the danger of developing policy and programs outside of a theoretical framework.

NOTHING IS AS PRACTICAL AS A GOOD THEORY
By Ronald L. Akers

Social Learning Theory and the Treatment and Prevention of Delinquency

I concluded a recent article on the relationship between theory and practice by outlining some questions to ask when examining existing programs and policies for theoretical linkages. These included the following questions regarding past and current programs for control, treatment, or prevention of crime and delinquency (Akers 2005, 34–36):

1. Which of these programs and policies are based explicitly and clearly on a theory of crime and delinquency?...

2. Which policies and programs are based on a combination of different theories...

3. Which programs are based only implicitly on theoretical assumptions, not recognized or articulated by those who put the program into place or operate it? Can the underlying theoretical principles behind the program be identified?

These questions are related to the purposes of this chapter. I begin with a review of some basic assertions about the relationship between theory and practice in criminology, Then, after providing an overview of social learning theory of crime and delinquency, I review prevention and treatment programs that are self-consciously and clearly based on the cognitive-behavioral principles and processes in social learning theory (whether or not they are combined with other compatible theories) relevant to questions 1 and 2. Programs based on these principles have been shown by good research to be at least moderately effective, and I include references to that research. I give somewhat more detailed descriptions of some good examples of theory-based programs taken from the work of the Oregon Social Learning Center (OSLC) and from the work of the Social Development Research Group (SDRG) in Seattle. The OSLC programs are explicitly founded on social learning theory but also have elements that are consistent—at least, implicitly—with social bonding theory (Hirschi 1969). The SDRG programs are explicitly based on a foundation of both social learning and bonding theories. Finally, I review Gang Resistance Education and Training (GREAT) and Drug Awareness and Resistance Education (DARE) as programs that relate to question 3.1 That is, as nearly as I am able to decipher them, neither of these programs is based on clear statements of principles or assumptions of a theory of crime and deviance. Neither has been found by sound evaluation research to be effective in producing the desired and expected outcomes. I draw directly from what I have previously written over many years on social learning theory—its empirical validity and its practical usefulness and issues related to theory and practice. I apologize for any overlap and redundancy to those readers who are familiar with the prior work (see Akers 1973, 1985, 1992, 1998, 2005, 2006; Akers and Jensen 2003; Akers and Sellers 2004; Akers et al. 1979; Sellers and Akers 2006).

Relationship between Theory and Practice in Criminology

I take the title of this chapter from a book by Hans Lennart Zetterberg (1962) that I read in graduate school many years ago in which he says:

The phrase "nothing is as practical as a good theory" is a twist of an older truth: Nothing improves theory more than its confrontation with practice. It is my belief that the development of applied social theory will do much good to basic theoretical sociology. This is obvious enough as we deal with those parts of theoretical sociology that are put to practical use; they become refined in the process. (189)

Some forty years later, John H, Laub (2004) echoed this sentiment for criminology: "Despite efforts by many to divide theory and research from policy, the fact is theory, research, and policy are deeply intertwined and central to the lives of everyone involved in explaining crime and advancing justice and public safety" (18). The usual academic distinction between "pure" theoretical and "applied" practical social science has some validity and relevance for criminology and sociology. As these insightful quotes remind us, however, the distinction is flawed because it too often obscures the integral relationship between the two.

There are a number of scientific criteria for evaluating criminological theories, the most important of which is the extent to which an explanation of crime and deviance is consistent with the known facts of crime and is supported by empirical data from direct tests of its propositions. The usefulness or applicability of a theory to doing something about the problems of crime and delinquency is another important criterion (Akers 1994; Akers and Sellers 2004). Does the theory provide principles that can be used to control, prevent, or modify offending behavior? The question is most often asked with regard to actions, policies, or programs in the formal social control (criminal and juvenile justice) systems. But it can also be asked regarding informal social control that can be undertaken by parents, schools, churches, peers, and neighborhood and community groups and organizations, as well as by private practitioners and enterprises, to enhance conformity and prevent, change, or control criminal and deviant behavior.

All formal and informal efforts to prevent, deter, lessen, modify, or otherwise "do something about" delinquency, crime, drug abuse, violence, and other forms of antisocial and deviant behavior relate in some way to explanations of what causes that behavior at the individual or group level (Akers and Sellers 2004; Barlow 1995). Of course, the emphasis is on practicality and trying to find what works; programs rely on common-sense hunches, intuition, and guesses along with some mixture of theoretical insights. They are not meant to be, and we cannot expect them to be, theoretically pure. Too often, however, this pragmatism produces a combination of techniques and approaches in the same program or facility that is fraught with "paradoxes," conflict, and confusion (Abrams, Kim, and Anderson-Nathe 2005), and it is difficult to determine what exactly the theories are on which the practices might be based. This, in turn, makes it difficult to determine the conclusions that could be reached about a particular theory if the program were found to be a success or a failure. This unduly undermines the link between theory and practice and can be avoided by clearer articulation of theory when establishing or operating programs and policies. "Evidence-based practice" has become a catch phrase today in criminology and sociology, but it is a sound principle of application (see Welsh and Farrington 2006). Of course, certain practices should never be put in place because they do not conform to moral and ethical standards of fairness, justice, and human rights, regardless of how effective they might be or how much they are based on empirically validated theory, (For a more complete discussion of these issues, see Akers 2005.)

Brief Overview of Social Learning Theory

My version of social learning theory is an integration of Edwin H. Sutherland's (1947) sociological theory of differential association and behavioral principles of conditioning and reinforcement from psychology originally formulated by Robert L. Burgess and Akers (1966) as "differential association-reinforcement" theory and as I have developed it since then (see Akers 1973, 1985, 1994, 1998; Akers and Sellers 2004; Akers el al. 1979; Jensen and Akers 2003). Social learning principles have been used to explain criminal and delinquent behavior. They have also been applied to treatment and prevention by other social behaviorists working with explanatory models that are compatible with and differ only somewhat from social learning theory as I have proposed it (see Andrews and Bonta 1998, 2003; Patterson and Dishion 1985; Patterson, Reid, and Dishion 1992; Reid, Patterson, and Snyder 2002).

Social learning is a general social-psychological theory that offers an explanation of the full range of criminal and deviant behavior (onset, persistence, desistence, and change) and embraces social, nonsocial, and cultural factors operating to both motivate and control criminal behavior and to both promote and undermine conformity. The social, cognitive, and behavioral principles in the theory "are fundamental principles of performance [that account for]... the acquisition, maintenance, and modification of human behavior" (Andrews and Bonta 1998, 150). They are not confined to accounting for learning and performing novel behavior. Contrary to the way it is sometimes depicted, the theory does not simply try to account for the "positive causes" of crime, which would thereby render it unable to answer questions of why people do not commit crime (Gottfredson and Hirschi 1990; Hirschi 1969). Rather, it offers answers to both the question of why people do and why people do not violate norms; it incorporates factors and variables that facilitate as well those that counteract crime and delinquency. The basic proposition is that the same learning process in a context of social structure, interaction, and situation produces both conforming and deviant behavior. The probability of criminal or conforming behavior is a function of the balance of these risk and protective influences on behavior—not only those that operate in an individual's learning history, but also on those that operate at a given time in a given situation and those that predict future behavior (Akers 1998, 59). Deviant and criminal behavior is acquired, performed, repeated, maintained, and changed through all of the same cognitive and behavioral mechanisms as conforming behavior.

Social learning theory accounts for the individual becoming prone to deviant or criminal behavior, stability or change in that propensity, committing the behavior in some situations and not others, and for processes of offense specialization (discrimination) and versatility (generalization). Therefore, the theory is capable of accounting for the development of stable individual differences, as well as for changes in the individual's behavioral patterns or tendencies to commit deviant and criminal acts over time and in different situations. In the Social Structure—Social Learning (SSSL) Model, the social learning process is hypothesized to mediate the effects of society, culture, and social structure on rates of crime, deviance, and delinquency (Akers 1998); social learning processes are micro-level mechanisms most relevant to the macro-level mechanisms proposed in structural theories of crime (Akers and Jensen 2006; Jensen and Akers 2003).

While referring to all dimensions of the underlying behavioral process (e.g., operant and classical conditioning, reinforcement schedules, stimulus satiation and deprivation) I have relied mainly on four principal explanatory concepts: differential association, definitions (and other discriminative stimuli), differential reinforcement, and imitation to explicate the social learning process (Akers 1985, 1998; Akers et al. 1979).

Differential reinforcement, or instrumental conditioning, refers to the frequency, amount, and probability of experienced and perceived contingent rewards and punishment for behavior, *Imitation* refers to the process in which the behavior of others and its consequences are observed and modeled. *Stimulus discrimination/generalization* designates the process by which overt and covert stimuli, verbal and cognitive, act as cues or signals for behavior to occur. The reinforcement and discriminative stimuli are mainly social (such as socially valued rewards and punishments contingent on the behavior and other social stimuli), but they are also nonsocial (such as unconditioned physiological reactions to environmental stimuli and physical effects of ingested substances and the physical environment). The content of the learning by these mechanisms includes the simple and complex behavioral sequences and the *definitions* (beliefs, attitudes, justifications, orientations) that in turn become discriminative for the commission of deviant and criminal behavior. *Differential association* has both behavioral-interactional and normative dimensions and refers to the direct and indirect, verbal and nonverbal communication, interaction, and identification with groups and individuals that comprise or control the individual's major sources of reinforcement, most salient behavioral models, and most effective definitions for the commission and repetition of behavior. The most important of these groups are the primary ones of family, friends, and peer groups, though they may also be secondary and reference groups, including "virtual peer groups" formed through the Internet, land and cell phones, movies, television, and other social media (Warr 2002). The relative frequency, intensity, duration, and priority of associations affect the relative amount, frequency, and probability of reinforcement of conforming or deviant behavior and exposure of individuals to deviant or conforming norms and behavioral models.

There is a large body of research that typically finds strong to moderate relationships between social learning variables (singly and in combination) and criminal, delinquent, and deviant behavior, mainly in American samples but also in studies in European, Asian, and other societies. There has been little research evidence that runs counter to social learning hypotheses (see reviews in Akers 1998; Akers and Jensen 2006; Akers and Sellers 2004).

Social Learning Principles in Prevention and Treatment Programs

Social learning theory proposes that criminal and delinquent behavior is acquired and sustained through association, reinforcement, definitions, imitation, and other learning processes. The application of social learning theory is found in programs designed, directly or indirectly, to affect associations, reinforcement, definitions and attitudes, modeling and imitation, discriminative stimuli, and other learning and variables by which behavior is acquired and changed. The general prediction is that the greater the degree to which an intervention project is designed or otherwise reflects these social learning principles, the greater the effectiveness of the program in preventing, controlling, or countering delinquent or criminal behavior.

Some Early Programs

Donald R. Cressey (1955) recognized more than fifty years ago, in his concept of "retroflexive reformation," that most group-based approaches to rehabilitation for juveniles and adults, whether those responsible for them recognized it or not, were based on the principle of differential association—that is, the assumption that group dynamics can be directed to influence individual offenders to change their definitions, attitudes, and orientations to make them less favorable to law breaking. Cressey argued:

> The most effective mechanism for exerting group pressure on members will be found in groups so organized that criminals are induced to join with non-criminals for the purpose of changing other criminals. A group in which Criminal A joins with some non-criminals to change criminal B is probably most effective in changing Criminal A, not B; in order to change Criminal B, criminal A must necessarily share the values of the anti-criminal members. (117)

A decade later, Don Gibbons (1965), in what may have been the first sociologically oriented book proposing general principles and treatment strategies for "changing the law breaker," made a similar argument:

> Group therapy encourages the participants to put pressure on each other for behavioral change and to get the group to define new conduct norms.... [G]roup therapy represents a kind of primary group relationship in which behavioral change is attempted through the same mechanisms by which attitude formation and behavioral change takes place in conventional primary groups. (151)

One of the first systematic uses of created peer groups to change delinquents' attitudes and behavior was in the Highfields project (Weeks 1958), which used Guided Group Interaction (GGI) in a residential facility for adjudicated delinquent boys. GGI reflects the principle of differential association applied in peer group (guided by adult staff) sessions in which common problems can be discussed in a group atmosphere that intends to encourage non-delinquent attitudes and behavior. At the end of the program, the Highfields boys had developed attitudes more favorable to obeying the law, and those who had changed their attitudes the most were more likely to succeed and stay out of trouble later. The Highfields boys did somewhat better than a comparison group of boys who had been committed to the state reformatory school (even when adjustments for in-program failures were made) in avoiding reinstitutionalization, but this was primarily due to the differences observed among the black youth.

The Provo Experiment (Empey and Erickson 1972) offered a semi-residential alternative to regular juvenile probation and to incarceration in a state training school for adjudicated delinquent boys. The boys assigned to the facility were subjected to group techniques similar to GGI that were meant, with guidance from adult counselors, to develop a pro-social, anti-delinquent peer culture in the facility and to use peer group interaction and influence to foster modifications in the boys' motivations and definitions toward conforming, and away from delinquent, behavior. The evaluation of the Provo project was designed to have court-adjudicated delinquent boys randomly assigned to one of the three conditions: (1) Pinehills, the semi-residential facility; (2) the secure-custody state training school; or (3) a regular juvenile probation caseload in the community. However, the experimental design did not last because the juvenile-court judge began purposely, rather than randomly, assigning boys to Pinehills once he learned that the Pinehills boys had significantly lower recidivism than those boys assigned to the state training school. The Pinehills boys did better than the state training school boys six months after release and even four years later. However, after four years the Pinehills boys did little better than the juveniles placed on community probation (Lundman 1993).

The Teaching Family model (and its predecessor, Achievement Place) operated in a home with a married couple as surrogate parents and six to eight delinquent or "at risk" youth living with them as a family. A "token economy" was installed in which the youth could earn reward points for proper behavior or have points taken away for improper behavior in the home or at school. The group home parents were responsible for teaching social, academic, and prevocational skills and maintaining positive, mutually reinforcing relationships with the adolescents. In addition, the youths operated a peer-oriented self-government system in the home. Thus, in addition to the shaping of behavior by the teaching parents (applying the principle of differential reinforcement), the Teaching Family model promoted conforming behavior through exposure to a pro-social peer group (applying the principle of differential association). The Teaching Family was quite effective in maintaining good behavior in the school and in the community while the youth were in residence. Outcome evaluations, however, found that the delinquency-inhibiting effects on the adolescents did not survive release from the environment of the Teaching Family homes back to their previous family and neighborhood environments because there was no after-care program (Braukmann and Wolf 1987).

Three Programs of the Oregon Social Learning Center

These earlier programs had some acknowledged and plain social learning underpinnings, but none was as able to tie theory and practice together as carefully and successfully over so many years as have Gerald R. Patterson and his colleagues at the Oregon Social Learning Center (OSLC; Dishion, McCord, and Poulin 1999; Dishion, Patterson, and Kavanagh 1992; Patterson 1975; Patterson and Chamberlain 1994; Patterson, Capaldi, and Bank 1991; Patterson, Debaryshe and Ramsey 1989; Reid, Patterson, and Snyder 2002; Snyder and Patterson 1995). The OSLC has conducted research on, and applied the principles of, social learning theory in family, peer group, and school programs for the treatment and prevention of childhood and adolescent misbehavior. The OSLC model proposes that the child's behavior and interaction with others are "learned in the family, and under more extreme conditions carr[y] over to a child's interactions with others outside the family, including peers and teachers" (Dishion, Patterson, and Kavanagh 1992, 254–255). This learning is more apt to result in misbehavior in the home and delinquency outside the home when the interaction between parent and child can be characterized as "coercive": "Poor parent discipline practices increase the likelihood of child coercive responses, and high rates of child coercion impede parents' attempts to provide evenhanded, consistent, and effective discipline. It is in this sense that parental limit setting for behaviors such as lying, stealing, or fighting often fail in the quagmire of the child's arguments, excuses, and counteraccusations" (258).

The OSLC's Adolescent Transition Program (ATP) was a successful intervention with at-risk youth that targeted family disciplinary and socialization skills in parent-focused and parent–teen groups compared with teen-focused groups and self-directed change. Parents were enlisted (voluntarily) into training sessions and provided services to help them develop more effective socialization and disciplinary skills to develop and maintain a home environment in which pro-social behavior is modeled and rewarded and aggressiveness or other misbehavior is punished. "Social learning parent training is a step-wise, skill-based approach for developing effective parenting skills and strategies for maintaining change." (Dishion et al. 1992, 263) In addition, at risk youth age 10–14 were involved in group and individual sessions (under the guidance of therapists), again voluntarily, designed to promote pro-social peer associations, attitudes, and self-control. The program had some of the intended outcomes, with improvements in parenting skills and reductions in antisocial behavior among the youth, but formation of peer-focused groups in which older delinquents were included increased deviant behavior among the younger youth in the group, which is not a surprising outcome when modeling and imitation effects are considered (Dishion, Patterson, and Kavanagh 1992; Dishion et al. 1999).

The participants in the OSLC's Multidimensional Treatment Foster Care (MTFC) program were chronic, high-frequency, and serious youthful offenders who had been adjudicated by the juvenile court as delinquents (Chamberlain, Fisher, and Moore 2002; Eddy and Chamberlain 2000). The judge allowed them to be assigned randomly to regular group home foster care or to foster-care parents who had been specially recruited and trained by the OSLC to use "behavior management methods...to implement and maintain a flexible and individualized behavior plan for each youth within the context of a three-level point system that made youth privileges contingent on compliance with program rules and general progress" (Eddy and Chamberlain 2000, 858). The foster parents were trained "to notice and reinforce youngsters" for proper behavior in a positive way. In addition, each youth took part in weekly sessions "focused on skill building in such areas as problem solving, social perspective taking, and nonaggressive methods of self-expression" (Chamberlain, Fisher, and Moore 2002, 205–206), working directly with behavioral therapists. All aspects of the intervention program were coordinated and supervised by case managers to monitor the participation of the youth and to insure that the procedures and techniques were carried out as intended by the program design. After the youth completed the program, they were returned to their biological or stepparents, who also received support and training in parenting skills to help them manage the youths' behavior and maintain the behavioral and attitudinal gains made in the MTFC. Evaluation of the program found that the treatment group had significantly lower levels of both self-reported and official delinquency than the control group up to three years later. Moreover, the research showed that the effects of the intervention procedures on program outcome were mediated by their effects on the social learning variables—that is, reductions in differential association with delinquent peers and increases in parental supervision of the children's behavior and positive reinforcement for good behavior (Chamberlain, Fisher, and Moore 2002; Eddy and Chamberlain 2000).

While the MTFC was a treatment program for court-adjudicated delinquents, Linking the Interests of Families and Teachers (LIFT) was an OSLC delinquency-prevention project. While high-risk areas of the community were targeted, LIFT used a "universal strategy" in which services were made available to all first- and fifth-graders (as the transitional grades into elementary and middle schools, respectively), their parents, and teachers in those areas. No attempt was made to identify individual youth at risk and single them out for preventive intervention. LIFT secured the cooperation of schools serving the high-risk neighborhoods and the voluntary involvement of children and families in those neighborhoods. The program was based on the theoretical principle that "the driving force in a child's conduct problems are the reinforcement processes that occur in his or her dat-to-day relationships.... [A]ntisocial behavior develops as an interaction between the child's antisocial behavior and the reactions of those with whom he or she interacts on a daily basis" (Reid and Eddy 2002, 222). Therefore, the program focused on modifying the ways in which the youth interacted with peers, with parents and siblings, and with teachers and classmates at school. "The three major components of the LIFT are (a) classroom-based child social and problem skills training, (b) playground-based behavior modification, and (c) group-delivered parent training" (Eddy, Reid, and Fetrow 2000, 165). The program had some modest to strong effects almost immediately on reductions in physical aggression on the playground and improved behavior in classrooms in the participating schools. Also, in the longer term, by the time the fifth-graders were in middle school and the first years of high school, the LIFT participants had experienced significantly fewer police arrests, lower levels of self-reported drug use, and fewer associations with deviant peers (as observed by the teachers) than did the youth in the control group.

Two Programs of the Seattle Social Development Research Group

As can be seen from these descriptions, and as is fully evident from its name, these and other projects of the OSLC are transparently and explicitly predicated on social learning principles. However, the training of parents in good practices for supervising and disciplining their children to prevent delinquent behavior is also consistent with principles of self-control (Gottfredson and Hirschi 1990) and social bonding (Hirschi 1969) theories. Indeed, much to my consternation, control theorists often refer to the work of the OSLC as supportive of social bonding or self-control theory while usually neglecting to point out that it is the Social Learning Center, not the Social Control Center. Although the implications of the two theories for intervention in peer groups are very different (control theory would advise paying no attention to foster learning of conforming, non-deviant behavior in peer groups and concentrate only on enhancing attachment to peers), there are commonalities in the practical implications of social learning and social bonding for family interventions (and to some extent for school-based interventions). The Social Development Model (SDM) programs are explicitly formulated on a combination of social learning and social bonding theories. This model has been developed and implemented in a series of delinquency and substance-use prevention programs by J. David Hawkins, Richard F. Catalano, and their associates in the SDRG at the University of Washington, Seattle (Brown el al. 2005; Hawkins, Von Cleve, and Catalano 1991; Hawkins et al. 1992, 1999, 2005; Weis and Hawking 1981). The SDM combines strengthening social attachment and commitment (social bonding theory) with positive reinforcement, modeling, and learning pro-social attitudes and skills and avoiding learning delinquent patterns (social learning theory) as applied in families, schools, and peer groups.

The first major program applying the SDM by the SDRG was the Seattle Social Development Project (SSDP). The SSDP was designed to enhance opportunities, develop social skills, and provide rewards for good behavior in the classroom and in families. The teachers in the intervention classrooms were trained to use "proactive classroom management," in which teachers were trained to "establish consistent classroom expectations and routines;…give clear, explicit instructions for behavior; recognize and reward desirable student behavior and efforts to comply; [and] keep minor classroom disruptions from interrupting instruction" (Hawkins et al. 2005, 27), as well as practice "interactive teaching" (e.g., state explicit learning objectives and model skills to be learned). Small groups of students were formed to participate in "cooperative learning" teams that were given positive recognition for both individual and group improvements, and other innovative techniques were used to strengthen bonds to school and teach the students academic and social skills for interacting properly with others. These included interpersonal problem solving and "refusal" skills to help the children recognize peer and other social influences on their behavior, identify consequences of behavior, and involve peers in conforming behavior. Parenting-skills training was also offered on a voluntary basis to parents of students that included learning ways to monitor their children's behavior, to teach and support pro-social and anti-delinquent definitions and attitudes, to discipline with proper application of punishment for their children's misbehavior and of positive rewards for their good behavior (differential reinforcement) while providing a positive family environment and encouraging commitment to school (differential association and social bonding).

The program was evaluated by comparing the intervention and control groups when they were in the fifth grade (Hawkins et al. 1992) and then again when they reached 18 (Hawkins et al. 1999). The findings on outcomes in the fifth grade show that the intervention group (20 percent) was somewhat less likely than the control group (27 percent) to have initiated alcohol use. Also, relatively fewer students in the intervention group (45 percent) than in the control group (52 percent) had engaged in some other forms of misconduct or problem behavior. By the time the students were 18, the two groups did not differ in self-reported nonviolent delinquency, smoking, drinking, and use of other drugs or in official arrest and court charges. However, the two groups did differ significantly in self-reported violent delinquency (48.3 percent versus 59.1 percent), heavy drinking (15.4 percent versus 25.6 percent), and sexual activity (72.1 percent versus 83 percent) with multiple partners (49.7 percent versus 61.5 percent). Participants were then followed into young adulthood (age 21) with both self-reported and court record data collected. "Full-intervention group participants were significantly less likely to be involved in a high variety of crime, to have sold illegal drugs in the past year, and to have an official lifetime court record at age 21 years" (Hawkins el al. 2005, 28–29).

The SDM has also been applied in the SDRG's Raising Healthy Children (RHC) project (Brown et al. 2005) in the middle- and high-school years:

> As a theory-based intervention, RHC is guided by the social development model (SDM) which *integrates empirically supported aspects of social control, social learning, and differential association theories into a framework for strengthening prosocial bonds and beliefs*. Within this framework, the SDM emphasizes that prevention should (a) begin before the formation of antisocial beliefs and behaviors; (b) recognize the importance of individual and family characteristics as well as larger social contexts of community, school, and peer influences; and (c) identify and address the changing needs of its target population with regard to risk and protective factors that change in influence during the course of development.... [F]our distinct points of intervention were targeted by RHC: (a) opportunities for involvement with prosocial others (e.g., family, teachers, and peers who did not use substances); (b) students' academic, cognitive, and social skills; (c) positive reinforcements and rewards for prosocial involvement; and (d) healthy beliefs and clear standards regarding substance use avoidance. (700, emphasis added)

Five schools were randomly assigned to the intervention program and five schools were assigned to the control group. The teachers in the intervention schools were given training in teaching and classroom management strategies and techniques for developing positive learning, reading, social, and problem-solving skills to promote students' bonding to school and pro-social peer associations, During the time, the students were in the elementary school and in the first year of middle school. The approach to intervening with individual students was to offer after-school opportunities for academic tutoring, studying "clubs," and other individual and group sessions to develop "healthy behavior" and "pro-social beliefs" (Brown et al., 2005).

Parents were given the opportunity to participate in sessions that sought to reduce family conflict and enhance family bonding while countering associations with deviant peers and deviant attitudes. The RHC program seemed not to make a difference in using or abstaining from, but it did significantly lower the frequency of use of alcohol and marijuana during the middle-school to high-school years.

Social Learning and Cognitive-Behavioral Approaches: Overview of Evidence on Effectiveness

To a greater or lesser degree, the theoretical foundation for these earlier and more recent treatment and prevention programs just reviewed (one or more of the principles of differential association, definitions and attitudes, role modeling and imitation, differential reinforcement, and other dimensions of the social learning process, sometimes in combination with other theoretical principles) have also been reflected, although often less explicitly, in a range of other group therapies; positive peer counseling programs; gang interventions; family and school programs; teenage drug, alcohol, and delinquency prevention and education programs; and other private and public programs (see Akers 1992; Andrews and Bonta 2003; Hersen and Rosqvist 2005; Lundman 1993; Morris and Braukmann 1987; Pearson et al. 2002.)

No program has been found always to be highly effective, and even the successful programs have modest effects. However, as D. A. Andrews and James Bonta (1998, 2003) report, the preponderance of evaluation research findings show that the "*cognitive behavioral and social learning approaches* [are more effective than] nondirective relationship-oriented counseling or psychodynamic insight-oriented counseling [and that] behavioral treatments had a substantially greater average effect [mean effect size of .25] on recidivism than did non-behavioral treatments [mean effect size of .04]" (Andrews and Bonta 1998, 262–263, 267–268, 282–290; emphasis added). Meta-analysis and other research literature support the same conclusions. There is "strong and consistent support for theories, such as differential association/ social learning theory, that link offending to antisocial associations and to the internalization of antisocial values. A consistent finding across meta-analyses, including cross-cultural studies, is that 'cognitive-behavioral' programs tend to achieve higher reductions in recidivism than other treatment modalities" (Cullen et al, 2003, 353), Assessments of the research literature and meta-analysis of findings have led many others to reach similar conclusions about the effectiveness of applied program grounded in social learning principles (Ellis and Sowers 2001; Gendreau, Smith, and French 2006; Lipsey and Landenberger 2005; Losel 2007; Pearson et al. 2002; Triplett and Payne 2004).

"The core criteria of successful programs in developmental prevention are similar to those in offender treatment. For example, such programs have a sound theoretical basis in social learning theory, follow a cognitive-behavioral approach, are well structured, and address multiple risk and protective factors" (Losel 2007, 4). And R. Ellis and K. Sowers write:

> The use of cognitive-behavioral interventions is consistent with the conclusion of other meta-analyses that intervention based on *social learning theory* is particularly effective (Losel 1996). Social learning theory asserts that behavior is learned through several processes, including modeling, *imitation*, and

differential reinforcement (Bandura 1977). In *modeling* a child observes an adult engaging in a behavior. If the child sees that the adult experiences positive consequences, he is likely to imitate the behavior.... He is also likely to associate with people who encourage his violent behavior (*differential association*). Eventually, he develops ideas (cognitions) that support violence.... Cognitions that support specific behaviors are known as '*deffinitions*' (Akers 1985). Definitions justify those behaviors by explaining why they are useful, necessary, or merited. Definitions, then, could be seen as one form of the problematic cognitions that the therapist needs to address. (2001, 91–92; emphasis in the original)

Two Programs with Police Officers in the Classroom: Unstated and Unclear Theoretical Rationales

All of the programs described thus far have clearly stated, or readily observable, links to principles and processes of social behavior as found in my and others' social learning models of the causes of criminal and delinquent behavior (and sometimes to those of other theories such as social bonding). This linkage is most strongly and clearly made by the OSLC and the SDRG in their programs. In each of these, the theoretical perspective and assumptions in the design of the programs and the specific ways in which the practical actions taken relate to theory are explicit, sound, and well made. The linkage is also apparent in other treatment and prevention programs that lake a cognitive-behavioral approach. There are many other treatment and prevention programs, both longstanding and newly developed, however, for which theoretical principles or assumptions are left unstated or poorly articulated by their designers and implementers. I will briefly review two well-known and well-funded examples: Gang Resistance Education and Training (GREAT) and Drug Abuse Resistance Education (DARE). Both of these rely on uniformed police officers' going to school classrooms over a period of time to teach a curriculum that is meant to educate preadolescents and adolescents so that they will "refuse" or "resist influences that can lead them into gang activity (GREAT) or substance use (DARE).

GREAT is a gang- and delinquency-prevention program that originally consisted of nine officer-run classroom sessions, including lessons on conflict resolution, resisting peer pressure, and recognizing the negative effect of gangs on the quality of life in the community. Based on disappointing evaluations of effectiveness (Esbensen 2004; Esbensen et al. 2001), GREAT was later modified to include an expanded school curriculum and a family component (see http://www.great-online.org). It entails no direct intervention in gang activity or efforts to work directly with youth or with their families. The school programs have police officers teach the students about gangs, violence, and drugs to foster pro-social attitudes and to teach "refusal skills" that, it is hoped, allow the youth to avoid gangs and other deviant peer groups. Police officers also deliver the family component of the program, attempting to teach parents to apply good parental skills, provide pro-social role modeling, and control their childrens' access to television, movies, video games, and the Internet. Neither the original nor the revised program descriptions delineate social learning or any other specific theory of adolescent or delinquent behavior as guiding the curriculum for students or parents. It would seem that GREAT includes at least some implicit recognition of the social learning principles that differential peer association and attitudes (definitions favorable and unfavorable), modeling, and learning in the family are relevant to joining gangs and committing delinquency. At the same time, the parental monitoring and supervision taught in the program seems to be fashioned on social bonding theory. Moreover, some GREAT activities do not follow from, or even run counter to, what one would expect from social learning theory. What principle of learning is invoked in placing both school and family instruction in the hands of uniformed police officers? Social learning theory (backed by network analysis of gang membership and peer relationships) would suggest direct intervention with individual gang members or potential gang members, especially those who occupy central "cut points" (sole connecting links between different individuals and groups), as a potentially more effective approach (McGloin 2005; McGloin, Pratt, and Maahs 2004).

DARE is the largest and longest-running youth drug-use prevention program in the United States, with programs in other countries (see http://www.dare.com). Like GREAT, DARE is a cooperative effort between local police departments and school districts. This cooperation involves the schools' allowing uniformed police officers to come to the school classroom and teach a curriculum over a seventeen-week period in the fifth and sixth grades (e.g., social skills, drug knowledge, and self-esteem) with shorter sessions in middle school or junior high school (e,g., resisting peer pressure and resolving conflict) and senior high school (e.g., making choices and managing anger). Opportunities are also provided for some after-school activities and for programs for parents (Sherman et al. 1998). As the name implies, DARE is designed mainly to equip students to recognize, and develop the ability to "resist," peer influence to use drugs and alcohol, with the expectation that this will also prevent or reduce other forms of delinquency. Police officers are assigned full time to the project and present one-hour classroom lessons that stress the consequences of using drugs and teach students how to say no to drugs and alcohol. The activities in the program from the beginning have included not only instruction but also student role-playing to demonstrate strategies for resisting "peer pressure" and other influences to take drugs, group discussions about ways to enhance self-esteem, behavioral alternatives to drugs, decision making, and understanding media influences (Bureau of Justice Statistics 1988; Dejong 1986; Triplett and Payne 2004).

Although unequivocal claims of DARE's high level of effectiveness are often made, it has been difficult to find clear, scientifically valid evidence that the program has reduced the problems of adolescent substance use and delinquency in the communities where it has been instituted (Akers 1992; Rosenbaum 2007; Triplett and Payne 2004). The fairly long history of disappointing findings with regard to the central goals of affecting adolescent substance use has led to a reassessment of governmental investment and support for the program and calls by some to discontinue or greatly reduce it. This has been met with resistance from the police, schools, and communities involved in DARE (Rosenbaum 2007).

The DARE curriculum was supposedly "grounded in three main 'psychosocial' approaches to prevention: psychological inoculation, resistance skill training, and personal and social skills training" (Rosenbaum 2007, 816). However, the theoretical assumptions of the program, including assumptions that would lead one to believe that classroom exposure to the range of topics in the curriculum and related activities led by uniformed police officers will prevent adolescent substance abuse, were left unspecified when the program was initiated (Bureau of Justice Statistics 1988) and are still not clearly delineated (see http://www .dare.com). Social skills training and instruction on ways to "resist" or counteract peer influences and efforts to promote anti-drug attitudes would seem at first glance to be based at least implicitly on some aspects of social learning theory (differential peer association and definitions). However, the curricular focus in DARE on teaching adolescents to resist "peer pressure" runs counter both to the concept in social learning theory of differential peer association and to the empirical evidence supporting the predicted effects of peer influence on adolescent substance use in research on the theory (Akers 1992). In addition, training in decision-making skills based on factual information on drugs suggests rational choice theory. A portion of the curriculum that deals with enhancing individual self-esteem and anger management would seem to reflect psychological personality theory or general strain theory (Agnew 1992). The prominence of police officers (and the symbolism of law enforcement functions in apprehending and punishing drug law violators) would imply some reliance on deterrence theory. The reference on the Web site to "stunning brain imagery—tangible proof of how substances diminish mental activity, emotions, coordination and movement" suggests both a return to the old idea that kids will make the right decision if you just "give them the facts" about drugs and the "scared straight" idea that showing "this is your brain on drugs" negative effects will deter use. These are plausible inferences about the theoretical underpinnings of DARE, but there is nothing in the program that shows how teaching of anti-drug attitudes is based on social learning or any other theory of the causes of substance use. Thus, it is difficult to determine at this time what the theoretical assumptions are in the GREAT and DARE programs. Further analysis and more careful examination of the rationale of the programs by those funding and running them might produce a clearer understanding concerning on which, if any, theory the programs rely.

I find little explicit reference to social learning principles in either program, but perhaps closer attention to social learning principles and incorporation of program elements more clearly relevant to those principles in the future would improve effectiveness. I would suggest doing away with or modifying the reliance on in-class curricula taught by police officers and paying more careful attention to how influence, modeling, imitation, and social reinforcement by peers and others truly operate in drug behavior and avoiding sole reliance on the notion of "peer pressure," a popular but inarticulate theoretical construct. I would suggest borrowing from the successful programs of the OSLC and the SDRG with regard to the pro-social modeling and behavioral reinforcement practices and procedures they use in the in-school programs, direct contact with families to train them in effective parenting and socialization of children, after-school programs for youth, and other elements, as well as the more successful cognitive-behavioral approaches to changing attitudes and behavior used in other substance-use and delinquency-prevention programs.

Concluding Observations

A good theory is useful for guiding practice, and good practice both reflects and informs theory. I propose here that social learning theory is such a theory. It is an empirically valid theory on which sound and effective crime and delinquency prevention and treatment programs have been and can be formulated. I have concentrated on examples of American programs that are based, at least in part, on social learning principles but have given a couple of examples of programs for which it is uncertain which theoretical principles inform them. There is a body of evidence that supports the conclusion that past and current applications of the cognitive-behavioral principles in social learning theory have at least a modest impact and are more effective than alternative programming. That does not mean that all programs with discernible social learning elements in them have been effective or even that one can always determine the theoretical underpinnings of applied programs, whether successful or not. As Ruth Triplett and Brian Payne (2004) point out, even sound theory can be misunderstood or misapplied in a way that inhibits programs from producing the effects they could have. Starting with social learning theory does not guarantee that the goals of a program, policy, or strategy meant to prevent or change criminal, delinquent, and deviant behavior will be achieved. However, I would hypothesize that the more explicitly and directly the design of the prevention or treatment strategy is predicated on or informed by all of the social learning principles (alone or in combination with principles from other compatible theories), the greater the fidelity to the theory (Reid, Patterson, and Snyder 2002) of the actions taken by the operators and participants in the program to that design and the greater the extent to which midstream modifications in the program (whether induced externally or precipitated internally) moves it closer to really affecting the targeted social behavioral processes, the more likely it is that the programs will have some success in preventing and treating delinquent and criminal behavior. In short, I would say that social learning theory is a prime exemplar of the maxim with which I began: There is nothing as practical as a good theory.

References

Abrams, L. S., K. Kim, and B. Anderson-Nathe. 2005. Paradoxes of treatment in juvenile corrections. *Child and Youth Care Forum* 34:7–25.

Agnew, R. 1992. Foundation for a general strain theory of crime and delinquency. *Criminology* 30:47–88.

Akers, R. L. 1973. *Deviant behavior: A social learning approach.* Belmont, Calif.: Wadsworth Publishing

———. 1985. *Deviant behavior: A social learning approach.* 3rd ed, Belmont, Calif,: Wadsworth Publishing.

———. 1992. *Drugs, alcohol, and society: Social structure, process and policy.* Belmont, Calif.: Wadsworth Publishing.

———. 1994. *Criminological theories: Introduction and evaluation.* Los Angeles: Roxbury Publishing.

———. 1998. *Social learning and social structure: A general theory of crime and deviance.* Boston: Northeastern University Press.

———. 2005. Sociological theory and practice: The case of criminology. *Journal of Applied Sociology/Sociological Practice* 22:24–41.

———. 2006. Aplicaciones de los principios del aprendizaje social, Algunos programas de tratamiento y prevencion de la delincuencia. In *Derecho penal y criminologia como fundamento de la politica criminal: Estudios en homenaje al professor Alfonso Serrano Gomez,* Ed. J. G. Dalbora and A. S. Maillo, 1117–1138. Madrid: Dykinson.

Akers. R. L., and G. F. Jensen (Eds.). 2003. *Social learning theory and the explanation of crime: A guide for the new century.* Vol. 11. *Advances in criminological theory.* New Brunswick, N.J.: Transaction Publishers.

———. 2006. Empirical status of social learning theory of crime and deviance: The past, present, and future. In *Taking stock: The status of criminological theory.* Vol. 15, *Advances in criminological theory.* Ed. F. T. Cullen, J. P. Wright, and K, R, Blevins, 37–76, New Brunswick, N.J.: Transaction Publishers.

Akers, R. L., M. D. Krohn, L. Lanza-Kaduce, and M. Radosevich. 1979, Social learning and deviant behavior: A specific test of a general theory. *American Sociological Review* 44: 635–655.

Akers. R, L., and C. Sellers. 2004. *Criminological theories: Introduction, evaluation, and application.* 4th ed. Los Angeles: Roxbury Publishing.

Andrews, D. A., and J. Bonta. 1998, *The psychology of criminal conduct.* 2nd ed. Cincinnati: Anderson Publishing.

———. 2003. *The psychology of criminal conduct.* 3rd ed. Cincinnati: Anderson Publishing.

Bandura, A. 1977, *Social learning theory.* Englewood Cliffs, N.J.: Prentice Hall.

Barlow, H. (Ed.). 1995. *Crime and public policy: Putting theory to work.* Boulder, Colo.: Westview Press.

Braukmann, C. J., and Wolf, M. M. 1987. Behaviorally-based group homes for juvenile offenders. In *Behavioral approaches to crime and delinquency: A handbook of application, research, and concepts*. Ed. E. K Morris and C. J. Braukmann, 135–159. New York: Plenum Press.

Brown, E. C., R. F. Catalano, C. B. Fleming, K. P, Haggerty, and R. D. Abbott. 2005. Adolescent substance use outcomes in the raising healthy children project: A two-part latent growth curve analysis. *Journal of Consulting and Clinical Psychology* 73: 699–710.

Bureau of Justice Statistics. 1988. *An invitation to project DARE: Drug Abuse Resistance Education*. Program brief. Washington, D.C.: U.S. Department of Justice.

Burgess, R. L., and R. L. Akers. 1966). A differential association reinforcement theory of criminal behavior. *Social Problems* 14: 128–147.

Chamberlain, P., P. A. Fisher, and K. Moore. 2002. Multidimensional treatment foster care: Applications of the OSLC Intervention Model to high risk youth and their families. In *Antisocial behavior in children and adolescents: A developmental analysis and model for intervention*. Ed. J. B. Reid, G. R. Patterson, and J. Synder, 203–218. Washington, D.C.: American Psychological Association.

Cressey, D. R. 1955, Changing criminals: The application of the theory of differential association. *American Journal of Sociology* 61: 116–120.

Cullen, F. T., J. P. Wright, P. Gendreau, and D. A. Andrews. 2003. What treatment can tell us about criminological theory: Implications for social learning theory. In *Social learning theory and the explanation of crime: A guide for the new century*. Vol. 11, *Advances in criminological theory*. Ed. R. L. Akers and G. F. Jensen, 339–362. New Brunswick, N. J.: Transaction Publishers.

Dejong, W. 1986. Project DARE: 'Teaching kids to say "no" to drugs and alcohol. Report, National Institute of Justice, U.S. Department of Justice, Washington, D.C.

Dishion, T. J., J McCord, and F. Poulin. 1999. When interventions harm: Peer groups and problem behavior. *American Psychologist* 54:755–764.

Dishion T. J. G. R. Patterson and K. A. Kavanagh 1992. An *experimental test of the coercion behavior*. Intervention *from birth through adolescence*. Ed. J. McCord and R. E. Tremblay, 253–282. NewYork: Guilford Press.

Eddy, J. M., and P. Chamberlain. 2000. Family management and deviant peer association as mediators of the impact of treatment condition youth antisocial behavior. *Journal of Consulting and Clinical Psychology* 68:857–863.

Eddy, J. M., J. B. Reid, and R. A. Fetrow. 2000. An elementary school based prevention program targeting modifiable antecedents of youth delinquency and violence: Linking the Interests of Families and Teachers (LIFT), *Journal of Emotional and Behavioral Disorders* 8:165–176.

Ellis, R., and K, Sowers. 2001. *Juvenile justice practice: A cross-disciplinary approach to intervention*. Belmont Calif.: Wadsworth/Brooks Cole Publishing.

Empey, L. T., and M. L. Erickson. 1972. *The Provo experiment: Evaluating community control of delinquency*. Lexington, Mass.: Lexington Books.

Esbensen, F. D. 2004. Evaluating G.R.E.A.T.: A school-based gang prevention program. National Institute of Justice. Research for Policy, U.S. Department of Justice, Washington, D.C., June.

Esbensen, F. D., W. Osgood, T. J. Taylor, D. Peterson, and A. Freng. 2001. How great is G.R.E.A.T.? Results from a longitudinal quasi-experimental design. *Criminology and Public Policy* 1:87–118.

Gendreau, P., P. Smith, and S. K. French. 2006. The theory off effective correctional intervention: Empirical status and future directions. In *Taking stock: The status of criminological theory*. Vol. 15, *Advances in criminological theory*. Ed. F. T. Cullen, J. P. Wright, and K. R. Blevins, 419–446. New Brunswick, N.J.: Transaction Publishers.

Gibbons, D. 1965. *Changing the lawbreaker: The treatment of delinquents and criminals.* Englewood Cliffs, N.J.: Prentice-Hall.

Gottfredson, M., and T. Hirschi. 1990. *A general theory of crime.* Palo Alto, Calif.: Stanford University Press.

Hawkins, J. D., R. F. Catalano, R. Kosterman, R. Abbott, and K. G. Hill. 1999. Preventing adolescent health-risk behaviors by strengthening protection during childhood. *Archives of Pediatric and Adolescent Medicine* 153:226–234.

Hawkins, J. D., R. F. Catalano, D. M. Morrison, J. O. O'Donnell, R. D. Abbott, and L. E. Day. 1992. The Seattle Social Development Project: Effects of the first four years on protective factors and problem behaviors. In *preventing antisocial behavior: Interventions from birth through adolescence.* Ed J. McCord and R. E. Trembley, 139–161. New York: Guilford Press.

Hawkins, J. D., R. Kosterman, R. F. Catalano, K. G. Hill, and R. D. Abbott. 2005. Promoting positive adult fuctioning through social development intervention in childhood: Long-term effects from the Seattle Social Development Project. *Archives of Pediatric Adolescent Medicine* 159:25–31.

Hawkins. J. D., E. Von Cleve, and R. F. Catalano, 1991. Reducing early childhood aggression: Results of a primary prevention program. *Journal of the Academy of Child and Adolescent Psychiatry* 30:208–217.

Hersen, M., and J. Rosqvist (Eds.). 2005. *Encyclopedia of behavior modification and cognitive behavior therapy.* Vol. 1, *Adult clinical applications.* Vol. 2, *Child clinical applications.* Vol. 3, *Educational applications.* Thousands Oaks, Calif.: Sage Publication.

Hirschi, T. 1969. *Causes of delinqueny.* Berkeley: University of California Press.

Jensen, G. F., and R. L. Akers. 2003. "Taking social learning global": Micro-macro transitions in criminological theory. In *Social learning theory and the explanation of crime: A guide for the new century.* Vol. 11. *Advances in criminological theory.* Ed. R. Akers and G. Jensen.

Laub, J. 2004. The life course of criminology in the United States. The American Society of Criminology 2003 presidential address. *Criminology* 42:1–26.

Lipsey, M. W., and N. A. Landenbeger. 2005. Cognitive-behavioral interventions. In *Preventing crime: What works for children, offenders, victims, and places.* Ed. B. C. Welsh and D. P. Farrington, 57–71, Dordrecht: Springer.

Losel, F. 1996. Changing patterns in the use of prisons. *European journal of Criminal Policy and Research* 4:108–127.

———. 2007. It is never too early and never too late: Toward an integrated science of development intervention in criminology. *Criminologist* 32, no. 5 (September–October): 3–8.

Lundman, R. J. 1993. *Prevention and control of juvenile delinquency.* 2nd ed. New York: Oxford University Press.

McGloin, J. M., T. C. Pratt, and J. Maahs. 2004. Rethinking the IQ–delinquency relationship: A longitudinal analysis of multiple theoretical models. *Justice Quarterly* 21:603–631.

Morris, E. K., and C. J. Braukmann (Eds.). 1987. *Behavioral approaches to crime and delinquency: A handbook of application, research and concepts.* New York: Plenum Press.

Patterson G. R. 1975. *Families: Applications of social learning to family life.* Champaign, III. Research Press.

Patterson, G. R., D. Capaldi, and L. Bank. 1991. The development and treatment of childhood aggression. In *The development and treatment of childhood aggression.* Ed. D. Pepler and R. K. Rubin, 139–168. Hillsdale, III.: Erlbaum.

Patterson, G. R., and P. Chamberlain. 1994. A functional analysis of resistance during parent training therapy. *Clinical Psychology: Science and Practice* 1:53–70.

Patterson, G. R. B. D. Debaryshe, and E. Ramsey. 1989. A developmental perspective on antisocial behavior. *American Psychologist* 44:329–335.

Patterson, G. R., and T. J. Dishion. 1985. Contributions of families and peers to delinquency. *Criminology* 23:63–79.

Patterson, G. R., J. B. Reid, and T. J. Dishion. 1992. *Antisocial boys*. Eugene, Ore.: Castalia Publishing.

Pearson. F. S., D. S. Lipton, C. M. Cleland, and D. S. Yee. 2002. The effects of cognitive-behavioral programs on recidivism. *Crime and Delinquency* 48:476–496.

Reid, J. B., and M. Eddy. 2002. Preventive efforts during the elementary school years: The linking of the interest of families and teachers (LIFT) Project. In *Antisocial behavior in children and adolescents: A developmental analysis and model for intervention*. Ed. J. B. Reid, G. R. Patterson, and J. Snyder, 219–233. Washington. D. C.: American Psychological Association.

Reid, J. B., G. R. Patterson, and J. Snyder (Eds.). 2002. *Antisocial behavior in children and adolescents: A developmental analysis and model for intervention*. Washington, D. C.: American Psychological Association.

Rosenbaum, D. P. 2007. Just say no to D.A.R.E. *Criminology and Public Policy* 6:815–824.

Sellers, C. S., and R. L. Akers. 2006. Social learning theory: Correcting misconceptions. In *the essential criminology reader*, Ed. S. Henry and M. M. Lanier, 89–99. Boulder, Colo.: Westview Press.

Sherman, L, W., D. L. Gottfredson, D. L. MacKenzie, P. Reuter, and S. D. Bushway. 1998. *Preverenting crime. What works, what doesn't. what's promising. Research in brief.* Washington, D.C.: National institute of Justice.

Snyder, J. J., and G. R. Patterson. 1995. Individual differences in social aggression: A test of a reinforcement model of socialization in the natural environment. *Behavior therapy* 26:371–391.

Sutherland F. H. 1947. *Principles of criminology* 4th ed. Philadelphia. J. R. J. innisoft.

Triplett, R., and B. Payne. 2004. Problem solving as reinforcement in adolescent drug use: Implication for theory and policy. *Journal of Criminal Justice* 32:617–630.

Wart, M. 2002. *Companions in crime: The social aspect of criminal conduct*. Cambridge: Cambridge University Press.

Weeks, H. A. 1958. *Youthful offenders at highfields.* Ann Arbor: University of Michigan Press.

Weis, J. G., and J. D. Hawkins. 1981. Preventing delinquency: The social development model. *Preventing delinquency.* Washington, D.C.: U.S. Government Printing Office.

Welsh, B. C., and D. P. Farrington. 2006. Evidence-based crime prevention. In *preventing crime: What works for children, offenders, victims, and places.* Ed. B. C. Welsh and D. P. Farrington, 1–7. Dordrecht: Springer.

Zetterberg, H. L. 1962. *Social theory and social practice.* New York: Bedminster Press.

DISCUSSION QUESTIONS

By John M. Stogner

1. How does Akers's work differ from that of Sutherland? Do they make any different assumptions? Do the policy recommendations differ?
2. Does Akers's theory explain the age–crime curve? Or why males commit more crimes than females?
3. Does Akers's description of definitions differ from Sutherland's?
4. Are the programs based on the principles of social learning generally successful? What obstacles have they faced?
5. Why is it inefficient to institute policies not based on theory or based on perspectives that lack empirical support?

CHAPTER TEN

Hirschi's Social Bond Theory

NOEL S. BOST

STUDENT INTRODUCTION
By John M. Stogner

In the 1950s and early 1960s, a number of criminologists had proposed that crime was connected to the absence or weakness of personal and social controls. In other words, they argued that some individuals chose to engage in delinquent behaviors because they lacked either the requisite internal controls or connections to others that would prevent them from succumbing to temptation. The works of Albert Reiss (1951), Ivan Nye (1958), and Walter Reckless (1961) created the foundation for this control perspective and the theories of Travis Hirschi. Briefly, the theories within this perspective generally begin with the assumption that deviance, rather than conformity, is natural behavior. As such, the goal of control-based theories is not to determine what motivates deviant behavior for those who violate the law; instead, they focus on what prevents nonoffenders from engaging in those acts. This distinction may be largely semantic, as each perspective attempts to account for variation along a continuum ranging from complete conformity to extreme deviance; however, this framework may have facilitated theoretical imagination and theoretical diversity that might otherwise have been lacking.

Hirschi's social bond theory, the subject of his 1969 book *Causes of Delinquency*, is one of the leading control theories—perhaps only superseded by another of his own works (discussed in the next chapter). Hirschi argues that people choose to abstain from delinquency because they have a strong bond to society. They resist their natural impulses to violate the law because of the ways in which they are connected to others. Those who are weakly bound to society are not constrained in the same way; their behavior is unencumbered. Thus, the simplest statement of Hirschi's theory is that delinquency is the result of an individual's bond to society being weak or broken. Hirschi describes an individual's bond to society as having four elements: *attachment* to others, *commitment* to conventional society, *involvement* in conventional activities, and *belief* in the society's normative values. He thoroughly defines these elements—each of which can be quantified with self-report data.

As you read Bost's summary of Hirschi's social bond theory, take note of its underlying assumptions, both explicit and implied. Consider how these assumptions led to the development of a theory conceptualized very differently from Akers's work (which had been introduced just three years prior). Reflect on the distinctions between social learning theory and social bond theory, considering whether the two actually make distinct predictions about human behavior. Take care to understand each element of the social bond as described by Hirschi and contemplate how each might be best measured. Finally, review the information related to empirical assessments of Hirschi's propositions in order to understand that social bonding is generally supported, but may not adequately and consistently account for gender and racial disparities in offending.

HIRSCHI'S SOCIAL BOND THEORY
By Noel S. Bost

Introduction

Hirschi's theory of social bond (1969) explored several factors that could possibly link placement experience and delinquency.1 His theory provides a valuable conceptual framework for understanding many of the mechanisms at work in explaining the occurrence of delinquent offending among youth in out-of-home care, including African Americans and females within this group. One of the most influential and scientifically tested theories of youth crime,2 the key concepts of social bond theory comprise constructs that are reliable, logical, and parsimonious (Akers, 1997; Leonard & Decker, 1994). The following discussion demonstrates the utility of social bond theory for explaining violent offending among youth who are aging out of the out-of-home care system, including African American and female youth offenders among this population.

Key Elements Of Hirschi's Social Bond Theory

The fundamental premise of social bond, according to Hirschi (1969), is that delinquent behaviors are the consequence of an individual's weak or broken bonds to society. Individuals who are most tightly bonded to social groups such as the family, school, and peers are less likely to commit delinquent acts. In general, the social bond is established early in childhood through a natural attachment to parents, peers, teachers, and others who manifest and model expected social conformity and respected sanctions. In his view of human beings as rational decision-makers guided by motivations to maximize pleasure and avoid or reduce pain, Hirschi's theoretical ideas derive from principles of classical criminology and sociology. Additionally, Hirschi's social bond theory adapts Durkheim's notion of the power and influence of social governance on social conformity, and Hobbes' belief that individuals are socially motivated to create community and to conform to socially derived norms (Lilly, Cullen, & Ball, 1995). In relation to Hobb's question of conformity, the explanation of delinquency is based not on 'why youth engage in delinquent acts' but 'why do youths not engage in delinquent acts.' In essence, "deviance is taken for granted, conformity must be explained." (Hirschi, 1969, p. 10). In effect, deviance is seen as the natural state of humans who are thus disposed to deviate unless they form a strong bond from which they develop a sense of morality and conformity.

---

[1]This chapter relies heavily on the method used by Boudreau (2002) to structure discussion of Hirschi's Social Bond. M. Boudreau, "Examining the Impact of the Social Bond for Serious and Violent Young Offenders." Thesis Paper, Simon Fraser University.

[2]Akers, 1997; Bynum & Thompson, 2002; Friedman & Rosenbaum, 1988; Hawdon, 1999; Junger & Marshall, 1997; Kempf, 1993; Le Blanc & Caplan,1993; Leonard & Decker,. 1994; Lilly, Cullen, & Bull, 1995; Wright, Caspi, Moffitt, & Silva, 1999.

In conceptualizing the mechanisms by which conformity is developed, Hirschi describes the development of the social bonds as a process whereby during early childhood, individuals internalize conventional values and learn to gain access to legitimate social roles (Hirschi, 1969). This process of social bond formation continues throughout the early life span into adolescence. In his conceptualization, Hirschi (1969) notes that all are not alike in proficiencies of formulating bonds. The process occurs differently for each individual in terms of the stages in a youth's life, strength of the bond, and stability of the bond.

According to Hirschi (1969), four key elements characterize the social bond: attachment to significant others; commitment to conventional behavior; involvement in conventional activities; and belief in society's normative system. While there is possible interconnectedness among the elements for example, attachment and commitment may vary inversely in the event that parental attachment prevents a youth from developing commitments to school or occupational pursuits (Shoemaker, 2005) Hirschi suggests that each element is positively associated with one another. Thus, each aspect of the social bond represents a restraint against engaging in delinquent behavior.

Attachment to Significant Others

Attachment describes the quality of the relationship or affectionate ties an individual has with others in society. Hirschi (1969) reasoned that the strength of attachment particularly towards parents (but also peers and school as well) was inversely related to delinquency. Attachment to significant others has been heralded as the most important element of the social bond (Le Blanc & Caplan, 1993) as it represents the social bond that developmentally occurs first among the elements—by way of parents or other caregivers. For Hirschi, strong affectional ties to others, characterized by the level at which an individual cares about the expectations of parents, peers, and/or teachers, preclude an individual from engaging in delinquent activities (Hirschi, 1969; Kempf, 1993; Le Blanc & Caplan, 1993). The likelihood of delinquent behavior decreases as an individual's attachment to significant others increases. Hirschi highlights the importance of interpersonal and institutional attachments to parents, peers, and the school.

Attachment to Parents. Hirschi points to many elements of the bond to the parent, but notes that all of them may not be equally important in the control of delinquent behavior. For example, direct supervision or control over youth by the parent is of little substantive or theoretical importance because delinquent acts require little time, and most adolescent youth spend little time under the direct supervision of their parents. The three dimensions for measuring attachment to parents that are offered by Hirschi include 1) "virtual supervision" or the psychological parental impact; (2) the intimacy of communication between parent and child; and (3) the youth's affectional identification with their parents.

Virtual supervision can be illustrated by a scenario where in the face of temptation to commit a delinquent act, a youth is likely to ask himself or herself, "What will my parents think?" One who gives no consideration of the parents' expectation or anticipated reaction is likely to commit the delinquent act. Intimacy of communication reflects a youth's willingness to share their thoughts, feelings, and plans for the future with their parents (Hirschi, 1969). An open level of communication between a youth and his or her parent is equated to highly valued parental expectations and opinions by the youth, and consequently, the lower likelihood that a youth will risk disappointing these expectations by engaging in delinquent acts. Intimacy of communication also encompasses the extent to which parents are willing to share their own thoughts and feelings toward the youth (Hirschi, 1969; Le Blanc & Caplan, 1993).

Affectional identification is considered by Hirschi to be the "crucial" element of the bond to the parent. As this dimension of parental attachment deals with a youth's love or respect for his or her parents, Hirschi suggests that even if a child considers a parent's opinion when confronting the temptation of delinquency, if the youth does not care for the parent, he or she may conclude that detection of the act by the parent is not sufficiently important to deter engagement in the act (Hischi, 1969). Conversely, youth who love and respect their parents are less likely to engage in delinquent acts.

Attachment to School. Attachment to school represents the next dimension of attachment discussed by Hirschi (1969). School attachment is measured by the youth's attitudes toward educational institutions, "academic competence,"[3] concern and regard for teachers' opinions, and an acceptance of the authority of the school staff and personnel (Akers, 1997; Hirschi, 1969; LeBlanc & Caplan, 1993). To illustrate the impact of attachment to school, Hirschi presents a simple "causal chain" which "runs from academic incompetence to poor school performance to disliking of school to rejection of the school authority to the commission of delinquent acts" (Hirschi, 1969, p. 132). While Hirschi provides exclusive measures for the other three elements of the social bond, "academic achievement in school (as indicated by grades, test scores, and self-perceived scholastic ability) is taken as indicative of commitment, involvement, and belief, as well as attachment" (Akers, 1997, p. 88). According to Hirschi, youth with negative school experiences may resort to delinquent behavior as a means of reducing the associated stress and frustration.

Academic ability and performance, which focuses on a youth's level of academic success, represents the next dimension of attachment to school. According to Hirschi, "it would be puzzling if attachment and commitment to a system were not related to possession of those characteristics the system rewards and, indeed, spends much of its effort attempting to foster." (Hirschi, 1969, p. 112). As such, it is not the poor academic performance itself, but the fact that poor academic performance results in weakened or broken bonds to school, such as lower teacher expectation, bad reputation with teachers, etc. In time, academically incompetent youth have less serious social consequences associated with engaging in delinquency compared to academically competent youth.

Self-perceived academic competence represents the third dimension of school attachment (Hirschi, 1969). This aspect of school attachment equates youths' positive perception of their own ability to succeed in school with avoiding delinquent behavior. For Hirschi (1969), youth with a demonstrated positive attitude about their own school competence are more likely to have a positive school outlook, which in turn leads to commitment to school and avoidance of delinquent behaviors. Another assumption related to attachment to school includes the concern that a youth has for the opinion of teachers. In this case, a youth who has little or no concern about a teacher's opinion of him or her is more likely to engage in delinquent acts. Hirschi (1969) also hypothesized that a youth's acceptance of the school's authority to set rules and policies by which the youth and fellow students must abide is related to delinquency. In short, rejecting the school's authority to impose rules and sanctions lead to disregard for these rules, thus denial of the broader conventional ideals to which they correspond.

---

[3]Hirschi specifies the use of "academic competence" rather than "intelligence" because 1) the test scores he uses to measure school attachment are not intelligence tests; 2) the assumption that it is the differences in academic ability rather than the sources of these ability that affects an individual's life is sufficient for his argument; and 3) a basic trait of brightness or stupidity is not required in the model.

Attachment to Peers. The final dimension of attachment to significant others is attachment to peers. Hirschi asserts that a majority of delinquent acts are committed with companions. In other words, most delinquents have delinquent friends. This is explained by the assumption that attachment to others requires adherence to conventional norms. Individuals who lack the social and interpersonal skills required to form meaningful attachment to others and are incapable of committing to positive individualistic success values resort to associations with others who similarly lack the capacity for attachment and commitment (i.e. other delinquents) (Hirschi, 1969). Delinquents are not inconsistent in their abilities to form attachments. They are less likely to be attached to each other (Hirschi, 1969). Hirschi stipulates that for youth who are capable of forming attachments to others, the character of the object of attachment is of no consequence in determining adherence to or violation of conventional rules:

> [H]olding delinquency (or worthiness) of friends truly constant at any level, the more one respects or admires one's friends, the less likely one is to commit delinquent acts. We honor those we admire not by imitation, but by adherence to conventional standards. (Hirschi, 1969, p. 152).

Even for youth attached to delinquent peers, the stronger the attachment to those friends, the less likely he or she will tend to be delinquent. The delinquent tends to have "cold and brittle" relationships with everyone, to be socially isolated, and to be less attached to either conventional or delinquent friends than the non-delinquent (Hirschi, 1969, p. 141).

A final assumption of the peer attachment holds that, similar to parent attachment, affectional identification is paramount. In short, the more that a youth respects the opinions of their friends, and threat of negative peer reaction, the less likely the youth is to engage in delinquent acts (Hirschi, 1969).

Commitment to Conventional Lines of Action

Commitment, the second of Hirschi's (1969) social bond elements, refers to the extent to which individuals have built up an investment in conventional behavior or a stake in conformity (Akers, 1997). Investing takes the form of committing energy and effort into conventional activities and values. The more that a person is invested in conventional behavior, the more that he or she has to lose by engaging in nonconforming, unlawful behavior. In turn, he or she is more likely to avoid delinquency in the interest of protecting the investment. Thus, commitment refers to a rational element in the choice to avoid or commit crime. Hirschi (1969) specifies that "the mere wish to be "something or somebody" is not enough to affect behavior seriously unless the person supports or has supported his words with deeds…The test is not that a man have lofty ambitions, but that he strive mightily" (p. 178). The three key dimensions that comprise commitment include individual achievement orientation, educational and occupational expectations, and passage into adult status. Achievement orientation reflects a youth's desire to do well in school as evidenced by concern for academic grades and achievement. Youth with such interest are more likely to avoid delinquent acts. Commitment to educational and employment expectations refers to a youth's foresight into his or her future goals and aspirations. The social bonds are strengthened because the youth does not want to jeopardize aspirations and expectations of a bright future by straying from a promising academic and/or employment path to arrive there. Passage into adult status is identified as the negative element of commitment. When youth prematurely engage in adult-like activities such as drinking, smoking, and/or owning a car, they impinge on or represent a lack of commitment to educational goals (Hirschi, 1969).

Involvement in Conventional Activities

Involvement reflects the behavioral element of the social bond. It refers to the pre-occupation with and active participation in conventional activities. Such, behaviors include doing homework, spending time with friends, and recreation (Hirschi, 1969). Hirschi hypothesizes that the more one is involved in conventional prosocial activities, the less time they have to engage in deviant behavior. Hirschi (1969) observes amount of time involved in these activities in order to assess level of involvement in conventional activities.

Belief in Society's Normative System

The final element of Hirschi's social bond theory is belief. This element reflects the extent to which an individual believes in socially acceptable values and rejects those that are unconventional (Hirschi, 1969). Having respect for and adherence to the values of the law and legal system are examples of beliefs that would encourage one's compliance with social expectations and rejection of delinquent behaviors. In contrast, an individual who has weakened conventional beliefs or who has not developed strong beliefs is more likely to engage in delinquent acts. Hirschi measured this dimension of belief by accounting for one's attitude toward rules, laws, and the legal system, as well as the respect that an individual has for others who are in positions of authority.

Another aspect of belief involves the extent to which a youth minimizes or excuses his or her violation of nonnormative behavior, which Hirschi terms techniques of neutralization (Hirschi, 1969). These behaviors are used as a means of allowing an individual to mitigate anxiety and mental discomfort that might be associated with offensive actions by rationalizing or minimizing the seriousness of what he or she has done. Along a continuum of actions to rationalize nonnormative behavioral choices, techniques of neutralization may be seen as less radical than fatalism, Hirschi's final dimension of belief. This behavior involves the complete rejection of conventional societal norms. Rationally, fatalism is directly related to involvement in delinquent activity.

Hirschi's Research Findings on the Social Bond

In testing his own theory, Hirschi (1969) employs tabular analysis on a sample of 3,605, primarily White, male youth from the Richmond Youth Project. He reports primary findings that support the hypothesis that each of the identified elements of the social bond, with the exception of peer involvement, co-vary with the incidence of delinquency. In essence, the weaker the social bond, encompassing attachment, commitment, or involvement, the more likely a youth is to engage in delinquent acts (Hirschi, 1969). Hirschi also found that youths' association with delinquent peers was strongly linked to the likelihood of committing delinquent acts. In response to this unanticipated finding, Hirschi modified his hypothesis that association with peers, regardless of their background, would lead to less delinquent acts to the stipulation that attachment to *prosocial* peers would in fact reduce the likelihood of offending. Hirschi maintains his position that youth with low levels of bonding are more likely to associate with peers who, likewise, score low on bonding and are thus themselves susceptible to delinquent acts.

Social bond theory is not without its critics, many of whom note that Hirschi's study was based on a sample of mostly White and exclusively male youth, raising questions about the adequacy of social bond theory to delinquent behavioral patterns of youth among demographic group representations beyond White males, namely African Americans and females (e.g., Lotz & Lee, 1999). There is also a need to understand the function of social bond theory among youth from nontraditional family arrangements as this is a structural arrangement that characterizes youth in out-of-home care placement. The remainder of this chapter discusses study findings that have tested the utility of social bond theory on broken families and/or unconventional parents; African-Americans and other racial minorities, and females. The findings are assumed relatable to the conditions and experiences of youth in out-of-home care.

Broken Families and the Social Bond

Perhaps one of the most persistent explanations of delinquent behavior is the breakdown of the family. The interest in family factors and delinquency has typically involved both the structure of the family and the nature of relationships occurring within the family (see Geismar & Wood, 1986; and Wright & Wright, 1994, for reviews of some of this literature; Shoemaker, 2005). The structure of the family includes the broken home—that is, a home where one (or both) natural parent is permanently absent because of events such as death, desertion, or divorce—and intact homes where both parents are present. While some study findings support the parental attachment element of the social bond model as an important explanatory (or at least mediating) premise underlying the relationship between broken families and delinquency (Adlaf & Ivis, 1997; Biron & LeBlanc 1977; Goldstein, 1984; Nye, 1958; Sokol-Katz et al., 1997), others find that the social bond model cannot adequately explain the relationship between broken or nontraditional families and delinquency (Cernkovich & Gioradano 1987; Chen & Kaplan, 1997; Dornbusch et al., 1985; Gove & Crutchfield, 1982; Rosen, 1985; Van Voorhis et al., 1988).

Hirschi's (1969) analysis of self-report delinquency among junior and senior high school students in California failed to demonstrate an association between broken homes and delinquency. In addition to earlier reported findings from Hirschi's (1969) study that an inverse relationship between parent attachment and delinquency exists, ties to the family were inversely related to delinquency, even when parents were "unconventional" (i.e., on welfare or unemployed). A number of subsequent studies that investigated whether parental attachment might intervene between family structure and delinquency found support for Hirschi's finding. For example, Biron and LeBlanc's (1977) initial analysis revealed that, controlling for age and gender, the structural aspects of family were significantly related to home-based delinquent behavior. However, when parental supervision was introduced into their models, the original relationship between family structure and home-based delinquency became statistically non-significant.

Similarly, Sampson and Laub (1994) found that significant correlations between the structural indicators of family life and delinquent behavior ended with the introduction of family process variables (discipline, maternal supervision, and parent-child attachment) into their multivariate regression models. Initial analysis reported in a study by Adlaf and Ivis (1997) found that familial disruption was significantly correlated with four substance abuse measures and a composite delinquency scale. However, when family quality variables, including parental attachment, were entered into a multivariate regression equation, family structure remained a significant predictor of only one of the five outcome measures. Finally, Cernkovich and Gioradano (1987) reported that several variables related to the concept of parental attachment were significant predictors of delinquent behavior. These researchers found that none of these variables varied significantly across the three categories of family structure in their research. Similarly, Van Voorhis et al. (1988) found that several variables related to Hirschi's (1969) social control theory were correlated with delinquency. Family structure was not related to the majority of these variables (Kierkus & Baer, 2002).

Other investigators report findings rejecting Hirschi's initial premise. Dornbusch et al. (1985) found that youth from non-intact families had significantly lower levels of social control than children from two parent homes. Using multiple regression analysis to examine the impact of parent attachment, the authors found that this element of social control did not affect the strength of the relationship between family structure and delinquency. Similarly, Gove and Crutchfield (1982) used multivariate analysis to examine the influence of family structure and social control on delinquency and found family attachment did not reduce the strength of the association between family structure and delinquent behavior (Kierkus & Baer, 2002).

More recent research has been conducted on the grounds that significant methodological concerns have rendered the findings of earlier studies inconclusive (see Kierkus & Baer, 2002 for an explanation of these limitations; Shoemaker, 2005). A number of these more recent efforts seem to suggest that family attachment in spite of broken homes is an important determinant of delinquent behavior. For example, using a representative sample of school children from the province of Ontario (n=1,891), Kierkus & Baer (2002) found that, controlling for age, gender, and SES, family structure is a significant predictor of most self-reported delinquent behaviors. However, after adding parental attachment into the regression equation, the strength of the relationships between family structure and delinquency are greatly reduced. The authors conclude that the parental attachment element of social bond theory represents a plausible explanation of the link between family structure and delinquency. Mack, Leiber, Featherstone and Monserud (2007), using data from the National Longitudinal Study of Adolescent Health (Add Health), examined parental data on White, African-American, and Hispanic youth respondents (n = 9,636). The investigators found that while type of household, characterized by broken homes (due to divorce, parent never married, death) was not a significant predictor of nonserious or serious delinquency, maternal attachment was found to be the most important predictor of delinquency among youth from all family types.

Race/Ethnicity and the Social Bond

Hirschi's social bond theory purports to be constant and applicable across all racial and ethnic boundaries (Junger & Marshall, 1997). However, Hirschi devoted little effort toward evaluating this assumption. In fact, to date, nearly forty years since Hirschi introduced his version of social bond theory, studies examining the impact of racial and ethnic influences on social bonding variables and delinquency remain rare. Of those that do focus on race, some have concluded that race or ethnicity is not significant (Junger & Marshall, 1997; Cernkovich & Giodano, 1992), while others have discovered that the theory best explains Caucasian involvement in criminal and/or delinquent behavior (Lotz & Lee, 1999; Silverman, Nakhaie, & Lagrange, 2000).

Cernkovich and Giodano (1992) used a neighborhood sample (n = 942) to examine potential racial differences with respect to the level of school bonding and the effect of school bonding on delinquent behavior. The authors found no significant differences of the effect of school bonding on delinquency across racial groups. Similarly, Junger and Marshall (1997) used a sample of 788, Surinamese, Moroccan, Turkish, and Dutch male youth in the Netherlands and tested the presence of variation in delinquent offending among the four ethnic groups. Findings showed that the social bond equally accounted for variance in self-reported delinquency among each of the four ethnic groups.

Other studies report differences in the explanatory power of the social bond theory across racial groups. For instance, using a sample of 2,772 adolescents, Lotz and Lee (1999) reported that while weak attachment and commitment to school in the form of "negative school experience" predicted delinquency for White youth in the sample, it showed no predictive value for African American youth. Finally, using a sample of junior and senior high school students in Alberta, Canada (n=2,495), Silverman, Nakhaie, and Lagrange (2000) reported that the social bond model does not account for delinquency among Aboriginal youth as it does among youth of other racial groups represented in the sample.

The literature cited above is clear on two positions. (1) Studies that examine the utility of social bond across racial groups are sparse; and (2) disparities between their findings preclude arriving at a definitive position on the applicability of the social bond theory across various racial groups.

Gender and the Social Bond

Studies that focus on gender differences with respect to the social bond are also rare, though not as rare as those focused on race. In fact Hirschi's (1969) empirical test of social bond theory involved male respondents, exclusively. Despite a gradual increase in studies that apply social bond theory to females, study efforts in this area remain negligible (Alarid, Burton, & Cullen, Cernkovich & Giordanao, 1992; Friedman & Rosenbaum, 1988; Junger & Marshall, 1997; Kempf, 1993; Rosenbaum, 1987; Rosenbaum & Lasley, 1990; Samuelson, Hartnagel & Krahn, 1995). While a few studies report that social bond theory functions similarly for both males and females (Cernkovich & Giordanao, 1992; Sommers & Baskin, 1994; Thompson, Mitchell, & Dabber, 1984), others indicate that the social bond is not equally applicable for both males and females (Alarid, Burton, & Cullen, 2000; Rosenbaum, 1987; Rosenbaum & Lasley, 1990; Friedman & Rosenbaum, Samuelson, Hartnagel, & Krahn, 1995; Seydlitz, 1990). Still other research suggests that certain aspects of the bond affect males and females differently (for example, Huebner and Betts, 2002).

Sommers and Baskin (1994) assess social bonding variables on a sample of 85 females who were arrested and/or incarcerated for a violent crime. By conducting interviews with these females, they conclude that weak school and parental attachment are key factors related to female involvement in violent crime. Similarly, using selfreport surveys, Cernkovich & Giordanao's (1992) study compared the effect of the school bonding aspect of the social bond theory on both males (49%) and females (51%) and found that school bonding explains the variance in delinquency at comparable levels for both genders. In other words, school bonding has a consistent effect for both genders' involvement in delinquent behavior.

Similarly, examining the attachment aspect of the theory among a sample of 724 male and female high school and incarcerated youth, Thompson, Mitchell, and Dobber (1984) found that attachment to parents, peers, and school was related to lower levels of delinquency for both males and females.

Other studies find different gender effects of the social bond. In Rosenbaum's (1987) self-report study of 1,612 youth, social bonding theory more adequately explained drug and property crimes among females than among males; however, it accounted for an equal amount of violent behavior in males and females. Similarly, using data from the National Survey of Youth, Seydlitz (1990) examined the parental attachment aspect of the social bond theory on a sample of 872 male and female youth. Seydlitz found that "virtual supervision" is a stronger predictor of delinquency for males than females at age 15, while "intimacy of communication" is a more adequate predictor for females than males at age 18. Finally, Rosenbaum and Lasley (1990) apply social bonding theory to 1,508 male and female high school youth made up of three groups: those with no police or court records; those with only police records; or those with police and court records. Rosenbaum and Lasley's study suggests that strong attachment and commitment to school explains significantly more conforming behavior in males than in females. They also found that a lack of involvement in conventional activities explains more male than female involvement in criminal or delinquent behavior.

Other studies suggest that attachment bonds have different effects for males and females. For instance, in a study of attachment to families, Canter (1982) found that while girls reported stronger bonds to parents than boys, the protective function of parent attachment was greater for boys. Anderson et al. (1999) found that attachment to parents reduced the severity of adolescent boys' delinquency, whereas attachment to peers and school reduced the severity of adolescent girls' delinquency. Huebner and Betts (2002) examined the utility of social bond theory's "attachment" and "involvement" bonds as protective factors to examine gender differences in reports of delinquency and academic achievement in a sample of 7th to 12th graders. The findings suggest that although several of the involvement bond variables of social control theory are predictive of both delinquency and academic achievement for both genders, only the attachment bond variables provide such an overall protective function for females.

Much like research that examines the impact of racial differences on the social bond, studies that investigate the effects of gender report a range of findings that can loosely be categorized as those that find no gender affects, those that find differences along lines of gender and those that find varying affects according to different elements and dimensions of the social bond theory. In the absence of more investigations in this area, findings are mixed, thus no definitive position can be taken with regard to the applicability of social bond theory across gender demographics.

Summary

Factors that are provided as possible explanation for the placement experience and delinquency link were developed primarily from Hirschi's theory of social bond (1969). Through testing his own theory, Hirshi provides empirical evidence toward the conclusion that poor attachment to positive parental influences, poor school commitment, and lack of involvement in prosocial activities predict delinquency. Moreover, application of the social bond theory to youth in out-of-home care placement is supported by research that demonstrates its utility among samples that share certain characteristics of youth who make up this subgroup, namely demographic minorities such as African Americans and individuals from nontraditional family arrangements (such as broken homes, and in at least one finding, homes where parental behaviors may be considered "unconventional").

DISCUSSION QUESTIONS
By John M. Stogner

1. Hirschi describes the social bond as having four elements rather than there being four (or more) separate social bonds. Is this distinction meaningful? What are the implications of the theory being presented in this way?

2. Are Akers's social learning theory and Hirschi's social bond theory compatible? What are the biggest differences between the two? Do they suggest opposing testable hypotheses?

3. Does Hirschi believe that individuals' behaviors are influenced by those of their peers?

4. If Hirschi's work is largely accurate, how could it be used to reduce crime rates (i.e., what are the policy recommendations of social bond theory)?

5. Does social bond theory address (explicitly or by inference) the urban–rural disparities in crime rates? That is, can it explain why fewer crimes per capita are committed in rural areas?

CHAPTER ELEVEN

Self-Control Theory

TRAVIS HIRSCHI AND MICHAEL R. GOTTFREDSON

STUDENT INTRODUCTION
By John M. Stogner

Michael Gottfredson and Travis Hirschi's 1990 contribution to the control perspective was even more parsimonious than Hirschi's earlier social bonding theory. Similar to social bonding, their theory assumes that deviance is a natural human behavior only avoided when an individual is constrained in some way. Whereas Hirschi's initial theory focused on connections to society, his work with Gottfredson highlighted the importance of internal control. The theory's central proposition is that individuals engage in delinquency because they lack self-control. According to Gottfredson and Hirschi, self-control is the ability to resist temptation, to deter gratification, and to minimize risk. They argue that those who fail to develop the trait are impulsive, shortsighted, insensitive, physical, nonverbal, and risk-takers. They attribute variation in offending solely to variation in self-control; those lower in self-control commit more offenses because their behavior is not adequately constrained.

Thus, low self-control is a critical risk factor. Gottfredson and Hirschi are bold in their predictions, claiming that it is *the factor* that separates offenders from nonoffenders. In their view, criminal opportunities abound and crime requires few skills—individuals do not refrain from criminality because of a lack of opportunity; they refrain because of self-control. Gottfredson and Hirschi do not suggest that this self-control is a dynamic trait. Instead, they suggest it is relatively stable after early childhood. How self-control is developed is therefore quite important to their work. They argue that good parenting practices help children to develop self-control. Specifically, they suggest that parents who are attached to their young children, supervise their behavior, identify age-inappropriate behaviors, and punish misbehavior in a fair and consistent manner will typically raise children with higher levels of self-control. The theory proposes that the level of self-control formed during childhood will impact behavior across the life-course.

Self-control theory may seem simplistic given that deviance is attributed to a single factor: low self-control; however, this simplicity is also part of its appeal. The idea that the failure to develop a single trait during childhood is largely responsible for all later misbehavior is easily tested. Similarly, it allows Gottfredson and Hirschi to make clear and explicit recommendations for policy. Yet, as you read, note that the theory is more complex than it appears on the surface. Attempt to understand exactly how they conceptualize low self-control, why they claim other factors are less important, and why they do not consider opportunity to be a factor. Consider how self-control theory compares to social bonding theory and works within the learning perspective. Finally, evaluate the potential drawbacks of utilizing self-control theory's policy recommendations.

SELF-CONTROL THEORY

By Travis Hirschi and Michael R. Gottfredson University of Arizona

I n the summer of 1998, three white men in east Texas chained a black man to the rear of a pickup truck and dragged him for several miles along the backroads near his hometown. The victim's remains were found strewn along the road the next morning. When arrested that same day, the three men had in their possession a large quantity of meat they had stolen during a burglary of a packing plant. According to media reports, all had served time in prison and all had been drinking heavily at the time the crimes were committed. In federal law, murder involving race hatred is punishable by death. In Texas law, murder involving kidnapping (forcing the movement of the victim) is also subject to the death penalty. Many calls for speedy execution of the offenders were heard in the days that followed. These calls were not limited to one area of the country or to one ethnic group. In fact, a good guess would be that about 95 percent of the U.S. population favored the death penalty in this case. Through his lawyer, one of the arrested men quickly denied participation in the act.

A theory of crime should be able to make sense of these facts, however rare and horrible they may be. A general theory should also make sense of the far more common crimes and delinquencies at the other end of the seriousness scale: truancy, shoplifting, underage smoking, bicycle theft, cheating on tests.

What are "the facts" in this case? You may have heard that theories favor some facts and ignore others. If so, what you have heard is true. Facts accepted by one theory may be rejected or ignored by other theories. Self-control theory focuses on the typical features of criminal acts and on the criminal record of the offender. In the case in question, self-control theory would emphasize the following: (1). The offenders had long records of involvement in criminal and deviant acts. (2). They did not limit themselves to one kind of crime, but engaged in a wide variety of criminal and deviant acts, even in a short period of time (burglary, murder, kidnapping, drinking excessively, driving under the influence). (3). Everyone believes that these acts are criminal or deviant and that some of them deserve severe punishment. (4). The potential costs to the offenders of the crimes described are considerable and long term; the benefits are minimal and of short duration. (5). Despite the enormity of the crimes described, no special skill or knowledge is required to commit them. (6). Although three offenders were involved in these crimes, they did not act as an organized group. Indeed, one offender took the first opportunity to claim that he did not participate in the most serious offense.

Self-control theory would largely ignore the two features of the homicide that made it so newsworthy: its unusual brutality and its element of race hatred. Self-control theory pays little attention to the seriousness of crimes and is not interested in the motives of offenders. It is also relatively uninterested in the social or economic backgrounds of the perpetrators. The theory would lead us to guess that the offenders in this case were uneducated and unskilled, but it would do so because it assumes that people committing such crimes are unlikely to have exerted the effort required to obtain an education or a high level of occupational skill, not because poverty forced them into the acts in question. In short, self-control theory takes the social and economic conditions of offenders as a reflection of their tendency to offend, not as a cause of their offending. By the same token, the theory would pay little attention to the time and place of the crime. In its view, there is nothing special with respect to crime about east Texas or the end of the twentieth century.

Which of the facts listed is most important? We begin to answer this question by asking another: What fact best predicts crime? The answer is previous crime. If you want to know the likelihood that a person will commit criminal or deviant acts in the future, you can do no better than count the different kinds of criminal and deviant acts he or she has committed in the past. This is the central fact on which self-control theory is based. It says to the self-control theorist that all criminal and deviant acts, at whatever age they are committed, whatever their level of seriousness, have something in common. It says also that people differ in the degree to which they are attracted to or repelled by whatever it is crime and deviance have to offer.

We know that criminal and deviant acts have something in common because participation in any one of them predicts participation in all of the others. People who smoke and drink are more likely than people who do not smoke or drink to use illegal drugs, to cut classes, to cheat on tests, to break into houses, to rob and steal. People who rob and steal are more likely than people who do not rob and steal to smoke and drink, use illegal drugs, break into houses, and cheat on tests. What do robbery, theft, burglary, cheating, truancy, and drug use (and the many forms of criminal and deviant behavior not listed) have in common? They are all quick and easy ways of getting what one wants. They are all also, in the long run, dangerous to one's health, safety, reputation, and economic well-being.

The features common to various crimes and deviant acts would not cause them to predict one another unless these features were reflected in some relatively enduring tendency of individuals. People must differ in the likelihood that they will take the quick and easy way regardless of long-term consequences. This enduring difference between people the theory calls *self-control*. Those who have a high degree of self-control avoid acts potentially damaging to their future prospects, whatever the current benefits these acts seem to promise. Those with a low degree of self-control are easily swayed by current benefits and tend to forget future costs. Most people are between these extremes, sometimes doing things they know they should not do, other times being careful not to take unnecessary risks for short-term advantage.

So, a *fact* at the heart of the theory is the ability of previous criminal and deviant acts to predict future criminal and deviant acts. The *concept* at the heart of the theory is self-control, defined as the tendency to avoid acts whose long-term costs exceed their immediate or short-term benefits.

The Theory

To construct such a theory, it was first necessary to distinguish between crime and criminality, a distinction forced upon us by the age distribution of crimes. Crimes rise and fall during the life course, but *differences* in the tendency to commit criminal acts do not follow this pattern. Children in trouble with teachers in the 2nd and 3rd grades are more likely to be in trouble with juvenile authorities at 15 and 16; they are more likely to serve prison terms in their 20s; they are more likely to have trouble with their families and jobs at all ages.

So, to discuss the facts sensibly, we need something that may change with age and something that may not. The changeable element is crime. Crimes are acts or events that take place at specific points in space and time. We began this chapter describing an event in east Texas in the summer of 1998. Three men tied another man to a battered pickup truck and dragged him to his death. That is a crime: murder. A witness in a criminal trial lies under oath. That is a crime: perjury. A man drives after drinking ten cans of beer. That is a crime: driving under the influence. Crimes are very common. Each year in the United States, the police report about 15 million arrests to the Federal Bureau of Investigation (FBI).

The unchangeable element is criminality, the tendency of people to engage in or refrain from criminal acts. Because criminality is a propensity or tendency, it cannot be counted, but it can be observed or measured. From such observation, we know that few people would allow themselves to be involved in the murder of a stranger. (In context, the oft-repeated statement that "everybody does it" is obviously foolish. It is usually foolish elsewhere as well.) We know that more people might, under the right circumstances, commit perjury. And we know that many would and do drive after drinking more than the law allows. In fact, experience shows that everyone is capable of criminal or deviant acts. More meaningfully, however, it shows that some are more likely than others actually to commit them. Criminality is a matter of degree.

With this distinction, the task of theory is clear: It is to identify and explain criminality and to relate it to the commission of criminal acts.

We begin by looking more closely at crimes and deviant acts. What do murder, perjury, and driving under the influence (and theft, assault, cheating on tests, burglary, robbery, forgery, and fraud) have in common? The Chinese have a saying: "Crime is as easy as falling down a mountain." Indeed, most crimes require no special learning or knowledge. Children invent them without help. Young people are their major practitioners. A fiendish and relatively complex murder may be committed by (1). wrapping a chain around an outnumbered man; (2). hooking it to a pickup bumper; (3). driving away. Most people know or could learn on the spot how to wrap and hook a chain, and most adults know how to drive. Perjury may be accomplished by saying "No" when what actually happened would require "Yes." The capacity for perjury is thus present the moment the child is able to affirm or deny the occurrence of an event. Driving drunk requires only the ability to drink and the ability to drive. The highest rates of drunk driving are found among those still learning these skills.

Most crimes take little time or effort. They are rarely the product of lengthy and elaborate preparation. Among our examples, drunk driving appears to be the most time-consuming but would not normally be considered hard work. In the United States, homicide is most often committed with a gun. In the typical case, the decision to aim and fire is made instantaneously, on the spot. Compared to this, our east Texas homicide was unusually difficult, possibly requiring several minutes to accomplish. Perjury too may take only a split second. The consequences of perjury may be complicated, but the difficulties following the commission of a criminal or deviant act should not be confused with the act itself.

Indeed, another characteristic of criminal and deviant acts is that they entail just such long-term complications, difficulties, or costs. These costs or penalties are called *sanctions*. Following the British philosopher Jeremy Bentham ([1789] 1970), we identify four kinds of sanctions. *Physical* sanctions are those that follow naturally from the act, without the active intervention of others. Examples include hangovers and diminished health from the consumption of drugs, disease from promiscuous sexual activity, injuries from the actions of victims attempting to defend their persons or property, and diminished earning capacity from repeated truancy. *Moral* or *social* sanctions are those imposed by family, friends, neighbors, employers, clients, and constituents in the court of public opinion. They include divorce, shaming, shunning, and reduced responsibility and trust. *Political* or *legal* sanctions are those imposed by governments and organizations for violations of law. They include fines, imprisonment, and even execution. They also include expulsion and impeachment. *Religious* sanctions are those imposed by supernatural authorities, now and in the hereafter. Their form varies from one religion to another, but they are usually pictured as long-term and serious.

We often refer to the *risk* of legal and moral sanctions because they cannot be imposed unless the offender is convicted or caught in the act. This suggests the possibility of cost-free crime and deviance, depending on the luck of offenders or their ability to avoid detection. Indeed, religious sanctions are sometimes explained as an effort to solve this problem, as devices that punish deviant behavior whether or not it is seen by others. Self-control theory does not require supernatural or religious sanctions for several reasons: (1). It emphasizes often serious physical or natural sanctions whose application does not require third-party knowledge or intervention; (2). It emphasizes the generality of deviance, the tendency of people to repeat offenses and to be involved in a wide variety of them. As the level and variety of deviant activity increase, detection and automatic penalties become more and more certain; (3). It emphasizes the spontaneous and unplanned nature of criminal and deviant acts, a characteristic inconsistent with successful long-term concealment.

We now see another reason that reckless, deviant, criminal, and sinful acts tend to go together, to be committed by the same people: They all produce potentially painful consequences. Distinctions among deviant acts on the basis of the sanction system most concerned with them are to some extent arbitrary and misleading. Murder is a crime punished by the legal system, but it is also reckless, deviant, and sinful. In fact, one reason it is judged a crime is to control the natural tendency of the victim's family and friends to seek their own revenge. Perjury (lying under oath) is sometimes said to be the quintessential criminal act, but lying in other contexts is also subject to natural, social, and religious penalties. Driving under the influence of alcohol has only recently become a major concern of the criminal justice system. Not long ago, it was widely practiced and considered only mildly deviant. This should not be taken to mean that it was not punished. Whatever its legal or moral status, few acts are more reckless than drunk driving. Since the invention of the automobile, in the United States alone, drunk driving has killed hundreds of thousands of its practitioners (as well as countless others).

The idea that murder, perjury, drunk driving, and marijuana smoking (and all other criminal and delinquent acts) have something in common is sometimes met by such statements as: "Marijuana smoking is not murder!" "Sex is not shoplifting!" "Perjury is not driving under the influence!" Self-control theory does not say these acts are the same thing. It says they have something in common. This common element may be identified more clearly by focusing on the logical structure of criminal and deviant acts.

The logical structure of an act is the set of conditions necessary for it to occur. Each distinct criminal or deviant act has a unique set of necessary conditions. For example, smoking marijuana requires attractive (for reasons of cost, quality, and reputation) and available marijuana. It also requires an offender unrestrained by the consequences of marijuana use. Homicide is more complex. It requires interaction between an offender and a victim, an offender with the means of taking the life of another, an offender insufficiently restrained to prevent the crime, a victim unable to remove himself from the scene, and absence of life-saving third-party intervention. (Life-saving intervention would make the crime attempted murder or aggravated assault.) Perjury is ultimately simple. It requires only a question asked of a person who has sworn to tell the truth, where that person is insufficiently restrained to prevent the crime. Driving under the influence combines the logical structure of two distinct acts. It requires a drug (usually alcohol) that is available and attractive to the offender, a vehicle that is accessible to the offender, an offender capable of operating the vehicle while intoxicated, and an offender insufficiently restrained to prevent the crime.

The element common to these acts (and all other criminal and deviant acts) is an unrestrained offender, a person willing to risk long-term costs for immediate personal benefits. Self-control theory says there is nothing extraordinarily attractive about the benefits of crime, that they may be found in noncriminal activities as well, and that in practice crime is not an efficient method of producing them. It says further that awareness and appreciation of the benefits of crime are not restricted to offenders. Everyone enjoys money, sex, power, excitement, ease, euphoria, and revenge. Everyone can see that crime provides a direct and easy way of obtaining them. So, according to the theory, the difference between offenders and nonoffenders is in their awareness of and concern for the long-term costs of crime—such things as arrest, prison, disgrace, disease, and even eternal damnation.

The idea that crime satisfies special needs and that offenders are strongly motivated to accomplish their purposes is accepted in many theories of crime and discussions of crime control policy. The source of this idea may be the obvious imbalance between the short-term and uncertain rewards of crime and its long-term and more certain penalties. Offenders often appear to trade a cow for a bag of beans, to risk powerful positions for brief sexual pleasures or small monetary gains. To strike such bargains, the logic goes, offenders must be driven by emotions (seductions and compulsions) of considerable strength. Self-control theory solves this "problem" by reducing the offender's awareness of or concern for the long term. What distinguishes offenders from others is not the strength of their appetites but their freedom to enjoy the quick and easy and ordinary pleasures of crime without undue concern for the pains that may follow them.

From the nature of crime, and acts analogous to crime, we thus infer the nature of criminality. People who engage in crime are people who tend to neglect long-term consequences. They are, or tend to be, children of the moment. They have what we call low self-control.

Where does low self-control come from? All of us, it appears, are born with the ability to use force and fraud in pursuit of our private goals. Small children can and do lie, bite, whine, hit, and steal. They also sometimes consider horrendous crimes they are too small to carry off. By the age of 8 or 10, most of us learn to control such tendencies to the degree necessary to get along at home and school. Others, however, continue to employ the devices of children, to engage in behavior inappropriate to their age. The differences observed at ages 8 to 10 tend to persist from then on. Good children remain good. Not so good children remain a source of concern to their parents, teachers, and eventually to the criminal justice system. These facts lead to the conclusion that low self-control is natural and that *self-control* is *acquired* in the early years of life.

Children presumably learn from many sources to consider the long-range consequences of their acts. One important source, we previously called natural sanctions, penalties that follow more or less automatically from certain forms of behavior. The list is long. It include burns from hot stoves,' bruises from falling down stairs or out of trees, and injuries from efforts to take things thought by others to belong to them. Obviously, natural sanctions can be dangerous and painful. In fact, the natural system is so unforgiving that parents and other adults spend a lot of their time protecting children from it.

But the major sources of self-control, in our view, are the actions of parents or other responsible adults. Parents who care for their children watch them as best they can. When they *see* their children doing something they should not do, they correct, admonish, or punish them. The logical structure of successful socialization thus has four necessary conditions: care, monitor, recognize (deviant behavior), and correct. When all of these conditions are present, the child presumably learns to avoid acts with long-term negative consequences, whatever their legal or moral status. When any one of them is missing, continued low self-control may be the result. Delinquency research provides strong support for these conclusions. It shows that the greater the attachment of the parent to the child, the lower the likelihood of delinquency. It shows that careful supervision and adequate discipline are among the most important predictors of nondelinquency. By extension, this child-rearing model goes a long way toward explaining all of the major family factors in crime: neglect, abuse, single parents, large number of children, parental criminality. All of these are measures of the extent of parental concern for the child or are conditions that affect the ability of the parent to monitor and correct the child's behavior. As would be expected, they are also major predictors of behaviors we call analogous to crime: truancy, quitting school, smoking, excessive drinking, and job instability.

We are now ready to use the theory to explain criminal, deviant, and reckless acts. Persons deficient in self-control are attracted to acts that provide immediate and apparently certain pleasure with minimal effort, whatever their collateral consequences. Criminal, deviant, and reckless acts fit this definition. In many, force and fraud speed up the process and reduce the effort required to produce the desired result. In others, mind-altering chemicals provide shortcuts to happiness. In still others, the pleasure inheres in the act itself or in the risks it entails.

Persons sufficient in self-control avoid such acts because they find that their collateral consequences outweigh their benefits. Force and fraud in the service of self-interest are opposed by the law and by most people (including those lacking self-control). Drugs entail risks to self and others inconsistent with long-term goals. And reckless behavior gains its charm from the very possibility that it may put an end to future prospects, whatever they may be.

Theories explain facts by stating general propositions from which specific facts may be derived. For example, in Newton's theory, apples fall to earth *because* every particle of matter in the universe is attracted by every other particle. The larger the particle, the stronger the attraction. We often condense this explanation into one word, *gravity*, but the truth and value of the explanation are not reduced by this practice. By the same logic, in self-control theory, people commit criminal acts because they fail to consider their long-term consequences. This explanation, too, may be condensed into a single concept, (low) self-control, but its truth and value are not reduced by this practice.

Other theories of course also explain crime by stating general principles from which specific acts can be derived. For example, traditional strain theory would say that people commit criminal acts because they have been blocked from attaining success by noncriminal or conventional means. And social learning theory might explain crime by saying that people commit criminal acts because they have learned such behavior from their peers. Choosing among theories is not, then, so much a matter of their logic as of their relative ability to predict the facts about crime and criminals.

Tests of Self-Control Theory

Our version of self-control theory was published in 1990, which makes it a new or contemporary theory. Given the traditions of the field, new theories are by definition untested. They are hypotheses or conjectures whose fate depends on the results of research not yet conducted. This suggests that new theories are more problematic than theories that have withstood efforts to test or falsify them. Actually, the reverse should be true. If theories are logical systems based on current understandings of the facts, new theories should be especially consistent with the results of current research. And the use of old theories to explain facts they once ignored or denied should be viewed with considerable suspicion.

Self-control theory is based on and, therefore, "predicts" the following facts:

- Differences between high- and low-rate offenders persist over the life course. Children ranked on the frequency of their delinquent acts will be ranked similarly later in life. This is not to say "once a criminal always a criminal." It is to say that differences in tendencies to commit crime, like differences in height, maintain themselves over long periods of time. This is among the best-established facts in criminology (Nagin and Paternoster 1991; Gendreau, Little, and Goggin 1996).
- Efforts to treat or rehabilitate offenders do not produce the desired results. The search for effective treatment programs of course continues. But research continues to show that once tendencies to engage in crime and delinquency have been established, successful treatment is, at a minimum, extraordinarily difficult (Martinson 1974a; Sechrest et al. 1979. For a strongly contrary view, see Andrews et al. 1990).
- Intervention efforts in childhood offer the greatest promise of success in crime reduction (Tremblay et al. 1992).
- The law enforcement or criminal justice system has little effect on the volume of criminal behavior. Offenders do not attend to increases in the number of police or in the severity of penalties for violations of law (Andrews et al. 1990).
- Crimes may be prevented by increasing the effort required to commit them (Murray 1995).
- Crime declines with age among all groups of offenders and in almost all types of offending (Cohen and Land 1987; Gottfredson and Hirschi 1990).
- Offenders do not specialize in particular forms of crime. Career criminals are extremely rare (Wolfgang et al. 1972; Britt 1994).
- Offenders have higher accident, illness, and death rates than nonoffenders (Farrington and Junger 1995).
- Offenders are more likely than nonoffenders to use legal and illegal drugs (Boyum and Kleiman 1995).
- Offenders are more frequently involved in noncriminal forms of deviance (Evans et al. 1997).
- Offenders are more weakly attached than nonoffenders to restrictive institutions and long-term careers—families, schools, jobs (Glueck and Glueck 1968).
- Compared to nonoffenders, offenders are disadvantaged with respect to intellectual or cognitive skills (Hirschi and Hindelang 1977).
- Family structure, family relations, and childrearing practices are important predictors of deviant behavior (Glueck and Glueck 1950; Loeber and Stout-hamer-Loeber 1986).

In our view, these facts have been repeatedly confirmed by research. In our view, self-control theory is consistent with all of them, something that cannot be said for any of its competitors.

Policy Implications of the Theory

The control theory approach to policy is to analyze the features of the criminal act and the characteristics of offenders and to pattern prevention efforts accordingly. The major relevant characteristics of offenders are youthfulness, limited cognitive skills, and low self-control. Because the rates of such important crimes as burglary, robbery, theft, shoplifting, and vandalism all peak in mid-to late adolescence and fall to half their peak levels as early as the mid-twenties, effective crime control policies will naturally focus on the interests and activities of teenagers. Because the cognitive skills of offenders are relatively limited, their criminal acts are typically simple and easily traced. As a result, policies targeting sophisticated offenders or career criminals are unnecessarily complex and inefficient. Because offenders have low self-control, they are easily deterred by increasing the immediate difficulties and risks of criminal acts and are generally unaffected by changes in the long-term costs of criminal behavior. Consequently, steering wheel locks are more effective than increased penalties in reducing auto theft, and moving in groups is more effective than increased police presence in preventing robbery.

The characteristics of criminal acts relevant to their prevention have been listed earlier. Crimes provide immediate, obvious benefit, are easily accomplished, and require little skill, planning, or persistence. They involve no driving force beyond the satisfaction of everyday human desires. Because people do not suffer when criminal opportunities are unavailable to them, crimes can be prevented by making them more complex or difficult. For example, increasing the cost of alcohol or banning its use in particular settings will often produce the desired result with little effort. Guarding parking lots or apartment complexes can also be effective in preventing theft and vandalism.

Although it focuses on an element common to all forms of crime and deviance, low self-control, self-control theory actually supports an offense-specific approach to crime prevention. Procedures for preventing one type of crime may be inapplicable to others. Effective efforts to control hijacking have no impact on vandalism or burglary. Offense-specific approaches begin by analyzing the conditions necessary for a particular act to occur. Graffiti, for example, requires spray paint and large, accessible, paintable, generally observable surfaces that are unguarded for a predictable period of time. It also requires an unrestrained offender. Graffiti may be controlled by removing any one of its necessary physical conditions or by altering the behavior of unrestrained offenders. Clearly, efforts directed at offenders—treatment, deterrence, incapacitation—will be highly inefficient compared to programs that restrict access to paint and to paintable surfaces.

Self-control theory is based on the idea that behavior is governed by its consequences. As we have seen, this idea is also central to the criminal justice system, according to which crime may be reduced by increasing the likelihood and severity of such legal sanctions as fines and imprisonment. Nevertheless, self-control theory leads to the conclusion that the formal criminal justice system can play only a minor role in the prevention and control of crime. Because potential offenders do not consider the long-term legal consequences of their acts, modification of these consequences will have little effect on their behavior. Because criminal acts are so quickly and easily accomplished, they are only rarely directly observed by agents of the criminal justice system. As a result, even large increases in the number of such agents would have minimal effect on the rates of most crimes.

These and other considerations led us to advance the following recommendations for crime control policy (from Gottfredson and Hirschi 1995):

1. Do not attempt to control crime by incapacitating adults. A major factor in the decision to incarcerate offenders is the number of prior offenses they have committed. The result is that adults are

much more likely to be imprisoned than adolescents. Most people would agree that prior records should be considered, but the age distribution of crime (see Figure 2) shows us that putting adults in prison is ineffective because by then it is too late. They are too old. The average age of persons sentenced to prison is the late twenties, more than ten years after the peak age of crime.

2. Do not attempt to control the crime rate by rehabilitating adults. As has been shown above, there are two very good arguments against treatment programs for adult offenders. The first is the age effect, which makes treatment unnecessary. The second is that no treatment program for adults has been shown to be effective. If nothing but time works, it seems ill-advised to pretend otherwise.

3. Do not attempt to control crime by altering the penalties available to the criminal justice system. Legal penalties do not have the desired effect because offenders do not consider them. Increasing their certainty and severity may make citizens and policymakers feel better about the justice system, but it will have a highly limited effect on the decisions of offenders.

4. Restrict the unsupervised activities of teenagers. Crime requires opportunity and unrestrained individuals. Much can be gained from limiting access of teenagers to guns, cars, alcohol, unwatched walls, unattended houses, and to each other. One of the great success stories of the last quarter of the century was the reduction in fatal auto accidents that followed increases in the drinking age. Curfews, truancy prevention programs, school uniforms, and license restrictions—all of these have potential value for the same reason.

5. Limit proactive policing including police sweeps, police stings, intensive arrest programs, and aggressive drug policies. Control theory sees crime as a product of human weakness. It sees no point in creating opportunities for crime in order to identify those suffering from such weakness. It sees no point in exploiting such weakness merely for the benefit of the law enforcement establishment.

6. Question the characterization of crime offered by agents of the criminal justice system and uncritically repeated by the media. The evidence suggests that offenders are not the dedicated, inventive, and clever professionals law enforcement and the media often make them out to be. In fact, control theory questions the very existence of huge juvenile gangs and highly organized criminal syndicates. Where, the theory asks, do people unable to resist the pleasures of drugs and theft and truancy and violence find the discipline to construct organizations that force them to resist such pleasures?

7. Support programs designed to provide early education and effective child care. Programs that target dysfunctional families and seek to remedy lack of supervision have been shown to have promise. This does not contradict the control theory notion that self-control is acquired early in life. The finding that nothing works in the treatment area may be limited to programs focusing on adolescents and adults.

8. Support policies that promote and facilitate two-parent families and that increase the number of caregivers relative to the number of children. Large families and single-parent families are handicapped with respect to monitoring and discipline. As a consequence, their children are more likely to commit criminal acts and are especially more likely to become involved with the criminal justice system. A major source of weak families is unmarried pregnancy among adolescent girls, which is itself important evidence of low self-control. Programs to prevent such pregnancies should therefore be given high priority.

Criticisms of the Theory

Self-control theory is among the most frequently tested theories in the field of crime and delinquency. It is also frequently criticized. These criticisms are concentrated around three more or less traditional issues: (1) the definition of the dependent variable—crime and deviant behavior; (2) the logical structure of the theory; and (3) the ability of the theory to deal with particular offenses.

The Dependent Variable

Self-control theory attempts to explain short-term self-interested behavior that entails the risk of long-term sanctions. Because it is framed without regard to the law, this definition includes acts that may not be defined as criminal and may exclude acts defined as criminal by the jurisdiction in question. Examples of the first are behaviors we have labeled "analogous to crime" (e.g., premarital pregnancy, divorce, job-quitting, accidents). Examples of the second are terrorism and espionage, acts committed on behalf of political organizations. The definition also excludes the use of force or fraud in the public interest or as required by the legal system (e.g., killings by soldiers, undercover activities by police, forced removals of property owners by university officials).

This definition of crime is very different from the traditional definition, according to which crime is restricted to and includes all behavior "in violation of law." How can we exclude behavior that is clearly criminal by the laws or norms of all societies (terrorism) and include behavior that is rarely if ever punished by the state (accidents)? The answer is that we have no choice in this matter. Theories define the behavior they explain and their definition cannot be changed without changing them. Terrorist acts are excluded from self-control theory because they are assumed to reflect commitment to a political cause or organization. Terrorists do not act without regard for the broad or long-term consequences of their acts. On the contrary, their purpose is to alter the status quo. However heinous the consequences of their acts, and however severely they are punished by the state, they do not meet the requirement common to acts explained by control theory—that they be committed by an unrestrained offender.

The seriousness of this criticism of self-control theory will depend on the range and frequency of acts it fails to cover. As far as we can see, this number is small, especially when compared to the theory's coverage of the very large number of acts ignored by traditional definitions of crime.

Logical Structure

Self-control theory says that crime is the best predictor of crime and that self-control is the element common to the crimes of interest. These statements are often described as tautological, a serious criticism of the theory in the eyes of many social scientists. One meaning of *tautology* is "repetition; saying or, by extension, doing the same thing again." *The Oxford Universal Dictionary* lists an example from 1687: "Our whole Life is but a nauseous Tautology." This statement introduces another meaning of the term: The repetition described is trivial, pointless, or worse.

That crimes repeat themselves may be tautological, and some criminologists have indeed labeled this fact "trivial and theoretically pointless" (Akers 1998, 168-169). But such repetition is neither logically nor empirically necessary. It cannot therefore possibly be a valid criticism of control theory. Theories are not responsible for the nauseousness of the behavior they attempt to explain.

Another meaning of *tautology* is that the logical relations among concepts may be derived from their definitions. Thus, if low self-control is defined by willingness to engage in behavior with long-term negative consequences, and *crime* is defined as behavior with long-term negative consequences, a relation between low self-control and crime is logically necessary or tautological. The theory repeats the definition and vice versa. We do not deny the tautological or circular nature of self-control theory. On the contrary, we believe that pure theory is always tautological in this sense of the term (Hirschi and Selvin [1967] 1994). Definitions entail theories. Theories entail definitions. It cannot be otherwise. The source of confusion appears to be the belief among social scientists that tautological theories cannot be falsified. This belief, in our view, is demonstrably false.

Applicability of the Theory to Particular Crimes

In constructing self-control theory, we tried to concentrate on the characteristics of ordinary crimes. This led us to emphasize their triviality and predictability, the ease and speed with which they are committed, the small losses and smaller gains they typically involve. The purpose was to avoid the distractions that come from looking first or mainly at large, serious, or apparently bizarre crimes, crimes that attract the attention of the media and criminal justice system. This strategy has led some critics of the theory to the conclusion that it applies only to the ordinary, mundane crimes from which it was constructed. We believe this conclusion ignores the success of our strategy in revealing features shared by rare and common, serious and trivial offenses. Indeed, we began this essay with a rare and most serious offense to show that it fell easily within the scope of the theory.

Other crimes said at one time or another to fall outside the scope of the theory include income tax evasion, white-collar crime, corporate crime, organized crime, and gambling. Tests of these alleged exceptions seem to us straightforward. Those involved in crimes where self-control is not a factor should be otherwise indistinguishable from the law-abiding population. As of now, it seems to us, the evidence on these matters points in directions favorable to the theory. Those involved in such apparently exceptional crimes tend to have been involved in other forms of crime and deviance as well (Le Blanc and Kaspy 1998).

References

Akers, Ronald. (1998). Social Learning and Social Structure: A General Theory of Crime and Deviance. Boston: Northeastern University Press.

Andrews, D.A., Ivan Zinger, Robert D. Hoge, James Bonta, Paul Gendreau, and Francis T. Cullen. (1990). "Does correctional treatment work? A clinically relevant and psychologically informed meta-analysis." Criminology, 28:369–404.

Bentham, Jeremy. [1789] (1970). An Introduction to the Principles of Morals and Legislation. Reprint. London: The Althone.

Boyum, David and Mark A. R. Kleiman. (1995). "Alcohol and other drugs." Pp. 295–326 in J.Q. Wilson and J. Petersilia (eds.), Crime. San Francisco: ICS.

Britt, Chester L. (1994). "Versatility." Pp. 173–192 in T. Hirschi and M.R. Gottfredson (eds.), The Generality of Deviance. New Brunswick, NJ: Transaction.

Cohen, Lawrence C. and Kenneth C. Land. (1987). "Age structure and crime: Symmetry versus asymmetry and the projection of crime rates through the 1990s." American Sociological Review, 52:170–183.

Coleman, James. (1990). Foundations of Social Theory. Cambridge, MA: Belknap.

Evans, T., F. Cullen, V. Burton, R. Dunaway, and M. Benson. (1997). "The social consequences of self-control: Testing the general theory of crime." Criminology, 35:475–504.

Farrington, David P. and Marianne Junger (eds.). (1995). Criminal Behavior and Mental Health, 5(4): Special Issue.

Gendreau, Paul, Tracy Little, and Claire Goggin. (1996). "A meta-analysis of the predictors of adult offender recidivism: What works!" Criminology, 34:575–607.

Glueck, Sheldon and Eleanor Glueck. (1940). Juvenile Delinquents Grown Up. New York: Commonwealth Fund.

_____. (1950). Unraveling Juvenile Delinquency. Cambridge, MA: Harvard University Press.

_____. (1968). Delinquents and Nondelinquents in Perspective. Cambridge, MA: Harvard University Press.

Goring, Charles. (1913). The English Convict. Montclair, NJ: Patterson Smith.

Gottfredson, Michael R. and Travis Hirschi. (1990). A General Theory of Crime. Stanford, CA: Stanford University Press.

_____. (1995). "National crime control policies." Society, 32:30–37.

Hirschi, Travis. (1969). Causes of Delinquency. Berkeley: University of California Press.

_____. (1975). "Labeling theory and juvenile delinquency: An assessment of the evidence." Pp. 181–203 in Walter Gove (ed.), The Labeling of Deviance. Halsted.

Hirschi, Travis and Michael Gottfredson. (1983). "Age and the explanation of crime." American Journal of Sociology, 89:552–584.

Hirschi, Travis and Michael J. Hindelang. (1977). "Intelligence and delinquency: A revisionist review." American Sociological Review, 42:571–187.

Hirschi, Travis and Hanan C. Selvin. [1967] (1994). Delinquency Research: An Appraisal of Analytic Methods. New Brunswick, NJ: Transaction.

Le Blanc, Marc and Nathalie Kaspy. (1998). "Trajectories of delinquency and problem behavior. Comparison or social and personal control characteristics of adjudicated boys on synchronous and nonsynchronous paths." Journal of Quantitative Criminology, 14:181–214.

Loeber, Rolf and Magda Stouthamer-Loeber. (1986). "Family factors as correlates and predictors of juvenile conduct problems and delinquency." Pp. 29–149 in M.H. Tonry and N. Morris (eds.), Crime and Justice: A Review of Research. Chicago: University of Chicago Press.

Martinson, Robert. (1974a). "What works? Questions and answers about prison reform." The Public Interest, Spring, 35:22–54.

_____. (1974b). The myth of treatment and the reality of life process. April. Paper delivered at the Eastern Psychological Association, Philadelphia.

Murray, Charles. (1995). "The physical environment." Pp. 349–361 in J.Q. Wilson and J. Petersilia (eds.), Crime. San Francisco: ICS.

Nagin, Daniel S. and Raymond Paternoster. (1991). "On the relationship of past to future participation in delinquency." Criminology, 29:163–189.

Osgood, D. Wayne, Patrick M. O'Malley, Jerald G. Bachman, and Lloyd D. Johnston. (1989). "Time trends and age trends in arrests and self-reported illegal behavior." Criminology, 27:389–417.

Quetelet, Lambert A.J. [1833] (1969). A Treatise on Man. Gainesville, FL: Scholars' Facsimiles and Reprints.

Sechrest, Lee, Susan O. White, and Elizabeth Brown (eds.). (1979). The Rehabilitation of Criminal Offenders: *Problems and Prospects*. Washington, DC: National Academy of Sciences.

Toby, Jackson. (1957). "Social disorganization and stake in conformity: Complementary factors in the predatory behavior of hoodlums." Journal of Criminal Law, Criminology, and Police Science, 48:12–17.

Tremblay, Richard E., Frank Vitaro, Lucie Bertrand, Marc LeBlanc, Helene Beauchesne, Helene Boileau, and Lucille David. (1992). "Parent and child training to prevent early onset of delinquency: A Montreal Longitudinal-Experimental Study." Pp. 117–138 in J. McCord and R. Tremblay (eds.), Preventing Antisocial Behavior. New York: Guilford.

Wolfgang, Marvin, Robert Figlio, and Thorsten Sellin. (1972). *Delinquency in a* Birth Cohort. Chicago: University of Chicago Press.

DISCUSSION QUESTIONS
By John M. Stogner

1. How is low self-control defined? Is this definition overly broad; that is, does it intertwine traits that do not always cluster together?

2. If low self-control is the most important influence on offending, and self-control is relatively stable, how can self-control theory account for the age–crime curve?

3. Does/how could self-control theory account for rural–urban disparities in crime rates?

4. How does self-control theory differ from social bonding theory? How do their policy recommendations differ?

5. How could self-control be measured? What do you believe to be the best way of measuring self-control?

CHAPTER TWELVE

Durkheim, Anomie and Strain

TIM NEWBURN

STUDENT INTRODUCTION
By John M. Stogner

In the following chapter, Tim Newburn summarizes the anomie/strain perspective and its leading theories. Newburn first describes the work of Emile Durkheim, the so-called founding father of sociology. Although his works in the late 1800s often focused on suicide rather than acts we view as criminal today, Durkheim offered extensive insights into the relationship between social structure, societal evolution, and crime and is still considered to have been one of the most influential academics on the subject. Among his greatest contributions was describing *anomie* resulting from a society's moral and legal constraints failing to keep up with the needs of an advancing and evolving society. Put simply, rapid social change, according to Durkheim, was responsible for anomie and increases in crime. Robert K. Merton would later build on Durkheim's arguments in a brief piece entitled "Social Structure and Anomie." This 1938 work identifies stable societal conditions that contribute to crime and deviance. More specifically, Merton suggests that societies that place differential emphasis on goal achievement and the institutionalized means of achieving those goals will have higher crime rates.

Robert Agnew's general strain theory marked the next significant advance within the perspective. Agnew argued that goals other than monetary success influence behavior and saw negative relationships with others as having the potential to motivate deviant behavior. He describes three sources of criminogenic strain, or stressors that make crime likely, and the process by which these strains lead to deviance. Put simply, Agnew argues that some stressful situations lead to negative emotional states and create a pressure for resolution; people experiencing stress feel a need to deal with or alleviate that stress. His theory defines circumstances and traits that make deviant rather than prosocial coping more likely and has been empirically supported in scientific studies. Messner and Rosenfeld's institutional anomie theory, the fourth major work in this perspective, has yet to be empirically evaluated to the same degree as Agnew's work, but it does offer a number of interesting insights. Most importantly, the authors argue that the overriding influence of economic pressures in some societies weakens the ability of noneconomic institutions to appropriately socialize individuals.

As you read the following material, make sure to distinguish each theorist's ideas from those of the others. Works within this perspective may define key terms differently, so it is critical to understand each theory both in isolation and in comparison to the others in order to avoid confusion. Take particular note of the relationship between social change and crime as described by Durkheim and the adaptations to strain as described by Merton. Agnew's general strain theory is more complex than it initially appears—carefully examine the traits of strains more likely to lead to deviance, the specific strains argued to be most important, and the way strains are argued to lead to crime. Finally, consider Messner and Rosenfeld's claims about institutional anomie and whether their arguments have feasible policy applications.

DURKHEIM, ANOMIE AND STRAIN
By Tim Newburn

Introduction

Though Marx has had a considerable influence on criminological thought, he had little directly to say about crime. Emile Durkheim, by contrast, had a considerable amount to say about crime. His ideas can be said to have had a significant bearing on the Chicago School, on Robert Merton and strain theory, and on more contemporary theories of punishment. Indeed, a convincing case can be made that Durkheim is one of the great underestimated figures in criminology (Smith, 2008). As with the rest of his work, Durkheim's preoccupation was with the ways in which the *social* aspects of phenomena might be understood and illustrated. His major writings on crime emerge from his work on the division of labour and on the nature of social solidarity.

Durkheim and Criminology

Crime, for Durkheim, was those actions that offended against collective feelings or sentiments. Crime is not something that is unchanging, or has some essence. Rather, the notion of 'crime' reflects particular social conventions and these vary according to time and place. Moreover, it is not the case that 'crimes' are everywhere equally harmful to society; that is, crimes cannot be conceived as matters that are specifically injurious to the wider community. Rather, they are best understood, he argued, as violations of a moral code—what he referred to as the *conscience collective* of society. It is because this moral code is violated that punishment is required. As Garland (1990: 30) explains it:

> The criminal act violates sentiments and emotions which are deeply ingrained in most members of society—it shocks their healthy consciences- and this violation calls forth strong psychological reactions, even among those not directly involved. It provokes a sense of outrage, anger, indignation, and a passionate desire for vengeance.

According to Durkheim a certain amount of crime is normal in any society:

> Crime is present not only in the majority of societies of one particular species but in all societies of all types. There is no society that is not confronted with the problem of criminality. Its form changes; the acts thus characterized are not the same everywhere; but, everywhere and always, there have been men who have behaved in such a way as to draw upon themselves penal repression. (Durkheim, 1938: 65-6)

Crime, for Durkheim, plays a number of important functions. First, it has an *adaptive* function in that it introduces new ideas and practices into society thereby ensuring that there is change rather than stagnation. It also has a *boundary* maintenance function, reinforcing social values and norms crudely, through its stimulation of collective action against deviance it helps to reaffirm the difference between right and wrong. To this extent crime should be considered to be a normal element in any properly functioning society.

> Let us make no mistake. to classify crime among the phenomena of normal sociology is not to say merely that it is an inevitable, although regrettable phenomenon, due to the incorrigible wickedness of men; it is to affirm that it is a factor in public health, an integral part of all societies. (Durkheim, 1938: 67)

His phrase—crime 'is a factor in public health' seems odd at first sight. Surely, crime is bad, negative, unhelpful, destructive? Durkheim's argument was intended as a corrective to those views that took crime to be entirely anti-social, strange or parasitic. Rather, he pointed out that it had a social role. However unpalatable it may seem, sociologically we must recognise the functions it performs. It is, for example, part of our social 'glue'. By proscribing certain forms of behaviour we simultaneously indicate what acceptable behaviour looks like. By punishing, we reinforce legal and moral rules. Thus, too little crime, by implication, could be as concerning as too much. This is an observation of huge importance to criminologists. As Durkheim observes in an important passage, there is no prospect of crime disappearing:

> In a society in which criminal acts were no longer committed, the sentiments they offend would have to be found without exception in all individual consciousnesses, and they must be found to exist with the same degree as sentiments contrary to them. Assuming that this condition could actually be realized, crime would not thereby disappear; it would only change its form, for the very cause which would thus dry up the sources of criminality would immediately open up new ones. (Durkheim, 1938: 67)

Very quickly it becomes clear in such a discussion that crime has no essence. It varies by time and by place. The sociological study of crime, therefore, immediately must become much more than simply looking at patterns and trends, discussing practical responses to crime and how they might be altered or improved. Crime, in the hands of a sociologist such as Durkheim, becomes an important tool that can tell us much about the nature of the social order in which we live. The types of behaviours that we legislate against—and call crimes- and the specific ways in which we respond to them—the types and amounts of punishment- are indicators of the nature of our society.

One of the clearest illustrations of this style of sociological thinking can be found in Durkheim's focus on the importance of the nature of social reactions to crime. Here, Durkheim was highlighting what has become an important criminological truth:

> We must not say that an action shocks the conscience collective because it is criminal, but rather that it is criminal because it shocks the conscience collective. We do not condemn it because it is a crime, but it is a crime because we condemn it. (Durkheim, 1972: 123-4)

This observation runs through much criminological theory, not least labelling theory, some radical criminologies and, indeed, control theory.

Durkheim and Social Change

If crime and punishment have the ability to provide us with important insights into the nature and functioning of society, the periods of dramatic social change will surely be reflected in the penal sphere. In *The Division of Labour* in *Society* Durkheim analysed and sought to understand the profound changes affecting modern industrial societies. What occurred as relatively primitive societies were superseded by more complex ones. In his analysis, Durkheim identified two ideal typical social formations which he terms 'mechanical' and 'organic', each typifying differing forms of social solidarity.

Ideal types are abstractions designed to help identify and explain patterns that appear in the real world, rather than straightforward, faithful descriptions of that world. Weber described ideal types as one-sided accentuations, and as syntheses of particular phenomena, arranged in order to provide a unified construct useful for analysis. These terms—'mechanical' and 'organic' solidarity- and other ideal types that we will meet, are best seen as didactic models, used to help us understand particular social phenomena by focusing on certain core characteristics.

In more primitive societies, characterised by mechanical solidarity, there is, he argued, a relatively undifferentiated division of labour. People live fairly common, shared lives in which work is generally identical and values are shared. Under conditions of mechanical solidarity, he argued, the social order was largely organised through similarity, and social norms were enforced through retributive sanctions. Such sanctioning served to identify and exclude offenders, to treat them as outsiders.

Such societies are gradually superseded by more complex formations characterised by what Durkheim referred to as organic forms of solidarity. Within such societies there is a relatively highly differentiated division of labour, and social solidarity is organised around difference rather than similarity. Such social transformation is reflected in the systems of law and punishment characteristic of the different types of social solidarity. Under mechanical solidarity the primary function of law is to enforce uniformity and to limit or even prevent deviation from the common pattern. Under conditions of organic solidarity on the other hand the primary function of law is to regulate the interactions between the different parts of society and between members.

What we have here, then, is a sophisticated attempt to examine how social bonds are reciprocal ties and obligations are maintained (a) in times of very rapid social change, and (b) in societies that are highly internally differentiated. Durkheim was writing in the aftermath of the industrial revolution, in a period in which all major writers (as varied as Karl Marx and Charles Dickens) were struggling to understand the nature of the social transformation in front of them. In this regard, Durkheim confronted head-on one of the great questions of the moment: what is it that will provide social solidarity and coherence in these new times? One can see similar questions being asked of globalisation now. Is the new global order breaking down all the old certainties? Will these new social arrangements bring with them the collapse of social structures? Are we losing the ability to regulate behaviour and maintain order?

The transformation of social systems toward those characterised by organic solidarity is accompanied by a decline in retributivism. This is viewed by Durkheim as involving an increasing valuation of human dignity—akin to what Elias (1978) referred to as a 'civilizing process'

Now, for Durkheim, the modernisation of society, involving a shift from mechanical to organic solidarity, is far from straightforward. In particular, there is a danger, Durkheim argued, that the forms of regulation that bound less complex societies together wouldn't be replaced quickly and effectively enough by new forms

Emile Durkheim (1858–1917)

Copyright in the Public Domain.

Born in eastern France, Durkheim was the son of a rabbi. Indeed, not only his father, but his grandfather and great-grandfather had been rabbis also, and it was expected that Emile would also follow this path.

He studied at the Ecole Normale Superieure and in his early twenties became a teacher of philosophy. By the age of 29 he got a job at the University of Bordeaux where he taught the very first sociology course in France. It wasn't until 1902, when Durkheim was 44, that he became a Professor of Philosophy and Education at the University of Paris.

The *Division of Labour in Society, arguably* Durkheim's greatest work, was published in 1893, and this was quickly followed by *The Rules of Sociological Method* (1895), *Suicide: A Study in Sociology* (1897) and, later, *The Elementary Forms of the Religious Life* (1912).

Durkheim died in 1917 not long after his son, also a gifted academic, had been killed in the First World War.

of moral regulation. One potential consequence of this is *anomie,* where moral constraints are insufficient effectively to limit individual desires. The link with crime and deviance is clear. We return to anomie below.

Assessing Durkheim

It is not only through the notion of anomie that Durkheim has exerted a very particular and profound influence over criminological theory. More generally, his observation about the 'normality' of crime and the importance of societal reaction in framing what is to be considered criminal are now cornerstones of the sociological approach to the study of crime and crime control. Smith (2008:339) argues that the following seven key insights in criminology arguably have their origins in Durkheim's work:

- Deviance is, in part, the product of weak moral integration and poor social regulation.
- Deviance is a social fact that is patterned and regular when viewed in aggregate. In a sense we can think of a certain amount of crime as 'normal' and 'inevitable', perhaps even as 'useful' for any given social organisation.
- Definitions of deviance and perceptions of its severity are cross-culturally variable.
- Social change, such as the transition to modernity, can often generate anomie and with this an increase in levels of crime.
- The law reflects the cultural values of a society, although the strength of this connection can of course vary.

- Crime is meaningful. It generates emotional responses and is perceived as a violation of a moral code.
- Punishment has a ritual and expressive dimension.

Before moving on, however, there are a number of criticisms of Durkheim's work that have been made and which we must briefly consider. First, Durkheim's work arguably underplays the way in which systems of punishment are shaped by the nature and distribution of power within society. That is to say, it is possible, as radical critics might argue, that rather than punitive responses tending to be directed at actions which transgress generally held social norms, it is actions which run counter to the interests of particular groups that tend to be punished. Second, but relatedly, the assumption of consensus which underpins the notion of conscience collective is precisely that, an assumption, rather than something that Durkheim demonstrated empirically.

Third, it is debatable whether Durkheim's arguments about the functional utility of crime actually apply to all types of crime. Thus, it is possible to identify criminal acts that simply don't call forth the type of moral outrage that Durkheim took to be illustrative of challenges to the collective conscience. Finally, critics have also pointed to the circularity in the functionalist character of elements of Durkheim's explanation of why laws are enacted and criminals punished. As Garland (1983: 52-3) notes:

> The discussion of crime reproduces all the circularity of Durkheim's basic arguments. We are told that crime consists in acts 'universally disapproved by members of each society'. Clearly, as an empirical statement this is questionable; one must presume that the offenders themselves do not wholly partake in this universal spirit of disapproval. However, Durkheim tells us that he refers only to healthy consciences, that is, to those which share the sentiments of the collective conscience. But since violation of the collective conscience is the very quality which gives certain acts the attribute of criminality, the appeal to 'healthy consciences' as a proof is an empty form of tautology.

Merton and Anomie

One influential commentator judged Robert K. Merton's anomie theory 'the single most influential formulation in the sociology of deviance' (Clinard, 1964: 10). It has however fallen 'distinctly out of fashion, perhaps permanently so in any explicit form. Like functionalism, from which it derives, it has become a routine conceptual folly for students to demolish before moving on to more rewarding ground' (Downes and Rock, 2003: 104). Indeed, Downes and Rock argue that it has been Robert Merton's version of anomie theory that has been subject to the most vociferous criticism, rather than Durkheim's approach.

Although Durkheim was by no means entirely consistent in his portrayal of anomie, as we have seen he viewed it as the product of rapid social change unaccompanied by corresponding growth in systems of moral regulation. Anomie for Durkheim, then, is that state of affairs brought about by insufficient normative regulation. Building on this idea, but within the specific context of having lived through the depression experienced by America in the 1930s, Robert Merton saw anomie as resulting from the absence of alignment between socially desired aspirations, such as wealth, and the means available to people to achieve such objectives. Merton, like the researchers of the Chicago School that we will meet in the next chapter, sought a more sociological explanation of crime as a corrective to the generally individualised explanations that still tended to dominate. Merton's aim was to:

> discover how some social structures exert a definite pressure upon certain persons in the society to engage in non-conforming rather than conforming conduct. If we can locate groups peculiarly subject to such pressures, we should expect to find high rates of deviant conduct in these groups, not because the human beings comprising them are compounded of distinctive biological tendencies but because they are responding normally to the social situation in which they find themselves. (Merton, 1969: 255)

Merton's theory was built on a critique of particular elements of American culture. The emphasis on consumption and the tendency towards greed, ever-increasing material desires and dissatisfaction, which some critics would take to be defining negative characteristics of modern capitalism, also lie at the heart of much of anomie theory's portrayal of the sources of deviance. It was this focus that distinguished it from the ecological approach adopted by many of the Chicago School sociologists with their concern with neighbourhoods and the social structure of the city. In an oft-quoted statement, Merton observed that 'a cardinal American virtue, ambition, promotes a cardinal American vice, deviant behaviour' (Merton, 1949: 137, quoted in Downes and Rock, 2003: 94). At the heart of this is the 'American dream'.

Anomie and the 'American Dream'

At the core of the ideology of the American dream was the idea that prosperity and success were available to all those who worked hard. The depression of the 1930s, however, had given the lie to the idea of America as a prosperous, egalitarian society, though President Roosevelt's New Deal sought to maintain faith in the vision of opportunity for all. Mertonian anomie theory emerged in this period. It got a further boost in the early 1960s from the Kennedy government and its concern with civil liberties and opportunity. According to Merton any society identifies certain culturally preferred goals. In American society this is material success:

> It would of course be fanciful to assert that accumulated wealth stands alone as a symbol of success just as it would be fanciful to deny that Americans assign it a high place in their scale of values. In some large measure money has been consecrated as value in itself…. [However it is] acquired, fraudulently or institutionally, it can be used to purchase the same goods and services. (Merton, 1968: 190)

However, not everyone can realistically achieve such goals. There is not the means for everyone to succeed. The dissonance between socially desired ends and limited means produces a 'strain to anomie'—effectively a range of behavioural adaptations to these social and psychological circumstances. In Merton's terms this strain to anomie is the product of the 'contradiction between the cultural emphasis on pecuniary ambition and the social bars to full opportunity'. Merton summarised his argument as follows:

> The dominant pressure of group standards of success is, therefore, on the gradual attenuation of legitimate, but by and large ineffective, strivings and the increasing use of illegitimate, but more or less effective, expedients of vice and crime. The cultural demands made on persons in this situation are incompatible.

On the one hand, they are asked to orient their conduct toward the prospect of accumulating wealth and on the other, they are largely denied effective opportunities to do so institutionally. The consequences of such structural inconsistency are psychopathological personality and /or antisocial conduct, and/or revolutionary activities. (Merton, 1938: 71)

Mode of adaptation	Culture goals	Institutionalised means
I Conformity	+	+
II Innovation	+	–
III Ritualism	–	+
IV Retreatism	–	–
V Rebellion	+ / –	+ / –

Table 12.2. Merton's typology of modes of individual adaptation

The bulk of individuals will continue to conform, he suggested, despite the strain to anomie. However, 'certain phases of social structure generate the circumstances in which infringement of social codes constitutes a "normal" response' (Merton, 1938: 672). The strain to anomie is stronger for certain social groups than others. The social structure effectively limits the possibilities for some groups more than it does for others—in short, the lower classes. In this fashion, it has been argued that Merton is forwarding a *Cultural* argument to explain the nature of crime in American society and a *structural* argument to explain its uneven distribution (Vold *et al.,* 2002).

For those who don't conform there are four *deviant adaptations:* innovation, ritualism, retreatism and rebellion. These are distinguished by whether culturally prescribed goals and institutionally available means are accepted or rejected. The five sets of relationships can be illustrated as follows (see Table 12.2).

Innovation is the application of illegitimate means to the achievement of socially approved and legitimate ends. The innovator accepts the social goal of material success, but has not the legitimate means for achieving it: 'such anti-social behaviour is in a sense "called forth" by certain conventional values of the culture *and* by the class structure involving differential access to the approved opportunities for legitimate, prestige-bearing pursuit of the culture goals' (Merton, 1938: 679). Deviance is the consequence.

In this sense, much organised crime shares both the overall aims, and indeed many of the means, of standard capitalist activity. It differs in that it operates outside the law in some important ways. Innovators accept the cultural goals, but don't use the standard institutionalised means. The protagonists in a number of Hollywood portrayals of American Mafiosi—Francis Ford Coppola's *Godfather* movies and Scorsese's *Goodfellas,* for example—continue to espouse many traditional values and goals whilst using culturally illegitimate means for their achievement. Confronted with the 'absence of realistic opportunities for advancement' Merton argued, some people are particularly vulnerable to the 'promises of power and high income from organized vice, rackets and crime' (Merton, 1968: 199).

Arguably, it is in the area of corporate and white-collar crime that this particular adaptation often appears. Accounts of insider trading, corporate fraud, major failures in industrial health and safety are all replete with illustrations of individuals focused upon achieving material and career success, whilst failing to operate within rules and laws. Protagonists like Gordon Gekko in the 1987 movie *Wall Street* and Sherman McCoy in Tom Wolfe's novel *Bonfire of the Vanities,* published in the same year, captured the greed and rampant materialism of that era— a period many critics felt promoted the idea of success at all costs (Downes, 1989).

By contrast, *ritualism* concerns those circumstances in which the cultural goals disappear—they are lost sight of - whilst attachment to the institutional means becomes seemingly ever stronger. It is deviant because, although the means conform to social expectations, the search for the socially valued goal of financial success has been abandoned. This is a routinised nature of elements of bourgeois life, a sticking to the rules at all costs, and a scaling down of aims to the point where they can be achieved effortlessly. Merton's example here was the bureaucratic mindset.

Retreatism, the least common of the adaptations according to Merton, involves the rejection of both the objectives and means, and concerns people who 'are in society but not of it'. Merton's examples are the hobo, the drug taker and elements of the tramp played so famously by Charlie Chaplin: 'always the butt of a crazy and bewildering world in which he has no place and from which he constantly runs away into a contented do nothingness' (Merton, 1949: 25 1). As such it may be characterised by drug use/ addiction, alcoholism, homelessness and so on. It is an adaptation, Merton felt, that tends not to involve the victimization of others, and is often a private, rather than a public, response. Retreatism became something of a subcultural style in the 1960s with the advent of the hippie movement.

The final adaptation is *rebellion.* This is a more radical alternative, seeking to replace both the means and the ends as a way of resolving the strain to anomie. This might be the political radical proposing an entirely new set of culturally approved goals and means for their achievement. Unlike some criminological theories, Merton was explicit in his acknowledgement that anomie theory was 'designed to account for some, not all, forms of deviant behaviour customarily described as criminal or delinquent' (Merton, 1968: 195).

Assessing Merton's Anomie Theory

Despite its enormous influence, it was some two decades before Merton's famous article began to resonate powerfully through criminology. It did so partly as a result of Albert Cohen's *Delinquent Boys* (1955), Richard Cloward and Lloyd Ohlin's *Delinquency and Opportunity* (1960), as well as Merton's reworking of the original article. As Downes and Rock argue, anomie theory has had an odd shelf-life: for its first few decades after Merton's original exposition in 1938 it was accepted rather uncritically. Since the early 1960s, however, the reverse has been true with its rejection arguably being more critical than is deserved. Again, rather like functionalism, anomie theory may not be referred to explicitly very much these days, but seasoned observers can see its footprints everywhere:

> It has an anonymous presence in jock Young's essay in labelling theory, *The Drugtakers,* and appears under its own name as one of the principal themes in his account of the making of left realism in the 1980s. It is the invisible prop to the Birmingham Centre for Contemporary Cultural Studies' radical work on class, youth, and deviance in Britain. (Downes and Rock, 2003: 105)

Numerous potential shortcomings have been identified in Merton's anomie theory (we return to this at the end of the chapter). As Akers and Brezina (2010: 97) observe, 'surprisingly, Merton's theory has not been well tested. A proper test of theory would require measures of the relative emphasis placed on monetary success and the extent to which individuals achieved or expected to achieve such success.'

Although Merton's work and Durkheim's were only 'loosely coupled' (Cullen and Messner, 2011), some of the criticisms of Mertonian anomie theory reflect differences between the two uses of the term 'anomie'. There was, as we have seen, something of a shift in the use of the term anomie, which is neatly captured in the following passage from Steven Box (1981: 97–8):

> Merton's analysis...appears to follow Durkheim's usage of the concept of anomie. But the appearance is, I think, deceptive, for during the argument Merton shifts his meaning of anomie away from a Durkheimian position towards one which is peculiarly his own. Initially, Merton appears to be discussing the *emphasis on normative means* of achieving cultural values. . . . However, later in his analysis, Merton appears to shift the focus of his attention away from an *emphasis on normative means to differential access to opportunity structures,* such as schools and employment organizations, through which cultural values can be properly and legally realized. . . . The emphasis on normative means is fundamentally Durkheimian because, by implication, it suggests that human aspirations have to be regulated and channelled.

Merton's initial use of the term was faithful to this conception, Box argues, in that at its core the emphasis is upon an overriding cultural goal—worldly material success. The difficulty for Merton was how to explain the apparent overinvolvement of people from lower social classes in criminal and deviant activity if this cultural goal was universally accepted.

Robert K. Merton (1910–2003)

Born Meyer Robert Schkolnick in Philadelphia on American Independence day 1910, Merton's parents were working-class Jewish immigrants from Eastern Europe. The family lived above the father's dairy products shop in South Philadelphia. It was common at this time to Americanize names and Merton initially changed his to Robert K. Merlin (as a young man he worked as a magician) before a friend advised him that it was rather 'hackneyed'.

Inquiring as to why Merton should have focused his attention of the unintended consequences of the American dream, Lilly and colleagues point to his social origins. Born into considerable poverty, Merton gained a scholarship to Temple University in Philadelphia, published his famous article 'Social Structure and Anomie' whilst teaching at Harvard University, aged 28, and became a Professor at Columbia University three years later. Though speculative, 'this personal journey', they suggest, 'may have helped focus Merton's attention on the prominent role in the national culture of social ascent' (Lilly et al., 2002: 53).

Among others, he coined the phrases 'self-fulfilling prophecy', 'role model' and 'reference group'. Merton is also credited with being the creator of the idea of focus groups as a research tool. Merton's son, Robert C. Merton, won the Nobel Prize for Economics in 1997.

Merton needed to transform the conception of anomie; he did this by shifting from an underemphasis on normative means to a discussion on the differential access to legitimate opportunity structures, particularly education and occupational opportunities. Anomie was no longer a condition of deregulation or norm-lessness, but one of *relative deprivation*. Individual motivation behind deviant behaviour emerged out of the frustrations of such deprivations and these emotions existed because individuals had internalized the 'American Dream'. (Box, 1981: 99-100)

Later strain theory

It was Albert Cohen's work which picked up on Merton's theory and introduced the notions of culture and subculture to the study of delinquency. Cohen was critical of Merton's approach because of its failure in his eyes to explain the nature or content of juvenile delinquency. Relative deprivation, identified as the major impetus to adult deviance in Merton's usage of the term anomie, is less useful, Cohen argued, in explaining juvenile motivations. Crucially, rather than being oriented towards the legitimate goals of adult society, many young people engage in behaviour which is 'nonutilitarian, malicious and negativistic' (1955: 25). It is not material success that delinquents are searching for, but meaning in some other way. We return to this idea in greater detail in the next chapter when we consider subcultural theory.

Rather than anomie, Cohen suggests that competition and frustration around status is the key to understanding youthful delinquency. It is here the parallels with Merton are visible. Cohen argues that in contemporary society issues of status are largely settled according to criteria such as educational success. However, not everyone is equally placed in this competition. The terms and criteria used by teachers and others are far from straightforwardly objective and they distinguish between children in both moral and social terms, i.e., crudely, according to middle-class standards. Significant proportions of working-class children are therefore faced with a number of status difficulties and linked feelings of shame or guilt on the one hand and resentment on the other. These young people are placed under severe strain. The issue is how such difficulties can be resolved. One solution is to form attachments with others in similar situations, to form gangs or other groupings and to reject some of the core adult values. This is the basis, in Cohen's terms, for the formation of delinquent youth subcultures.

Cloward and Ohlin

Influenced by Merton and by Albert Cohen, as well as by Edwin Sutherland's notion of differential association, the next milestone in strain theory was Richard Cloward and lloyd Ohlin's *Delinquency and Opportunity*, published in 1960. Their debt to Merton can be seen in one of their central questions (1960: 32): 'Under what conditions will persons experience strains and tensions that lead to delinquent solutions?' At the heart of their answer is the observation that in 'a system that stresses ability as the basis of advancement, the failures who view themselves as equal in ability to those who succeed tend to feel unjustly deprived' (1960: 117). That is to say, where people are led to believe that the ability they have will enable them to gain access to education and thereby to occupational success, but where opportunities are limited and decisions are frequently based on other criteria such as class, ethnicity and sex, the outcome is that a proportion of the population feel anger at their unreasonable exclusion. The solution again is the rejection of core middle-class values.

However, as we noted earlier, Cloward and Ohlin also sought to incorporate elements of Sutherland's differential association theory. They do so by arguing that there are numerous means of resolving the adjustment or *strain* problems. The particular delinquent solution adopted will depend upon the nature of illegal or criminal means available in the particular environment. In this way:

> The concept of differential opportunity structures permits us to unite the theory of anomie, which recognizes the concept of differentials in access to legitimate means, and the 'Chicago tradition', in which the concept of differentials in access to illegitimate means is implicit . . . . The approach permits us to ask, for example, how the relative ability of illegitimate opportunities affects the resolution of adjustment problems leading to deviant behaviour. (Cloward and Ohlin, 1960; reproduced in Jacoby, 2004: 286-7)

Strain theory was remarkably influential in its time. Lloyd Ohlin, for example, was appointed by Robert Kennedy when he was Attorney General, to help develop Federal crime policy, and his and Cloward's work later formed the basis for much of President Lyndon Johnson's action in the war on poverty in the mid-1960s. The apparent lack of success of many of these programmes led President Nixon to abandon them and led many critics to focus their attention on strain theory.

General Strain Theory

More recently, Robert Agnew has sought to build on Merton's ideas. Agnew suggests that there are at least four reasons why strain theory had declined in popularity:

- It has tended to focus on lower-class delinquency.
- It has neglected all but the most conventional goals (middle-class status and wealth).
- It overlooked barriers to achievement other than social stratification (these might include gender, race, intelligence and many others).
- It has found it difficult to explain why some people who experienced strain didn't turn to criminal activity. Arguably, strain and frustration are experienced by many who continue to conform.

As a consequence Agnew sought to develop a more general strain theory, though his specific focus was upon adolescent delinquency and drug use. His extension and elaboration of strain theory involves the identification of two types of strain over and above the central problem of failing to achieve one's personal goals. The first, slightly at variance with Merton's theory, he suggests arises from the 'actual or anticipated removal (loss) of positively valued stimuli from an individual' (1992: 57). The withholding of something that is valued- privileges, opportunities, relationships -is the source of strain. The second form of strain is the result of 'actual or anticipated presentation of negative or noxious stimuli' (1992: 58) such as relationships at home, work or elsewhere, that are abusive.

The greater the extent of strain, the more likely the adaptive response is to be deviant. In this context, delinquency and drug use are means of coping with negative relationships and emotions. The likelihood of deviant adaptations may be offset, Agnew argues, by the existence of support from other sources, the availability of alternative goals, and personal characteristics such as high levels of self-control and fear of

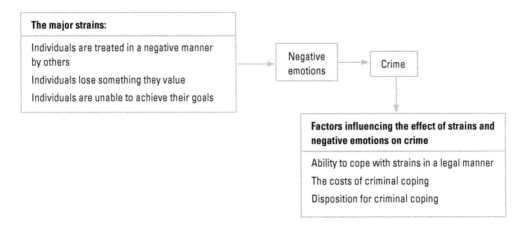

FIGURE 12.1. The central propositions of general strain theory
Source : Agnew (2006: 19).

adverse consequences. Relatedly, Agnew (2001) identifies a number of factors that increase the likelihood that strain will lead to crime and delinquency:

- Where the strain is perceived to be 'unjust'; where people feel that they have been treated unfairly they are more likely to become angry, and anger, according to Agnew's strain theory, is linked with increased likelihood of offending.
- When strain is high in magnitude it is more difficult to ignore and to manage in ways that are legitimate.
- Where the strain is caused by, or is associated with, low sodal control it is more likely to result in a deviant adaptation.
- Strains may also lower levels of social control.
- Where the strain creates pressure to engage in 'criminal coping'- such as strain induced by criminal victimization leading to a desire for revenge.

General strain theory identifies a range of strains that are particularly condudve to crime (Akers and Brezina, 2010: 103-4):

- *Parental rejection-* Parents who reject their children do not express love or affection for them, show little interest in them, provide little support to them and often display hostility toward them.
- *Supervision/discipline* that is erratic, excessive and/or harsh (use of humiliation/insults, threats, screaming and/or physical punishments).
- *Child abuse and neglect,* including physical abuse; sexual abuse; and the failure to provide adequate food, shelter, medical care and affection/attention (neglect).
- *Negative secondary school experiences,* including low grades, negative relations with teachers, and the experience of school as boring and a waste of time.
- *Abusive peer relations,* including insults, ridicule, threats, attempts to coerce and physical assaults.
- *Work at jobs in the secondary labour market* Such jobs commonly involve unpleasant tasks, little autonomy, coercive control, low pay, few benefits, little prestige and very limited opportunities for advancement.

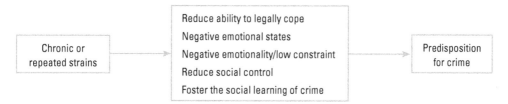

Figure 8.2 The mechanisms by which chronic or repeated strains increase the predisposition for crime
Source: Agnew (2006).

FIGURE 12.2. The mechanisms by which chronic or repeated strains increase the predisposition for crime
Source: Agnew (2006).

- *Unemployment,* especially when it is chronic and blamed on others.
- *Marital problems,* including frequent conflicts and verbal and physical abuse.
- *The failure to achieve selected goals,* including thrills/exdtement, personal autonomy, masculine status and the desire for much money in a short period of time.
- *Criminal victimisation.*
- *Residence in severely deprived communities,* which is associated with exposure to a host of strains- including criminal victimization and economic problems.
- *Homelessness.*
- *Discrimination* based on characteristics such as race/ethnidty, gender and religion.

What is particularly problematic is chronic or repeated strains. Agnew argues that such chronic strains are likely to create a predisposition to crime. They do this in a number of ways. Through repetition they reduce the ability of individuals to cope with strain. Thus, if one is regularly bullied it may, over time, become increasingly difficult to resist resorting to violence in response. Chronic strains may lead to the development of negative emotional traits such as anger, depression, fear and frustration, each of which may be condudve to crime. Agnew quotes a passage from Elijah Anderson's *Code of the Street* in support of this:

> Frustrations mount over bills, food, and, at times, drink, cigarettes, and drugs. Some tend toward self-destructive behaviour; many streetoriented women are crack-addicted ('on the pipe'), alcoholic, or repeatedly involved in complicated relationships with the men who abuse them. In addition, the seeming intractability of their situation, caused in large part by the lack of well-paying jobs and the persistence of racial discrimination, has engendered deep-seated bitterness and anger in many of the most desperate and poorest blacks, especially young people ... the frustrations of persistent poverty shorten the fuse in such people, contributing to a lack of patience with anyone, child or adult, who irritates them. (Anderson, 1990: 10–11)

Agnew summarises these arguments in Figure 12.2.

Messner and Rosenfeld

A variant on Agnew's general strain theory, called *institutional anomie theory*, is proposed by Messner and Rosenfeld (2001). Focusing, like Merton, on the 'American dream' they suggest an anomie sodety has been created which privileges success over all other socialy approved goals:

> A primary task for noneconomic institutions such as the family and schools is to inculcate beliefs, values and commitments other than those of the marketplace. But as these noneconomic institutions are relatively devalued and forced to accommodate to economic considerations, and as they are penetrated by economic standards, they are less able to fulfil their distinctive socialization functions successfully. (Messner and Rosenfeld, 2001: 150)

At its simplest, their argument is that 'the American Dream itself exerts pressures toward crime by encouraging an anomic cultural environment, an environment in which people are encouraged to adopt an "anything goes" mentality in the pursuit of personal goals' (2001: 61). There are a number of specific features of the American dream, they suggest, that are crucial. These are:

- the emphasis on *achievement* and on the winner takes-all mentality;
- the *individualism* that focuses attention on rights rather than responsibilities;
- the *materialism* that fetishises wealth;
- the fact that these values permeate the whole of society—which they call *universalism*.

The effect of these cultural values is to privilege economic goals over others—for example, educa- tion becomes increasingly devoted to servicing the labour market and the family becomes increasingly dominated by work. The tendency to focus on ends rather than means makes it increasingly difficult for institutions such as schools and families to exert appropriate social control. Messner and Rosenfeld's argument owes much to earlier strain theory but also reflects the critical criminologist's discontent with the nature of contemporary capitalism. In addition, they reflect Durkheim's central point about the *normality* of crime:

> There is nothing necessarily 'sick', pathological, dysfunctional, or disorganized about a society organized to produced high rates of crime...a particular level and type of crime are a normal outcome of a specified set of cultural and social arrangements.... A *low* level of predatory crime would be a sign of 'something wrong' with a society that places a premium on the individual competitive pursuit of financial gain, encourages people to create ever more efficient means of besting others, and offers comparatively little protection or comfort to the unsuccessful. We would be on the lookout for something out of the ordinary, something abnormal, about unusually low or falling crime rates in a society organized for crime. (Rosenfeld and Messner, in Henry and Lanier, 2005: 168)

In contemporary society, crime, for Messner and Rosenfeld, is a product of the dominance of freemarket economics, its elevation of material success above all other goals and its cultural tendency toward anomie. Social controls are weakened and the use of illegitimate means to attain culturally desired goals increases as such means themselves become progressively legitimised. They argue that societies which protect their members from the worst excesses of free-market economics therefore tend to have lower crime rates than others where there is less restriction on the market. Recent research (Downes and Hansen, 2006; Cavadino and Dignan, 2006) tends to provide support for just such a proposition. Thus, Downes and Hansen (2006) in a study of crime rates and welfare spending across 18 societies concluded that:

> countries that spend a greater proportion of GDP on welfare have lower imprisonment rates and that this relationship has become stronger over the last 15 years. The consistency in these findings across the United States and the other 17 countries studied makes it difficult to believe that this relationship is simply accidental or coincidental.

Assessing Strain Theory

As we noted at the outset, in many respects strain theory has fallen out of fashion. It had major influence in the 1960s but has waned since, though Agnew's general strain theory has revitalised discussion of such ideas in some quarters. Nevertheless, strain theories contain a number of important features and it is important to recognise them.

- They draw our attention to the social, cultural and economic circumstances that lead to crime.
- They point to the *necessary* relationship between particular forms of social organisation and particular levels of crime.
- Merton's formulation drew attention to the unintended consequences of the social goal of individual economic achievement. Critics of the market society and of consumer capitalism are in many respects working in a similar tradition.
- Anomie and strain theory's predominant concern with the vulnerability of working-class or poorer communities sits comfortably with the liberal sensibilities of much sociological criminology and, undoubtedly, accounts for some of its intuitive appeal.

There are, however, numerous criticisms of strain theory:

- The tendency to rely on official statistics as an indicator of the nature and distribution of crime and, connected with this, the tendency generally to focus on lower-class crime is argued to be misleading. Strain theory tends to ignore the crimes of the powerful, for example, or simply the crimes of the middle classes.
- It is argued that anomie theory exaggerates the consensus that surrounds financial success as a socially and culturally defined objective; there are other, competing means by which success can be measured. Indeed, Merton dearly recognised the existence in American society of a range of 'counter-cultures' (lower middle-class preference for security over competition; the craftsman's emphasis on skill and 'expressivity' over financial reward) but nevertheless assumed a generalised acceptance of the American dream.
- For the radical theorist, anomie theory fails to look closely enough at the socio-political circumstances of crime. Thus, according to Taylor, Walton and Young, the major shortcoming of Merton's analysis was its failure to go beyond the identification of the central contradiction of American capitalism to ask why the situation existed and continued. They quote Laurie Taylor (1971: 148):

It is as though individuals in society are playing a gigantic fruit machine, but the machine is rigged and only some players are consistently rewarded. The deprived ones then either resort to using foreign coins or magnets to increase their chances of winning (innovation) or play on mindlessly (ritualism), give up the game (retreatism) or propose a new game altogether (rebellion). But in the analysis nobody appeared to ask who put the machine there in the first place and who takes the profits. Criticism of the game is confined to changing the payout sequences so that the deprived can get a better deal. . . . What at first sight looks like a major critique of society ends up by taking the existing society for granted. The necessity of standing outside the present structural/cultural configurations is not just the job of those categorized in the rebellion mode of adaptation—it is also the task of the sociologist.

- In a similar vein, it is argued, again notably by Taylor *et al.,* that anomie theory over-predicts lower-class crime (and, arguably, lower-class *strain*) but it is less clear whether anomie theory is able to account for crimes of the middle class and wealthy.
- It is similarly unclear that the theory can deal with the very wide variety of forms of offending (the wide variety of *adaptations*) that exist—are sexual violence and theft the product of the same strain to anomie that leads to vandalism, for example?
- Early strain theory tends to focus on structural conditions and, consequently, pays relatively little attention to human agency- Agnew's general strain theory endeavours to deal with this criticism.
- The theory underplays the importance of social control (and self-control) in the production and moulding of deviance, i.e. it pays insufficient attention to the particular social circumstances and opportunities which affect crime.
- Merton ignored the possibility of achievements exceeding expectations, rather than simply failing to reach them–what Downes and Rock call the 'anomie of success' (2003: 137).
- Some deviance, rather than being the product of 'strain', appears rather to be part and parcel of the routine operation of work or organisations, or even the state. How, for example, might anomie theory deal with state human rights abuses?

DISCUSSION QUESTIONS

By John M. Stogner

1. Durkheim's emphasis on rapid social change (and its relationship to crime) followed the Industrial Revolution in Europe. What periods of rapid change have occurred since his death? Were these associated with increases in crime?

2. Could Merton's typology of adaptations be applied to other behaviors (e.g., the use of performance-enhancing drugs by athletes)?

3. Critics of Agnew's general strain theory claimed that the theory (particularly its initial form) was not falsifiable. Why might this be the case?

4. How might Messner and Rosenfeld's institutional anomie theory account for changes in American crime rates since World War II?

5. Describe the policy recommendations of each major theoretical work within the anomie/strain perspective.

CHAPTER THIRTEEN

Labelling Theories

ROGER HOPKINS BURKE

STUDENT INTRODUCTION

By John M. Stogner

The following two chapters explore social reactions to behaviors considered deviant and the ramifications of those reactions. Instead of examining what factors influence deviance (or conformity), theories within the labeling perspective present the way in which society responds to certain actions as the critical issue. This is not to say that labeling-based theories do not assist in the explanation of deviance; they clearly present hypotheses about future behavior. One of their central assumptions is that the reactions to a criminal event influence the likelihood of similar events occurring in the future. However, labeling theories primarily examine how certain events come to be considered deviant or illegal and who gets labeled as a criminal, offender, or delinquent for minor violations. Labeling theories often create a negative depiction of the juvenile and adult criminal justice systems—suggesting that they are largely responsible for many of the problems that they are tasked with managing.

Howard Becker's 1963 book, *Outsiders: Studies in the Sociology of Deviance*, can be considered a defining work for the labeling perspective. Becker presents an intriguing view of crime and criminality. Rather than assuming that there are absolute and consistent criteria for deviance, he describes crime as a social construct. He famously argues that "social groups create deviance by making rules whose infraction constitutes deviance." Becker did not consider acts to be deviant, but labeled as deviant by others. Put another way, crimes are only crimes because society has labeled them as such, and criminals are simply those who society has successfully labeled as criminal. Becker explores the nature of these labels and how the powerful can create rules and labels to be applied to those with less power. The reason Becker's work is considered a criminological theory is because he also postulates about the effect of labels on future offending (although he suggests that his work is not a complete or overarching theory). He describes how being labeled as deviant affects the way others react and interact with that individual—eventually affecting how the individual sees himself or herself. "Criminal" or "deviant" eventually becomes a *master status* that influences every social interaction. This may lead to isolation, loss of social capital, blocked vocational opportunities, and increased association with delinquents. Becker argues that, because of the label's direct and indirect effects, some individuals engage in more illicit behavior than they would have if not initially labeled.

As you read the following chapter, carefully explore Becker's arguments and consider what his theory may mean for policy. Also closely examine the descriptions of the works of Frank Tannenbaum and Edwin Lemert; their works are insightful and were instrumental in the development of other labeling-based theories. Consider how social movements and the broader political climates may have influenced their works and that of Becker. To better understand the material, you should evaluate the arguments of labeling theorists using the criteria described in Chapter 1 and contemplate the limitations of their works. Finally, explore the concepts of a *moral panic* and *moral entrepreneurs*. Many legal and policy changes have been driven by elite, interest-group, or grassroots panics—thus affecting what is labeled as deviant in our society.

LABELLING THEORIES
By Roger Hopkins Burke

L abelling theories have their foundations in the various concepts and insights provided by interactionism, phenomenology and ethnomethodology—we encountered above—and focus on three central concerns. First, there is a consideration of why and how it is that some acts come to be defined as deviant or criminal while others do not. Thus, to this end there is an examination of legal codes and practices, and the social and professional interest groups that shape the criminal law. Second, it is recognised that certain people and groups are more likely to attract deviant, criminal and stigmatising labels than others. There is thus an examination of the differential applications of laws and labels by the various social control agencies and the relationship of this to organisational context. Unfortunately, these early, well-known and highly influential labelling theorists—with the limited exception of Becker (1963), Kitsuse (1962), Piliavin and Briar (1964) and Cicourel (1968)—did not address these concerns as thoroughly as they might have done, although they contributed significantly to the development of the radical criminology discussed in the following chapter, while the later far less well-known and significantly less influential labelling theorists such as Hartjen (1974), Ditton (1979) and Arvanites (1992) focus very much on the issue of state power. Most of the energy of the most active phase of the highly influential earlier labelling theory was nevertheless directed towards the third concern that assesses the experience of being labelled for the recipients of the label. We will consider each of these concerns in turn.

The Social Construction of Crime

Before labelling theories achieved prominence, most criminologists had a non-problematic conception of crime. Criminal behaviour was simply a form of activity that violates the criminal law. Once crime was thus defined, theorists—working in the predestined actor model tradition—could concentrate on their main concern of identifying and analysing its causes. This whole approach was nevertheless far too simplistic for proponents of the labelling perspective who argued that what is defined as 'criminal' is not fixed but varies across time, culture and even from one situation to the next. From this perspective, the conventional morality of rules and criminal laws in any given society should be studied and questioned and not merely accepted as self-evident.

Labelling theorists fundamentally argue that no behaviour is *inherently* deviant or criminal, but only comes to be considered so when others confer this label upon the act. Thus, it is not the intrinsic nature of an act, but the nature of the societal reaction that determines whether a 'crime' has taken place. Even the most commonly recognised and serious crime of murder is not universally defined in the sense that anyone who kills another is everywhere and always guilty of murder. The essence of this position is neatly summarised in a well-known passage by Becker (1963: 4) whom, unlike most other labelling theorists, was concerned with the creators and enforcers of criminal labels and categories:

> Social groups create deviance by making the rules whose infraction constitutes deviance, and by applying those rules to particular people and labelling them as outsiders. From this point of view... the deviant is one to whom the label has been successfully applied; deviant behaviour is behaviour that people so label.

Becker argued that rules—including criminal laws—are made by people with power and enforced upon people without power. Thus, even on an everyday level, rules are made by the old for the young, by men for women, by whites for blacks, by the middle class for the working class and we might add here, by schools for their students and parents for their children, an observation to which we return later in this chapter. These rules are often imposed upon the recipients against their will and their own best interests and are legitimised by an ideology that is transmitted to the less powerful in the course of primary and secondary socialisation. As a result of this process, most people internalise and obey the rules without realising—or questioning—the extent to which their behaviour is being decided for them.

Becker also argues that some rules may be cynically designed to keep the less powerful in their place while others may have simply been introduced as the outcome of a sincere—albeit irrational and mistaken—belief on the part of high-status individuals that the creation of a new rule will be beneficial for its intended subjects. Becker termed the people who create new rules for the 'benefit' of the less fortunate 'moral entrepreneurs'.

Becker noted two closely interrelated outcomes of a successful 'moral crusade': first, there is the creation of a new group of 'outsiders', those who infringe the new rule; second, a social control agency emerges charged with enforcing the rule and with the power to impose labels on transgressors, although more often this simply means an extension of police work and power. Eventually the new rule, control agency and 'deviant' social role come to permeate the collective consciousness and are taken for granted with the outcome being the creation of negative stereotypes of those labelled 'deviant'.

Becker (1963) cites the campaign by the US Federal Bureau of Narcotics (FBN) to outlaw marijuana use through the Marijuana Tax Act of 1937 which was justified on the grounds of protecting society—particularly young people—from the ill effects of this drug and relied heavily on propaganda of one sort or another to get its message across. In Becker's view the campaign was undertaken primarily as a means of advancing the organisational interests of the FBN. Moreover, the successful conclusion of the campaign led to 'the creation of a new fragment of the moral constitution of society, its code of right and wrong' (Becker, 1963: 145).

Other studies have looked at the process whereby previously 'acceptable' forms of behaviour have been brought within the remit of the criminal law. Platt (1969) showed how contemporary approaches to 'juvenile delinquency'—indeed even the very concept itself—were the outcome of a nineteenth century moral crusade undertaken by largely upper-class women. This successful campaign established juveniles as a separate category of offender with their own courts, which in turn enabled the scope of the powers of intervention enjoyed by the state to be extended beyond mere breaches of the criminal law to cover 'status offences' such as truancy and promiscuity.

Tierney's (1982) analysis of domestic violence also provides evidence of the process of criminalisation. She argues that 'wife battering' only emerged as an important social issue worthy of criminal justice intervention after the mid-1970s, mainly because of the increasing strength of the women's movement and the determination to secure the provision of refuges, legislation and other measures aimed at protecting women.

In short, what these and similar studies show, is not the inherent harm of behaviour or its pervasiveness that prompts changes in the law, but rather the concerted efforts of sufficiently motivated and powerful social groups to redefine the boundaries of what is considered acceptable and legal.

Others have adopted a macro perspective in order to explain these pro- cesses. Thus, Erikson (1962) draws upon Durkheim in arguing that all social systems place certain boundaries on culturally permissible behaviour and deviancy is simply that which is defined as crossing these parameters. Indeed, deviant behaviour may be the only way of *marking* these boundaries. Thus, transactions between deviants and social control agents are 'boundary maintenance mechanisms' which attract a good deal of publicity and by acting outside of these system boundaries deviants demonstrate to society where the perimeters lie while, at the same time, giving those inside a sense of identity or 'belongingness'. These processes in turn help to preserve social stability. Thus, in viewing deviance as essentially 'boundary maintenance activity', the work of Erikson marks a point of convergence between the labelling perspective and the functionalism of Durkheim.

Quinney (1970) also employed a macro sociological perspective but one that combined labelling theory with conflict theory, differential association and deviant subculture theories. He was also influ- enced by Durkheim's notion of mechanical and organic solidarity in proposing two ideal types of society (or social organisation): *singular* and *segmental*. According to Quinney, in a singular or homogeneous society all crime must necessarily occur outside any value system since by definition all members of the society adhere to this value system. In a segmental or heterogeneous society some segments will share common values with others, but because there is unlikely to be a complete consensus, value systems will be in conflict to a certain extent. Thus, the criminal laws and their enforcement are a product of this conflict and the associated unequal distribution of political power.

Quinney argues that society is segmentally organised or pluralistic and, therefore, the criminal law tends to represent the values of politically powerful sections of society. Moreover, he suggests a direct relation between the possibility of someone being labelled as criminal and their relative position in the social structure.

The Recipients of Deviant Labels

It is conventional wisdom that those who break the law will be labelled as criminal. Becker (1963) nevertheless exposed the inadequacy of this perception, noting that the innocent are sometimes falsely accused, and more importantly, only some of those who violate the criminal law are eventually arrested and processed through the system. Kitsuse (1962) found—in a study of homosexuality that has much wider criminological ramifications—that it is not the behaviour *per se* that is the central issue. It is the interactional process through which behaviour is both defined as deviant and through which sanctions are initiated. Thus distinguishing deviants from non-deviants is not primarily a matter of behaviour but is contingent upon 'circumstance or situation, social and personal biography, and the bureaucratically organised activities of social control' (Kitsuse, 1962: 256).

A number of important studies conducted in the USA confirmed that the actual behaviour is not the only factor in determining whether a deviant or criminal label is conferred. Official responses are shaped by a range of extra- legal variables, such as appearance, demeanour, ethnic group and age, for example, Piliavin and Briar (1964) looked at police encounters with juveniles and found that arrest decisions were based largely on physical cues—manner, dress and general appearance—from which the officer inferred the character of the youth. *Structural* factors, such as gender, social class, ethnic group, and time of day were also significant, thus a young, working-class, black male in a 'high delinquency area' at night was seen to have a very high chance of being at least stopped and questioned, if not arrested. The young man is quite simply *assumed* to be delinquent unless he can prove otherwise (Piliavin and Briar, 1964: 206). More recent studies undertaken in the UK have also shown that some police officers show class and/or race bias in the performance of their duties (see for example Smith and Gray, 1986; Institute of Race Relations, 1987).

Cicourel (1968) found that in the course of their interactions with juveniles, the 'background expectations' of the police—that is, their commonsensical theories as to the typical delinquent—led them to concentrate on certain 'types' of individuals. A further factor in determining how that encounter developed was found to be dependent on how the individual officer defined his or her own role. Those who defined their role in terms of a 'due process' model that emphasises the rights of the defendant attempted to follow the *letter* of the law and, therefore, tended to react only to specific, concrete evidence of the commission of a crime. In contrast, when officers perceived their role primarily in terms of a 'crime control' model that considers the control of crime to be of primary importance they were more concerned with the *spirit* of the law. Thus, they were more likely to respond on the basis of their subjective definition of a situation and the personalities involved.

Cicourel found this process to be essentially class-biased, as it was generally working-class areas and their inhabitants that most closely mirrored the typifications and expectations of the police. Moreover, other criminal justice practitioners, such as probation officers, social workers, court officials and the organisational context within which they work reinforced such practices. Cicourel found probation officers and social workers subscribed to a theory of delinquency causation that focused on factors such as 'broken homes', 'permissive parenting' or 'poverty'. Thus, juveniles with this sort of background were seen as the likeliest candidates for a delinquent career and were often, albeit unwittingly, launched upon one. These findings had serious implications for the validity of crime statistics.

Many criminologists from quite different perspectives had previously acknowledged that official statistics were not a wholly accurate reflection of the reality of crime, for example, there was much concern over the hidden figure of unrecorded crime. Official statistics had been widely viewed as reasonably objective and thus providing a reliable basis for discerning patterns in crime and suggesting associations. From a labelling perspective official statistics were seen to be just another interpretation of the world and their only utility lay in the light they inadvertently shed on the agencies of social control that 'constructed' them. Quinney (1970) suggested four societal structures—age, gender, class and ethnic group—that would enhance the likelihood of someone receiving a criminal label and thus, there is a high probability that a young black working-class male will be defined as deviant. Moreover, the reality that this group is over-represented in the official crime statistics is not surprising since these figures are produced by agencies whose personnel, operating criteria and rationale are drawn from the more politically powerful segments of society. What Quinney was essentially arguing is that some people have the facilities for applying stigmatising labels to other people, ostensibly because these other people violate norms the labellers wish to uphold. This is only possible because these others are identified as members of society with little or no political power.

The Consequences of Labelling for the Recipients

It was noted earlier that labelling theories have for the most part concentrated on their third area of concern which is assessing the consequences of the labelling process for the future conduct of the recipient and this aspect is certainly the most widely discussed and best documented.

Frank Tannenbaum (1938)—who is usually regarded as founder of the labelling perspective—noted that of the many young males who break the law only some are apprehended. His 'dramatisation of evil' hypothesis described the process whereby a community first defines the *actions* of an individual as evil, but eventually goes on to define the *individual himself* as evil, thus casting suspicion on all his future actions. The evil is further 'dramatised' by separating the individual from his usual group and administering specialised treatment to 'punish' or 'cure' the evil. This leads to further isolation and the confirmation and internalisation of his new 'tag'. Eventually he will redefine his self-image in line with the opinions and expectations of others in the community and thereby come to perceive himself as criminal. This idea that in reacting to people as 'criminal', society actually encourages them to become so, and that criminal justice intervention can deepen criminality is the central contention of the labelling approach.

Edwin Lemert (1951) made a crucial distinction between *primary* and *secondary* deviance. The former—with affiliations to the predestined actor model—could arise out of a variety of sociocultural, psychological or even physiological factors. However, because these initial acts are often extremely tentative and certainly not part of an organised way of life, offenders can easily rationalise them as a temporary aberration or see it as part of a socially acceptable role, for example, a worker may observe that everyone pilfers a little from work. Thus such behaviour will be of only marginal significance in terms of the status and self-concept of the individual concerned. In short, primary deviants do not view their deviance as central to themselves and do not consider themselves to be deviant.

If, however, these initial activities are subject to societal reaction—and with each act of primary deviance the offender becomes progressively more stigmatised through 'name calling, labelling or stereotyping'—then a crisis may occur. One way of resolving this crisis is for the individual to accept their deviant status and organise their life and identity around the facts of deviance and it is at this stage that the person becomes a 'secondary deviant'. In short, it is proposed that a youth who steals something and is not caught may be less likely to persist in this behaviour than one that is apprehended and officially sanctioned. Deviance is simply the end result of a process of human interaction. Primary deviance may or may not develop into secondary deviance. It is the number of criminal transgressions and the intensity and hostility of societal reaction that determines the outcome.

It was with the influential work of Becker (1963), Erikson (1966) and Kitsuse (1962)—and their use of Merton's concept of the 'self-fulfilling prophecy': a false definition of a situation, evoking a new behaviour that makes the original false assumption come true—that the labelling perspective was to gain widespread popularity. These writers argued that most offenders are falsely defined as criminal. That is not to say that they are innocent in the sense of having not committed offences, but rather that the system, and thus society, not only judges their actions as criminal and 'bad', but extends this judgement to them as people. The consequences are that once someone has been deemed by society to be 'bad', there is an expectation that this 'badness' must again find expression in some way or another, leading to the commission of further offences. Armed with these stereotypes of offenders as wholly criminal and incapable of law-abiding behaviour, the general population reacts to them on this basis and treats them accordingly. Consequently, offenders may face discrimination in employment, often even where their offence bears no relation to the type of work being sought. Moreover, a person's previous social status, such as parent, spouse or worker, is hidden under the criminal label until that becomes their 'master status' or controlling public identification.

In summary, labelling theorists claim that the false definition of offenders as uncompromisingly criminal fulfils this very prophecy by evoking hostile and negative societal reactions that render conformity difficult, and criminality attractive. Thus, the processes and means of social control that are intended to induce law-abiding behaviour can have the ironic and unintended consequence of achieving the very opposite. It would be meaningless to suggest, that in general, labelling theorists view the processes outlined above as in any way deterministic or unavoidable. It is quite possible that some offenders may react to being labelled and stigmatised by refraining from the type of conduct that elicited such a reaction but as Downes and Rock (1998: 183) pertinently observe:

> Interactionism casts deviance as a process which may continue over a lifetime, which has no necessary end, which is anything but inexorable, and which may be built around false starts, diversions and returns. The trajectory of a deviant career cannot always be predicted. However constrained they may seem to be, people can choose not to err further.

The key point from a labelling perspective is that *many* offenders *do* internalise their criminal labels and thus stable or career criminality arises out of the reaction of society to them.

Moral Panics and Deviance Amplification

The labelling perspective has also been applied at the group level and a useful analytical tool in this context is that of the *deviancy amplification* feedback or spiral (Wilkins, 1964) where it is argued that the less tolerance there is to an initial act of deviance, the more similar acts that will be defined as deviant. This process will give rise to more reactions against offenders resulting in more social *alienation* or *marginalisation* of deviants. This state of affairs will generate more crime by deviant groups, leading to decreasing tolerance of deviants by conforming groups.

Deviancy amplification feedback is central to the phenomenon known as the 'moral panic' which Jock Young (1971) first used in his study of recreational drug users in north London and which was later developed by Stanley Cohen (1973) in his study of the societal reaction to the 'mods and rockers' disturbances of 1964. These studies marked a significant break with those approaches to delinquency—favoured by proponents of the predestined actor model—that were primarily concerned with finding the causes of delinquent behaviour. By contrast, definitional and structural questions relating to why certain groups define certain acts as deviant, and the consequences of this process, were asked.

Cohen (1973) found the press to be guilty of exaggeration and distortion in their reporting of the events in Clacton over the Easter bank holiday weekend in 1964. The sense of outrage communicated by such misrepresentation had set in motion a series of interrelated responses. First, there was increased public concern about the issue, to which the police responded by increasing their surveillance of the groups in question—mods and rockers. This resulted in more frequent arrests, which in turn appeared to confirm the validity of the original media reaction. Second, by emphasising the stylistic differences and antagonisms between the groups, the press reaction encouraged polarisation and further clashes between the groups.

Various moral entrepreneurs call for action to be taken against the groups involved in the outbreaks of lawlessness and usually pronounce that current controls are inadequate. Cohen (1973) shows that these entrepreneurs exaggerate the problem in order to make local events seem ones of pressing national concern and an index of the decline of morality and social standards. The extension of control leads to further marginalisation and stigmatisation of deviants which in turn leads to more demands for police action and so on into a deviancy amplification spiral. Cohen located the nature and extent of reaction to the mods and rockers in the social context of Britain during the 1960s. In particular, ambivalence about social change in the post-war period, the new affluence and freedom of young people and their apparent rejection of traditional social norms such as employment and the family are used as a context for the panic.

The concept of moral panic is also central to Hall *et al.*'s (1978) study of 'mugging' although the concept is used within a very different theoretical framework. While conceding that there can be no deviance without an agency of condemnation and control, it is argued that the notion of moral panic is limited if employed without reference to the social and political structures that empower a dominant minority to construct and implement the process of labelling. Within labelling theories moral panic is thus expressed in terms of a 'society' that creates rules and within the Marxism that informs Hall *et al.*'s approach, it is expressed in terms of a 'state' that has the power to criminalise (Cohen, 1985: 272). Given its theoretical basis, this analysis falls more within the scope of the radical theories discussed in the following chapter.

Goode and Ben-Yehuda (1994) have more recently challenged the assumption of earlier theorists that moral panics are in some way engineered at the behest—and in the interests—of dominant élites and distinguish three different models. First, there is the grass roots model where a panic has its origins within the general public and which expresses a genuinely felt—albeit objectively mistaken—concern about a perceived threat. Second, the elite- engineered model is where dominant groups deliberately and consciously generate concerns and fears that resonate with their wider political interests. Third, the interest-group model is where rule-creators and moral entrepreneurs launch crusades that coincide neatly with their own professional concerns and interests. Goode and Ben-Yehuda (1994) identify the following five characteristics of a moral panic: (i) a disproportionate reaction; (ii) concern about the threat; (iii) hostility to the objects of the panic; (iv) widespread agreement or consensus that the threat is real; and (v) the unpredictability—or volatility—of moral panics in terms of scale and intensity.

Others have criticised the whole notion of moral panics as a conceptualisation of social reaction. Left realists—the subject of Chapter 16 in this book—maintain that crime and the fear of crime should be taken seriously and not dismissed as just an expression of media over-reaction or panic. For example, Waddington (1986) criticised the empirical basis of Hall *et al.*'s (1978) influential study of street robberies, arguing that incidents of 'mugging' were increasing at the time and therefore asked what a proportionate response to the problem should have involved. Others have identified problems with the use of the concept of moral panic to capture reaction to diverse themes or issues. For example, Watney (1987) has questioned the use of the concept to characterise media and policy reactions to HIV/Aids. McRobbie and Thornton (1995) argue that the whole idea of a moral panic needs to be reconsidered in an environment where there may be an institutionalised need for the media to generate 'good stories' and that these can easily become part of a promotional culture that 'ironically' uses sensationalism for commercial purposes.

Criticisms of Labelling Theories

As the labelling approach became more influential during the 1960s and early 1970s it attracted criticism from a variety of sources. Plummer (1979) noted that because the perspective is so loosely defined, it could harbour several diverse theoretical positions and therefore leave itself open to internal contradiction and criticism from all theoretical sides. Such ambiguity and eclecticism thus led some critics to claim that labelling is at best a vague perspective that does not contain consistent and interrelated concepts and which fails to make precise distinctions between mere description and causal statements (Taylor, Walton and Young, 1973). On the other hand, proponents of labelling theory such as Schur (1971) contend that the strength of the approach lies in its ability to analyse aspects of social reality that have been neglected, offer directions for research and thus complement other theoretical approaches.

Others argue that labelling theories fail to clearly define deviance. According to Gibbs (1966), labelling theorists claim that an act is deviant only if a certain reaction follows, yet at the same time refer to 'secret deviants' and 'primary deviants', and suggest that certain groups of people are licensed to engage in deviant behaviour without negative reactions. This implies, it is argued, that deviance can be identified not merely in terms of societal reactions to it but in terms of *existing social norms.* There may be ambiguity about certain kinds of 'soft' deviance—where criminal definitions are relative to time and place—but there can be no such ambiguity regarding 'hard' deviance, such as violent assault, robbery and burglary, which have always been universally condemned. 'Hard' deviants at least are fully aware that what they are doing is deviant or criminal but freely choose this course of action because it is profitable or exciting. Labelling is therefore an irrelevance.

Taylor, Walton and Young (1973) accept the notion that deviance is not simply an inherent property of an act but they do not agree that it is as arbitrary as labelling theorists imply. They take the view that the deviant is not a passive actor but a decision-maker whose rule breaking reflects initial motives and choices, and thus has meaning. This approach overlaps with a further criticism that observes the emphasis to be on the negative repercussions of labelling which implies an individual totally at the mercy of official labellers. A consequence of this overemphasis on societal reaction at the expense of individual choice has been the tendency to elevate the offender to the status of victim. Labelling theories have 'the paradoxical consequence of inviting us to view the deviant as a passive nonentity who is responsible neither for his suffering nor its alleviation—who is more 'sinned' against than sinning' (Gouldner, 1968: 38). Yet, as previously noted, labelling theories do not on the whole argue that the effects of labelling are determinant, but rather that negative societal reaction can, and in many cases will, deepen criminality. Thus as Downes and Rock (1998: 190) quite correctly observe, 'criticisms of the species offered by Gouldner really reflect a response to only the most narrow versions of interactionism'. As for the charge that labelling theorists take the side of the deviant and overlook the 'real' victims of crime some, most notably Becker (1967), make no apologies for this and argue that they are merely balancing out traditional approaches within criminology that are severely biased *against* the deviant.

Many of the criticisms of labelling theories would seem more justified had the approach been promoted as a developed theory rather than as a perspective comprising loosely connected themes. In the light of this, perhaps the most telling criticism of the perspective is that, though it focused on societal reaction, it stopped short of offering a systematic analysis of social structure and power relations. While acknowledging that political interest and social disadvantage influenced societal reaction, labelling theorists failed to make explicit the connection of the criminal justice system to the underlying capitalist economic order and the inequalities of wealth and power rooted therein. Some of these issues are addressed by later more recent labelling theorists and by the radical theorists we will encounter in the following chapter.

Labelling Theories Revisited

In more recent years the notions and concepts of labelling theories have been modified and developed. First, more recent attention has been devoted to informal labelling such as that carried out by parents, peers, and teachers which it has been argued has a greater effect on subsequent criminal behaviour than official labelling. Ross Matsueda (1992) and Heimer and Matsueda (1994) discuss the reasons why individuals may be informally labelled as delinquents and note that such labels are not simply an outcome of interaction with the criminal justice system—for example, arrest—but are crucially influenced by the individual's offending behaviour *and* their position in society. Powerless individuals such as urban, ethnic-minority, lower-class adolescents are far more likely to be negatively labelled by parents and peers than more affluent middle-class young people. Matsueda (1992) also argues that informal labels affect the subsequent level of crime committed by individuals because these help shape their perceptions of how others see them. Thus, if they believe that others see them as delinquents and troublemakers, they are more likely to act in accord with this perception and engage in offending behaviour.

Some have observed that a shift seems to have occurred around 1974 in which labelling theorists came to retreat from their underdog focus and move away from the study of 'nuts, sluts, and perverts' (Liazos, 1972) and came to accommodate legalistic definitions and focus on state power. Thus, modern labelling theorists came to recognise that societies socially construct and create crime by passing legislation and, therefore, the substantive nature of the law is a legitimate object of study. These are sometimes referred to as criminalisation theories (Hartjen, 1974) and while they have some resemblance to societal reaction—or labelling perspectives—they are more closely linked to a field of study that some call the sociology of law perspective or the study of law as a mechanism of social control. Labelling theories that focus on state power can be considered as branches of controlology (Ditton, 1979) which refers to a group of theories with some interest in crime waves and moral panics but mostly take the view that criminal justice agencies are part of broader social control mechanisms, like welfare, mental health, education, the military, and the mass media, all of which are used by the state to control 'problem' populations (Arvanites, 1992). Controlology has its theoretical foundations in the work of Foucault (1971, 1977) who argued that various instruments of social control—more humane, enlightened, reasonable responses to deviance—are packaged and sold by the state to cover up the inherent coercion and power in the system. The state is thus always trying to portray a 'velvet glove' where its ultimate goal is to exercise its 'iron fist' to control troublesome populations, in other words, the pervasive 'hard' and 'soft' 'policing' strategies of the 'disciplinary-control-matrix' (Hopkins Burke, 2004b; 2008) which is discussed in more detail in the third part of this book.

Link (1987), Link *et al.* (1987), and Link *et al.* (1989) have used labelling theory to understand how we view and respond to the mentally ill and observe that in the USA public attitudes have been conditioned so that such people are perceived in negative and devalued ways with the outcome being that many who need psychiatric help—and those who care for them—will either try to hide this reality from family friends, colleagues and their employers, or will withdraw from groups or people who they think might reject them.

Some have suggested that the criminal justice system and the public are increasing the stigmatisation of—particularly young—offenders and thus heightening the most negative effects of labelling. De Haan (2000) observes that levels of violence in society appear to be rising—even in the Netherlands where previously there had been reasonable tolerance of such behaviour—and explains this occurrence as a process of relabelling previously non-problematic actions as more serious. Indeed, it seems that there is an increasingly universal intolerance of violence and such behaviour is being dealt with much more harshly. Triplett (2000) claims that an increase in violent offences in the USA during the 1980s and 1990s had been accompanied by changes in the criminal justice system moving less serious offences—particularly status offences such as truancy—up the sentencing tariff, and by a change in the way in which (especially young) violent offenders come to be seen as evil. She observes that these judgements have been subsequently attached to all young offenders who have subsequently become isolated and excluded from mainstream society. Meossi (2000) argues that this demonising of offenders—observed both in Italy and the USA—tends to correlate closely with periodic economic downturns and Halpern (2001) asserts that the subsequent rise in crime levels leads to harsher treatment of offenders thus devaluing people through labelling which can itself lead to further acceleration in offending behaviour.

While many studies have been conducted to apply labelling theory to various types of deviance, Kenney (2002) considers it in relationship to the victims of crime and found that sympathy offered to a victim may be received as condescension and may result in a feeling of a loss of power. The victim may lose self-esteem as a result of this loss of power and if he or she seeks help from friends and loved ones, they may fear feeling or being viewed as incompetent. Once the individual has been labelled as a 'victim' they may well find that work colleagues, friends, and even family begin to avoid them due to feelings of guilt or not knowing how to react which can lead to further isolation of the victim. Many victims do not receive the support they seek from loved ones and may wonder if their feelings are normal. Similarly, Li and Dennis Moore (2001) concluded from their study of the relationship between disability and illicit drug use that discrimination against persons with disabilities leads to higher rates of illegal drug use by these people.

Others have utilised the concept of labelling in a more positive mode. Braithwaite (1989) thus introduces the concept of 'reintegrative shaming' where it is proposed that offenders should be shamed not in order to stigmatise them but to make them realise the negative impact of their actions on both individual victims and the wider community and then encourage others to forgive them and accept them back into society. Reintegrative shaming is an influential concept that underpins reparation and restorative justice programmes and has been widely introduced—in particular with young offenders—in New Zealand (see Morris, Maxwell and Robertson, 1993), Australia (see Strang, 1993; Forsythe, 1994; Hudson *et al.*, 1996), parts of the USA (see Alford, 1997) and Britain (see Dignan, 1999, Young and Goold, 1999; Maxwell and Morris, 2001). It is discussed in more detail in Chapter 15. Some have suggested that such a policy would only work in rural communities with strong community bonds but Braithwaite (1993) considers that it could be even more effective in cities which are invariably constituted of many closely-knit micro-mechanical solidarities or communities (see Hopkins Burke and Pollock, 2004). Moreover, Braithwaite (1993) and Simpson, Lyn Exum and Smith (2000) consider reintegrative shaming to be an appropriate response to some white-collar and corporate violations of the law and propose that its application would be a considerable advance on a long established tradition of ignoring such cases.

DISCUSSION QUESTIONS
By John M. Stogner

1. If labels do indeed increase the likelihood of future offending, how might we reform the justice system to reduce secondary deviance?
2. How does the work of Becker relate to the broader social and political issues of his day?
3. How do labeling-based theories relate to other leading explanations of crime and deviance?
4. Describe behaviors that were labeled as deviant but are now considered acceptable. Similarly, describe formerly normative behaviors that are now considered deviant. Was the change the result of the acts themselves changing? How do these changes affect those that have committed these behaviors?
5. Can you describe a situation where a moral panic (as defined by Cohen or Goode and Ben-Yehuda) led a behavior to be labeled as deviant?

CHAPTER FOURTEEN

Crime, Shame, and Reintegration

JOHN BRAITHWAITE

STUDENT INTRODUCTION
By John M. Stogner

Australian criminologist John Braithwaite argues that whether an act is labeled inappropriate or deviant should not be the central focus of societal reaction theories. In fact, he suggests that all illicit acts are condemned or shamed to some degree. He proposes that it is the quality and form of this shame that impacts future behavior, noting that the result can be either an increase or decrease in the likelihood of deviant behavior. Shame and disapproval can lead poor behavior to worsen, but Braithwaite also sees potential for them to decrease future offending if properly utilized. Put another way, it is not whether a label is applied to an action, but how it

is applied that matters according to Braithwaite's work.

Braithwaite describes shaming as a consequence of offending; it is an attempt of society to show disapproval, evoke remorse, and make the offender aware that the behavior is considered inappropriate. He argues that shaming has the negative effect described by other labeling theorists (i.e., increases the likelihood of future offending) when it is stigmatizing, separates the offender from the community, or restricts social capital. He labels this reaction *disintegrative shaming*, but notes that positive outcomes can come from *reintegrative shaming*. Reintegrative shaming involves the expression of forgiveness by community members; it shows the offender that he or she is valued. Braithwaite cautions that the criminal act rather than the individual should be defined as immoral within this process. He further argues that for shaming to be reintegrative, the offender must take an active role in the process and perhaps complete acts of restitution. Put simply, Braithwaite's work suggests that it is necessary to lead individuals to the conclusion that they are a good person who has committed a bad act rather than a bad person in need of punishment.

As you read the selection from Braithwaite's book, note the core tenets of his theory and his view on how societal reaction can decrease future offending. You should pay careful attention to his arguments about what conditions make shaming more likely to be disintegrative rather than reintegrative (i.e., low *interdependency* and low *communitarianism*). Also, consider the policy applications of reintegrative shaming theory and whether they are feasible; Braithwaite's theory is supportive of restorative justice programs and policies. Consider how our culture treats juvenile offenders and whether these processes are consistent with Braithwaite's recommendations. Finally, examine whether Braithwaite's work is consistent with the traits of a good theory and our knowledge of crime and delinquency as presented in Chapter 1.

CRIME, SHAME, AND REINTEGRATION
By John Braithwaite

The theory in this book suggests that the key to crime control is cultural commitments to shaming in ways that I call reintegrative. Societies with low crime rates are those that shame potently and judiciously; individuals who resort to crime are those insulated from shame over their wrongdoing. However, shame can be applied injudiciously and counterproductively; the theory seeks to specify the types of shaming which cause rather than prevent crime....

The first step to productive theorizing about crime is to think about the contention that labeling offenders makes things worse. The contention is both right and wrong. The theory of reintegrative shaming is an attempt to specify when it is right and when wrong. The distinction is between shaming that leads to stigmatization—to—outcasting, to confirmation of a deviant master status-versus shaming that is reintegrative, that shames while maintaining bonds of respect or love, that sharply terminates disapproval with forgiveness, instead of amplifying deviance by progressively casting the deviant out. Reintegrative shaming controls crime; stigmatization pushes offenders toward criminal subcultures....

The theory of reintegrative shaming posits that the consequence of stigmatization is attraction to criminal subcultures. Subcultures supply the outcast offender with the opportunity to reject her rejectors, thereby maintaining a form of self-respect. In contrast, the consequence of reintegrative shaming is that criminal subcultures appear less attractive to the offender. Shaming is the most potent weapon of social control unless it shades into stigmatization. Formal criminal punishment is an ineffective weapon of social control party because it is a degradation ceremony with maximum prospects for stigmatization.

The nub of the theory of reintegrative shaming is therefore about the effectiveness of reintegrative shaming and the counterproductivity of stigmatization in controlling crime. In addition, the theory posits a number of conditions that make for effective shaming Individuals are more susceptible to shaming when they are enmeshed in multiple relationships of interdependency; societies shame more effectively when they are communitarian. Variables like urbanization and residential mobility predict communitarianism, while variables like age and gender predict individual interdependency. (A schematic summary of these aspects of the theory is presented in Figure 14.1).

Some of the ways that the theory of reintegrative shaming builds on earlier theories should now be clear. Interdependency is the stuff of control theory; stigmatization comes from labeling theory; subculture formation is accounted for in opportunity theory terms; subcultural influences are naturally in the realm of subcultural theory; and the whole theory can be understood in integrative cognitive social learning theory terms such as are provided by differential association....

Preventing Crime

We have seen that the micro process of shaming an individual has consequences far beyond the life of that individual. The social process of gossip links a micro· incident into a macro pattern. A shaming incident reinforces cultural patterns which underwrite further cultural products like a moralistic children's story,

---

a television program, school teacher's homily. The latter modalities of public (societal) shaming exert pressure for further private (individual) shaming.

The reasons why reintegrative shaming works in preventing crime might be summarized as follows:

1. The deterrence literature suggests that specific deterrence associated with detection for criminal offending works primarily through fear of shame in the eyes of intimates rather than fear of formal punishment.

2. Shame not only specifically deters the shamed offender, it also generally deters many others who also wish to avoid shame and who participate in or become aware of the incident of shaming.

3. Both the specific and general deterrent effects of shame will be greater for persons who remain strongly attached in relationships of interdependency and affection because such persons will accure greater interpersonal costs from shame. This is one reason why reintegrative shaming makes for more effective social control than stigmatization.

4. A second reason for the superiority of reintegrative shaming over stigmatization is that the latter can be counterproductive by breaking attachments to those who might shame future criminality and by increasing the attractiveness of groups that provide social support for crime.

5. However, most compliance with the law is not achieved through either specific or general deterrence. Most of us comply with the law most of the time, not because we rationally weigh our fear of the consequences of detection against the benefits of the crime, but because to commit the crime is simply unthinkable to us. Shaming is the social process which leads to the cognition that a particular type of crime is unthinkable. Cultures where the social process of shaming is muted are cultures where citizens often do not internalize abhorrence for crime.

6. A third reason for the superiority of the reintegrative shaming over stigmatization is that a combination of shame at and repentance by the offender is a more powerful affirmation of the criminal law than onesided moralizing. A shaming ceremony followed later by a forgiveness and repentance ceremony more potently builds commitment to the law than a shaming ceremony alone. Nothing has greater symbolic force in community-wide conscience-building than repentance.

7. Because shaming is a participatory form of social control, compared with formal sanctioning which is more professionalized than participatory, shaming builds consciences through citizens being instruments as well as targets of social control. Participation in expressions of abhorrence toward the criminal acts of others is part of what makes crime an abhorrent choice for ourselves to make.

8. Once consciences have been formed by cultural processes of shaming and repentance, pangs of conscience become the most effective punishment for crime because whereas conscience delivers a timely anxiety response to every involvement in crime, other negative reinforcers, including shame, are delivered unreliably or with delay.

9. Shaming is therefore both the social process which builds consciences, and the most important backstop to be used when consciences fail to deliver conformity. Formal punishment is another backstop, but a less effective one than reintegrative shaming.

10. Gossip within wider circles of acquaintances and shaming of offenders not even known to those who gossip are important for building consciences because so many crimes will not occur in the direct experiences of limited groups like families. Societal incidents of shaming remind parents and teachers of the need to moralize with their children across the whole curriculum of crimes.

11. Public shaming puts pressure on parents, teachers and others to ensure that they engage in private shaming which is sufficiently systematic, and public shaming increasingly takes over the role of private shaming once children move away from the influence of the family and school. The latter is one reason why public shaming by courts of law has a more important role to play with strictly adult offenses like crimes against the environment than with predominantly juvenile offenses like vandalism.

12. Public shaming generalizes familiar principles to unfamiliar or new contexts. It integrates new categories of wrongdoing, which may arise from technological change into pre-existing moral frameworks. Public shaming transforms the loss of life in a battle at My Lai into a "war crime" and a "massacre," and through our distant involvement in the incident of shaming, the moral category of illegal killing acquires some expanded meanings.

13. Cultures with heavy emphasis on reintegrative shaming establish a smoother transition between socialization practices in the family and socialization in the wider society. Within the family, as the child grows, social control shifts from external to internal controls; punishment oriented cultures set this process more starkly in reverse in the public domain than do shame oriented cultures. To the extent that crime control can be made to work by continuing to catalyze internal controls it will be more effective agents of social control than police forces.

14. Gossip and other modalities of shaming can be especially effective when the targets of shame are not directly confronted with the shame, but are directly confronted with gestures of forgiveness or reintegration. Citizens who have learnt the culture do not have to be shamed to their faces to know that they are the subject of gossip, but they may need to be directly offered gestures of acceptance before they can be confident that they are again part of the community of law abiding citizens. In other words, shaming which is excessively confrontational renders the achievement of reintegration a tall order. There is thus something to be said for hypocrisy: our friends are likely to recover from a suspicion that we have stabbed them in the back, but stabbing them in the front can be divisive!

15. The effectiveness of shaming is often enhanced by shame being directed not only at the individual offender but also at her family, or her company if she is a corporate criminal. When a collectivity as well as an individual is shamed, collectivities are put on notice as to their responsibility to exercise informal control over their members, and the moralizing impact of shaming is multiplied. For reasons which will be elaborated in the next chapter, a shamed family or company will often transmit the shame to the individual offender in a manner which is as regenerative as possible. From the standpoint of the offender, the strategy of rejecting her rejectors may resuscitate her own self-esteem, but her loved ones or colleagues will soon let her know that sinking deeper into the deviant role will only exacerbate the shame they are suffering on her behalf.

The Theory of Reintegrative Shaming

Figure 14.1 provides a schematic summary of the theory. In the first part of this chapter clear definitions are attempted for the key concepts in Figure 14.1 The cluster of six variables around interdependency at the top left of Figure 14.1 are characteristics of individuals; the three at the top right are characteristics of societies; while high levels of crime and shaming are variables which apply to both individuals and societies. The theory as summarized in Figure 14.1 thus gives an account both of why some kinds of individuals and some kinds of societies exhibit more crime.

Summary of the Theory of Reintegrative Shaming

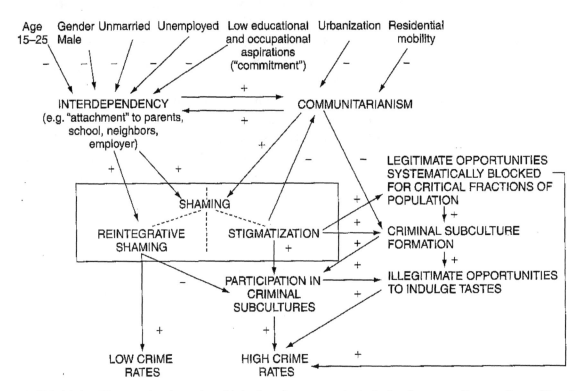

FIGURE 14.1. The mechanisms by which chronic or repeated strains increase the predisposition for crime

Source: Agnew (2006).

We could get a more parsimonious theory by collapsing the similar constructs of interdependency (an individual-level variable) and communitarianism (a societal variable) into a single construct, but then we would no longer have a framework to predict both which individuals and which societies will have more crime. On the desirability of being able to do this I can only agree with Cressey:

> A theory explaining social behavior in general, or any specific kind of social behavior, should have two distinct but consistent aspects. First, there must be a statement that explains the statistical distribution of the behavior in time and space (epidemiology), and from which predictive statements about unknown statistical distributions can be derived. Second, there must be a statement that identifies, at least by implication, the process by which individuals come to exhibit the behavior in question, and from which can be derived predictive statements about the behavior of individuals. (Cressey, 1960:47)

Key Concepts

Interdependency is a condition of individuals. It means the extent to which individuals participate in networks wherein they are dependent on others to achieve valued ends and others are dependent on them. We could describe an individual as in a state of interdependency even if the individuals who are dependent on him are different from the individuals on whom he is dependent. Interdependency is approximately equivalent to the social bonding, attachment and commitment of control theory.

Communitarianism is a condition of societies. In communitarian societies individuals are densely enmeshed in interdependencies which have the special qualities of mutual help and trust. The interdependencies have symbolic significance in the culture of group loyalties which take precedence over individual interests. The interdependencies also have symbolic significance as attachments which invoke personal obligation to others in a community of concern, rather than simply interdependencies of convenience as between a bank and a small depositor. A communitarian culture rejects any pejorative connotation of dependency as threatening individual autonomy. Communitarian cultures resist interpretations of dependency as weakness and emphasize the need for mutuality of obligation in interdependency (to be both dependent and dependable). The Japanese are said to be socialized not only to *amaeru* (to be succored by others) but also to *amayakasu* (to be nurturing to others) (Wagatsuma and Rosett, 1986).

Shaming means all social processes of expressing disapproval which have the intention or effect shamed and/or condemnation by others who become aware of the shaming. When associated with appropriate symbols, formal punishment often shames. But societies vary enormously in the extent to which formal punishment is associated with shaming or in the extent to which the social meaning of punishment is no more than to inflict pain to tip reward-cost calculations in favor of certain outcomes. Shaming, unlike purely deterrent punishment, sets out to moralize with the offender to communicate reasons for the evil of her actions. Most shaming is neither associated with formal punishment nor perpetrated by the state, though both shaming by the state and shaming with punishment are important types of shaming. Most shaming is by individuals within interdependent communities of concern.

Reintegrative shaming is shaming which is followed by efforts to reintegrate the offender back into the community of lawabiding or respectable citizens through words or gestures of forgiveness or ceremonies to decertify the offender as deviant. Shaming and reintegration do not occur simultaneously but sequentially, with reintegration occurring before deviance becomes a master status. It is shaming which labels the act as evil while striving to preserve the identity of the offender as essentially good. It is directed at signifying evil deeds rather than evil persons in the Christian tradition of "hate the sin and love the sinner." Specific disapproval is expressed within relationships characterized by general social approval; shaming criminal behavior is complemented by ongoing social rewarding of alternative behavior patterns. Reintegrative shaming is not necessarily weak; it can be cruel, even vicious. It is not distinguished from stigmatization by its potency, but by (a) a finite rather than open-ended duration which is terminated by forgiveness; and by (b) efforts to maintain bonds of love or respect throughout the finite period of suffering shame.

Stigmatization is disintegrative shaming in which no effort is made to reconcile the offender with the community. The offender is outcast, her deviance is allowed to become a master status, degradation ceremonies are not followed by ceremonies to decertify deviance.

Criminal subcultures are sets of rationalizations and conduct norms which cluster together to support criminal behavior. The clustering is usually facilitated by subcultural groups which provide systematic social support for crime in any of a number of ways—supplying members with criminal opportunities, criminal values, attitudes which weaken conventional values of law-abidingness, or techniques of neutralizing conventional values.

Short Summary of the Theory

The following might serve as the briefest possible summary of the theory. A variety of life circumstances increase the chances that individuals will be in situations of greater interdependency, the most important being age (under 15 and over 25), being married, female, employed, and having high employment and educational aspirations. Interdependent persons are more susceptible to shaming. More importantly, societies in which individuals are subject to extensive interdependencies are more likely to be communitarian, and shaming is much more widespread and potent in communitarian societies. Urbanization and high residential mobility are societal characteristics which undermine communitarianism.

The shaming produced by interdependency and communitarianism can be either of two types—shaming 'that becomes stigmatization or shaming that is followed by reintegration. The shaming engendered, is more likely to become reintegrative in societies that are communitarian. In societies where shaming does become reintegrative, low crime rates are the result because disapproval is dispensed without eliciting a rejection of the disapprovers, so that the potentialities for future disapproval are not dismantled. Moreover, reintegrative shaming is superior even to stigmatization for conscience-building....

Shaming that is stigmatizing, in contrast, makes criminal subcultures more attractive because these are in some sense subcultures which reject the rejectors. Thus, when shaming is allowed to become stigmatization for want of reintegrative gestures or ceremonies which decertify deviance, the deviant is both attracted to criminal subcultures and cut off from other interdependencies (with family, neighbors, church, etc.). Participation in subcultural groups supplies criminal role models, training in techniques of crime and techniques of neutralizing crime (or other forms of social support) that make choices to engage in crime more attractive. Thus, to the extent that shaming is of the stigmatizing rather than the reintegrative sort, and that criminal sub cultures are widespread and accessible in the society, higher crime rates will be the result. While societies characterized by high levels of stigmatization will have higher crime rates than societies characterized by reintegrative shaming, the former will have higher or lower crime rates than societies with little shaming at all depending largely on the availability of criminal subcultures.

Yet a high level of stigmatization in the society is one of the very factors that encourages criminal subculture formation by creating populations of outcasts with no stake in conformity, no chance of self-esteem within the terms of conventional society-individuals in search of an alternative culture that allows them self-esteem. A communitarian culture, on the other hand, nurtures deviants within a network of attachments to conventional society, thus inhibiting the wide spread outcasting that is the stuff of subculture formation.

For clarity of exposition the two types of shaming have been presented as a stark dichotomy. In reality, for any society some deviants are dealt with in ways that are more stigmatic while others receive more reintegrative shaming. Indeed, a single deviant will be responded to more stigmatically by some, more reintegratively by others. To the extent that the greater weight of shaming tends to stigmatization, the crime producing processes on the right of Figure 14.1 are more likely to be triggered; to the extent that the balance of shaming tips toward reintegration, informal processes of crime control are more likely to prevail over these crime-producing processes.

The other major societal variable which fosters criminal subculture formation is systematic blockage of legitimate opportunities for critical fractions of the population. If black slum dwellers are systematically denied economic opportunities because of the stigma of their race and neighborhood, then criminal subcultures will form in these outcast neighborhoods. It can be seen that stigmatization (as opposed to social integration) as a cultural disposition may contribute to the systematic blockage of these economic opportunities; but cultural variables like stigmatization will be of rather minor importance compared with structural economic variables in determining opportunities. I have argued that the blockages in this part of the theory are not restricted to closed opportunities to climb out of poverty; systematically blocked opportunities for ever greater wealth accumulation by the most affluent of corporations often lead to corporate criminal subculture formation....

Criminal subcultures are the main mechanism for constituting illegitimate opportunity structures—knowledge on how to offend, social support for offending or communication of rationalizations for offending, criminal role models, subcultural groups which assist with the avoidance of detection and which organize collective criminal enterprises. However, illegitimate opportunities are greater in some societies than others for a variety of further reasons which are not incorporated within the theory. While the effects of legitimate and illegitimate opportunities on crime are mostly mediated by participation in criminal subcultures, the blockage of legitimate opportunities combined with the availability of illegitimate opportunities can independently increase· crime. Whether illegitimate opportunities to engage in crime are supplied by participation in criminal subcultures or otherwise, they must be opportunities that appeal to the tastes of tempted individuals for them to result in crime.

This summary is crudely simple because it ignores what goes on within the shaming box in Figure 14.1. That is, it ignores the treatment... of the social processes that combine individual acts of shaming into cultural processes of shaming which are more or less integrative: gossip, media coverage of shaming incidents, children's stories, etc. In turn, the summary has neglected how these macro processes of shaming feedback to ensure that micro practices of shaming cover the curriculum of crimes....

Shunting the Colliding Locomotives of Criminological Theory

This sharp contrast with the inability of the existing dominant theories to explain much of what we know about crime is achieved, ironically, through the addition of just one element—the partitioning of shaming-as a shunt to connect these diverging theoretical tracks. Through putting the old theoretical ingredients together in a new way, we can do better at accounting for the facts than can any of these traditions separately. Moreover, we can do better compared with adding together their separate (contradictory!) elements as partial explanations within an atheoretical multi-factor model.

The top left of Figure 14.1 incorporates the key variables of control theory; the far right-opportunity theory; the middle and bottom right—subcultural theory; the bottom, particularly the bottom left-learning theory; the right side of the middle box-labeling theory. With one crucial exception (reintegrative shaming), there is therefore no originality in the elements of this theory, simply originality of synthesis.

Through the effect of interdependency in reducing crime, we can capture the explanatory successes of control theory in accounting for primary deviance. Through shunting stigmatization away from other forms of shaming (as that sort of shaming which triggers subcultural participation) we proffer a more promising approach to the explanation of secondary deviance in labeling and subcultural theory terms. We achieve a more specified theory of differential association with conventional others versus others who share a subculture. Conceived another way, it is a theory of differential shaming. Most shaming is by conventional others on the anti-criminal side of a tipping point. When stigmatization produces secondary deviance, it is because the balance of shame has tipped; for those who share the subculture there is sufficient approval for crime… to outweigh the shaming of conventional society.

DISCUSSION QUESTIONS
By John M. Stogner

1. Do the juvenile justice system and the accompanying societal reaction typically shame offenders in a way that is reintegrative or stigmatizing? What about the adult system?
2. What aspects of American culture makes instituting policies based on reintegrative shaming theory (i.e., restorative justice) unlikely?
3. Why would Braithwaite suggest that shaming is more likely to be reintegrative in rural communities?
4. Can Braithwaite's ideas be extended to businesses to increase corporate compliance with policies and regulations?
5. How does reintegrative shaming theory relate to social learning, social bonding, and/or general strain theory?

CHAPTER FIFTEEN

The Influence of Neighborhoods on Crime

ZACHARY R. HAYS

STUDENT INTRODUCTION
By John M. Stogner

Without question, human behavior is influenced by the environment. The way in which individuals behave is at least partially contingent on setting and place. Put another way, who we are and how we act has a great deal to do with where we are and where we were raised. Chapter 15 offers a brief summary of place-based theories, better labeled the *neighborhood perspective*. These works attribute much of the variation in offending and crime rates to conditions, physical and social, within the neighborhood. That is, some qualities of neighborhoods facilitate offending whereas other qualities may be protective. Theories within this perspective typically do not define deviant behavior as unusual or abnormal; they generally consider crime to be the normal reaction of normal people to abnormal circumstances.

The following reading presents three important theoretical advances based on features of neighborhoods (a fourth neighborhood theory is explored in Chapter 16). First, Clifford Shaw and Henry McKay's social disorganization theory is presented. They proposed that the higher rates of crime in certain inner city areas were the result of that environment rather than the people who chose (or were forced) to live there. Shaw and McKay believed that a number of factors (e.g., concentrated disadvantage, poverty, etc.) prevented these communities from organizing around goals and expectations of normative behavior, which, in turn, prevented the neighborhood from effectively limiting crime. Kornhauser's subsequent contribution to the perspective includes a greater focus on *informal social control* and citizen intervention. Finally, Robert Sampson and colleagues argue that the higher crime rates in some neighborhoods can be partially attributed to low *collective efficacy*. Collective efficacy is defined as the perceived willingness of community members to intervene when a crime or challenge occurs and the mutually shared values and trust between community members. Collective efficacy theory likely represents one of the more significant advances in criminological theory in the last two decades.

As you read Chapter 15, imagine how the assertions of Shaw and McKay may have been interpreted at the time of their writing. You should explore what their work may have meant for policy and whether their assumptions about the level of organization in non-inner-city neighborhoods are accurate. Consider Kornhauser's contribution and discussion of informal social control; contemplate whether and how policy changes might lead to increases in neighborhood informal social control. Similarly, evaluate options for increasing neighborhood collective efficacy. Finally, consider how these theoretical frameworks relate to the overly simplistic "broken windows" theory that you have likely discussed in other classes.

THE INFLUENCE OF NEIGHBORHOODS ON CRIME
By Zachary R. Hays

W hile the lack of theory in policing research is a significant issue that needs to be addressed, another important theme that needs to be considered, and which is conspicuous in its relative absence from the police use of force literature, is the influence of neighborhood context. As the object of this book is to establish a relationship between police officers' use of force behaviors and the contextual factors associated with the neighborhoods in which they work, this research should contribute to that gap in the literature. Before discussing exactly how neighborhood context is expected to influence police behavior, however, it is useful to review the existing research on neighborhoods and crime, which will be relied upon heavily for the theoretical arguments made later in this book (see Chapter 4) linking the social disorganization tradition to police officers' use of force.

Although the theory of social disorganization is commonly, and appropriately, attributed to Clifford Shaw and Henry McKay, what this research refers to as *the social disorganization tradition* can be attributed to a much larger body of researchers. For the purposes of this book, the social disorganization tradition can therefore be defined as the combination of both Shaw and McKay's original theory *and* the works of a number of later researchers who have each made significant modifications to the concept of neighborhood social disorganization. Accordingly, throughout the remainder of this book, whenever any neighborhood contextual concepts attributable to any of the various researchers discussed in this chapter are mentioned, they will be referred to as coming from *the social disorganization tradition*, rather than coming from any particular researcher or group of researchers.

The Origins of Social Disorganization

The theory of social disorganization is rooted in Clifford Shaw and Henry McKay's research on juvenile delinquency in Chicago, Illinois, during the 1920s and 1930s. Their theory, however, is founded in works of other researchers who came from what is commonly known as *the Chicago School*, of which both Shaw and McKay were later a part. The Chicago School refers to any of the research or researchers that came out of the University of Chicago's Department of Sociology (especially related to the discipline of Urban Sociology) during the first half of the 20th century.

The Chicago School has long considered how the neighborhoods in which individuals live could influence how they behave. Years before Shaw and McKay would conceive of their much more widely-recognized theory of social disorganization, however, another group of researchers from the Chicago School mapped out the growth of Chicago using concentric zones emanating outwards from the center of the city's downtown area. Park, Burgess, and McKenzie (1925) identified five concentric zones which not only had very different demographic, social, and economic compositions, but very different levels of crime as well. They found that the zone immediately surrounding the downtown area (i.e., the central business district) was populated chiefly by recent immigrants to the United States who needed the close access to employment available downtown and the cheap housing prices found in the deteriorating housing stock that had once served the earliest inhabitants of Chicago. In addition to the poor quality of the housing in those neighborhoods, however, the researchers also observed that this zone had the highest rates of crime in all of Chicago. Subsequently, Park and colleagues named this zone the *transitional zone* because individuals would typically move out of the zone as soon as they had the financial means to do so in order to escape the crime problems, only to be quickly replaced by an even newer cohort of immigrants who were also in need of access to downtown employment and cheap housing.[15]

While most criminologists of the time believed that criminal behavior could be explained using characteristics of individuals, Park and colleagues' finding that the transitional zone consistently had the highest rates of crime in all of Chicago, regardless of who was living there at the time, paved the way for what was then a new way of thinking about crime. This new avenue for explaining criminal behavior was led by their colleagues, Clifford Shaw and Henry McKay. Based on Park and colleagues' finding, Shaw and McKay argued that, contrary to popular belief, it was not the people who lived in the transitional zone who caused rates of crime to be surprisingly high, rather it was the place in which they lived that gave rise to those high crime rates. In other words, Shaw and McKay believed that it was *places*, and not *people*, that were the key to explaining rates of crime.

Shaw and McKay's Theory of Social Disorganization

Using Park and colleagues' (1925) research as a foundation for their own work, Shaw and McKay's theory of social disorganization was a direct result of their attempts to explain the spatial variation in crime rates across the city of Chicago. This research ultimately led to their seminal work, *Juvenile Delinquency in Urban Areas* (1942), in which they first proposed linking neighborhood context to neighborhood juvenile arrest rates.[16] Although their original theory has received numerous additions and modifications, the fundamental argument remains the same—variation in neighborhood context influences the levels of crime, above and beyond the influences of the individual—level compositional factors related to the residents who live in them. Specifically, they argued that the negative effects of certain neighborhood structural characteristics would give rise to neighborhood residents being less likely and less able to come together, define, and ultimately achieve common goals, including the prevention of crime.

Furthermore, they argued that that the negative effects of those structural characteristics would lead to an increase in criminal values among neighborhood residents over time. Ultimately, it was the neighborhood's inability to collectively define and achieve common goals, as well as the increase in criminal values throughout the neighborhood that Shaw and McKay termed *social disorganization*.

---

[15] Individuals escaping the transitional zone typically moved to one of the three outer zones of Chicago identified by Park and colleagues–what they called the working class zone, the residential zone, and the suburban zone (listed from the nearest to the central business district to the furthest). Because these zones were not essential to Shaw and McKay's development of their theory of social disorganization, they are not discussed in any more detail here.

[16] While Shaw and McKay (1942) were primarily interested in explaining rates of juvenile delinquency and arrest rather than criminal behavior in general, their theory is commonly applied to the explanation of other forms of deviance and crime as well. Thus, for the purposes of this research, Shaw and McKay's original theory is considered to be an explanation for all types of crime, rather than juvenile delinquency only.

The three neighborhood structural characteristics that Shaw and McKay believed would lead to neighborhood social disorganization were poverty, racial and/or ethnic heterogeneity, and residential instability, which collectively measure what will be referred to in this book as n*eighborhood structural disadvantage.*[17] Shaw and McKay found that Chicago's transitional zone consistently had not only the highest rates of crime, but it also had the highest rates of neighborhood structural disadvantage. As a result of this observation, Shaw and McKay argued that variation in a neighborhood's level of structural disadvantage would predict its level of neighborhood social organization (or the lack thereof), which would, in turn, predict its rates of crime.

To explain it more plainly, Shaw and McKay argued that because structurally disadvantaged neighborhoods were composed of many poor individuals (i.e., high levels of poverty), who were more likely to be of a variety of different cultural backgrounds (i.e., high levels of racial/ethnic heterogeneity), they would be unwilling, or unable, to get to know each other and agree on any common set of values and goals for the neighborhood as a whole. Then, exacerbating this problem, as many of the immigrants that populated the transitional zone assimilated into American culture and found better paying jobs, they would move away from the inner city and the transitional zone only to be replaced by new (poor racial/ethnic minority) families. The constant in—and out—flow of new residents (i.e., high levels of residential instability) further complicating the remaining residents' ability to come together, get know each other, and form a common set of goals and values. Then, as this process repeated itself over the years, Shaw and McKay argued that it would quickly become nearly impossible for residents of those structurally disadvantaged neighborhoods to collectively define a set of rules regulating which behaviors were acceptable or unacceptable in their neighborhood. Consequently, the researchers expected that structurally disadvantaged neighborhoods would become more vulnerable to deviant and criminal activities since rules of behavior that did not exist could not be enforced. Unfortunately, Shaw and McKay would never explicitly give neighborhood residents' inability to regulate the behavior of individuals a specific name. Fortunately, however, later researchers would come to call the phenomena a *lack of informal social control* (e.g., Kornhauser 1978; Morenoff et al. 1997; Sampson et al. 1997; Sampson et al. 1999).

The lack of informal social control in structurally disadvantage neighborhoods was only one half of what Shaw and McKay meant when they said social disorganization, though. In order to help explain why neighborhoods within the transitional zone continued to consistently have high rates of crime over long periods of time, Shaw and McKay posited that neighborhood structural disadvantage not only reduced informal social control within a neighborhood, but that it also increased the deviant and criminal values among its residents. They contended that once high rates of crime had entered a neighborhood and become a regular occurrence, some residents would become accustomed to, and perhaps even tolerant of, a certain amount of criminal activity. Eventually, they believed that a subculture which actually embraced deviant and criminal values would form because no other residents of structurally disadvantaged neighborhoods would be willing to challenge those alternative values since there was no set of common values

---

[17] Although Shaw and McKay do not coin a collective term for the three structural precursors of neighborhood social disorganization that they identified—poverty, racial/ethnic heterogeneity, and residential instability—for the remainder of this book, when *neighborhood structural disadvantage* is mentioned, it refers to the combined influence of all three of those neighborhood structural characteristics.

with which to begin. Effectively then, Shaw and McKay believed that deviant and criminal values might not only exist in disadvantaged neighborhoods, they could actually thrive and be transmitted from one generation of residents to another.[18] Thus, for Shaw and McKay, neighborhood social disorganization represented not only the inability of neighborhood residents to informally control deviant or criminal behavior, but also an increase in deviant and criminal values over time.

Unfortunately, while Shaw and McKay were able to observe a relationship between neighborhood structural disadvantage and juvenile arrest rates in Chicago, they never specifically sought to identify or empirically test any measures of neighborhood social disorganization. That is, even though they theorized about how social disorganization might mediate the relationship between neighborhood structural disadvantage and rates of crime, they never proposed how neighborhood informal social control efforts or deviant and criminal values might be operationalized. Subsequently, Shaw and McKay were only able to empirically link neighborhood structural disadvantage to increased rates of juvenile delinquency and arrests (but not their actual concept of neighborhood social disorganization). Then, perhaps as a result of this omission, their theory fell out of favor among criminologists for several decades until the work of some new researchers once again sparked interest in the field of neighborhoods and crime.

The Informal Social Control Reformulation

More than three decades after Shaw and McKay unveiled their original theory of social disorganization, Kornhauser (1978) published her dissertation research on what she generally described as "the social sources of delinquency." In her dissertation, she both lauded and critiqued Shaw and McKay's original theory. While she agreed with their conclusion that places were important factors for explaining crime, she was also one of the first people to criticize Shaw and McKay for not clearly enough explicating the mechanisms through which they expected neighborhood structural disadvantage to lead to increased rates of crime (i.e., neighborhood social disorganization). And, it was through this criticism of Shaw and McKay's theory that Kornhauser ultimately made two of the most important contributions to the greater social disorganization tradition.

Kornhauser's first major contribution to the social disorganization tradition was her insistence that the Shaw and McKay's concept of *informal social control* should receive a greater emphasis. She argued that criminologists needed to more seriously consider how neighborhood residents' willingness to intervene on behalf of their neighborhood and regulate behaviors, without the help of formal sources of control (i.e., the police), might influence neighborhood rates of crime. Moreover, while her definition of informal social control was very similar to what Shaw and McKay (1942) described in their work (but never officially named), she focused less on residents sharing common goals and values, and argued that more attention should be paid to residents' collective willingness to *act* when their neighborhood was threatened. In other words, Kornhauser argued that neighborhood structural disadvantage would make residents less willing

---

[18] While important in the original theory, Shaw and McKay's arguments regarding the transmission of deviant and criminal values have worked their disorganization. For the widely-accepted argument regarding why the concept of deviant and criminal values should have never been included in their original theory, see the review of Kornhauser's (1978) contributions to the social disorganization tradition below

to place themselves in harm's way for the benefit of their neighbors, and consequently, the neighborhood would have no one to step forward and put a stop to any deviant or criminal behaviors. Only then, when no one was willing to act, did she believe that a neighborhood would become vulnerable to being taken over by criminal activity. Thus, Kornhauser's first major contributions to the social disorganization tradition was the increased emphasis that she placed on residents' ability to informally regulate behaviors in their neighborhood (i.e., neighborhood informal social control).

Kornhauser's second major contribution to the social disorganization tradition might actually be considered a case of addition by subtraction. She contended that Shaw and McKay's (1942) subcultural argument regarding the inter-generational transmission of criminal values contradicted their other arguments regarding how neighborhood structural disadvantage would lead to increased rates of crime. She argued that, because Shaw and McKay expected that the residents of structurally disadvantaged neighborhoods were unable to come together and form and enforce common values that would condemn deviant behaviors and crime, they should just as well be unable to come together and d enforce common values that would *promote deviant behaviors and crime.* Simply put, she questioned why Shaw and McKay believed that neighborhood residents could come to an agreement that deviant and criminal behaviors should be acceptable, when they had argued in the some piece that those same people could not come together to agree on anything else.

In addition to this critique of the subcultural component of Shaw and McKay's original theory of social disorganization, Kornhauser also criticized the researchers for trying to explain the consistently high rates of crime in structurally disadvantage neighborhoods through the inter-generational transmission of criminal values. She argued that because structurally disadvantaged neighborhoods had high levels of residential instability, each successive wave of immigrants (or other new groups) who moved into those neighborhoods should continue to experience social disorganization and consequently have high rates of crime. Then, if residential instability could explain high rates of crime over time, she believed that using the transmission of culture as an explanation for the same phenomenon was not only redundant, but unnecessary. Based on this logic, Kornhauser argued that if neighborhood residential instability could explain high levels of social disorganization and crime over time, then there was never really any need to introduce the concept of inter-generationally transmitted criminal values (i.e., criminal subcultures) and strongly recommended that it should therefore be purged from the tradition (although some argue that it should be brought back—e.g., Anderson 1999; Warner 2003).

Kornhauser's two major contributions to the evolution of the social disorganization tradition were therefore 1) that a stronger emphasis be placed on the role neighborhood informal social control efforts, and 2) that the subcultural element of Shaw and McKay's original theory be cut out. Despite what contemporary social disorganization theorists now recognize as being invaluable contributions, however, at the time in which Kornhauser's dissertation was published, the social disorganization tradition remained relatively unpopular. It was not until two new social-disorganization-based explanations of neighborhood crime rates emerged in the early 1990s that the tradition finally experienced a popular revival.

The Emergence of a Collective Efficacy Framework

The most recent modification to the social disorganization tradition comes in the form of another mediating mechanism of the relationship between neighborhood structural disadvantage and neighborhood crime rates—*collective efficacy*. The concept of collective efficacy is attributed to Sampson and a number of his colleagues (Morenoff et al. 2001; Sampson et al. 1999; Sampson et al. 1997). Despite the recent theoretical and empirical development of the systemic model, Sampson and colleagues argued that social ties among neighborhood residents were not as important for linking neighborhood structural disadvantage to neighborhood rates of crime as previous researchers had suggested (Bursik and Grasmick 1993; Hunter 1985; Sampson and Groves 1989).

Sampson and colleagues also believed that Kornhauser's (1978) exclusive focus on neighborhood informal social control was too narrow, however. As a result, they believed that only an agreement on common goals and values, and more importantly, a mutual trust amongst neighbors that every resident of the neighborhood would be willing to intervene and exercise informal social control efforts would be sufficient to prevent social disorganization and ultimately crime. Moreover, they believed that residents did not need to have frequent or strong social ties with their neighbors, as long as they trusted them to engage in informal social control efforts when necessary. Sampson and colleagues therefore defined neighborhood collective efficacy as the combination of two concepts—informal social control (i.e., the willingness to intervene on behalf of the neighborhood) *and* social cohesion (i.e., the sharing of common beliefs, values, and a mutual trust among residents).[20]

Using these concepts, Sampson and colleagues hypothesized that high levels of neighborhood structural disadvantage would impair residents' ability to get together, define common goals and values, and most importantly, trust each other. They then argued that, even if residents had strong social networks within their neighborhood, if they could not trust the individuals within those networks to engage in informal social control, they would be unwilling to make any effort themselves. As a result of this lack of mutual trust, Sampson and colleagues believed that informal social control efforts in the neighborhood would be weakened, leaving the residents vulnerable to deviant and criminal activities, even in the presence of strong social ties.

It should be noted that, unlike the previous modifications and reformulations of Shaw and McKay's original theory discussed previously, Sampson and colleagues' concept of neighborhood collective efficacy actually serves as a measure of neighborhood social *organization*. In other words, whereas Kornhauser and the proponents of the systemic model generally defined neighborhood social disorganization as the presence of *low* levels of informal social control, Sampson and colleagues combined *high* levels of informal social control with their concept of social cohesion so that they were measuring the inverse of social *dis*-organization. Rather than using neighborhood social disorganization to predict high rates of crime then, Sampson and colleagues effectively used neighborhood collective efficacy to predict lower neighborhood crime rates. Despite this departure from earlier conceptualizations of neighborhood social disorganization,

---

[20] Although social cohesion may appear to be very similar in nature to the systemic model's notion of social ties, the focus here is more on the relationship among *all* neighborhood residents, rather than a few strong ties among friends and family members. In essence, Sampson and colleagues' concept of social cohesion is consistent with the notion of weak ties described in detail by Bellair (1997) (see als tter 1973).

the concept of collective efficacy is nonetheless consistent with the larger social disorganization tradition since its proponents are still trying to explain why neighborhood structural disadvantage might be related to neighborhood rates of crime.

Like systemic model researchers, Sampson and colleagues also contributed to the theoretical development of the social disorganization tradition by conducting empirical tests of the mechanisms that they proposed. Unlike tests of the systemic model, however, research on neighborhood collective efficacy has been largely supportive of the framework. Perhaps not surprisingly then, Sampson and colleagues' contributions to the development of the social disorganization tradition include not only the conceptualization and empirical assessment of their collective efficacy concept, but also the revival of scholarly and popular interest in the study of neighborhoods and crime.

Empirical Tests of the Social Disorganization Tradition

Since Shaw and McKay first proposed their original theory of social disorganization, numerous studies have empirically analyzed many of the concepts and mechanisms associated with the tradition, including neighborhood structural disadvantage, informal social control, the systemic model (i.e., social ties), and collective efficacy (i.e., informal social control *and* neighborhood social cohesion). Beginning with the individual effects of neighborhood structural disadvantage's component measures (poverty, racial/ethnic heterogeneity, and residential stability), researchers have consistently found very strong support for nearly all of the social disorganization concepts reviewed above in regards to their capacity to explain neighborhood rates of crime.

Although astute social disorganization tradition researchers recognize that Shaw and McKay never actually hypothesized that neighborhood structural disadvantage was directly related to neighborhood crimes (as reviewed above, they expected the effect to be mediated by a loss of informal social control and an increase in criminal values), nearly all of the empirical research on the subject has nonetheless attempted to discern both the direct and indirect effects of neighborhood structural disadvantage on rates of crime. And, almost without exception, such research has observed a positive and significant relationship between the component measures of neighborhood structural disadvantage and neighborhood crime rates. More simply put, researchers have found that as neighborhood levels of poverty, racial/ethnic heterogeneity, and residential instability[21] increase, so do levels of crime and delinquency (e.g., Bursik and Grasmick 1993; Krivo and Peterson 1996; Morenoff et al. 1997; Peterson, Krivo, and Harris 2000; Sampson and Groves 1989; Sampson et al. 1997; Sampson et al. 1999; Sampson et al. 2001; Shaw and McKay 1942; Silver 2000; Warner and Rountree 1997; Veysey and Messner 1999; for a comprehensive review see Sampson, Morenoff, and Gannon-Rowley 2002).

---

[21] While the role of neighborhood structural disadvantage in general is one of the most well-established in all of the neighborhoods and crime literature, the independent effect of residential instability has been observed to be the weakest (Sampson et al. 2002). Nonetheless, with a large body of supporting literature, all three measures of neighborhood structural disadvantage should be included in any study of neighborhood context, and are therefore also included in this analysis of police use of excessive force.

Research examining the specific influence of neighborhood informal social control efforts on crime rates has been largely supportive as well. As Kornhauser (1978) first hypothesized, the empirical research has shown that when residents are willing to intervene on behalf of their neighborhood to prevent deviant and criminal behaviors, crime rates tend to be low (Hunter 1985; Bursik 1999; Kornhauser 1978; Velez 2001; Veysey and Messner 1999). Moreover, much of the research that has included measures of neighborhood informal control as a part of Sampson and colleagues' collective efficacy has also found it to be negatively and significantly related to rates of crime.[22] Neighborhood informal social control therefore appears to be an important contextual factor for predicting levels of crime as well.

Finally, Sampson and colleagues (1997) both theorized and found empirical evidence challenging the importance of neighborhood social ties. To briefly reiterate their position, Sampson and colleagues firmly believed that neighborhood residents did not need to have strong or frequent social ties, as long as they shared a mutual trust that their neighbors were willing to exercise informal social control efforts when necessary. And, just as they expected, Sampson and his various colleagues found strong empirical support for their hypothesis that high levels of collective efficacy within a neighborhood would reduce those neighborhoods' crime rates (Morenoff et al. 1997; Sampson et al. 1997; Sampson et al. 1999; Sampson et al. 2001; Sampson et al. 2002), even in the absence of large social networks or strong social ties amongst neighbors. However, one might be skeptical of Sampson and colleagues' research which had all supported the collective efficacy framework since they were the same researchers who developed it in the first place. Auspiciously, other neighborhoods and crime researchers have also consistently found support for the collective efficacy framework, though, lending both credence and generalizability to Sampson and colleagues' own research.

A number of other social disorganization researchers have recently conducted empirical tests of the collective efficacy framework and each has observed a strong, negative, and significant relationship between the concept and a variety of aggregate-level measures of crime and deviance (Browning 2002; Browning et al. 2004; Cancino 2005; Reisig and Cancino 2004; Triplett et al. 2003). Thus, while a not unsubstantial body of research has called into question the relative importance of neighborhood social ties,[23] the ameliorative role of collective efficacy on neighborhood rates of crime appears to be above reproach. Neighborhood collective efficacy has therefore been, and continues to be today, one of the most prominent modifications of the social disorganization tradition.

---

[22] As one of the primary goals of this research is to test Sampson and colleagues' concept of collective efficacy as an explanation for police officers' use of excessive force, rather than examining the independent effect of neighborhoods informal social control efforts, it is analyzed only as a component of the collective efficacy measure. For more details on how the concept of informal social control is utilized within this research, see Chapter 5.

[23] Based on the empirical evidence reviewed here, neighborhood social ties appear to be less influential than some researchers had originally envisioned. Nonetheless, in order to fully test the viability of the social disorganization tradition as a theoretical framework for explaining police officers' use of excessive force, measures of both neighborhood social ties (i.e., the systemic model) *and* collective efficacy (measured as informal social control and neighborhood social cohesion) are n this research.

DISCUSSION QUESTIONS
By John M. Stogner

1. What is the difference between collective efficacy and informal social control? Does one subsume the other?

2. What leads a neighborhood to be disorganized? Can social disorganization be remedied without addressing the bigger issues (e.g., poverty)? How?

3. How do the concepts of social disorganization and collective efficacy differ? Are they just two extremes of the same concept? Is one likely to be more stable than the other?

4. What should policymakers do to increase neighborhood collective efficacy?

5. How do neighborhood-based theories relate to learning, anomie/strain, and control theories? What assertions do they make that conflict with one another?

CHAPTER SIXTEEN

Decent and Street Families

ELIJAH ANDERSON

STUDENT INTRODUCTION
By John M. Stogner

Following extensive fieldwork and social observation in inner-city Philadelphia, ethnographer Elijah Anderson argues that the higher rate of interpersonal violence within poor African American urban communities is due to the adoption of a set of rules, expectations, and beliefs that are somewhat accepting of violence. He proposes that discrimination, poverty, alienation, lack of adequate employment opportunities, weak law enforcement efforts, and the availability of recreational drugs have all contributed to the development of a system where respect has become valued currency. One's reputation within these communities

becomes paramount—even to the degree that insults, slights, and other shows of disrespect may require retaliation or retribution. Anderson suggests that the development and endorsement of this *code of the streets* is a survival strategy for the challenges faced by individuals within the impoverished inner-city communities. Whereas some may classify Anderson's work as a subcultural theory, better suited as a reading within the learning perspective, the theoretical propositions within *Code of the Street* are best classified as a neighborhood theory because they argue that the social structure of neighborhoods influence the willingness to engage in violence.

Anderson's depiction of inner-city life in Philadelphia is intricately detailed. His comprehensive presentation of the community and vivid description of its members helps paint a picture consistent with his theoretical arguments. In the selected section, he describes members of the community classifying themselves and their peers as *decent* or *street*. Street families, according to Anderson's research, are disorganized and endorse violence; children learn that winning a physical altercation yields rewards. In contrast, decent families are organized, strict, and draw on their faith; they typically do not endorse attitudes supportive of violence, but learn (and may even express) the code of the streets for defensive purposes. Anderson details how the lack of supervision and inconsistent parenting practices in street families facilitates the internalization of the code of the street. He describes their social interactions and the need to display "juice" and "nerve" that may eventually lead to violence or victimization.

As you read the selected chapter from Anderson's book, note how he does not suggest that the internalization of a belief system endorsing violence is restricted to African American communities. As a careful researcher, he does not generalize his findings beyond the data, but there are no indications that his assertions could not be extrapolated to other communities. In fact, the general issues described by Anderson seem to be similarly present in disadvantaged white and Hispanic communities (albeit the communities may use different terminology). Also consider the utility of adopting the code of the streets as a protective or defensive strategy. Anderson argues that children raised in both street and decent families strive to appear tough and capable in order to avoid victimization, but that this behavior actually puts them at increased risk. Examine how Anderson presents males and females, and consider how the code of the street may be differentially accepted by males and females and how it may differentially affect their behavior. Finally, consider the policy implications of Anderson's work. Given his presentation of disadvantaged African American communities, what can be done to limit violence?

DECENT AND STREET FAMILIES
By Elijah Anderson

Almost everyone residing in poor inner-city neighbor hoods is struggling financially and therefore feels a certain distance from the rest of America, but there are degrees of alienation, captured by the terms "decent" and "street" or "ghetto," suggesting social types. The decent family and the street family in a real sense represent two poles of value orientation, two contrasting conceptual categories.[1] The labels "decent" and "street," which the residents themselves use, amount to evaluative judgments that confer status on local residents. The labeling is often the result of a social contest among individuals and families of the neighborhood. Individuals of either orientation may coexist in the same extended family. Moreover, decent residents may judge themselves to be so while judging others to be of the street, and street individuals often present themselves as decent, while drawing distinctions between themselves and still other people. There is also quite a bit of circumstantial behavior—that is, one person may at different times exhibit both decent and street orientations, depending on the circumstances. Although these designations result from much social jockeying, there do exist concrete features that define each conceptual category, forming a social typology.

The resulting labels are used by residents of inner-city communities to characterize themselves and one another, and understanding them is part of understanding life in the inner-city neighborhood. Most residents are decent or are trying to be. The same family is likely to have members who are strongly oriented toward decency and civility, whereas other members are oriented toward the street—and to all that it implies. There is also a great deal of "code-switching": a person may behave according to either set of rules, depending on the situation. Decent people, especially young people, often put a premium on the ability to code-switch. They share many of the middle-class values of the wider white society but know that the open display of such values carries little weight on the street: it doesn't provide the emblems that say, "I can take care of myself." Hence such people develop a repertoire of behaviors that do provide that security. Those strongly associated with the street, who have less exposure to the wider society, may have difficulty code-switching; imbued with the code of the street, they either don't know the rules for decent behavior or may see little value in displaying such knowledge.

At the extreme of the street-oriented group are those who make up the criminal element. People in this class are profound casualties of the social and economic system, and they tend to embrace the street code wholeheartedly. They tend to lack not only a decent education—though some are highly intelligent—but also an outlook that would allow them to see far beyond their immediate circumstances. Rather, many pride themselves on living the "thug life," actively defying not simply the wider social conventions but the law itself. They sometimes model themselves after successful local drug dealers and rap artists like Tupac Shakur and Snoop Doggy Dogg, and they take heart from professional athletes who confront the system and stand up for themselves. In their. view, policemen, public officials, and corporate heads are unworthy of respect and hold little moral authority. Highly alienated and embittered, they exude generalized contempt for the wider scheme of things and for a system they are sure has nothing but contempt for them.

Members of this group are among the most desperate and most alienated people of the inner city. For them, people and situations are best approached both as objects of exploitation and as challenges possibly "having a trick to them," and in most situation their goal is to avoid being "caught up in the trick bag." Theirs is a cynical outlook, and trust of others is severely lacking, even trust of those they are close to. Consistently, they tend to approach all persons and situations as part of life's obstacles, as things to subdue or to "get over." To get over, individuals develop an effective "hustle" or "game"plan," setting themselves up in a position to prevail by being "slick" and outsmarting others. In line with this, one must always be wary of one's counterparts, to assume that they are involved with you only for what they can get out of the situation.

Correspondingly, life in public often features an intense competition for scarce social goods in which "winners" totally dominate "losers" and in which losing can be a fate worse than death. So one must be on one's guard constantly. One is not always able to trust others fully, in part because so much is at stake socially, but also because everyone else is understood to be so deprived. In these circumstances, violence is quite prevalent—in families, in schools, and in the streets—becoming a way of public life that is effectively governed by the code of the street.

Decent and street families deal with the' code of the street in various ways. An understanding of the dynamics of these families is thus critical to an understanding of the dynamics of the code. It is important to understand here that the family one emerges from is distinct from the "family" one finds in the streets. For street oriented people especially, the family outside competes with blood relatives for an individual's loyalties and commitments. Nevertheless, blood relatives always come first. The folklore of the street says, in effect, that if I will fight and "take up for" my friend, then you know what I will do for my own brother, cousin, nephew, aunt, sister, or mother—and vice versa. Blood is thicker than mud.

Decent Families

In decent families there is almost always a real concern with and a certain amount of hope for the future. Such attitudes are often expressed in a drive to work "to have something" or "to build a good life," while at the same time trying to "make do with what you have." This means working hard, saving money for material things, and raising children—any "child you touch"—to try to make something out of themselves. Decent families tend to accept mainstream values more fully than street families, and they attempt to instill them in their children. Probably the most meaningful description of the mission of the decent family, as seen by members and outsiders alike, is to instill "backbone" and a sense of responsibility in its younger members. In their efforts toward this goal, decent parents are much more able and willing than street-oriented ones to ally themselves with outside institutions such as schools and churches. They value hard work and self-reliance and are willing to sacrifice for their children: they harbor hopes for a better future fur their children, if not for themselves. Rather than dwelling on the hardships and inequities facing them, many such decent people, particularly the increasing number of grandmothers raising grandchildren (see Chapter 6), often see their difficult situation as a test from God and derive great support from their faith and church community.

The role of the "man of the house" is significant. Working-class black families have traditionally placed a high value on male authority. Generally, the man is seen as the "head of household," with the woman as his partner and the children as their subjects. His role includes protecting the family from threats, at times literally putting his body in the line of fire on the street. In return he expects to rule his household and to get respect from the other members, and he encourages his sons to grow up with the same expectations. Being a breadwinner or good provider is often a moral issue, and a man unable to provide for a family invites disrespect from his partner. Many young men who lack the resources to do so often say, "I can't play house," and opt out of forming a family, perhaps leaving the woman and any children to fend for themselves.

Intact nuclear families, although in the minority in the impoverished inner city, provide powerful role models. Typically, husband and wife work at low-paying jobs, sometimes juggling more than one such job each. They may be aided financially by the contributions of a teenage child who works part-time. Such families, along with other such local families, are often vigilant in their desire to keep the children away from the streets.

In public such an intact family makes a striking picture as the man may take pains to show he is in complete control-with the woman and the children following his lead. On the inner-city streets this appearance helps him play his role as protector, and he may exhibit exaggerated concern for his family, particularly when other males are near. His actions and words, including loud and deep-voiced assertions to get his small children in line, let strangers know: "This is my family, and I am in charge." He signals that he is capable of protecting them and that his family is not to be messed with.

I witnessed such a display one Saturday afternoon at the Gallery, an indoor shopping mall with a primarily black, Hispanic, and working- to middle-class white clientele. Rasheed Taylor, his wife, Iisha, and their children, Rhonda, Jimmy, and Malika, wandered about the crowded food court looking for a place to sit down to eat. They finally found a table next. to mine. Before sitting down, Mr. Taylor asked me if the seats were available, to which I replied they were. He then summoned his family, and they walked forward promptly and in an orderly way to take the seats. The three children sat on one side and the parents on the other. Mr. Taylor took food requests and with a stern look in his eye told the children to stay seated until he and his wife returned with the food. The children nodded attentively. After the adults left, the children seemed to relax, talking more freely and playing with one another. When the parents returned, the kids straightened up again, received their food, and began to eat, displaying quite and gracious manners all the while. It was very clear to everybody looking on that Mr. Taylor was in charge of this family, with everyone showing him utter deference and respect.

Extremely aware of the problematic and often dangerous environment in which they reside, decent parents tend to be strict in their child-rearing practices, encouraging children to respect authority and walk a straight moral line. They sometimes display an almost obsessive concern about trouble of any kind and encourage their children to avoid people and situations that might lead to it. But this is very difficult, since the decent and the street families live in such close proximity. Marge, a slight, forty-three-year-old, married, decent parent of five who resides in such a neighborhood, relates her experience:

But you know what happens now? I have five children. Or I had five children—my oldest son got killed in a car accident. My children have always been different [decent]. And sometimes we have to act that way [street] that other people act to show them that you're not gonna be intimidated, that my child is gonna go to the store, they're gonna come out here and play, they're gonna go to school. You don't wanta do that, but you can't go to them and talk. 'Cause I've tried that. I've tried to go to people and say, "Listen. These are children. Let's try to make them get along." I remember years ago my sons had some expensive baseball mitts and bats that was given to them. I didn't buy them. They got them from Mr. Lee because he had the baseball team. And so he gave my sons some baseball bats and gloves. At that time the park at Twenty-seventh and Girard was Fred Jackson Stadium; they call it Ruth Bloom now. My sons played base-ball there. So one little boy wanted to borrow some of the gloves and the bat. I told my children,

"Don't let him hold [use] the gloves and the bat." But they let him hold them anyway. So he told them that when he finished with them he would put them on the porch. I told them they were never going to see them again, and they were never put on the porch. So I went to his mother, that was my neighbor, and I approached her very nicely and I said, "Johnny didn't bring Terry and Curtis's gloves and bat back." You know, she cursed me out! I was shocked. [She said,] "He doesn't have to take a so-and-so bat and a ball." And that woman really shocked me and hurt my feelings. I said, "For get it. Just forget it." She was really ignorant. But I had to even though I didn't get ignorant [get on her level] 'cause my son was there-but I had to say *some* negative things to her to let her know that I was just shocked. But I've been here [residing in this neighborhood] twenty-two years, and in twenty-two years I've had at least ten different, separate incidents that I had to go out and talk to somebody, to the point that I told my children, "No more." Somebody's gonna get hurt 'cause they don't know when to stop.

OK, my daughter, Annette, she went to Germantown High. So she was in about the ninth grade, had never had a fight in her life. She came from the store one day, and she told me about this girl that kept pickin' on her. She came up on the porch, and she said, "Mommy, come to the door. I want to show you this girl that keeps picking on me." Of course. Anybody that bothered them, I always wanted to see who it was in case I had to go see their parents or whatever. So I came and looked over the railing on the porch, and me and my daughter were lookin' down the street in that direction, not really at her [which could have been taken as offensive]. The girl came up and said, "Who the fuck are you lookin' at?" I said to my daughter, "Don't say any thing." So I said to the girl, "You better go home. You better take your little but home." OK. So she did go home. That afternoon, my daughter was sitting on the steps of the porch and reading a book—now this is a child who never had a fight, gets good grades. I think I raised her extremely well. She's a biochemist now. She's sitting on the step, reading her little book, and the girl came up to her, said something to her. I wasn't even out there, and so by the time my sons came to get me, my daughter and her were fighting. That was the first fight that she ever had in her life, and she was in the ninth grade. So I went out there and separated them. The girl went around the corner. When she came back, she had twenty different people with her. But I knew what was gonna happen. So-those same baseball bats I told you about—I told my son to get the baseball bats from the hallway. I said, "We're not gonna get off the porch, but If we have to, if they come up here, we're gonna have to do something." So they came back, and I had to actually coax them off like I was a little tough, like I'm not gonna take it. And I said to my sons, "If they come up here, we're gonna pay they as back," and all that kind of stuff. And that's how I got them off us. I mean, it was about twenty of them, friends, family, neighbors.

As I indicated above, people who define themselves as decent tend themselves to be polite and considerate of others and teach their children to be the same way. But this is sometimes difficult, mainly because of the social environment in which they reside, and they often perceive a need to "get ignorant"—to act aggressively, even to threaten violence.' For whether a certain child gets picked on may well depend not just on the reputation of the child but, equally important, on how "bad" the child's family is known to be. How many people the child can gather together for the purposes of defense or revenge often emerges as a critical issue. Thus social relations can become practical matters of personal defense. Violence can come at any time, and many persons feel a great need to be ready to defend themselves.

At home, at work, and in church, decent parents strive to maintain a positive mental attitude and a spirit of cooperation. When disciplining their children, they tend to use corporal punishment, but unlike street parents, who can often be observed lashing out at their children, they may explain the reason for the spanking. These parents express their care and love for teenage children by guarding against the appearance of any kind of "loose" behavior (violence, drug use, staying out very late) that might be associated with the streets. In this regard, they are vigilant, observing children's peers as well and some times embarrassing their own children by voicing value judgments in front of friends.

These same parents are aware, however, that the right material things as well as a certain amount of cash are essential to young people's survival on the street. So they may purchase expensive things for their children, even when money is tight, in order that the children will be less tempted to turn to the drug trade or other aspects of the underground economy for money.

The Decent Single Mother

A single mother with children-the majority of decent families in the impoverished sections of the inner city are of this type-must work even harder to neutralize the draw of the street, and she does so mainly by being strict and by instilling decent values in her children. She may live with her mother or other relatives and friends, or she may simply receive help with child care from her extended fancily. In raising her children, she often must press others to defer to her authority; but without a strong man of the house, a figure boys in particular are prepared to respect, she is at some disadvantage with regard not only to her own sons and daughters but also to the young men of the streets. These men may test her ability to control her household by attempting to date her daughters or to draw her sons into the streets. A mother on her own often feels she must be constantly on guard and exhibit a great deal of determination.

Diane, a single mother of four sons, three of whom are grown a case in point. Diane is forty-six years old, of average height, heavyset, and light-complexioned. One of her sons is a night watchman at the utility company, and another is a security guard at a down town store. Diane herself works as an aide in a day care center. In describing her situation, she has this to say:

> It really is pretty bad around here. There's quite a few grandmother taking care of kids. They mothers out here on crack. There's quite a few of 'em. The drugs are terrible. Now, I got a fifteen-year-old boy, and I do everything I can to keep him straight. 'Cause they [drug dealers and users] all on the corner. You can't say you not in it, 'cause we in a bad area. They be all on the corner. They be sittin' in front of apartments takin' the crack And constantly, every day, I have to stay on 'em and make sure everything's OK. Which is real bad, I never seen it this bad. And I been around here since '81, and I never seen it this bad. At nights they be roamin' up and down the streets, and they be droppin' the caps [used crack vials] all in front of your door. And when the kids out there playin', you gotta like sweep 'em up. It's harder for me now to try to keep my fifteen-year-old under control. Right now, he likes to do auto mechanics, hook up radios in people's cars, and long as I keep 'im interested in that, I'm OK But it's not a day that goes by that I'm not in fear. 'Cause right now he got friends that's sellin' it. They, you know, got a whole lot of money and stuff. And I get him to come and mop floors [she works part-time as a janitor], and I give him a few dollars. I say, "As long as you got a roof over yo' head, son, don't worry about nothin else."
>
> It's just a constant struggle tryin' to raise yo' kids in this time. It's very hard. They [boys on the street] say to him, "Man, why you got to go in the house?" And they keep sittin' right on my stoop. If he go

somewhere, I got to know where he's at and who he's with. And they be tellin' him [come with us]. He say, "No, man, I got to stay on these steps. I don't want no problem with my mama!" Now, I been a single parent for fifteen years. So far, I don't have any problems. I have four sons. I got just the one that's not grown, the fifteen-year-old. Everyone else is grown. My oldest is thirty-five. I'm tryin'. Not that easy. I got just one more, now. Then I'll be all right. If I need help, the older ones'll help me. Most of the time, I keep track myself. I told him I'll kill him if I catch him out here sellin'. And I know most of the drug dealers. He better not. I'm gon' hurt him. They better not give him nothin'. He better not do nothin' for them. tell him, "I know some of your friends are dealers. [You can] speak to 'em but don't let me catch you hangin' on the corner. I done struggled too hard to try to take care of you. I'm not gon' let you throw your life away."

When me and my husband separated in '79, I figured I had to do it. He was out there drivin' trucks and never home. I had to teach my kids how to play ball and this and that. I said, "If I have to be a single parent, I'll do it." It used to be the gangs, and you fought 'em, and it was over. But now if you fight somebody, they may come back and kill you. It's a whole lot different now. You got to be street-smart to get along. My boy doesn't like to fight. I took him out of school, put him in a home course. The staff does what it wants to. [They] just work for a paycheck.

You tell the kid, now you can't pick their friends, so you do what you can. I try to tell mine, "You gon' be out there with the bad [street kids], you can't do what they do. You got to use your own mind." Every day, if I don't get up and say a prayer, I can't make it. I can't make it. I watch him closely. If he go somewhere, I have to know where he at. And when I leave him, or if he go to them girlfriends' houses, I tell the parents, "If you not responsible, he can't stay." I'm not gon' have no teenager making no baby.

These comments show how one decent inner-city parent makes sense of the breakdown in civility, order, and morality she sees occurring in her community and how she copes. When Diane was a child, and even when her older sons were growing up, gang fights were common, but they generally took the form of an air-clearing brawl. Today many community residents feel that if you run afoul of a gang or an individual, somebody may simply kill you. Note that the schools are included among the institutions seen to have abdicated their responsibilities, a widespread belief among many inner-city parents.

The Street Family

So-called street parents, unlike decent ones, often show a lack of consideration for other people and have a rather superficial sense of family and community. They may love their children but frequently find it difficult both to cope with the physical and emotional demands of parenthood and to reconcile their needs with those of their children. Members of these families, who are more fully invested in the· code of the street than the decent people are, may aggressively socialize their children into it in a normative way. They more fully believe in the code and judge themselves and others according to its values.

In fact, the overwhelming majority of families in the inner-city community try to approximate the decent-family model, but many others clearly represent the decent families' worst fears. Not only are their financial resources extremely limited, but what little they have may easily be misused. The lives of the street-oriented are often marked by disorganization. In the most desperate circumstances, people frequently have a limited understanding of priorities and consequences, and so frustrations mount over bills, food, and, at times, liquor, cigarettes, and drugs. Some people tend toward self destructive behavior; many street-oriented women are crack-addicted ("on the pipe"), alcoholic, or involved in complicated relationships with men who abuse them.

In addition, the seeming intractability of their situation, caused in large part by the lack of well-paying jobs and the persistence of racial discrimination, has engendered deep-seated bitterness and anger in many of the most desperate and poorest blacks, especially young people. The need both to exercise a measure of control and to lash out at somebody is often reflected in the adults' relations with their children. At the very least, the frustrations associated with persistent poverty shorten the fuse in such people, contributing to a lack of patience with anyone—child or adult—who irritates them.

People who fit the conception of street are often considered to be lowlife or "bad people," especially by the "decent people," and they are generally seen as incapable of being anything but a bad influence on the community and a bother to their neighbors. For example, on a relatively quiet block in West Oak Lane, on the edge of a racially integrated, predominantly middle-class neighborhood, there is a row of houses inhabited by impoverished people. One of them is Joe Dickens, a heavyset, thirty-two-year-old black man. Joe rents the house he lives in, and he shares it with his three children—two daughters (aged seven and five) and a three-year-old son. With patches on the brickwork, an irregular pillar holding up the porch roof, and an unpainted plywood front door, his house sticks out on the block. The front windows have bars; the small front yard is filled with trash and weeds; the garbage cans at the side of the house are continually overflowing.

Even more obtrusive is the lifestyle of the household. Dickens's wife has disappeared from the scene. It is rumored that her crack habit got completely out of control, and she gravitated to the streets and became a prostitute to support her habit. Dickens could not accept this behavior and let her go; he took over running the house and caring for the children as best he could. And to the extent that the children are fed, clothed, and housed under his roof, he might be considered a responsible parent.

But many of the neighbors do not view him as responsible. They see him yelling and cursing at the kids when he pays attention to them at all. Mostly, he allows them to "rip and run" unsupervised up and down the street at all hours, riding their Big Wheels and making a racket. They are joined by other neighborhood children playing on the streets and sidewalks without adult supervision. Dickens himself pays more attention to his buddies, who seem always to be hanging out at the house—on the porch in warm weather—playing loud rap music, drinking beer, and playing cards.

Dickens generally begins his day at about 11 A.M., when he may go out for cheesesteaks and videos for his visitors. In fact, one gets the impression that the house is the scene of an ongoing party. The noise constantly disturbs the neighbors, sometimes prompting them to call the police. But the police rarely respond to the complaints, leaving the neighbors frustrated and demoralized. Dickens seems almost completely indifferent to his neighbors and inconsiderate of their concerns, a defining trait of street-oriented people.

Dickens's decent neighbors are afraid to confront him because they fear getting into trouble with him and his buddies. They are sure that he believes in the principle that might makes right and that he is likely to try to harm anyone who annoys him. Furthermore, they suspect he is a crack dealer. The neighbors cannot confirm this, but some are convinced anyway, and activities around his house support this conclusion. People come and go at all hours of the day and night; they often leave their car engines running, dash into the house, and quickly emerge and drive off. Dickens's children, of course, see much of this activity. At times the children are made to stand outside on the porch while business is presumably being transacted inside. These children are learning by example the values of toughness and self absorption: to be loud, boisterous, proudly crude, and uncouth-in short, street.

Maxine's family is another example. On a block that has managed to retain a preponderance of decent households, one house had stood vacant for some time. One day the absentee landlord showed up and started making minor repairs, painting the porch railings, and carrying out trash bags. Sometime later, Maxine, a large brown-skinned woman, was spotted sweeping up in the backyard, helped out by a heavyset middle-aged black man. The block's residents took note. Had the home been sold? Had the landlord found new tenants? Who were they? What were they like? Finally, move-in day arrived. Maxine and her friend, along with her six children, appeared on the block with an old blue pickup truck loaded down with old furniture, including beds, tables, lamps, and black plastic bags full of stuff. Anxious neighbors watched while they unloaded the truck and moved the belongings into the house.

After they moved in, Maxine's children were the first to make their presence felt on the block, spending a large part of the day playing noisily without supervision outside. Soon, however, a larger problem developed: a middle-aged male whose relationship to Maxine was unclear appeared to move in. After he did so, people began to notice a series of comings and goings at various times of the day and night. There were also exchanges on the front porch, on the sidewalk and in the street. Though residents did not know the exact nature of these transactions, her neighbors assumed that they involved drugs, because everything else seemed to fit. In addition, at night those residing closest to Maxine could hear the sounds of a great commotion and the screams of her children. The block had become decidedly less peaceful- and dirtier. On trash-pickup day, Maxine's trash would often not be stored properly, and some of it would fall to the ground, where it would lie and fly around with the wind. She and her children would sometimes contribute to the litter by tossing empty bags and soda bottles from the porch as soon as they were done with them. This behavior further upset the neighbors.

But most upsetting of all was the blatant drug dealing now going on at Maxine's house. All of this came to a head one Saturday in May at about 1 p.m. On this nice spring afternoon, the peace of the block was disturbed by a young man who was wailing and banging on Maxine's front door. A few residents were out and about doing chores, and small children played and rode their tricycles and bikes up and down the block. "Gimme my drugs, bitch! Where my drugs at?" The young man cried as he banged on the door. The neighbors who were out began to look at Maxine's house. After hearing this noise and assessing the situation, one woman ran to collect her small daughter, who was in front of the house on her tricycle. Suddenly, a beat-up brown windowless van careened around the corner and ·came to a screeching halt in front of Maxine's house. Out jumped two young black men, who headed for Maxine's front door. Without knocking, they entered, as though they had been summoned to deal with the other young man. But no sooner had they entered than they emerged, running out, ducking and hiding behind nearby trees and cars. It was clear that they were afraid of being hit by some flying object—or possibly of being shot at. By now the commotion had brought together a small crowd. And after a little while the police were summoned, and they came. They parked their police van on the street near the brown van and proceeded to the front door. They entered and in a few minutes emerged with the first young man and placed him in the van. At this point the man began to scream and yell at Maxine. "I'll get you, bitch! You won't get away with this. I'll get you," he cried. "As soon as I get out, I'll get you!" The police van drove away, leaving the neighbors with their worst fears confirmed: Maxine had established the street lifestyle on their previously quiet block.

Street-oriented women tend to perform their motherly duties sporadically. The most irresponsible women can be found at local bars and crack houses, getting high and socializing with other adults. Reports of crack addicts abandoning their children have become common in drug-infested inner-city communities. Typically, neighbors or relatives discover the abandoned children, often hungry and distraught over the absence of their mother. After repeated absences a friend or relative, particularly a grandmother, will often step in to care for the children, sometimes petitioning the authorities to send her, as guardian of the children, the mother's welfare check, if she gets one. By this time, however, the children may well have learned the first lesson of the streets: you cannot take survival itself, let alone respect, for granted; you have to fight for your place in the world. Some of the children learn to fend for themselves, foraging for food and money any way they can. They are sometimes employed by drug dealers or become addicted themselves (see Chapter 3).

These children of the street, growing up with little supervision, are said to "come up hard." They often learn to fight at an early age, using short-tempered adults around them as role models. The street-oriented home may be fraught with anger, verbal disputes, physical aggression, even mayhem. The children are victimized by these goings-on and quickly learn to hit those who cross them.

The people who see themselves as decent refer to the general set of cultural deficits exhibited by people like Maxine and Joe Dick ens—a fundamental lack of social polish and commitment to norms of civility—as "ignorance." In their view ignorance lies behind the propensity to violence that makes relatively minor social transgressions snowball into more serious disagreements, and they believe that the street-oriented are quick to resort to violence in almost any dispute.

The fact that the decent people, as a rule civilly disposed, socially conscious, and self-reliant men and women, share the neighborhood streets and other public places with those associated with the street, the inconsiderate, the ignorant, and the desperate, places the "good" people at special risk. In order to live and function in the community, they must adapt to a street reality that is often dominated by people who at best are suffering severely in some way and who are apt to resort quickly to violence to settle disputes. This process of adapting means learning and observing the code of the street. Decent people may readily defer to people, especially strangers, who seem to be at all street-oriented. When they encounter such people at theaters and other public places talking loudly or making excessive noise, they are reluctant to correct them for fear of verbal abuse that could lead to violence. Similarly, they will often avoid confrontations over a parking space or traffic error for fear of a verbal or physical altercation. But under their breaths they may mutter "street niggers" to a black companion, drawing a sharp cultural distinction between themselves and such individuals.

There are also times when decent people try to approach the level of the ignorant ones by "getting ignorant" themselves, as Diane's story illustrates, making clear by their behavior that they too are entitled to respect and are not to be messed with. In these circum stances, they may appear more than ready to face down the ignorant ones, indicating they have reached their limit or threshold for violent confrontation. From such seemingly innocent encounters, actual fights can and do erupt, but often there is an underlying issue—typically involving money. Don Moses is a sixty-year-old gypsy taxi driver who has lived in various local black communities his entire life. Don has the reputation of being a decent man, attending church when he can and trying to treat everyone with respect. He knows the city "like the back of my hand." He related to me the following of the levels of violence in his neighborhood:

Somebody's mother, daughter, father, child got shot. I hear it all the time. Hardly a night goes by that I don't hear gunshots. Sometimes you hear live voices and gunshots. You get the paper the next day—I remember the other night I was in the bathroom, and somebody shot—boom!—between out yards. The next day, that shot I heard, it was somebody getting shot. He went to the door, this guy did this guy wrong, kicked the door open, bam!—shot the guy. I just had a feeling—sometimes you hear a shot and you say, "I wonder who went down behind that." Sure enough, somebody did go down. Could have been anything the littlest thing. Could be somebody left the trash can with the lid off in front of his house. Anything.

A good example of that is a neighbor. I got along—and I've always prided myself on being able to get along with everybody, especially neighbors. I say you have to take care with everybody, especially neighbors. I say you have to take care with your neighbors and look out for them because who else is going to look out for your property if you're not there or your children. My neighbor and I, we got along very well. Last winter, my neighbor, who was a woman, her mother started an argument. She used to have this little bickering with me for no reason at all. She'd say something to me—I left the flashers on my car once: "Why don't you turn the flashers off? The first thing you wanta do if your battery runs down is ask Johnnie"—that's the girl's name—"to give you a jump: she can't be doing this." And I would politely say, "Thank you for telling me. I'll try my best to keep my thinking cap on."

It keept on until she finally found something to really jump on. Her son borrowed some money from me, and he didn't pay it back. Her daughter approached me and said "Look, my brother hasn't paid you back the money. I feel responsible for him, I was there. I'm gonna give you the money." Now, if you tell me that, I'm gonna be looking for you. So when I would see her, and I'd see her a couple times, "I don't have it now." So one time I was walkin' in the house, she told me, "Look, you're gonna have to see my brother for that money." So, I said, "Sure, it's fine. I'll see. We'll cross each other's paths sometime." So as fate would have it, one day he shows up and he and I had a few words. And he didn't have it on him. Three or four times he said he was gonna have it, and he didn't have it. So then that led into the time I was home and her and her mother blowed up. Her mother lit into me: "I don't know why you keep harassin' "—I really hadn't said anything to her for about a month after she said her brother would take care of it, I'd have to see him-I'd say, "No problem. It wasn't your debt. It was your brother's debt. You just happened to be there. The transaction took place in your place." Jesus, her mother lit into me. Now, I know that she instigated that by tellin' her mother, "Every time I see Don, he's askin' me for the money." I knew that's what happened. I didn't wanta let her know that I knew. She knew it, and she was trying to hush her mother up and pull me aside and talk to me. I started to get real angry with her mother because her mother had already prodded and tried to get something started with me, so she finally succeeded. All I said to her was, "Look, it really wasn't any of your business. I don't have anything to say to you about this. I don't wanta hurt your feelings. I don't wanta be disrespectful to you 'cause you're older than I. I don't want anything negative to jump off, and I don't want any problems with your daughter or your son." He was on the porch, and he gets the attitude: "What are you doin' talkin to my mother?" I said, "I didn't say anything. I didn't use no profanity. I didn't raise my voice. I wasn't disrespectful to her. I think she was very disrespectful to me." So he jumps up off the porch and goes into the house. I walked back to say something to him. He jumps up and goes into the house. Now, be pulled a gun on several people and I was lookin' for him to come out with a gun, but he didn't He didn't come out of the house. So after that—that's been a year ago—things kind of cooled off. We just started kind of talkin' to each other again. You don't wanta fight with your neighbor.

As Dan's account indicates, respect or props are very much an issue in the community, and if a person determines that he or she is not getting the proper deference, there can be trouble. In this case the man. Don had lent money to had not paid up, so his sister intervened perhaps very much aware that her brother could be viewed as disrespectmg Don by not paying off the debt. Then, on the porch the man ."copped" an attitude with Don about the supposed way he was treating his mother, but things cooled off and violence was averted. meanwhile, Don is still waiting for his money, but he is prepared to wait for the man who owes him to pay up voluntarily, mainly because the person is potentially violent- and street- and Don does not want to give him an excuse to feel he has been wronged enough to resort to violence. For the time being, Don knows that the "price" of repaying the debt owed to him may well be too high.

The inner-city community is actually quite diverse economically; various people are doing fairly well, whereas others are very poor but decent and still others are utterly and profoundly suffering, alienated, and angry. Such is the social terrain the decent family must navigate and negotiate in order to remain whole as well as secure. This situation creates a major dilemma for decent families who are trying to raise their children to remain decent even though they must negotiate the streets. These parents want their children to value educations, jobs, and a future, but they also want them to get their fair share of respect and the props that go with it- and not to be dissed or attacked or shot.

DISCUSSION QUESTIONS
By John M. Stogner

1. How is the code of the streets likely to differentially impact the behavior of males and females?
2. *The Code of the Street* was based on extensive qualitative fieldwork, but most criminological studies are quantitative. What does this mean for your interpretation of Anderson's work? How might this have impacted the academic community's interpretation of his work?
3. How does Anderson's work relate to the neighborhood-level theories presented in the preceding chapter?
4. In communities like those described by Anderson is it possible for any social interactions to result in a net gain in terms of respect (meaning all parties involved)?
5. Does the code of the streets apply to poor, rural African American neighborhoods/communities?

CHAPTER SEVENTEEN

Adolescence and Crime

MICHAEL L. BENSON

STUDENT INTRODUCTION
By John M. Stogner

Individuals clearly change as they grow older. You likely have different interests now than just a few short years ago, and your behaviors have likely also changed. Criminologists have long been aware of these changes and that the general process of maturation yields what has been labeled the age–crime curve. The majority of offenses are committed by individuals in late adolescence and early adulthood. As individuals grow older, they typically violate the law less frequently. In a way, this information partially blinded the field for some time. So much offending occurred during a brief window of development that only this window was the subject of many criminological works

and theories. Put another way, because so many crimes are committed by adolescents and young adults, crimes committed during other windows—and what makes the period adolescence/young adulthood special—were partially ignored. The life-course criminology perspective addresses this issue, noting that there is both change and continuity in individuals' behaviors as they age. It explores the general pattern of offending and factors that may account for the age–crime curve.

In the following chapter, Michael Benson presents compelling insight regarding the age—crime curve and the existence of offender groups responsible for a disproportionate amount of crime. He describes four leading theories that fall within the life-course perspective (note: Benson distinguishes between life-course and developmental perspectives, but this distinction is unnecessary). The most influential of these is likely the work of Robert Sampson and John Laub, which presents arguments referred to as the *age-graded theory of informal social control*. The theory was based on unique and impressive data containing information about the full lives of 500 formerly delinquent boys born in the 1930s. The age-graded theory of informal social control provides insight into why individuals' behaviors generally follow a trajectory but can also change quickly. Terrie Moffitt's developmental taxonomy has also received a great deal of attention. Moffitt argues that there are multiple types of offenders and offending trajectories, which necessitates multiple theories. She developed a biosocial theory for what she terms *life-course persistent offenders* and a social mimicry explanation for *adolescent-limited offenders*. In addition to these works, pay careful attention to the contributions of John Hagan and Terrence Thornberry.

As you read consider the relationship between works within the life-course perspective and the theories presented in the preceding chapters. Ask whether age-graded informal social control is truly distinct from social bonding theory and consider whether Moffitt's social mimicry theory is consistent with Akers's presentation of adolescent delinquency. Also examine the potential policy applications of each theory. Attempt to determine whether each work's insight can be utilized to effectively reform policy and reduce offending in the future. Consider Moffitt's argument that multiple theories are needed to understand multiple types of offenders and question whether there may be more than two offending types/trajectories.

ADOLESCENCE AND CRIME: CONTINUITY AND CHANGE
By Michael L. Benson

Overview

For many parents, teachers, and just about everybody else, teenagers can be a lot of trouble. During the teenage years, there is a rapid, almost explosive, increase in the prevalence of offending. Indeed, involvement in minor forms of delinquency is so widespread among teenagers that it is statistically normal (Moffitt 1993; Moffitt 1997; Wiesner and Capaldi 2003). It may seem odd and it certainly goes against the wishes of most parents, but the child who never does anything wrong is actually out of step with peers and may be a cause for concern. For criminologists, the teenage years are where the action is.

The age of onset—that is, the age at which a person commits his or her first offense—appears to peak between 15 and 17 (Nagin and Farrington 1992; Elliott 1994; Farrington 1994; Steffensmeier and Allan 2000). Regardless of whether offending is measured by self-reports or official statistics such as arrest rates, a large proportion of young people become involved in delinquent behavior during this period. From the perspective of life course theory, this two-year period is especially important because it is when most people start their trajectories in crime and delinquency. Luckily for society, these trajectories tend to be short-lived and characterized by relatively minor offenses (Farrington, Ohlin, and Wilson 1986). After a brief teenage walk on the wild side, the average person settles down to a life of more or less consistent conformity. But this pattern is not universal. Some individuals follow trajectories of much longer duration, involving much more serious types of offenses. Thus, as we will see, the teenage years are marked by both continuity and discontinuity in behavior. For most people, the teenage years encompass two important turning points: onset of offending and desistance from offending.

Although there is near-universal consensus on the general shape of the age—crime curve (Ellis, Beaver, and Wright 2009), scholars still debate a number of important details about the relationship between age and crime (Gottfredson and Hirschi 1990; Steffensmeier and Allan 2000). One particularly important matter concerns the theoretical interpretation of the relationship between age and crime. What causes or underlies the rapid increase in the prevalence of offending during the early teenage years? Just as important, what causes the almost equally rapid decline in offending near the end of the teenage years? A second important issue concerns the universality or invariance of the age—crime relationship. Is the relationship between age and crime the same in all societies and among all groups of people, or does it vary over time, place, demographic category, and type of crime? Do some individuals follow trajectories that do not coincide with the general trend? To put it another way, are there different types of trajectories in crime and deviance? And if so, how many types are there, what are their characteristics, and why do some people follow one trajectory while others follow different trajectories? These are important questions for life course criminology.

Societal Age–Crime Patterns

Our picture of the age—crime curve is based primarily on two data sources: arrest statistics and self-report surveys (Ellis, Beaver, and Wright 2009). Arrest statistics are the most common indicator of criminal behavior. The standard technique for examining arrests and age is to calculate age-adjusted arrest rates for a given time period, type of offense, and locality. An age-adjusted arrest rate is the rate at which persons of a particular age are arrested. Rates are usually expressed as the number of arrests per some constant number, such as 1,000. For example, using data from the 2007 Uniform Crime Report and estimated population data from the U.S. Census, we can calculate age-adjusted arrest rates for all offenses for selected age groups, as shown in Figure 17.1. These data are approximate, but they give us a feel for the relationship between age and crime and they replicate the pattern found in a large number of studies. Involvement in crime is highest during the second and third decades of life (Ellis, Beaver, and Wright 2009). For both males and females the graph describes an inverted *j* pattern (Tittle and Paternoster 2000, 326), though for females the *j* has a much lower peak. Starting at age 10, the age-adjusted arrest rate rises precipitously. Somewhere between the ages of 15 and 24 the rate peaks at about 149 for males and slightly below 60 for females. Then, it gradually slopes downward like an inverted *j*, until around age 55, when the age-adjusted rate for both sexes starts closing in on zero.

The calculation of age-adjusted arrest rates clearly shows that arrests occur much more frequently during the late teenage and early adult years than at any other time in the life course. But these data must be interpreted carefully. They do not show the age of onset, that is, the age at which most people are *first* arrested. Instead, the data show that given their representation in the population, people aged 15 to 24 are arrested more often than people aged 25 and over. However, this does not mean that most people are first arrested when they are 15, nor do the data show the prevalence rate for this age group. That is, we cannot assume, based on these data, that 149 out of every 1,000 15-to 24-year-olds are arrested, because some arrests undoubtedly involve repeat offenders—those who have been arrested more than once in a year.

To ascertain the age of onset of offending, a second technique must be used. This technique involves sampling individuals and either asking them to self-report on their first offense or else reviewing official records to see at what age each person first appears in the records. With this data, the hazard rate for

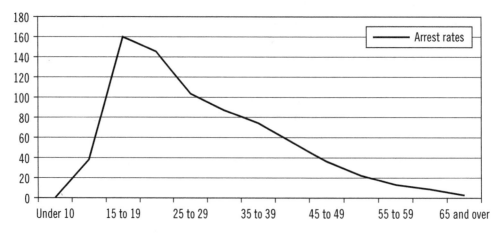

FIGURE 17.1. Arrest Rates per 1,000 by Age

first arrest (or first self-reported offense) can be calculated. The hazard rate is the rate at which persons in a sample experience some event, such as an arrest, determined from among those who have not yet experienced the event. For example, imagine that 100 males aged 20 are sampled and a check of official records reveals that at age 10 only one of them had been arrested. The hazard rate for first arrest at age 10 would be one in 100, or .01. Continuing to check the records, we find that at age 11 three more individuals were arrested. In this sample, then, the hazard rate for first arrest at age 11 would be 3 in 99, or .0303. This second rate is based on 99 individuals because the person who was arrested at age 10 is not eligible to have another first arrest. If we continued on in this fashion, we could calculate a hazard rate for first arrest for all ages up to the current age of our sample, which in this hypothetical example is age 20.

If we plot hazard rates against age, the result is a graph such as that shown in Figure 17.2. This figure, based on data from the National Youth Survey, shows the hazard rate for onset of serious offending by age and race (Elliott 1994). Because the graph plots the behavior of a relatively small number of people, it appears to be more erratic and jagged than the plots of national arrest statistics, which are based on millions of arrests. Nevertheless, for both African Americans and whites the general shape of the hazard rate curve resembles that of the familiar inverted *j* of age-adjusted arrest rates. Up to age 11, the hazard rate is very low, less than 0.5 percent for the total sample. At age 12 a steep increase begins that peaks at around age 16 (Elliott 1994). The rate then declines to under 1.0 percent by age 27. After age 27, very few people initiate careers in serious violent offending. People who are going to commit such offenses at any time in the life course almost always begin doing so before age 30.

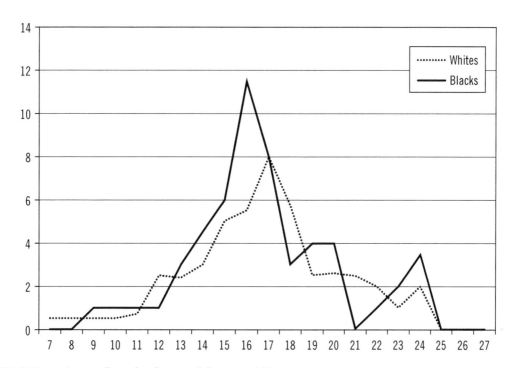

FIGURE 17.2. Hazard Rate for Onset of Serious Offending

Source: Elliott, Delbert S. 1994. "Serious Violent Offenders: Onset, Developmental Course and Termination." *Criminology* 32:1–22.

A very similar pattern was observed in the Cambridge Youth Study (West and Farrington 1977, 6–8). When the subjects in that prospective study of 411 lower-class males were 20 years old, Donald West and David Farrington examined official court records. They found that by age 20 a total of 120 youths, which is about 30 percent of the sample, had compiled 360 official joined them at age 11. The percentage of youths first convicted increased sharply up to a peak at age 14, when 21 of the subjects were convicted for the first time. After age 14, declining numbers of youths initiated criminal activity in each succeeding year. The peak age for convictions occurred at 18, when 42 different youths were convicted. Thus, in this sample, the prevalence of delinquency was highest at age 18. From that point on, the prevalence rate declined and fewer and fewer of the subjects in the study were criminally active.

Data from a variety of different sources and studies paint a similar picture. The peak age for onset of offending occurs somewhere between 14 and 15. The highest prevalence rate occurs a year or two after that. After age 20, it becomes highly unlikely that a previously law-abiding person will initiate a criminal career (Elliott, Huizinga, and Menard 1989; Elliott 1994). Almost everyone who is going to start has started by then (Moffitt 2006). And, by age 20, most of those who started earlier have either desisted or begun to reduce their levels of criminal activity.

Whether this pattern holds for all types of offenses, at all times, and in all places is debated. Gottfredson and Hirschi (1990) claim that the relationship between age and crime is invariant, meaning that it is found in all societies at all times. They further claim that the age—crime relationship is not subject to explanation by sociological variables. That young people commit more offenses than older people is simply a law of human nature. It is not something that is caused by the special experiences that youths undergo or by variation in standard sociological variables such as race or socioeconomic status. It just is.

Other scholars reject this extreme position (Steffensmeier and Allan 2000; Tittle and Paternoster 2000). Darrell Steffensmeier and Emilie Allan (106) argue that the claim of invariance is overstated. They contend that careful analysis shows considerable variation across offense types in the peak age and rate of decline from the peak age. To illustrate their point, Steffensmeier and Allan calculated age-adjusted arrest rates for three different offenses: burglary, fraud, and gambling. The peak age for burglary arrests occurs at about 19, but for fraud offenses it is closer to age 25. After peaking at age 19, the arrests rate for burglary decreases by over half just a few years later. The decline in the arrest rate for fraud, however, is much more gradual over time. Finally, the arrest rate for gambling does not appear to follow the standard inverted *j* pattern at all. It peaks at around age 20, declines slightly in the following few years, and then stabilizes for about 30 years. Thus, for people in their early twenties, the age-adjusted arrest rate for gambling was just under 2 percent. For people in their early fifties, it was also just under 2 percent. Contrary to the invariance hypothesis, the shapes of these three age—crime curves do not correspond with one another. In other words, the relationship between age and crime varies from one type of crime to another.

There are other differences in the age—crime curve that belie the idea that it is invariant. One important difference involves racial and ethnic minorities. The invariance hypothesis predicts that the relationship between age and crime is the same for all types of people. Thus, we would expect that the proportion of arrests accounted for by youths would be the same for whites and nonwhites. For example, if white youths between the ages of 15 and 20 account for 60 percent of arrests of white people for burglary, then African-American youths of the same ages should make up a roughly similar percentage of burglary arrests for African Americans. But they do not. The adult percentage of arrests for African Americans is larger than the adult percentage of arrests for whites across all crime categories (Steffensmeier and Allan

1995). For African Americans, the dramatic drop-off in offending that is expected to occur at the end of the teenage years is not so dramatic. The slope of the right side of the age—crime curve is more gradual, less sharply pitched downward for African Americans than for whites. This means that there is a greater probability that African-American as opposed to white offenders will continue to be involved in crime in adulthood. The reasons for the longer duration of criminal careers among African Americans are changes in the global economy. We will look into these matters later. But for now, we note that the relationship between age and crime appears to be different for African Americans than for whites.

One other aspect of the age—crime curve remains to be addressed, and that is whether the curve is invariant across cultures and historical periods. The evidence on this question is mixed. Gottfredson and Hirschi (1990, 124–126) examined data on age and crime from nineteenth-century England and Wales (1842–44), England in 1908, and the United States in 1977. The general shapes of the curves they examined are quite similar, with involvement in crime peaking during the late teen years and then sloping down gradually. Since the data come from different countries and span over 130 years, they concluded that this was impressive evidence of cross-cultural and historical stability.

Other analyses, however, suggest that the shape of the age—crime curve does vary both cross-culturally and historically. Societal age—crime curves appear to be influenced by variation in the degree of age stratification in society. Age stratification refers to distinctions made between age groups in regard to the roles that members of different age groups are expected to occupy and in the relative social status of different age groups. Contemporary industrialized societies, such as the United States, Canada, and Western Europe, are highly age stratified. For the most part, youths have low status and are excluded from assuming responsible and productive economic roles until well after they reach physical maturity. In contrast, age stratification is less pronounced in small preindustrial societies. In these societies, the transition from youth to adult status occurs earlier, and youths are expected to assume adult roles close to the time that they reach physical maturity. In these types of societies, the age—crime curve is flatter and less skewed than it is in contemporary industrialized societies (Steffensmeier, Allan, and Streifel 1989).

Even within the United States, the relationship between age and crime has changed gradually over the course of the past century. Darrell Steffensmeier and his colleagues (1989) examined UCR arrest statistics from 1940 to 1980. Their analyses suggest that there has been a gradual shift toward greater concentration of offending among youth. As the end of the twentieth century approached, age curves became more peaked than they had been earlier. In addition, the peak of the age—crime curve appears to occur at younger ages. Other research also suggests that the nature of youth crime has changed recently. An examination of the criminality of the two Philadelphia birth cohorts, the first born in 1945 and the second in 1958, uncovered a dramatic increase in violent crime among the later cohort (Tracy, Wolfgang, and Figlio 1990).

Considered as a whole, the research on age and crime suggests a general, but not invariant, pattern. Involvement in many crimes, especially the garden-variety street crimes that constitute UCR Index offenses, is most widespread among teenagers and young adults. Involvement in these offenses declines rapidly among older age groups. The majority of those who commit index-type crimes have relatively short careers. This inverted *j* pattern has been found in many countries and over a broad span of time (Tittle and Paternoster 2000). The inverted *j* pattern describes population-wide age—crime curves when all crimes are lumped together. However, when crime categories are considered separately, it appears that the peak age for certain crimes occurs later and the decline in involvement for older age groups is more gradual. These divergent patterns are observed particularly for white-collar type crimes and other crime categories not included in the UCR Crime Index. Variations in the standard inverted j pattern are also found among different population groups, cultures, and historical periods (Steffensmeier and Allan 2000).

The finding that the relationship between age and crime varies among different population groups and over historical periods is particularly important for the life course perspective. Consistent with a central premise of the life course perspective, this finding suggests that trajectories in crime are influenced by social and historical conditions and changes (Magnusson and Cairns 1996). If the age—crime curve did not vary over time and place, and if it did not vary across population groups, it would mean that social and historical conditions have little impact on crime trajectories. It would mean that macrosociological conditions such as the degree of race-based inequalities in a society or the structure of a society's age stratification system have no bearing on involvement in crime. The criminal careers of African-American males in Harlem would be the same as those of white males in Beverly Hills. Trajectories in crime would be the same for Generation X as for teenagers in colonial America. If results such as these were true, it would call into question the life course principle of historical time and place, that is, the idea that social and historical conditions shape trajectories in all domains of life.

However, the evidence reviewed on variations in the relationship between age and crime indicates it is unlikely that trajectories in crime are everywhere the same. Rather, they appear to be influenced by social and historical conditions. We elaborate on these influences in following chapters. To set the stage for that discussion, we turn now to a review of theoretical perspectives on adolescent trajectories in crime.

Adolescent Trajectories in Crime: Discovery of the Chronic Offender

Involvement in minor forms of crime and deviancy is so widespread among teenagers that it is statistically normal, especially for males (Moffitt 1990; Moffitt 1993). Sometime during their teenage years, most individuals regardless of race, ethnicity, or class background begin to rebel against authority and to break the law (Piquero and Brezina 2001). Many of the children who were nice kids when they were younger and who did not display antisocial tendencies, now become a source of headaches for their parents and teachers and a concern for law enforcement. For example, in the National Youth Survey, a significant proportion of respondents reported committing at least one delinquent act (Elliott and Huizinga 1983). Most teenage delinquencies are not serious. Rather, they involve such offenses as truancy, petty theft, alcohol abuse, and recreational drug use (Short and Nye 1958; Gold 1966). But serious violent crimes are not exactly rare either. The University of Michigan Institute for Social Research conducts an annual cross-sectional survey of high-school seniors called *Monitoring the Future*. In the 2008 survey, which is representative of all U.S. high school seniors, more than one out of five senior boys (20.7 percent) reported having been involved in serious fights in the previous year (Bachman, Johnston, and O'Malley 2009). In light of the near universality of deviance among the young, it is only a slight exaggeration to say that in every generation society is invaded by a host of uncivilized barbarians who must be tamed (Wilson 1975).

Although minor forms of delinquency are very common among teenagers, not all teenagers restrict themselves to trivial offenses. There is significant variation among teenagers in both the rate and seriousness of their offending. Some teenagers commit very serious crimes, and for some teenagers involvement in crime and deviance is not a new thing. Rather, it is a continuation of troublemaking and antisocial behavior that began long before they reached age 13. These individuals are continuing on trajectories that they started to pursue much earlier. The flood of newcomers to crime may obscure the continuity displayed by those who were regarded as problem children in early childhood.

An important result of the life course and other developmental approaches has been the discovery that there are different trajectories in crime. The exact number of trajectories is not yet agreed upon, nor are all of the characteristics of these trajectories well understood. Nevertheless, it is clear that for some offenders onset occurs earlier and desistance later than normal. Furthermore, some offenders commit much more serious offenses and at much higher rates than normal.

One of the earliest and most influential investigations to identify different trajectories in crime was the first Philadelphia cohort study conducted by Marvin Wolfgang, Robert Figlio, and Thorsten Sellin (1972). In this study, data were gathered on a cohort of 9,945 boys born in Philadelphia in 1945 who lived there until they reached age 18 in 1963 (Wolfgang, Figlio, and Sellin 1972). Official police records were used to identify delinquents. An official contact meant that the police had filed a report on a delinquent event in which the individual was involved. The researchers tracked the number of official contacts of each boy and evaluated the seriousness of each contact event. Wolfgang and his colleagues were able to identify non-offenders, onetime offenders, and multiple offenders, those with two or more contacts (Wolfgang et al. 1972, 65).

Nearly 35 percent of the sample, a total of 3,475 boys, had at least one official contact, and taken together the delinquent boys were responsible for one-time offenders. The remaining 54 percent (1,862) were repeat offenders. Not surprisingly, the repeat offenders accounted for the bulk of the total number of cohort offenses. They committed well over 8,000 offenses.

The fact that over one-third of the sample had an official police contact was surprising and indicated the widespread prevalence of delinquency. But even more surprising was the discovery of the chronic offender. Chronic offenders were defined as boys who had five or more contacts with the police. In this cohort, there were 627 chronic offenders. These offenders accounted for a hugely disproportionate share of the total number of offenses committed by the cohort. The 627 chronic offenders represent only 6.3 percent of all the individuals in the cohort, but they committed 5,305 offenses, which is over half of all the offenses committed by the entire cohort (Wolfgang et al. 1972, 88–89). The chronic offenders stood out from the rest of the delinquents in the cohort in more ways than just their frequency of offending. They also committed much more serious offenses. The "chronic 6 percent," as they have become known, accounted for between 70 and 80 percent of the cohort's homicides, rapes, aggravated assaults, and robberies.

The discovery of the chronic 6 percent spurred a host of other cohort studies designed to replicate and extend the results of the Philadelphia study. Wolfgang followed up his own research in a study of another cohort born in Philadelphia in 1958 (Tracy et al. 1990). The 1958 cohort was larger than the earlier one, including more than 27,000 subjects. Significantly, over 14,000 females were included in the second cohort.

As in the 1945 cohort, a small percentage of male youths (7.5 percent) were identified as chronic offenders. They accounted for 61 percent of all cohort offenses and an even larger share of the more serious offenses, such as homicide, rape, robbery, and aggravated assault. Chronic offending among females was rare. Of the females, only 1 percent were identified as chronic offenders (Tracy et al. 1990).

Since the pioneering studies in Philadelphia, other cohort studies have accumulated data that replicate Wolfgang's findings. Lyle Shannon followed three cohorts of youths born in 1942, 1949, and 1955 in Racine, Wisconsin. A small percentage of youths in the cohorts appeared to be chronic offenders. Shannon estimates that in each cohort, about 5 percent of the subjects account for three-quarters of the felonies committed by the total cohort (Shannon 1988). In the Cambridge study, West and Farrington also observed that a small number of recidivists accounted for a large share of arrests (West and Farrington 1977). Other cohort studies both in and out of the United States have similar findings: a small group of individuals (roughly between 5 and 8 percent) follow trajectories that involve a much higher rate of offending than normal. Indeed, as Terrie Moffitt (2006, 302) puts it, "Consensus about this group has emerged from all studies that have applied trajectory-detection analyses to a representative sample having longitudinal repeated measures of antisocial behavior."

Early analyses of longitudinal offending patterns identified three distinct groups: non-offenders, one-time or short-term offenders, and long-term chronic offenders. However, as researchers have more closely examined offending trajectories using more sophisticated statistical techniques, the number of distinct patterns identified has increased. In a reexamination of the Cambridge data, for example, Nagin and Land (1993) discovered evidence that the chronic group of offenders may comprise two subgroups: high-rate and low-rate chronics. The members of the low-rate chronic group were distinguished by the longevity of their criminal careers and by a flatter age—crime curve. During their teenage years, the low-rate chronics committed offenses at a rate that was actually lower than the short-term offenders. However, unlike the short-term offenders, the low-rate chronics continued to offend after age 20. By age 30, their offense rate was similar to that of the high-rate chronic offenders at the same age. Thus, the criminal careers of the low-rate chronic group did not appear to follow the typical age—crime curve. They had much flatter curves than normal (Nagin and Land 1993). A similar pattern was also found by Moffitt in the Dunedin data (Moffitt et al. 2002). Other researchers have identified even more groups (Blokland, Nagin, and Nieuwbeerta 2005).

Although advances in statistical techniques appear to have permitted investigators to identify groups and trajectories with increasing refinement, there is disagreement as to what these findings really mean or how they should be used to inform policy. If people can indeed be classified into different groups in regards to their trajectories in crime (e.g., early versus late starters or chronics versus desisters), it is not clear exactly how many groups there are. More importantly, it is not clear what the causal mechanisms are that determine who ends up in what group or whether group membership can be predicted early on with much success (Sampson and Laub 2005b). One school of thought holds that if we simply gather more and better data we will eventually be able to discern how many groups there are and their underlying causal mechanisms (Nagin and Tremblay 2005). An opposing point of view, however, holds that development is in a sense chaotic. That is, if we follow people who are supposedly in a "group" and gather more and more data on them, we will find that over time the trajectories of the people in the group will splinter into ever more branches of development (Raudenbush 2005). In other words, the composition of groups of offenders may be inherently unstable over time (Eggleston, Laub, and Sampson 2004).

Explaining Offending Trajectories: Development or Propensity?

Even though researchers disagree on how offending trajectories should be conceived and understood, the fact that different offending trajectories exist is no longer seriously debated. As Nagin and Land (1993, 329) put it, the "observation that individuals have criminal careers in the sense that there are persistent differences across individuals in their rates of offending over time is unassailable." Longitudinal studies from the Gluecks onward have demonstrated that most individuals who become involved in crime and delinquency do so for only a relatively short period of time during their teenage years. But a small proportion of offenders commit offenses for a longer period of time. The active phase of their offending careers may stretch from age 10 or 11 into adulthood. At issue is how to explain the different offending trajectories.

There are two broad conflicting schools of thought on the problem of explaining offending trajectories. These schools of thought are rooted in different views on the nature of offending groups. One school, represented most prominently by Robert Sampson and John Laub, takes what they call a life course approach (Sampson and Laub 2005a). The other school, championed by scholars such as Terrie Moffitt, Travis Hirschi, and Michael Gottfredson, takes a developmental propensity or general theory approach (Gottfredson and Hirschi 1990; Moffitt 1993). Within each of these general perspectives, there are, of course, variations in the proposed explanations for trajectories in crime.

Those who take a life course perspective on antisocial behavior make two main arguments. First, according to the life course approach the causes of antisocial behavior change over the life course (Bartusch et al. 1997). The factors that lead to early onset of offending are not the same as those that lead to onset at later ages. In effect, the life course perspective predicts that the different offending trajectories have unique causes, or at least that each trajectory has a few unique causes, although some causal mechanisms may overlap and operate across trajectories. Second, this school of thought places great emphasis on the importance of experiences that we undergo as we age. According to this perspective, individuals who come from similar backgrounds may nevertheless turn out dramatically different depending on the experiences they have as they go through life (Laub and Sampson 2003). What happens to people at each stage of the life course can have a causal impact on their behavior at that and subsequent stages. In effect, this means that membership in a particular offending group is always contingent (Raudenbush 2005). People can drop out at any time.

Developmental theorists place much less emphasis on variation in experience over time. This school of thought holds that there are distinct developmental trajectories that people get locked into. Thus, according to this perspective developmental trajectories are stable in the sense that once people enter a particular trajectory or developmental group their future progress is more or less determined. For example, Gottfredson and Hirschi argue that criminal behavior results from an underlying behavioral propensity that remains stable across the life span (Gottfredson and Hirschi 1990). At an early point in the life course, each individual's propensity toward crime and deviance is established. From that point on, this innate propensity drives behavior independent of other factors and is largely resistant to change. Thus, according to this school of thought, the different offending trajectories that are observed in adolescence reflect only variation in an underlying propensity toward crime. They are not caused by differences in experiences. On the other hand, in one of the most important and influential theoretical statements in the developmental perspective, Terrie Moffitt (1993) argued that there are two distinct trajectories, one called life-course persistent and the other called adolescent limited. We will discuss Moffitt's theory, which has evolved since her original statement, in greater detail below. For now, suffice it to say that although they are related there are important differences between the explanation for offending trajectories proposed by Moffitt (1993) versus that proposed by Gottfredson and Hirschi (1990).

The life course and developmental approaches to explaining trajectories in offending are not necessarily mutually exclusive. Individuals may indeed vary in some more or less stable propensity to commit offenses. Yet, how that propensity to offend is expressed may be shaped by external environmental contingencies. For example, individuals who share similar propensities but who experience different opportunities to offend can be expected to exhibit different levels of offending. Many life course theorists recognize that individuals vary in underlying propensities toward offending, but they argue that events and turning points in the life course nevertheless influence how propensities are expressed. They have proposed a variety of different theories to explain how underlying propensities are shaped by external conditions. Below, we review some of the best known and most influential of these theories.

Terrie Moffitt's Complementary Pair of Developmental Theories

Another important contemporary theory representing the developmental perspective is Terrie Moffitt's complementary pair of developmental theories. Moffitt (1993; 1997) argues that there are two qualitatively distinct types of offenders—*life-course persistent and adolescence-limited*. According to Moffitt, these two types of offenders follow distinctly different trajectories in crime and antisocial behavior over the life course, and their differing trajectories are caused by fundamentally different factors.

Moffitt theorizes that the life-course persistent trajectory is followed by a relatively small proportion of the population, somewhere between 4 and 9 percent of all males (Moffitt 1993). Offenders who follow this trajectory engage in a variety of antisocial behaviors throughout the life course (Moffitt 1997, 13). Their antisocial tendencies appear early in childhood and continue to be manifested through adolescence and into adulthood. As young children, these individuals stand out from other children as more aggressive and difficult to manage in the opinion of their parents and teachers. They come to the attention of the police when they are still preteens, and during their teenage years they commit more serious offenses than other teenagers. Finally, as adults, these individuals continue to lead very troubled lives. While their peers settle down, get married, have children, and get jobs, the lifecourse persistent offenders continue to follow patterns of antisocial behavior. They beat their wives, abuse their kids, and cheat on their taxes.

Moffitt's evidence for this type of offender comes from epidemiological studies of the prevalence of antisocial behavior at different stages in the life course and from longitudinal cohort studies of individual continuity in antisocial behavior. Epidemiological research on the prevalence of antisocial behavior consistently finds that between 4 and 9 percent of whatever age group is under investigation display high levels of antisocial behavior. Studies of preschool children, for example, find that about 5 percent are regarded by their parents as "very difficult to manage" (McGee et al. 1991). Costello (1989) found that in several countries roughly 4 to 9 percent of elementary school-aged boys were diagnosed with conduct disorder. As we noted above, in both the 1945 and 1958 Philadelphia cohort studies, 6 and 7.5 percent, respectively, of the males appeared to be chronic offenders (Wolfgang et al. 1972; Tracy et al. 1990). Finally, the prevalence of antisocial personality disorder among adult men is estimated to be around 5 percent (Robins 1985).

Thus, at different points in the life course, researchers using different indicators of antisocial behavior consistently find that between 4 and 9 percent of males stand out from their age peers.

Because epidemiological research is based on cross-sectional samples, it cannot tell us whether the individuals designated as antisocial at early and late ages are the same or different people (Moffitt 1997, 13). Proof that the preschoolers who are regarded by their parents as difficult to manage grow up to be the same individuals that psychologists diagnose with antisocial personality disorder can come only from longitudinal studies that follow the same persons over time. After reviewing this research, Moffitt (1997, 15) concludes that a "substantial body of longitudinal research consistently points to a very small group of males who display high rates of antisocial behavior across time and in diverse situations." Research clearly suggests that at least during the first few decades of life, life-course persistent individuals exist (Moffitt 2006).

Unlike the life-course persistent trajectory, which is followed by only a small proportion of people, the adolescence-limited trajectory is ubiquitous (Moffitt 1997, 15). Individuals who follow the adolescence-limited trajectory commit offenses for only a relatively short period of time during their teenage years. They start offending around age 14 or 15, committing for the most part minor delinquencies. They continue to commit offenses for two to three years and then desist. Prior to entering their teenage years, these individuals "have no notable history of antisocial behavior and little future for such behavior in adulthood" (Moffitt 1997, 16).

The adolescence-limited trajectory mirrors the shape of the general age—crime curve. Indeed, according to Moffitt (1993; 1997), adolescence-limited offenders are responsible for the shape of the age—crime curve. The apparent peak in the age—crime curve that is observed in arrest statistics is caused by an increase in the prevalence of offenders, not a sudden increase in the individual rate of offending (Moffitt 1997, 15). The large number of adolescence-limited offenders who join the small number of life-course persistent offenders makes it appear that offending peaks sharply in adolescence for everyone. In reality, though, the life-course persistent and adolescence-limited offenders have distinctly different trajectories.

Viewed over time, the trajectory of a life-course persistent offender should be flatter because this person offends at a relatively constant rate from early childhood through at least early adulthood. In contrast, the trajectory of an adolescence-limited offender peaks sharply during the middle teenage years because this person starts and then stops offending as a teenager. Thus, adolescence-limited offenders display discontinuity in behavior.

Adolescence-limited offenders differ from life-course persistent offenders in other ways as well. According to Moffitt, the antisocial behavior of adolescence-limited offenders is situation specific. That is, they behave well in some situations but not in others. For example, they may be good students in school during the week but drink and vandalize property on Friday and Saturday nights. Life-course persistent offenders, on the other hand, tend to have trouble getting along with others in many situations. Their antisocial behavior is said to be generalized.

Evidence for the adolescence-limited trajectory comes from numerous studies showing that a very large majority of teenagers commit minor delinquencies but then stop before they reach age 20. Self-report studies of representative samples consistently find that large majorities of individuals engage in crime and delinquency during their teenage years (Hirschi 1969; Elliott and Huizinga 1983; Moffitt 1994). In the Dunedin study, researchers interviewed the male subjects when the subjects reached age 18. A whopping 93 percent admitted involvement in some sort of delinquent activity in the past year (Moffitt 1997, 16). Statistically speaking, complete conformity is abnormal.

If there really are two types of offenders as envisioned by Moffitt, then this strongly implies that we need two theories. Accordingly, Moffitt (1993; 1997) proposes two separate etiological theories for life-course persistent and adolescence-limited antisocial behavior. Because Moffitt believes that antisocial behavior is stable in some individuals from very early childhood to adulthood, her theory of life course persistence focuses on factors present at the very earliest moments in the life course. Moffitt contends that the life-course persistent pattern of antisocial behavior arises out of the combination of a "vulnerable and difficult infant with an adverse rearing context" (Moffitt 1997, 17). She envisions a child with a difficult temperament who is born to parents who are ill equipped to handle the child's problems. The child's difficult temperament flows from what Moffitt calls neuropsychological deficits. These deficits may be genetic or non-genetic in origin. For example, the children of mothers who abuse drugs or alcohol or who receive inadequate nutrition or health care may suffer intrauterine developmental problems. Regardless of their source, deficits in neuropsychological conditions and processes may affect temperament in such areas as activity level and emotional reactivity; behavioral development in speech, motor coordination, and impulse control; and cognitive abilities in attention, language, and reasoning (Moffitt 1997, 18).

Children who suffer from neuropsychological deficits and who are born into disadvantaged or troubled families undergo negative encounters with their parents. The parents do not recognize or know how to properly respond to the child's problems. In interactions with the child, they do the wrong thing at the wrong time. Over time, this "chain of failed parent/child encounters" aggravates the behavioral problems or tendencies that flow from the child's innate neuropsychological deficits. Thus, a child with a neuro-psychological deficit that promotes impulsivity grows up to be very impulsive because his or her parents have not taken steps to help the child handle or ameliorate the behavioral effects of the condition. Life-course persistent antisocial behavior begins, then, with the interactions between problem children and problem parents. Moffitt's theory does not address how normal children—that is, those who do not have deficits—will be affected by inadequate parenting.

The early pattern of antisocial behavior persists into adolescence and later into adulthood. In part, this persistence is caused by the behavioral style that the individual developed as a child and carries over into later stages in the life course. The hyperactive child with poor self-control and limited cognitive abilities becomes an overactive adult who is self-indulgent and not very smart. When the person is a child, this constellation of traits leads to trouble, and it continues to do so as the person ages, producing continuous contemporary consequences. At each stage of the life course, this person's behavioral style gets him or her into trouble with others.

Persistence in antisocial behavior, and specifically criminal behavior, also results from the cumulating effects of problems and failure over time. Beginning early in life, individuals on a life-course persistent trajectory behave in ways that limit their future opportunities. Because they are so difficult to be around, life-course persistent individuals are often rejected and avoided by others. They have difficulty learning how to behave in a pro-social manner and so have few pro-social friends and little opportunity to practice conventional social skills. They do poorly in school and so never attain basic math and reading skills. Without these skills, their opportunities for legitimate employment are severely curtailed. Involvement in crime and delinquency leads to arrests and incarcerations, which further diminish opportunities for success in a conventional lifestyle. Cumulating conse-quences eventually ensnare the life-course persistent individual in a deviant lifestyle from which escape becomes ever more difficult as time passes (Moffitt 1997, 21–23).

The theory of life course persistence is designed to explain continuity in behavior over a long period of time, especially criminal and deviant behavior. The theory of adolescence-limited antisocial behavior confronts a different empirical regularity—the lack of continuity that characterizes the offending trajectories of most individuals. What accounts for the pattern of widespread onset of delinquency in early adolescence that is followed shortly thereafter by the equally widespread pattern of desistance from delinquent behaviors? Why do children who have little or no history of behavior problems develop such problems in adolescence, and then why do they seem to spontaneously recover just a few years later?

As with her theory of life course persistence, Moffitt begins her theory of adolescence-limited offending by noting the age at which antisocial behavior first appears in this trajectory and arguing that the important causal factors must begin operating at that time. In the adolescence-limited trajectory, delinquent behavior first appears early in the teenage years. The causal factors that begin operating at this time include biological changes (puberty and continuing brain development), the increasing importance of peer relationships, changes in age-graded societal expectations, and changes in teenagers' values, attitudes, and aspirations (Moffitt 1997, 25). Puberty brings with it an increased interest in sex and a rapid increase in physical strength (Steffensmeier and Allan 1995, 99). In addition, as we discussed earlier in this chapter, for teenagers the parts of the brain that produce emotions are developing more rapidly than the parts that control and modulate emotions. At about the same time that these biological changes are occurring, teenagers begin to spend less time with their parents and more time with their peers. The importance of parents as a point of reference and center of attention begins to decline, while peers move front and center as objects of concern and interest. Children move away from their parents not only because they come to like their peers more but also because society expects it of them. Between the ages of roughly 12 and 17, they are expected to "grow up" and no longer behave like children. However, they are not yet given the opportunity to assume productive adult roles. They occupy an ambiguous and confusing middle ground between childhood and adulthood (Steffensmeier and Allan 1995). Finally, in the realm of cognitive development, they become acutely aware of what they perceive to be inequities in society's expectations. To teenagers it is exceedingly unfair that while they are expected to behave like adults, they are not given the opportunity to be adults or to have the autonomy and freedom of movement that goes with adult status. All of these changes leave young teenagers looking for something else, some way out of their ambiguous and stressful position in society.

Although it is easy to agree with the idea that life for teenagers is ambiguous and stressful, this does not explain why they respond to this predicament with delinquency. To explain the onset of delinquency in the adolescence-limited trajectory, Moffitt introduces the idea of *social mimicry*:

> Social mimicry occurs when two animal species share a single niche and one of the species has cornered the market on a resource that is needed to promote fitness. In such circumstances, the 'mimic' species adopts the social behavior of the more successful species in order to obtain access to the valuable resource. (Moffitt 1997, 25)

Moffitt argues that the idea of social mimicry can be applied to adolescence-limited and life-course persistent delinquents. In the eyes of their peers, life-course persistent delinquents appear to have a very valuable "resource" and that resource is mature status. They seem to behave like adults. They smoke, drink, have sex, skip school, and resist adult authority. Seeing that life-course persistent delinquents get to act like adults and wanting to do the same themselves, adolescence-limited delinquents begin to mimic the behavior of life-course persistent delinquents, the "more successful species" in the ecology of teenagers. They begin committing minor delinquencies.

For youths following the adolescence-limited trajectory, delinquency is a way of cutting ties with childhood and staking a claim to adult status. It helps them deal with the stresses of the maturity gap and answers their needs for autonomy. By engaging in forbidden adult activities, teenagers clandestinely resist adult authority. These activities symbolize independence and, hence, are enormously rewarding to the adolescence-limited delinquent.

Despite all the fun, excitement, and thrills of misbehavior, adolescence-limited youths do not maintain their wrongdoing into adulthood. No doubt to the delight and relief of their parents, as adolescence-limited delinquents approach the end of their teenage years, they quit delinquent behaviors. Why? In Moffitt's view, the answer is that better routes to the valuable resource of mature status open up at the end of the teenage years. As teenagers near the end of their teenage years, and as they graduate from high school, society's expectations for them change once again. By age 20, they are expected to get jobs and support themselves or to be in college, preparing for a career. They attain some of the privileges and autonomy that they have desired for so long. Because of these changes, the adolescence-limited delinquent begins to perceive delinquency and its consequences from a new perspective. Delinquency is no longer seen as the only way to establish autonomy from adult authority. Autonomy is now freely given by society; indeed, it is thrust upon older teens. Furthermore, the legal and social consequences of delinquency become more serious at age 18, and adolescence-limited delinquents soon realize that continued involvement in crime is likely to harm their future life chances. The rewards of crime decline while its costs increase (Moffitt 1997, 35). Desistance becomes the rational thing to do.

For adolescence-limited delinquents, desistance is not only rational; it is, for most of them, also relatively easy. They have good options for change. Unlike life-course persistent delinquents, most adolescence-limited delinquents are able to avoid the damaging effects of contemporary and cumulative continuity. Because adolescence-limited delinquents do not suffer from personality disorders or cognitive deficits and because they have learned how to behave in a pro-social manner, it is relatively easy for them to fit into the expected routines of employment or college. They know how to get along with others and how to follow rules. In addition, because their delinquent careers are shorter than the careers of life-course persistent offenders, the process of cumulative continuity has less time to work. Adolescence-limited delinquents accumulate fewer of the negative consequences that accompany involvement in crime than life-course persistent delinquents. In some cases, though, the transition to adulthood for adolescent limited adolescents may be complicated if they have acquired what Moffitt calls "snares," such as criminal records or periods of incarceration (Moffitt 2006). Although these snares can compromise the life chances of adolescent limited offenders, their adult lives are considerably more successful than those of life-course persistent offenders.

Thus, as they enter adulthood, the paths of adolescence-limited and life-course persistent delinquents diverge. Most of the former begin to explore new pathways into conventional adult roles of employment, marriage, and family. The latter, however, discover that these options are closed to them. Life-course persistent delinquents find themselves stuck in an antisocial lifestyle (Moffitt 1997, 37).

Since Moffitt's original presentation of her taxonomic theory in 1993, it has undergone extensive empirical testing by Moffitt and her colleagues, as well as by other research teams (for reviews, see Moffitt 2006). In general, this research has supported many of the theory's original hypotheses, but there have been findings indicating the need for some revisions to the taxonomy. A brief summary of the empirical status of the theory taken from Moffitt (2006) is presented below.

1. There is widespread agreement among researchers that the life-course persistent antisocial individual exists. Researchers using a variety of different data sets from different countries and covering different age ranges uniformly find that a relatively small group of individuals, ranging from approximately 3 to 13 percent, show elevated levels of antisocial behavior early in life and persist in that behavioral style for as long as they are followed.

2. There is also considerable research to support the existence of the adolescence-limited trajectory. It appears that short-term involvement in crime or delinquency is normal among large majorities of males and females during the teenage years.

3. Consistent with the taxonomic theory, research suggests that the correlates of life-course persistent and adolescence-limited offending are different. Measures of neuropsychological deficits and family adversity predict life-course persistent offending but not adolescence-limited offending. In addition, adolescence-limited offenders seem to specialize more in status-oriented offenses than life-course persistent offenders, as predicted by the theory.

4. As the theory predicts, both total abstinence from offending and adult onset of offending appear to be quite rare. Very few people completely abstain from any sort of deviance and very few people start offending for the first time after their teenage years.

5. While there is a great deal of research supporting the validity of the life-course persistent and adolescence-limited trajectories, research suggests that these may not be the only trajectories that people follow. Several studies have found evidence for a third trajectory, sometimes called "low-level chronics" (D'Unger et al. 1998; Nagin, Farrington, and Moffitt 1995). Early in life these individuals appear to share some of the behavioral problems of life-course persistent people, but they do not display elevated levels of delinquent behavior in adolescence. Indeed, they are often less active in this regard than those following the adolescence-limited trajectory. However, unlike adolescence-limited individuals, low-level chronics often continue to offend, albeit at low levels, into adulthood. Not much is known about the characteristics of low-level chronics, but there is some evidence to suggest that they have personality disorders as adults (Moffitt 2006).

6. Although the existence of the adolescence-limited trajectory is well established, more research is needed to ascertain whether it is caused by the two processes postulated by Moffitt, that is, the maturity gap and social mimicry. In addition, further research is needed on snares and the differential rates of desistance among adolescent limited offenders.

Although they are both representatives of the developmental perspective, Moffitt's theory differs from the one proposed by Gottfredson and Hirschi in regards to the source of criminal propensities. Recall that for Gottfredson and Hirschi, the source of criminal propensities is low self-control, and it is caused exclusively by inadequate parenting early in life. While Moffitt may agree with Gottfredson and Hirschi that individual differences make some people more prone to commit crime than others, she disagrees with them on the source of these differences. In her view, the propensity toward crime results from the interaction of neuropsychological deficits and problem parenting. Unlike the general theory of crime, Moffitt's theory of life-course persistent offending explicitly acknowledges both genetic and non-genetic biological effects on crime. Also, unlike Gottfredson and Hirschi, Moffitt acknowledges that societal reactions to antisocial individuals may play a role in their persistence in crime and antisocial behavior. Cumulative disadvantages pile up for life-course persistent individuals in part because of how others respond to them. Rejection by employers, schools, and potential spouses or partners locks the life-course persistent offender into a particular social world that exacerbates their antisocial tendencies.

Sampson's and Laub's Age-Graded Theory of Informal Social Control

The most prominent representative of the life course perspective on trajectories in crime has been developed by Robert Sampson and John Laub. In a series of articles and two ground-breaking books, they have advanced an age-graded theory of informal social control to explain trajectories in crime and delinquency (Sampson and Laub 1993; 1997; Laub, Nagin, and Sampson 1998; Sampson and Laub 2003). Their theory is based on a careful reanalysis of the data that Sheldon and Eleanor Glueck collected on 500 delinquent boys born in Boston, Massachusetts in the 1930s. Although the Gluecks followed the boys until they were in their thirties, Laub and Sampson supplemented their data by gathering additional information on 475 of the original sample members into their seventies (Laub and Sampson 2003). They even contacted 52 of the men and interviewed them to find out how their lives had turned out.

The original statement of their theory was presented in their book *Crime in the Making: Pathways and Turning Points through Life*, published in 1993. Ten years later they revised and extended their original theory in another book, entitled *Shared Beginnings, Divergent Lives: Delinquent Boys to Age 70*. To explicate their theory, we start with their original statement and then introduce the modifications they made later.

As control theorists, Sampson and Laub start with the assumption that delinquency, crime, and deviance are natural. If people are not somehow controlled or prevented from following their natural inclinations, they will tend to behave in ways that society regards as antisocial or criminal. The theory of age-graded informal social control holds that the most important sources of control are informal bonds between people.

Sampson and Laub argue that at different stages in the life course individuals are potentially subject to different forms of informal social control. For children, informal family and school bonds are important. Children who are strongly bonded to their parents and who care about school are less likely to be involved in delinquency than children who have difficult relations with their parents or who do not like school. As children move through the life course, the major sources of informal social control change. Parents and school are not as important for young adults as they are for children and teenagers. For young adults, employment and marriage are potential sources of informal control. Variation in the strength of informal controls influences the likelihood and degree of involvement in crime and deviance at all stages of the life course.

Sampson and Laub recognize that ontogenetic differences between individuals—that is, persistent underlying differences in temperament and criminal potential—may account for some of the variation in criminal behavior. But, unlike Moffitt, they do not develop an explicit theory of what these "child-effect" personality or behavioral factors might be. Rather, they focus much more heavily on factors that are external to the individual, which they call "structural variables," related to the family. These structural variables include family size, household overcrowding, family socioeconomic status, mother's and father's deviance, mother's employment, family disruption, residential mobility, and whether the parents are foreign born. They argue that these structural variables influence "family process variables," which refer to how family members relate to one another and specifically how the parents relate to and interact with their children. Important dimensions of family process include the use of harsh and erratic discipline by the parents, the mother's supervision of the child, parental rejection of the child, and the child's attachment to the parents. The structural variables are conceived to affect the process variables, which in turn are conceived as the direct cause of delinquency. Thus, the process variables mediate the effects of the structural variables (Sampson and Laub 1993).

Besides the family, the other important sources of informal social control in early childhood are schools and peers. Sampson and Laub argue that structural variables also influence the child's performance in and attachment to school as well as relationships with delinquent peers. Children born into families that have certain structural characteristics are less likely to perform well in school or to be strongly attached to school (Sampson and Laub 1993, 110–111). Children from large, poor families that move often and in which the mother is employed appear to be particularly disadvantaged in regard to school attachment. Children from these types of families are also more likely to have friends who are delinquent. Both school attachment and delinquent peers, in turn, are related to delinquency.

Based on rigorous and exhaustive statistical analyses of the Gluecks' data, Sampson and Laub conclude that the direct causes of juvenile delinquency comprise child effects, process effects, and, to a lesser extent, structural effects (Sampson and Laub 1993, 119). Child effects, in the form of early antisocial behavior, are related to later delinquency but not as strongly as bad parenting, attachment to school, and attachment to delinquent peers. The effect of family structure is largely mediated by the process variables. Thus, delinquency can be curtailed by strong informal social controls based in family, schools, and friends. Teenagers who lack such controls are at great risk of finding themselves on a trajectory toward serious adult crime.

As teenagers move into young adulthood, two factors begin operating that shape adult patterns in crime. First, as young adults, they may become subject to new forms of informal social control. These new forms of control include employment and marriage. Individuals who are lucky enough to find good jobs or enter good marriages or both become subjugated to new informal controls. According to Sampson and Laub (1993), exposure to these adult forms of social control can redirect the criminal trajectories of individuals who were seriously delinquent as youths.

But the chances that a seriously delinquent youth will find a good job or marry a supportive spouse are less than ideal because of the second factor that begins operating in adulthood. Youths who are seriously delinquent accumulate disadvantages as they age. These cumulative disadvantages "snowball," or pile up, over time, making it increasingly more difficult for the individual to exit from a life of crime. These disadvantages are generated most directly by official sanctions, such as arrest, conviction, and incarceration, which label and stigmatize individuals. Being officially labeled as a serious delinquent dramatically reduces future educational and employment opportunities (Sampson and Laub 1997, 147). The individual becomes trapped in a cycle in which crime leads to failure in conventional activities, which in turn motivates further involvement in crime. Thus, Sampson and Laub (1993; 1997) hypothesize that there is an interaction between early criminal propensities and societal reactions that influences the adult life chances of delinquent youths. Continuity in criminal behavior is not solely the result of underlying criminal propensities; it also is caused by societal reactions.

The distinguishing feature of Sampson and Laub's theoretical work is their claim that social processes can cause even seriously delinquent individuals to desist from crime. They argue that even for very committed offenders change is possible, and change can occur relatively late in life (1997). Adult social bonds to work and family can inhibit adult criminality and deviance (Sampson and Laub 1990; 1993; Laub et al. 1998). How do these bonds develop? Why do some individuals experience a change in fortune for the better while others literally have nowhere to go but prison? Sampson and Laub are appropriately cautious about drawing any definitive conclusions. They acknowledge that they cannot rule out the possibility that selection effects account for both desistance and entry into a good marriage or good job (Sampson and Laub 1993, 241–42). So, it is difficult to know for sure whether stable marriages lead to desistance, or whether high criminal propensity leads to marital instability and continuity in offending in adulthood. In the end, they suggest that "both social selection and social causation . . . seem to be at work in the unfolding of human lives over time" (242).

Sampson and Laub have subsequently extended and modified their original age-graded theory of informal social control (Laub and Sampson 2003). Based on new data collected on the original Glueck sample (Glueck and Glueck 1950), they were able to follow the men into their sixties and seventies. They found that almost all of the men in the sample had eventually desisted from crime through a process that involved turning points, human agency, and the structuring effects of routine activities. We will describe their revised age-graded theory in more detail in the next chapter which deals with adulthood. But for now, we note that the research by Laub and Sampson casts some doubt on the idea that people follow fixed and immutable trajectories that are established early in life.

Terence Thornberry's Interactional Theory of Delinquency

Terence Thornberry argues that standard criminological theories ignore a basic feature of human behavior, to wit: it occurs in social interaction. The concept of interaction implies that human behavior involves "give-and-take," and that it has a back-and-forth aspect that plays out over time. During the process of interacting, all parties to the interaction are reciprocally affected. For example, a child's attachment to parents evolves over time as the parents and the child interact. What the child does at one point in time affects attachment at a later point, and in turn, what the parents do affects the child's feelings of attachment. Standard criminological theories, however, fail to take into account the back-and-forth character of human behavior. In standard models of delinquency, independent variables—such as attachment to parents—are assumed to effect dependent variables, such as delinquency. The causal effects are conceived as flowing only in one direction, from attachment to delinquency, and not from delinquency to attachment. This approach is mistaken because it ignores the interactional dimension of human development and behavior. It ignores the fact that a child's involvement in delinquency may affect attachment to parents, just as attachment to parents affects delinquency. Thornberry argues we should think of delinquency in interactional terms. We need to develop causal models of delinquency that take into account not only the effects of the independent variables on delinquency but also the effects of delinquency on the independent variables. In other words, we should develop reciprocal models of delinquency (Thornberry 1987).

The reciprocal model that Thornberry (1987, 873) proposes is similar to Sampson and Laub's age-graded theory of informal social controls. It is based on the premise that the "fundamental cause of delinquency is the attenuation of social controls over the person's conduct." His model incorporates three social control variables and three delinquency variables. Of the three social control variables, the most important one for explaining the onset of delinquency in early adolescence is attachment to parents. Attachment affects belief in conventional values and commitment to school, which are the two other social control variables. The three social control variables, in turn, affect associations with delinquent peers, delinquent behavior, and delinquent values. Following the standard logic of control-type theories, Thornberry argues that adolescents aged 11 to 13 who are strongly attached to their parents are likely to be committed to school and to believe in conventional values. Commitment and belief reduce the likelihood that the child will associate with delinquents, engage in delinquency, and hold delinquent values. Thus, children who are strongly attached to their parents are predicted to be at low risk for early onset of delinquency.

The interactional component in Thornberry's model lies in his stipulations that the social control variables are reciprocally related to each other and that the delinquency variables can act back upon the control variables. Regarding the reciprocal relationships between the social control variables, Thornberry assumes that over time attachment affects commitment and vice versa. Similarly, commitment to school affects belief in conventional values and the same is true in reverse. Children who are strongly attached to their parents are more likely to be committed to school, and over time commitment to school increases attachment to parents. This happy chain of socially conforming causality can be disrupted, however, if for some reason delinquent friends or activities enter the picture. Thornberry theorizes that if a child begins to associate with delinquent peers or engage in delinquent activities, these behaviors will have negative effects on the social control variables. Adolescents who begin hanging around with delinquents or engaging in delinquency are predicted to become less committed to school, to believe less in conventional values, and eventually to grow less attached to their parents.

The causal importance of different variables changes as children develop over the life course. For children in early adolescence, attachment to parents is conceived to be the most important variable. By middle adolescence, as children begin to mature and become less dependent on their parents, delinquent peers and delinquent values become more important. What happens in the home becomes less important than what happens outside the home. Thornberry does not argue that parents are irrelevant to teenagers but that they are less important in middle adolescence than in early childhood as a "locus of control and interaction" (1987, 879). The power of the family to shape behavior declines in middle adolescence and is supplanted by interactions with peers. At this stage of the life course, the causal importance of delinquent values increases. Delinquent values are now conceived to determine associations with delinquent peers and involvement in delinquent activities. Holding delinquent values steers youths toward other delinquents and toward delinquent acts. Delinquent values are also assumed to reduce commitment to school and to be incompatible with belief in conventional values. Thus, the major change that occurs in mid adolescence relates to the increased saliency of the delinquency variables relative to the family. The basic structure of Thornberry's theory, however, stays the same. The control variables and the delinquency variables are still seen as being locked in mutually reinforcing causal loops.

As individuals grow out of middle adolescence and into late adolescence (ages 18 to 20), new factors emerge to affect crime and delinquency and old ones recede in importance. According to Thornberry, two important new factors are commitment to conventional activities (employment, college, military service) and commitment to one's own family. These factors become potentially important sources of social control, while attachment to parents and commitment to high school become less important. During late adolescence, many individuals find work, begin to make plans to attend college, and begin to think seriously about marrying and raising their own families. In Thornberry's theoretical scheme, these developments are thought to naturally reduce involvement in delinquent activities and to lead to less time spent with delinquent peers. The transition to the world of work helps one build a stake in conformity, and so does getting married. Individuals who make these transitions on time embark on trajectories that are increasingly removed from crime and delinquency. However, if these transitions do not happen, then the effects of the delinquency variables amplify and the individual's criminal trajectory is likely to continue.

Although Thornberry's theory is primarily a social psychological theory of delinquency, he does not ignore the external social realities that influence the interactional processes lying at the heart of his approach. In particular, he notes that social class is systematically related to the "initial values," or starting positions, of the interactional variables in his model (1987, 885). Children born into lower-class families are more likely to experience disrupted family processes and environments. Hence, the likelihood that they will develop strong attachments to their parents is less certain. Lower-class children are also likely to live in neighborhoods where delinquents are present and where delinquent values may coexist with conventional values. In contrast, middle-class youth are more likely to have stable families and to live in suburbs or city neighborhoods that provide greater insulation against exposure to delinquent values and role models. Thus, social class is conceived to provide an environmental framework within which interactional processes develop.

John Hagan's Theory of Criminal Capital and Capital Disinvestment

One of the most important, provocative, and fertile ideas to arise in American sociology in the past 50 years is James S. Coleman's concept of *social capital*. Social capital is distinguished from human capital, which encompasses the skills, aptitudes, abilities, and credentials possessed by individuals that enable them to produce and succeed in life. It is also distinguished from physical capital, such as tools, machines, and factories. Social capital is not a property of individuals or of the physical implements of production. Rather, it inheres in the structure of relations between people (Coleman 1988). It is something that groups of actors can possess in relative degrees and that individual actors can tap into to serve their ends. Social capital can take the form of obligations and expectations of trustworthiness between group members. It also encompasses how information is transmitted among group members. Finally, social capital is created when groups have strong norms accompanied by sanctions (Coleman 1988). Groups or social structures can vary along all of these dimensions of social capital.

From the perspective of the individual, social capital, like all forms of capital, is useful because access to it enhances the individual's ability to pursue ends and to satisfy needs. Consider an example adapted from Coleman that illustrates how high levels of trust in a group can enhance individual productivity or need satisfaction. Imagine a mother in a neighborhood in which everyone knows and trusts one another. The mother can allow her young child to play without her being present in a local park because she knows that some other parent will be watching to make sure that nothing bad happens. The mother can take a few minutes to run an errand or clean the house or perhaps just relax for a moment. The mother's freedom to pursue these ends is made possible by the social capital that exists in her neighborhood, the high level of trust between residents. Imagine another mother in a different neighborhood, one in which residents do not know or trust one another. This mother does not have the freedom to let her children play outside unsupervised. Hence, the mother's ability to accomplish other tasks is diminished because of the time and energy she must devote to her child.

Social capital typically carries positive connotations, but criminologists were quick to realize that it could also have negative aspects for society. For example, organized criminal groups may have high levels of trust between members, which permits them to organize and coordinate criminal enterprises, such as large-scale drug dealing. This sort of criminal enterprise can be carried out only by individuals working in concert who can depend on one another. In this case, the group's social capital is used to further the criminal ends of its members to the detriment of society.

John Hagan has taken the concept of social capital and used it to construct a developmental theory of street crime in America (Hagan 1991; 1997a). His theory is distinguished from most others in the life course perspective by its explicit emphasis on historically based macro social and economic processes, most notably what he calls "capital disinvestment." Capital disinvestment is something that has happened to minority communities and neighborhoods over the course of the latter half of the twentieth century. The original cause of capital disinvestment was the economic slowdown that occurred in the last quarter of the twentieth century. During this period, three distinct processes of capital disinvestment eroded the ability of minority communities to provide good jobs for their members: residential segregation, racial inequality, and the concentration of poverty. The absence of opportunities in the legitimate economy forced the members of these communities to adapt and develop alternative means of capitalization. These alternative means included reliance on deviance service centers and the drug economy to provide jobs. The processes of capital disinvestment overlap one another. But each also produces its own distinct effects and requires separate explication.

According to Hagan (1997a), in the 1970s the U.S. economy began to slow down after a long period of postwar expansion. During this slowdown, core manufacturing jobs in auto plants and steel mills began to disappear from American cities in the Northeast and Midwest. Jobs in manufacturing had provided a means of economic advancement for African Americans and other minorities. Although the economy eventually created new jobs, these jobs were located in rural and suburban areas where African Americans were not welcome. Policies of residential segregation made it difficult for African Americans to leave inner-city neighborhoods and move to the suburbs, where the economy's new jobs were being created (Hagan 1997a, 290). Young minority males and females were, in effect, trapped in communities in which there were few opportunities in the legitimate economy (see also Wilson 1987).

In addition to being located in areas from which African Americans were segregated, the economy's new jobs increasingly required advanced education and high-level technical skills. It was not easy for African Americans to fulfill these requirements. Opposition to affirmative action laws gained in strength during the last quarter of the century and restricted the access of African Americans to college and to programs that might help them to secure good jobs in the legitimate economy. Racial differentials in earnings and educational achievement, which had been declining, began to grow again.

Race-linked inequality, always a feature of American society, became worse after the mid-1970s. According to Hagan, the rise in racial inequality led to feelings of "resentment, frustration, hopelessness, and aggression" in America's minority youths (Hagan 1997a, 291).

Finally, the third process of capital disinvestment is the concentration of poverty. Residential segregation and racial inequality combined to create hyper-ghettos. In hyper-ghettos, poverty is extreme and extensive. Community members lucky enough to have good jobs and a little money leave as quickly as they can. Only the most disadvantaged and discouraged are left behind. As a result, poverty is concentrated in hyper-ghettos, and the range in variation in economic resources becomes extremely narrow. Everyone is poor and everyone must struggle to survive.

The processes of capital disinvestment destroy conventional forms of social capital. In place of conventional forms of social capital, communities develop alternative forms of economic organization, which amount to what Hagan calls "forms of recapitalization" (Hagan 1997a, 296). By recapitalization, Hagan means that communities attempt to organize whatever resources are available so that they can be used to help community members achieve their goals. Often, according to Hagan, the only economic resources that disadvantaged communities have at their disposal are illicit. People who live in disadvantaged communities have nothing to offer the outside world in the way of conventional economic resources. Their labor is not wanted, they cannot produce anything conventional of value, and they have nothing conventional to sell. But they can offer the outside world something that is not available via the conventional economy. They can offer access to illegal services and commodities, such as prostitution, gambling, and especially narcotic drugs. These communities become deviance service centers for conventional society, places where illicit services and commodities are provided for a price.

Young people who live in disadvantaged communities are drawn to the promise of the deviance service industry. In their eyes, becoming involved in the drug economy or prostitution is a way to get ahead. It's a way to get money, fine clothes, and fancy cars. Jobs in the legitimate economy are not available to them or to their parents. The prospects of going to college seem dim. The deviance service industry is the most promising employer around and so young people, lacking access to other sources of social capital, take advantage of what is available. They take positions in the drug economy.

Hagan notes that deviance service centers are not a new urban phenomenon. Indeed, they have a long history in America. Throughout the nineteenth and early part of the twentieth century, different ethnic groups used the deviance service industry as a means of social mobility. Participation in organized crime was a way to acquire the financial resources necessary to move out of the ghetto and into mainstream society. But times have changed, and the deviance service industry is no longer the mobility ladder it once promised to be. Rather than providing a route out of the ghetto and out of a life of crime, participation in deviance and vice is more likely to embed young people in a criminal lifestyle.

The process of criminal embeddedness links the historical community-level processes of capital disinvestment and recapitalization to the life course trajectories of individuals. Young people who become involved in the deviance service industry, and especially the drug economy, isolate themselves from conventional employment and educational trajectories. They spend time with other criminals like themselves. Their social contacts are with others in the deviance industry and not with people who might provide access to legitimate employment or who might help them succeed in school. Cutting ties with conventional others is one aspect of criminal embeddedness. The other aspect is the high probability, indeed near certainty, that the individual will eventually be arrested and be officially labeled as a criminal offender. Being labeled a criminal makes it exceedingly difficult, if not impossible, for young members of socially stigmatized minority groups to ever find a way out of crime and into the middle class. Their life course trajectories are set in a downward spiral of cumulating disadvantages from which there is little hope of escape.

Thus, Hagan's theory focuses on how broad changes and patterns in the economy and social structure are linked to the life course trajectories of individuals. Capital disinvestment has created neighborhoods and communities that have relatively little conventional social or cultural capital. The parents of children who grow up in these communities are not well equipped to help their children develop human capital. Because the parents do not have strong links to the conventional labor market, they also have few resources to help their children find decent jobs in the legitimate economy. Young people see the deviance service industry as the most promising source of employment. Individuals who succumb to the lures of the deviance industry risk becoming embedded in criminal lifestyles that isolate them from conventional educational and employment trajectories. Their trajectories in crime are characterized by continuity into adulthood. Hagan explains the severity and longevity of the criminal trajectories of urban underclass youth by emphasizing the powerful shaping force of personal and neighborhood social disadvantages. Individual-level differences in personal constitutions do not figure prominently in his theory.

The powerful impact that capital disinvestment has had on the lives and development of children who grow up in inner-city ghettos is undeniable. Yet, even though inner-city ghettos undoubtedly make healthy development more difficult, we must avoid falling into the trap of environmental determinism. Even in the most disadvantaged communities, there are always variations in outcomes. The deviance service centers described by Hagan may indeed draw many young people into a life of crime, but not everyone succumbs to their charms. Despite the obstacles and disadvantages they face, many inner-city families try hard and successfully to protect their children from the lures of street life (Anderson 1990; Jarrett 1997). Good opportunities may be few and far between, but many young people do get jobs in the legitimate economy and try to rise above their circumstances via the traditional routes of work and education (Newman 1999). Genetic endowments do not by themselves determine developmental outcomes, and neither do environments. Developmental outcomes are always a matter of probabilities and interactions.

Summary

For criminologists, the teenage years are where the action is. As we have learned in this chapter, the early teenage years witness an explosion of deviant and lawbreaking behavior among a substantial proportion of every teenage cohort. The small percentage of youths who started engaging in crime before becoming teenagers build criminal momentum during the second decade of life. As they grow stronger, more autonomous, and more daring, they become a serious menace to society. But they are not alone. Sometime between the ages of 13 and 17, almost everyone gets into the act, as virtually all adolescents briefly engage in crime or delinquency. Thus, teenagers rightly command the attention of life course criminologists.

In this chapter, we have reviewed the evidence on age and crime. That age and crime are strongly related is not debated seriously by criminologists, but there is considerable dispute over the details of this relationship. The most thorough analyses indicate that at the aggregate level the shape of the age—crime curve varies over historical periods, societies, and demographic groups. Careful analysis also indicates that the relationship between age and crime is not the same for all individuals. The delinquent trajectories followed by many individuals mirror aggregate-level patterns in that they resemble an inverted *j*. Onset occurs in mid-adolescence, between the ages of 14 and 16. It is followed by a brief period of involvement in delinquency that then dwindles and finally ceases in late adolescence, around age 19 or 20. But some individuals follow trajectories that are flatter or less peaked than normal over time. These individuals tend to start earlier in life, to offend at higher rates than normal, and to continue to offend at the ages when most of their age peers are desisting.

Life course theorists have devoted considerable attention to explaining these different trajectories, and we have reviewed the major theories that they have proposed so far. A number of distinctions can be drawn between life course theories. Different theorists emphasize different causal factors. Terrie Moffitt, for example, places great importance on innate temperamental differences and early family experiences to explain variation in criminal trajectories. John Hagan, on the other hand, stresses the importance of macrohistorical and economic changes and their impact on the life chances of disadvantaged minorities. Robert Sampson, John Laub, and Terence Thornberry focus on shifts in the nature and balance of informal social controls over the life course. Despite these differences in emphasis, if we permit ourselves some theoretical license, we can begin to outline a general theory of crime and the life course.

Such a theory would begin with the family. Children who come from troubled families are more likely to embark on delinquent trajectories than children whose parents are calm, loving, and supportive. But it is a mistake to assume that parents alone are to blame if their children turn out wrong. The extent to which parents can provide calm, loving support to their children is influenced by two important factors. One factor is innate temperamental differences among children. Some children appear to be born with difficult temperaments, making it hard for parents to respond to them in a calm and loving fashion. The second factor that affects how parents relate to their children is the neighborhood environment. Parents whose economic circumstances force them to live in economically disadvantaged neighborhoods have a more difficult time raising their children than parents who have the financial means to live elsewhere. Disadvantaged neighborhoods may affect how families raise their children in a number of ways, such as by providing greater opportunities for delinquency and more exposure to delinquent role models.

For most children as they enter their teenage years, the salience of parents as the focus of control, support, and interaction begins to decline. At this point in the life course, peers move front and center as the primary object of teenagers' attention and concern. Teenage peers model and reinforce behavior for one another. Thus, peers are a major influence on trajectories in crime and delinquency during the teenage years.

Important changes also take place in the realms of biology and psychology during the teenage years. Biologically, these years bring sexual maturity and rapid increases in physical strength, and they bring significant developmental changes in the teenage brain associated with emotions, perceptions, and reasoning ability. Psychologically, they bring a desire for greater autonomy and independence from parents. The desire to be treated like an adult becomes paramount. These biological and psychological developments have much to do with the onset of delinquency among teenagers. They make certain types of offenses more feasible, such as those that require physical strength. They also serve as a source of motivation for other offenses and forms of deviancy in which teenagers attempt through rebellious behavior to stake a claim to adult status. In a highly age-stratified society such as the United States, there is a large gap between the timing of these biological and psychological transitions and the socially appropriate time for making the transition to adult status. The former transitions occur early in the teenage years, whereas the latter transition is delayed until the late teenage years or even the early twenties.

One consequence of the teenage drive for autonomy and independence is that teenagers venture out into the community without the protective supervision of their parents more often and for longer periods of time than do young adolescents. But the communities and neighborhoods into which they go are not all the same. Communities vary in a number of important ways that may strongly influence individual trajectories in crime and delinquency. They vary in the number and types of criminal and legitimate opportunities they offer, in the availability of deviant and legitimate role models, in the degree of police presence, and in the style of policing that is used. For teenagers in economically disadvantaged and racially segregated inner-city neighborhoods, all of these variables tend to converge in the wrong direction. These neighborhoods present a surfeit of criminal opportunities and few legitimate ones. Gangs are a strong presence, whereas fully employed adults are few and far between. The police do not hesitate to arrest, nor are the courts chary to convict and incarcerate adolescent troublemakers. Hence, compared to their middle-class suburban counterparts, youths in these neighborhoods are at much greater risk of becoming involved in serious crime and of becoming embedded early on in a criminal lifestyle.

DISCUSSION QUESTIONS
By John M. Stogner

1. How is age-graded informal social control distinct from social bonding? How are they similar?
2. Moffitt's developmental taxonomy was initially presented over 20 years ago. Given what you have learned from earlier sections on biosocial criminology, how might her explanation of life-course persistent offenders be different if the theory were developed today?
3. Is the focus on onset, persistence, and desistence of offending limited to life-course theories? Can the other works presented in this volume account for these issues (albeit not as explicitly as life-course theories)?
4. What policy reforms are suggested by Moffitt's work (including those that are explicit, implied, and logically derived)? Would all of these actions be considered ethical?
5. Are there explanations for the age–crime curve other than those mentioned in this chapter?

CHAPTER EIGHTEEN

Feminist Perspectives in Criminology

CLAIRE M. RENZETTI

STUDENT INTRODUCTION
By John M. Stogner

Until 40 years ago, criminological theories were markedly male—they were developed by males, debated by males, evaluated by males, and primarily created to better understand variation in the criminal behavior of young males. Female offending was seen as somewhat of an anomaly and rarely explored (although the field's reticence to research female offending may have also been influenced by logistical concerns; female offending being less common than male offending means data collection may be more challenging). Regardless, there is little doubt that gender is a defining characteristic for most individuals, impacting both how they act and how they are treated by others. The socially constructed expectations for each gender affect attitudes, beliefs, and opportunities. This, paired with the knowledge that males violate the law much more frequently than females, implies that gender must occupy a role within criminological theories. Gender may be used as a more distal variable whose effects are mediated by more proximal constructs (e.g., males having lower levels of self-control on average, gender being related to learning variables in SSSL, etc.) or be the central focus of a theory.

In the selected reading, Renzetti presents an overview of the feminist perspective within criminology. As you read, you will note that the perspective appears to be without a dominant or unifying theory (much like modern biosocial criminology). Several of the works described in the chapter detail how access to male roles has facilitated female crime, but fall short of being a fully developed theory. Renzetti's presentation is accurate; although there are a number of valuable arguments that explore gender differences in offending and how female behavior might be affected by factors distinct from those which influence male behavior, this perspective is evolving and has yet to reach a point where a single theory represents it effectively. Perhaps one of the strengths of feminist criminology is the diversity of the ideas and the breadth of its insight.

On a final note, the label of the feminist perspective may be misleading as it implies that these theories only attempt to explain variation in female behavior. This is an oversimplification; works on the subject typically focus on the relationship between gender, offending, and victimization. Feminist criminology is not the study of women but rather an assessment of gender and the gender experience as they relate to crime. In fact, some works that focus on the experience of male gender roles and expectations (e.g., Messerschmidt's *Masculinities and Crime*) are typically included within this grouping. Thus, the term *gendered criminology* might be more appropriate and accurate.

FEMINIST PERSPECTIVES IN CRIMINOLOGY
By Claire M. Renzetti

Introduction: What is Feminist Criminology?

In recent interviews with social activists working to address the problem of sex trafficking worldwide, I have posed the question, "Do you consider yourself a feminist?" The common reply from interviewees goes something like this: "No, I wouldn't say I'm a feminist; I think all people should be treated equally and respectfully." Before answering the question, "What is feminist *criminology*?," then, it would be useful to first answer the question, "What is *feminism*?," for there appears to be some confusion as to the meaning of this term. And it is undeniably a label that nowadays is loaded with social and political baggage.

The emergence of contemporary feminism is typically dated in the 1960s. At that time in the United States, Canada, Britain, and Europe, various social movements developed in response to widespread social injustice, including racial and ethnic inequality, colonialism, and the Vietnam War. Women were active participants in these movements, but quickly (and correctly) perceived that they frequently were not treated as equals by male participants. At the same time, women in what may be considered more mainstream social venues—for example government, business, and education—grew increasingly dissatisfied with how little genuine equality they enjoyed despite their formal legal rights. Not surprisingly, university campuses were often at the center of this social and political activism, and many academics—mostly, but not solely, women—began to take a careful look at their respective disciplines to learn how these might be actively or implicitly reproducing social inequalities, including gender inequality. Criminology was no exception.

From this introspection, a number of different perspectives emerged, all of which may be labeled feminist. There are several core principles, though, that feminist theories share. First, at the heart of feminism is the recognition that *gender* is a central organizing principle of social life. Gender may be defined as the *socially constructed* expectations or norms governing female and male behavior and attitudes that are usually organized dichotomously as *femininity* and *masculinity* and are reproduced and transmitted through socialization. Of course, biology influences the development of gender, too, but, although feminist perspectives recognize the complex interaction between biology and environment, feminism emphasizes the socially constructed, rather than innately determined, aspects of gender.

If gender is constructed dichotomously, then membership in gender categories is exclusive. In other words, a person is *either* feminine *or* masculine. Setting aside for the moment the problematic aspects of conceptualizing gender this way, an issue to which we will return later in the chapter, consider first the fact that the genders are not equally valued in the vast majority of societies. A second core principle of feminism, therefore, is that most societies, both on a macro (structural/institutional) level and on a micro (interpersonal) level, are characterized by *sexism*, that is, the differential valuing of one gender over the other. In most societies, this sexism is a built-in feature of a *patriarchal* social system in which men dominate women and what is considered masculine is more highly valued than what is considered feminine.

The academic disciplines exist within the patriarchal social system, so it is hardly surprising that women have been systematically excluded from many fields, including criminology, which are not considered "feminine" or appropriate for women. Moreover, women and girls have been systematically excluded from the studies conducted by members of male-dominated fields under the assumption that what women do, think, or say is unimportant or uninteresting (Lorber, 2009). Similar to other disciplines, beginning in the 1970s feminist criminologists highlighted the gender biases in widely used criminological theories and how women and girls have historically been overlooked in studies of crime and criminal justice (Chesney-Lind, 2006; Jurik, 1999). Consequently, another core principle of feminism is the inclusion of female experiences and perspectives in theorizing and research. This is not to say that male experiences and perspectives should be excluded; rather, feminists emphasize the critical importance of ensuring that female voices are heard, given that they have typically been silenced or simply ignored. A major goal of feminist research and theorizing is to uncover and explain similarities and differences in women's and men's behaviors, attitudes and experiences, which arise from their different locations in—and differentially imposed valuing by—the social structure. Although their different social locations constrain their responses or resistance to their relative circumstances, the ways that women and men choose to respond or resist—the ways they exercise *agency*—are, like all other aspects of social life, gendered.

The focus on gender, and not solely on women, is a critically important point because many people, as indicated by my interviewees' responses, think of feminism as "only" about women or "women's issues." It is certainly the case that feminist theorists and researchers have prioritized the study of women's attitudes, behaviors, and experiences because these have largely been neglected and excluded. Nevertheless, feminist perspectives include research and theorizing about both masculinities and femininities. Indeed, in studying women's *and* men's lives over the past four decades, feminist researchers have shown that not all groups of men benefit equally or in the same ways from gender privilege. As feminism has developed and matured, therefore, another significant principle to which many feminist theorists adhere is the necessity of analyzing how gender inequality *intersects* with multiple inequalities, including racism, classism, heterosexism, ageism, and ableism, to form an interlocking system of oppression that impacts women's and men's everyday lives, including their risk of criminal victimization and offending and their treatment as "clients" or employees of the criminal justice system (Burgess-Proctor, 2006; Risman, 2004).

Unlike other perspectives, feminism is not solely a set of theories; it is also a *social movement* informed by a theoretical framework with the goal of collective action to eliminate sexism and promote gender equity in all areas of social life. In conducting research and explaining their findings, feminist social scientists, including feminist criminologists, are engaged in what sociologist Joann Miller (2011) has called *purpose-driven research*: research that raises public awareness, in this case of gendered inequalities, and which produces usable knowledge that contributes to the social reconstruction of gender and gender relations so they are more equitable. Feminist researchers strive to acquire scientific knowledge through the research process that empowers individuals and groups to act to change behaviors and conditions which are harmful or oppressive.

This goal has important implications for how feminist research is conducted. Examples of feminist research will be discussed throughout this chapter, but suffice it to say here that, in general, feminist researchers reject the traditional model of science "as establishing mastery over subjects, as demanding the absence of feeling, and as enforcing separateness of the knower from the known, all under the guise of 'objectivity' " (Hess & Ferree, 1987, p. 13; see also Naples, 2003; Reinharz, 1992). Instead, feminist research is often characterized by *reciprocity* between the researcher and the research participants; rather than establishing relational distance from the research participants, the researcher engages in self-disclosure and may offer resources and helpful information, recognizing that research participants are frequently revealing private, sometimes traumatic aspects of their lives to a stranger and that they may, in fact, need assistance that the researcher can provide. Feminist researchers also try to take an *empathic stance* toward the participants in their studies; instead of imposing their own ideas or categories of response on their participants, they give participants a more active role in guiding the direction of the research and attempt to understand the phenomena they are studying from the participants' viewpoints.

This approach to research reflects another core principle of feminist perspectives: the research process is *dualistic*; that is, it has both subjective and objective dimensions. Feminists emphasize that no research is completely unbiased or value-free. No matter how objective researchers like to believe they are, they cannot help but be influenced by values, personal preferences, and aspects of the cultural setting and institutional structures in which they live. That said, research is not totally subjective either. Although a researcher may be influenced by values (i.e. judgments or appraisals), her or his goal is the collection of facts (i.e. phenomena that can be observed or empirically verified). Feminists challenge researchers to explicitly acknowledge the assumptions, beliefs, sympathies, and potential biases that may influence their work. They question not only the possibility, but also the desirability, of value-free science; however, although they reject this notion, they do not reject scientific standards in their research (Reinharz, 1992). And although the ideals of reciprocity and an empathic stance imply an emphasis on qualitative methods, such as ethnography and indepth interviewing, many feminist researchers, including feminist criminologists as we will see shortly, conduct quantitative studies using sophisticated statistical techniques to analyze their data, or mixed approaches that incorporate both quantitative and qualitative methods (see, for example, Campbell, 2011a,b).

So to return to the question that opened this chapter: "What is feminist criminology?" The short answer is that feminist criminology is a paradigm that studies and explains criminal offending and victimization as well as institutionalized responses to these problems as fundamentally gendered and which emphasizes the importance of using the scientific knowledge we acquire from our study of these issues to influence the creation and implementation of public policy that will alleviate oppression and contribute to more equitable social relations and social structures. Like many short answers, however, this one is inadequate and unsatisfying. As was noted at the outset, there is no single, unitary feminist perspective, but rather a diversity of feminist perspectives, each with variations on the core principles presented. Let us turn, then, to a discussion of some of the major feminist perspectives in criminology.

Feminist Criminologies

A number of typologies have been offered in an attempt to classify the many feminist perspectives currently being applied to the study of social life (see, for example, Lorber, 2009). Within criminology, it is argued that there are at least 12 distinct feminist theories (Maidment, 2006). Space constraints preclude a review of every theoretical perspective that may be considered feminist, so a select few—what I consider to be the major feminist criminological theories—will be discussed in this chapter. That said, it must be acknowledged that not all feminist criminologists agree on which theories to label "major"; some readers, therefore, will likely disagree with my selection, perhaps considering it too "conventional," and would choose other theories to highlight instead. Keep in mind, too, that the presentation of these theories is not chronological. Although some theories preceded others temporally and new perspectives built on these initial or early approaches, several theories were being developed and tested simultaneously, as is typically the case in criminology and other disciplines.

Liberal Feminist Criminology

In general, liberal feminism may be described as an "equal rights" approach in that the focus is largely on securing the same legal rights for women that men enjoy. Liberal feminists consider the major cause of gender inequality to be blocked opportunities, so the primary goal of their social activism has been dismantling gender discrimination in employment, education, government, and other social institutions. In addition, as women and men are taught specific—and unequal—gender roles, liberal feminists have sought to change traditional gender socialization practices so that men and women learn to be more alike in terms of their attitudes and behaviors.

Liberal feminism influenced several feminist criminological theories, particularly early in the development of feminist criminology. For example, emancipation theories of female offending (Adler, 1975; Simon, 1975) are rooted in liberal feminism. Emancipation theorists sought to explain what they perceived to be dramatic increases in female offending during the late 1960s and early 1970s. They attributed these changes to newly opened opportunities for women and girls, thanks to the women's liberation movement. In short, these theories argue that, just as legitimate opportunities opened for women and girls, so too did illegitimate or criminal opportunities. And because females were being encouraged to behave more like males, it should be no surprise that this would lead them to do so in less than positive ways as well, such as being more violent and committing more property crimes.

The value of any theory, of course, depends on how well it stands up to empirical testing. Emancipation theories were shown to be seriously flawed through research that demonstrated that, in fact, the gender gap in the crime rate was not closing as much as emancipation theorists believed, and that females were not becoming more like males in terms of the types of crimes they were committing. To be sure, women and girls were being arrested and imprisoned more frequently than in the past—and this trend has continued—but to a large extent this change reflected their greater likelihood of committing the property crimes for which they were traditionally charged (e.g. larceny, fraud) and drug offenses. Some feminist critics of the emancipation perspective have also argued that females' elevated arrest and incarceration rates are the result of policy and practice changes in the criminal justice system. More specifically, critics argue that the 1980s "war on crime" essentially became in practice a war on women and racial minorities, especially blacks, and that rising arrest and incarceration rates of women represent "equality with a vengeance" (Chesney-Lind, 2006). The question of whether females, or some groups of females, are treated more or less leniently by the criminal justice system continues to be debated and researched by feminist criminologists (see, for example, Spohn & Brennan, forthcoming), but empirical evidence clearly does not support the notion that a "downside" of the women's liberation movement is that it motivated women and girls to commit more crimes or to act "more like men."

Another liberal feminist theory is power-control theory (Hagan, 1989; McCarthy, Hagan, & Woodward, 1999). Power-control theory looks at how social class, as a mediating factor in gender socialization, may result in different rates of female and male offending, especially juvenile delinquency. In families characterized by patriarchal control—that is, families with a traditional gendered division of labor in which the husband/father is in the paid labor force and the wife/mother remains at home to care for the household and socialize the children—girls are socialized to be like their mothers (domestic, subdued, and, therefore, unlikely to take risks), whereas boys have considerably more freedom and more opportunities for risk-taking, including crime. Power-control theory posits that this arrangement is more common among working-class families. In families that are more egalitarian or "balanced" in terms of the gendered division of labor, in which both husbands/fathers and wives/mothers are in the paid labor force, girls and boys are treated more alike. Mothers in these families are still seen as primarily responsible for the gender socialization of their children and, the theory maintains, they less tightly control their daughters' opportunities and behavior and increase their control over their sons, such that the girls' and boys' behavior is likely to be more similar, including in terms of risk-taking and delinquency. Power-control theory sees this arrangement as more common among middle-class families.

Empirical support for power-control theory has been mixed at best (see, for example, Heimer & DeCoster, 1999; Morash & Chesney-Lind, 1991). The theory has also been critiqued for its simplistic conceptualization of social class and the gendered division of labor in the home and workplace, and for its lack of attention to racial/ethnic differences in gender socialization and to single-parent families, most of which are headed by women. Another significant weakness in power-control theory is its limited definition of patriarchal control, which is reduced to parental supervision (Chesney-Lind, 1997; Chesney-Lind & Sheldon, 1992). Patriarchal control, however, is far more complex and may take a variety of forms, ranging on a continuum from severe, brutal violence at one extreme, to what has been called "chivalry" or "benevolent sexism" at the other extreme. Let us consider, then, additional feminist criminological perspectives that recognize the importance and complexity of patriarchy and patriarchal control.

Radical Feminist, Marxist Feminist, and Socialist Feminist Criminology

One theoretical approach that broadens the scope of patriarchal control is radical feminist criminology. Radical feminism maintains that gender inequality or sexism is the most fundamental form of oppression and that it is females who are oppressed. Indeed, radical feminists argue that, throughout the world, females are the most oppressed group and that, regardless of race, ethnicity, or social class, men enjoy gender privilege, which includes the subordination and control of women. Patriarchal social structures, including the criminal justice system, serve to preserve male power and ensure female subordination, and one of the primary ways that this is accomplished is through the threat or actual use of violence. Radical feminist criminologists, then, have pioneered the study of women as crime victims, particularly as victims of violent crimes perpetrated by men, and the failure of the criminal justice system to protect women from men's violence.

Victimization by violent crime is gendered. Although males are more likely than females to be the victim of a violent crime, research by radical feminist criminologists and others consistently documents the alarming frequency of violence against women throughout the world and the multitude of forms it takes, including sexual harassment, sexual assault and rape, battering, and homicide (see Renzetti, Edleson, & Bergen, 2010). This research also shows that, ironically, although we advise girls not to talk to strangers, they are significantly more likely to be harmed by someone they know; in 70 percent of violent crimes committed against women, the victim knew her assailant, whereas in only 45 percent of violent crimes committed against men did the victim know his assailant (Truman & Rand, 2010; see also Kruttschnitt, 2001). According to radical feminist criminologists, however, despite these data the police, courts, and criminologists themselves have been preoccupied with male street crime, and the criminal justice system has been overwhelmingly ineffective in keeping women and girls safe, and holding men and boys accountable for the violence they perpetrate against them.

Work by radical feminist criminologists laid the foundation for the burgeoning research on violence against women that continues at present. Nevertheless, critics of radical feminist criminology maintain that this perspective still portrays the criminal justice system too negatively. Significant legislative and enforcement reforms have occurred over the past several decades (e.g. changes in rape laws designed to shift the focus of blame from the behavior of the victim to the behavior of the assailant, harsher penalties for batterers). Although some feminist researchers have identified gaps between these laws on paper and how they are actually implemented (e.g. Caringella, 2008), it cannot be denied that they have been beneficial to women.

Another criticism of radical feminist criminology is that it characterizes all men as oppressors, equally likely to harass, rape, or abuse women, even though it is the case that the majority of men do not violently victimize women and some profeminist men actively work to prevent and respond to such victimization. Moreover, this perspective overlooks women's violent offending, a point to which we will return shortly. And finally, by foregrounding gender as the paramount oppression, radical feminist criminologists inaccurately universalize the categories of "female" and "male," while overlooking the reality that gender inequality intersects with other types of inequality, particularly racism and social class inequality (Burgess-Proctor, 2006).

Marxist feminist criminologists differ from radical feminist criminologists in that they prioritize social class inequality over gender inequality. Marxist feminist criminologists maintain that societies with less social class inequality also have less gender inequality, because male dominance, like other types of discrimination, grows largely out of unequal economic conditions, specifically the exploitative class relations inherent in capitalism. Thus, from this perspective, if capitalism is replaced with a more egalitarian mode of production, this egalitarianism will be reflected in other spheres of social life, including gender relations.

However, some feminist criminologists see Marxist feminism as making an error similar to radical feminism: one form of inequality does not take precedence over another form of inequality. Oppression is not linear. Instead, in their everyday lives people *simultaneously* experience the effects of *multiple inequalities*, just as they also experience different forms and degrees of *privilege*. Socialist feminist criminology is one theoretical perspective that recognizes the importance of examining how the interaction of gender and social class inequalities influences criminal opportunities, victimization experiences, and responses by the criminal justice system to both offenders and victims. Messerschmidt (1993), for example, argues that the crimes individuals commit reflect both their social class position and their socialized conceptions of masculinity and femininity.

Socialist feminist criminologists were also the first to draw attention to the fact that the traditional criminological construction of offenders and victims as two distinct or dichotomous groups is largely inaccurate when gender is also taken into account (Jurik, 1999). Research shows that violent victimization, especially during childhood, is often a pathway to subsequent involvement in crime, more so for girls than for boys. For instance, Widom and Maxfield (2001) found a significant increase in arrest for violent crime among girls who were neglected and abused compared with girls who had not been neglected and abused, but this relationship did not hold for boys (see also Siegel & Williams, 2003). This pattern is found in studies of adult offenders as well (English, Widom, & Brandford, 2001; Morash, 2006).

However, although socialist feminist criminology attends to the dual importance and interactive effects of sexism and social class inequality, and highlights the salience of victimization in understanding pathways to criminal offending, particularly by women and girls, this perspective has been criticized nevertheless for depicting women and men as relatively homogeneous social categories, distinguishable only by social class differences. More recent feminist theories have drawn attention to the need to examine how race and ethnicity intersect with gender, social class, and other locations of inequality in order to understand both criminal offending and victimization, and the responses of the criminal justice system. It is to these theories that we turn to conclude this chapter.

Contemporary and Future Directions in Feminist Criminological Perspectives

As noted in the chapter introduction, gender is typically conceptualized in dichotomous terms: a person is *either* feminine *or* masculine. Recently, however, some feminist criminologists have adopted the reconceptualization of gender as *situated action* or *situated accomplishment* (West & Fenstermaker, 1995; West & Zimmerman, 1987); that is, gender is something one *does* in response to contextualized norms. From this perspective, males and females "do gender" in various situations, and make choices—albeit choices constrained by structural conditions and normative expectations—about how they will establish their masculinity and femininity respectively. Gender, then, is in flux; it changes over time, and from situation to situation, in response to normative demands and an individual's resources and perceptions of others' evaluations of him or her. This perspective also takes into account intersecting locations of inequality, such that individuals also simultaneously do race/ethnicity, social class, sexuality, and age, thereby producing multiple masculinities and femininities, "each shaped by structural positioning" (Miller, 2002, p. 435). Consequently, some feminist criminologists are theorizing that crime is a means for accomplishing gender in certain contexts, and these efforts to do gender also affect who is victimized. Consider, for instance, the recent studies of hate crime conducted by Bufkin (1999) and Perry (2001). In their analyses of the characteristics of hate crime perpetrators and their victims, as well as the characteristics of the crimes themselves (e.g. language used by perpetrators, the group nature of most hate crimes, use of alcohol by perpetrators), these feminist criminologists theorize that committing a hate crime is a means of accomplishing a particular type of masculinity, *hegemonic masculinity*, which is described as white, Christian, able-bodied, and heterosexual.

Other feminist criminologists call for even greater attention to the intersection of gender, social class, and race/ethnicity as well as other inequalities, emphasizing their interlocking nature in a "matrix of domination" (Collins, 2000). For example, black feminist criminology builds on both critical race feminist theory and black feminist theory more generally. This theoretical perspective is often referred to as a "standpoint theory," in that it focuses on the lived experiences of black women, recognizing their multiple intersecting identities and analyzing their oppression both within the black community and in the larger society, as well as their resistance to these forms of oppression. Potter (2006) identifies four themes in black feminist criminology—social structural oppression, interactions in the black community, intimate and familial relations, and the black woman as individual—and applies them in an analysis of intimate partner violence in the lives of black women to show how black women's intertwined racialized and gendered identities produce experiences of intimate partner violence that are different from the experiences of other groups of women and, therefore, require different responses. Even more broadly, Burgess-Proctor (2006) challenges feminist criminologists to embrace multiracial feminism in their work, emphasizing the critical importance of considering the *interactive* rather than additive effects of race, gender, class, age, sexuality, and other social locators on offending, victimization, and criminal justice processes. She offers numerous examples of criminological studies that demonstrate how the intersection of these factors affect the "production of crime," the relationship between victimization and offending, and criminal justice outcomes such as sentencing disparities.

A brief chapter such as this one can hardly do justice to the diversity of feminist perspectives within criminology, and I have overlooked many, such as pragmatic feminism (McDermott, 2002) and postmodern and poststructural feminism (Howe, 2000; Wonders, 1999). Nevertheless, this overview offers perhaps a sampling of some of the most influential and most promising feminist theoretical perspectives in criminology today. Undoubtedly, the work of feminists of color and also that of Third World feminists in non-Western or economically developing societies in Africa, Asia, and Latin America will enrich feminist criminology—and criminology as a discipline—in the years to come.

References

Adler, F. (1975). *Sisters in crime*. New York: McGraw-Hill.

Buf kin, J. (1999). Bias crime as gendered behavior. *Social Justice, 26,* 155–176.

Burgess-Proctor, A. (2006). Intersections of race, class, gender, and crime: Future directions for feminist criminology. *Feminist Criminology, 1,* 27– 47.

Campbell, R. (Ed.). (2011a). Special issue: Methodological advances in recruitment and assessment. *Violence against Women, 17*(2), 159–162.

Campbell, R. (Ed.). (2011b). Special issue: Methodological advances in analytic techniques for longitudinal designs and evaluations of community interventions. *Violence against Women, 17*(3), 291–294.

Caringella, S. (2008). *Addressing rape reform in law and practice*. New York: Columbia University Press.

Chesney-Lind, M. (1997). *The female offender*. Thousand Oaks, CA: Sage.

Chesney-Lind, M. (2006). Patriarchy, crime, and justice: Feminist criminology in an era of backlash. *Feminist Criminology, 1,* 6 –26.

Chesney-Lind, M., & Sheldon, R. G. (1992). *Girls' delinquency and juvenile justice*. Pacific Grove, CA: Brooks/ Cole.

Collins, P. H. (2000). *Black feminist thought* (2nd edn.). New York: Routledge.

English, D. J., Widom, C. S., & Brandford, C. B. (2001). *Childhood victimization and delinquency, adult criminality, and violent criminal behavior: A replication and extension*. Final report. Washington, DC: U.S. Department of Justice, National Institute of Justice.

Hagan, J. (1989). *Structural criminology*. New Brunswick, NJ: Rutgers University Press.

Heimer, K., & DeCoster, S. (1999). The gendering of violent delinquency. *Criminology, 37*, 277–318.

Hess, B. B., & Ferree, M. M. (1987). Introduction. In B. B. Hess & M. M. Ferree (Eds.), *Analyzing gender* (pp. 9–30). Newbury Park, CA: Sage.

Howe, A. (2000). Postmodern criminology and its feminist discontents. *Australian and New Zealand Journal of Criminology, 33*, 221–236.

Jurik, N. C. (1999). Socialist feminist criminology and social justice. In B. A. Arrigo (Ed.), *Social justice, criminal justice* (pp. 30 –50). Belmont, CA: Wadsworth.

Kruttschnitt, C. (2001). Gender and violence. In C. M. Renzetti & L. Goodstein (Eds.), *Women, crime and criminal justice* (pp. 77–92). Los Angeles: Roxbury.

Lorber, J. (2009). *Gender inequality: Feminist theory and politics*. New York: Oxford University Press.

Maidment, M. R. (2006). Transgressing boundaries: Feminist perspectives in criminology. In W. S. DeKeseredy & B. Perry (Eds.), *Advancing critical criminology: Theory and application* (pp. 43– 62). Landham, MD: Lexington Books.

McCarthy, B., Hagan, J., & Woodward, T. S. (1999). In the company of women: Structure and agency in a revised power-control theory of gender and delinquency. *Criminology, 37*, 761–788.

McDermott, M. J. (2002). On moral enterprises, pragmatism, and feminist criminology. *Crime & Delinquency, 48*, 283–299.

Messerschmidt, J. W. (1993). *Masculinities and crime*. Lanham, MD: Rowman & Littlefield.

Miller, J. (2002). The strengths and limits of "doing gender" for understanding street crime. *Theoretical Criminology, 6*, 433– 460.

Miller, J. A. (2011). Social justice work: Purpose-driven social science. *Social Problems, 58*, 1–20.

Morash, M. (2006). *Understanding gender, crime and justice*. Thousand Oaks, CA: Sage.

Morash, M., & Chesney-Lind, M. (1991). A re-formulation and partial test of power-control theory. *Justice Quarterly, 8*, 347–377.

Naples, N. A. (2003). *Feminism and method*. New York: Routledge.

Perry, B. (2001). *In the name of hate: Understanding hate crime*. New York: Routledge.

Potter, H. (2006). An argument for black feminist criminology: Understanding African American women's experiences with intimate partner abuse using an integrated approach. *Feminist Criminology, 1*, 106 –124.

Reinharz, S. (1992). *Feminist methods in social research*. New York: Oxford University Press.

Renzetti, C. M., Edleson, J. L., & Bergen, R. K. (Eds.) (2010). *Sourcebook on violence against women* (2nd edn.). Thousand Oaks, CA: Sage.

Risman, B. J. (2004). Gender as social structure. *Gender & Society, 18*, 429– 450.

Siegel, J. A., & Williams, L. M. (2003). The relationship between child sexual abuse and female delinquency and crime: A prospective study. *Journal of Research in Crime and Delinquency, 40*, 71–94.

Simon, R. J. (1975). *Women and crime*. Washington, DC: Government Printing Office.

Spohn, C., & Brennan, P. (forthcoming). Sentencing and punishment. In C. M. Renzetti, S. L. Miller, & A. Gover (Eds.), *Handbook of gender and crime studies*. London: Routledge.

Truman, J. L., & Rand, M. R. (2010). *Criminal victimization, 2009*. Washington, DC: U.S. Department of Justice, Bureau of Justice Statistics.

West, C., & Fenstermaker, S. (1995). Doing difference. *Gender & Society, 9*, 8 –37.

West, C., & Zimmerman, D. H. (1987). Doing gender. *Gender & Society, 1*, 125–151.

Widom, C. S., & Maxfield, M. G. (2001). *An update on the "cycle of violence."* Washington, DC: U.S. Department of Justice, National Institute of Justice.

Wonders, N. A. (1999). Postmodern feminist criminology and social justice. In B. A. Arrigo (Ed.), *Social justice, criminal justice* (pp. 109–128). Belmont, CA: Wadsworth.

DISCUSSION QUESTIONS
By John M. Stogner

1. Which criminological theories covered thus far do you believe are best able to account for both male and female offending? Are separate theories necessary for males and females?

2. John Hagan's power-control theory has been considered somewhat controversial/offensive. How do you evaluate his assertion that egalitarian homes facilitate equality in children's offending?

3. Is it possible that crime is a means of achieving masculinity for young boys/men?

4. Discuss at least four reasons why female offending has increased in the last few decades. Are girls catching up with boys?

5. How does the issue of race relate to gender in the context of criminological theory? Which is more important? Does race influence the role of gender in the etiology of both crime and victimization?

CHAPTER NINETEEN

Radical and Critical Criminology

TIM NEWBURN

STUDENT INTRODUCTION
By John M. Stogner

Much like Becker's work, theories that are classified as radical or critical question the notion of crime as an absolute. These works challenge the notion that some criminal acts are inherently bad or deviant. Instead, they focus on the reasons that certain acts are illegal and their violations punishable. Critical and radical criminological works examine the motivations behind the creation of laws, suggesting that the political interests and egocentrism of the affluent, instead of the greater public good, drive many policy decisions. Put another way, these works argue that those with wealth and status use their resources to ensure that a system exists that allows them to maintain power. Radical/critical criminology suggests that the wealthy manipulate the criminal justice system much like they often successfully lobby for tax and financial policies most beneficial to the affluent. Those in control strive to penalize the threatening actions of the lower class while avoiding policies that criminalize their own actions that violate human rights (often indirectly; e.g., corporate actions that endanger or fail to protect consumers).

Many of the works in the radical/criminal perspective go so far as to suggest that the criminal justice system is a tool used by the elite to maintain their status. They similarly suggest that the criminal justice system, along with unrestrained capitalism, only serves to further separate the "haves" from the "have nots." The solution, therefore, according to these theories, is to create a more equitable society where citizens reap the rewards of their labors more equally. They generally suggest that political reforms should focus on empowering the disadvantaged so that all have an equal voice in the demographic process, regardless of status or financial resources.

As you read, note the major influences within this perspective. Karl Marx's work has been particularly important in depicting the potential ramifications of class conflicts. Willem Bonger, Richard Quinney, and others have helped define the perspective. They have stressed that a capitalistic system leads to exploitation of the underclass by both the economic and criminal justice systems. Their works are supportive of socialist systems that Americans typically reject. Consider their arguments; ask whether they present a narrow view of capitalism. Evaluate whether their ideas are logical, feasible, or testable. Challenge the notion that exploitation and maltreatment are minimized in a society with a less competitive economy.

RADICAL AND CRITICAL CRIMINOLOGY
By Tim Newburn

Introduction

Much of what we discussed under the heading of 'control theories' in the previous chapter rested on the assumption that offenders are self-interested individuals who commit crimes when opportunities arise and circumstances make such criminal activity seem 'worth the risk'. Such approaches differ markedly from early sociological theories which place much less emphasis upon individual decision-making and, rather, focus on the social and cultural context in which crime is to be found. In this chapter we will examine a number of theoretical approaches which, again, differ in many ways from control theories, not least in the emphasis they place upon the *meaning* of crime.

Taylor, Walton and Young, at the forefront of radical criminology in Britain in the 1970s, took anomie theory and other approaches to task for 'predicting too little bourgeois and too much proletarian criminality' (1973: 107). In part, what they meant by this was that such approaches tend to focus upon those social conditions that are held to produce the types of crime that the working classes or poorer members of society are most likely to engage in, whilst paying little attention to other offences such as white-collar and corporate crime.

Crime and the Underdog

As we have seen labelling theory generated something of a debate about the nature and limitations of what has been referred to as *underdog sociology*. An early extension of labelling theory by Horowitz and Leibowitz (1968) increased the emphasis on the political nature of some deviant activity. They took the view that certain types of deviance could be seen as forms of social protest. Commenting on this work, Pearson (1975: 96) suggested that the implication was that deviant behaviour 'should be accorded political status. Or, more specifically, that deviance should be grasped as a primitive crypto-political action.'

Though this possibly overstates the case somewhat, it was nevertheless the case that in Britain in particular, a movement developed within one particular strain of sociological criminology which sought to adopt a more explicitly politicised position in relation to deviance and to see an element in it of resistance to existing social conditions. More generally, a radical criminology developed as a reaction in part to the functionalist sociology that had dominated up to this point with its assumptions, implicit or otherwise, about the necessity of policing and punishment. By contrast:

> Critical scholars refused to practise criminology as an auxiliary discipline to criminal law enforcement, and saw it as their task to examine the functioning of the criminal justice system as an instrument of the state to keep power relations as they are. (van Swaaningen, 1997: 79)

Marx and Marxism

Unlike Durkheim, Marx appears to have been relatively unconcerned by crime as a subject. That is not to say that Marxist thought has not been influential in criminology, merely that the influence is a result of Marx's general sociological theory rather than any direct observations he may have made about crime and criminality. Marx was a political economist/sociologist whose concern was with the nature of social divisions and the distribution of power within society. For Marx, it was to the *relations of production* that one should look in the search for the answers to such questions. Within industrial societies, the relations of production can be understood as a dyad, involving a capitalist class (or *bourgeoisie*) that owns the *means of production* and a working class (or *proletariat*) that has to sell its labour in order to survive. All other aspects of society come to reflect this basic division and the major state institutions work toward the maintenance and reproduction of this uneven and unequal system.

As Marx put it:

In the social production of their existence, men inevitably enter into definite relations, which are independent of their will, namely relations of production appropriate to a given stage of development of their material forces of production. The totality of these relations of production constitutes the economic structure of society, the real foundation, on which arises a legal and political superstructure and to which correspond definite forms of social consciousness. The mode of production of material life conditions the general character of the social, political, and intellectual life. It is not the consciousness of men that determines their existence, but their social existence that determines their consciousness. At a certain stage of development, the material productive forces of society come into conflict with the existing relations of production.... Then begins an era of social revolution. (Marx, 1976 [1857]: 5–6)

Here Marx sets out many of the fundamental ideas of his political economy. Societies can be seen to have gone through different stages of development (he was writing at the time of the growth of industrial capitalism). The economic structure of society is the basis on which all other aspects depend and, moreover, it is this that moulds and shapes human consciousness (what we think and believe). However, there are

Karl Marx (1818–1883), philosopher and revolutionary and author of *Das Kapital* and *The Communist Manifesto*. Though he had relatively little to say directly about crime, his ideas have had a profound impact on radical criminology.

Copyright in the Public Domain.

contradictions within the system. Capitalist society, for Marx, is one in which property and wealth become progressively concentrated in fewer and fewer hands. Society polarises into two groups—or classes—whose interests are fundamentally in opposition. Eventually, the contradictions of capitalism will become so serious that, following revolution, it will be replaced by a wholly new social system—*communism.*

For Marx, the essence of human nature was to be found in productive work—this is an essential part of what he referred to as our 'species being'. The denial of productive work, as happens to ever-larger numbers of people under capitalism, leads to demoralisation. Indeed, it leads to the emergence of a class of people, he argued, who are typified by criminal conduct and other forms of vice-ridden behaviour. This he termed the *lumpenproletariat.* The law, however, is not some neutral expression of what the philosopher Rousseau called 'the social contract'—that thing which binds free individuals together in an expression of collective interest. For Marx, the law is not something which upholds the rights and interests of all citizens, but is an expression of class domination: representing the interests of the dominant class.

One relatively simple—some might suggest *simplistic*—approach to crime that can be drawn from such an approach, is to see offending straightforwardly as a form of resistance by the disenfranchised to the capitalist order. The American political scientist James Q. Wilson (1975: xiii) caricatured such portrayals of crime as the 'expression of the political rage of the dispossessed, rebelling under the iron heel of capitalist tyranny'. It is true to say that Marx had been particularly concerned with working-class resistance to elements of industrial capitalism and, indeed, his collaborator, Engels, had argued in his most famous work, *The Condition of the Working Class in England,* that 'theft was the most primitive form of protest' (1969 [1892]: 240). This is sometimes referred to as the *primitive rebellion* thesis and, although you will rarely find it in crude form these days, you may still find echoes of such views in some contemporary accounts of some criminal activity.

Generally though, it is a subtler reading of Marx's ideas that tends to find its way into modern criminology. Arguments such as the centrality of class conflict to an understanding of social order, the notion that the dominant ideas of the moment are the ideas that serve the interests of the 'ruling class' (however such a thing is to be defined), and the centrality of property and the economy to class relations, all underpin radical, or conflict, theories of crime and criminal justice. All draw their inspiration more or less directly from Marx.

Willem Bonger

The Dutch scholar, Willem Bonger (see box), was one of the first criminologists to utilise the theory of political economy of Marx and his collaborator, Friedrich Engels. Bonger studied crime rates in Europe in the late nineteenth and early twentieth centuries and was highly critical of the form of social organisation he saw emerging. Capitalism, he argued, 'is a system of exploitation in which, in place of the exploited person being robbed he is compelled by poverty to use all his powers for the benefit of the exploiter' (1969: 28).

For Bonger, the economic inequalities found in contemporary capitalism, and the emphasis on financial success and the individualised, selfish pursuit of pleasure produced a form of 'egoism' which increased criminal conduct. Rather in parallel with Durkheim, Bonger identified the insufficient control of individuals in the new division of labour as a core problem of modern industrial times (what Durkheim sought to capture in his notion of *anomie.* However, unlike Durkheim, Bonger didn't see the solution to this as something to be found in more effective controls—as these controls reflect the nature of the society itself.

Like Marx, Bonger took the view that there was something fundamentally unjust about capitalist social organisation for 'hardly any act is punished if it does not injure the interests of the dominant class' (Bonger, 1969: 9). That is to say, the operation of the law in capitalist society acts to punish the poor whilst allowing the wealthy to act in selfish and greedy ways without fear of punishment. By contrast, in a socialist society crime would eventually be eliminated as the law would protect the interests of all rather than merely the propertied.

In a similar vein, Edwin Sutherland in the 1930s noted the extent to which major corporations were involved in activities that were, in principle, 'criminal' but which avoided being defined as such because of the economic and political muscle the organisations enjoyed. At approximately the same period, Thorsten Sellin (1938) published a book, *Culture Conflict and Crime,* which, though not Marxist in orientation, focused on conflict between dominant and subsidiary cultures as a means of understanding deviant activity. The law, Sellin argued, tends to reflect dominant cultural norms rather than some broader social consensus. This was not a class-based analysis but a theory which focused on differing normative standards among different communities and neighbourhoods. Much influenced by the work of the Chicago School and by Edwin Sutherland's notion of differential association he observed how conformity to one set of cultural norms may bring people into conflict with the institutions of the criminal justice system.

Willem Bonger (1876–1940)

The youngest of ten children, Bonger grew up in Amsterdam, where his father worked in insurance. He studied law at the University of Amsterdam where he came under the influence of scholars interested also in sociological thought and issues of crime and justice.

The author of a number of books, including *Race and Crime* (1939) and *An Introduction to Criminology* (1932), he is perhaps best known for *Criminality and Economic Conditions,* which was published in 1916. He was an influential author and academic and it has been argued that it 'was due to him that criminology in Holland became a separate field of science' (van Bemmelen, 1960).

Bonger was a fervent critic of oppressive regimes generally, and the Nazis in particular. He was identified by the Third Reich as an arch-enemy of the German state and, despite accepting that a German invasion of Holland would almost certainly end with his death, he refused to emigrate. When the German army entered Holland in early 1940 he wrote to his son, 'I don't see any future for myself and I cannot bow to this scum which will now overmaster us.' He committed suicide not long afterward.

What we have in the radical or critical criminologies which draw at least some of their inspiration from Marx, therefore, is work that is especially concerned with power relations in society and how crime and the criminal law relate to such power differentials. One of the core ideas running through much of such work is that of *criminalisation*. According to Spitzer (1975: 642, quoted in Box, 1983):

> Problem populations tend to share a number of social characteristics but most important among these is the fact that their behaviour, personal qualities, and/or position threaten the social relations of production.... . In other words, populations become generally eligible for management as deviant when they disturb, hinder, or call into question...capitalist modes of appropriating the product of human labour...the social conditions under capitalist production takes place...patterns of distribution and consumption...the process of socialization for productive and nonproductive roles...and...the ideology which supports the capitalist state.

More particularly, radical theory is critical precisely because it begins from the normative premise that current arrangements are unequal, exploitative and in need of substantial (radical) overhaul. Most criminological work that comes under this heading therefore is structuralist in character, seeing the deep-seated structural inequalities in society as the basis from which an analysis of crime and justice must proceed.

Although *radical* and *conflict theories* are largely discussed together in this chapter, there are a number of differences between them in practice. Generally speaking, it is held that conflict theory assumes human nature to be amoral whereas radical theorists hold a more benign view in which human nature is more positive, but the circumstances in which individuals find themselves shape behaviour in less acceptable ways. Conflict theories tend to view society as being divided into numerous groups whose interests differ, whereas the bulk of radical theorists, drawing at least in part on Marxism, tend rather to see the division as being primarily between two groups—differentiated by their relationship to property.

American Radicalism

A body of radical criminological work influenced by Marxist theory emerged in the USA in the late 1960s. It was associated with three people in particular: William Chambliss, Richard Quinney and Austin Turk. However, a survey of American radical criminology must begin somewhat earlier with the work of George Vold. Writing in the 1950s, and building on work by Edwin Sutherland, and by the German sociologist Georg Simmel, Vold focused on the centrality of political conflict in contemporary society and how group conflict is often the source of criminal activity. In this view the uneven distribution of power is vital. Vold felt that, although the idea of group conflict had some general relevance, it was most applicable to four types of crime (Brown *et al.*, 2004: 402):

- crimes arising from labour disputes;
- crimes arising from political protests;
- crimes arising from disputes between and within competing unions;
- crimes arising from racial and ethnic clashes.

Vold and Criminalisation

The issue raised implicitly by Vold in the quote earlier is that of 'criminalisation'—the assignment of the status *criminal* to particular individuals—and, more particularly, the socially uneven way in which this occurs.

What are the consequences of the uneven distribution of power and the fact, therefore, that some people have authority over others? Vold's approach began from the assumption that people in general are group-oriented and that they tend to develop strong attachment to particular groups. Groups inevitably come into conflict because of their differing interests, and this is a normal part of the functioning of any society.

Criminal activity is often something carried out for the benefit of a particular group, or indeed may be committed by groups, and can be understood in part as something that arises in the context of social and political inequality. Industrial or labour conflicts, for example, between management and workers have often led to the criminalisation of certain forms of behaviour—secondary picketing is one example—often reflecting the balance of power between the groups involved. As Vold argued in the first edition of his textbook, *Theoretical Criminology* (1958: 209):

> The whole political process of law making, law breaking, and law enforcement becomes a direct reflection of deep-seated and fundamental conflicts between interest groups and their more general struggles for the control of the police power of the state. Those who produce legislative majorities win control over the police power and dominate the policies that decide who is likely to be involved in the violation of the law.
>
> The task for the critical criminologist, therefore, becomes the analysis of the ways in which such conflicts of interest are played out to the detriment of the least powerful in our society, and the role of the criminal justice system in this process.

Austin Turk

Like Vold, Turk's conflict-oriented theory was stimulated by his perception that existing theories were unable to explain many of the problems and conflicts besetting contemporary American society. In the preface to his book *Criminality and Legal Order,* published in 1969, he said that:

> Embarrassment provided much of the initial push that led to the writing of this book. I was embarrassed at my lack of good answers when confronted by students who wondered, somewhat irreverently, why criminology is 'such a confused mish-mash'.... Some of these students were especially bothered by the 'unreality' of criminological studies, by which they meant the lack of sustained attention to connections between the theories and statistics about crime, and what they heard every day about relations among social conflicts, political manoeuvres, and law violation and enforcement. (quoted in Taylor *et al.*, 1973: 239)

Turk's sociology was heavily influenced by the work of the British sociologist Ralf Dahrendorf. In his conflict theory, Dahrendorf (1959) argued that members of society occupied one of two positions in any relationship: one of *domination* or one of *subjection*, and that these were not straightforwardly a reflection of property relations (as in traditional Marxist theory). Consequently, people see each other differently, conflict is inevitable, and both social norms and institutions develop in such a way as to protect the social status of those in dominant positions. Following Dahrendorf's reworking of Marxist theory, Austin Turk's conflict theory, rather than focusing on class conflict resulting from unequal access to property and the means of production, was concerned with the unequal distribution of authority in contemporary societies. He argued (1969: 43) that:

The stability of an authority relationship appears to depend far less upon subjects' conscious or unconscious belief in the rightness or legitimacy of the rank order than upon their having been conditioned to accept as a fact that authorities must be reckoned with as such.

The nature of social life is to be understood in part as a constant negotiation by individuals in different social positions as to how to behave in relation to each other. This learning of authority positions enables the social order to continue to exist. There are circumstances, Austin Turk argued, in which conflicts will arise between 'authorities' and 'subjects' and where criminalisation will be the consequence. Echoing elements of Becker's labelling theory, he argued that 'Nothing and no one is intrinsically criminal; criminality is a definition applied by individuals with the power to do so, according to illegal and extra-legal, as well as legal criteria' (1969: 10). He identified four types or levels of conflict:

- *Organised and sophisticated*—such as corporate and some organised crime.
- *Organised and unsophisticated*—such as youth offending and youth gangs.
- *Unorganised and sophisticated*—such as the con artist or fraudster.
- *Unorganised and unsophisticated*—such as thieves.

He argued that such conflict is most likely where the subjects are highly organised and relatively unsophisticated (such as in the case of delinquent gangs) and least likely where subjects are *unorganised* and *sophisticated* (such as in the case of professional con artists). A further mediating factor was the relative power of those seeking to enforce norms and those resisting them. In short, he argued that the greater the power differential, the greater the probability of criminalisation.

William Chambliss

Chambliss's work, especially his later work, is more explicitly Marxist in orientation than that of Turk, arguing that as the gap between the bourgeoisie and proletariat widens in contemporary capitalism, so it becomes necessary to use increasingly punitive measures to maintain order. Chambliss provides one of the clearest personal statements about the origins of his radical views:

> After I graduated from (UCLA) [University of California, Los Angeles], I hitchhiked across the country again to see my father. It was 1955, and in short order I was drafted into the army and sent to Korea with the Counter Intelligence Corps (CIC). I learned a lot about crime during that period. American and Korean soldiers raped, stole, assaulted, intimidated, and generally terrorised the Koreans. Because they had the power, nothing was done about it. . . . How could crime be understood from the paradigms I learned in psychology and sociology? (*The Criminologist*, 12, 1–9, quoted in Lilly *et al.,* 2002: 140)

Pursuing a Marxist-influenced analysis of crime and society, Chambliss and Seidman (1971) argued that the popular view that the law represents general social values and operates in the best interests of society is mistaken, indeed naive. Rather, they argued (1971: 73) that:

> Every detailed study of the emergence of legal norms has consistently shown the immense importance of interest group activity, not the 'public interest', as the critical variable in determining the content of legislation. To hold to the notion of natural laws emerging from the needs of society requires that we accept the highly questionable assumption that somehow interest groups operate in the best interests of society. It may be true that 'what's good for General Motors is good for society', if all the members of society benefit from the triumph of special interests. Rarely does this happen. Laws inevitably improve things for some people and make things worse for others.

They went on to argue that the more socially stratified a society becomes, the greater is the necessity for dominant social groups to enforce their supremacy through the coercive regulation of the conduct of others. By the mid-1970s Chambliss's position had further radicalised and he argued that 'crime diverts the lower classes' attention from the exploitation they experience and directs it toward other members of their own class rather than toward the capitalist class or economic system' and, furthermore and even more contentiously, that 'crime is a reality which exists only as it is created by those in the society whose interests are served by its presence' (1975: 152–3).

Some of Chambliss's most important work concerned the crimes of the powerful. In his book, *On the Take: From Petty Crooks to Presidents*, first published in 1978, he studied the relationship between organised crime and organised bureaucracy in Seattle. Based on participant observation in and around the city's bars, Chambliss eventually built a picture of a network of powerful people and groups involved in illegal activities. Some of this work is resonant of earlier studies from the Chicago School. Frederick Thrasher in his path-breaking study of Chicago's gangs in the late 1920s, for example, said:

> The politicians protect them in their practices and in return, receive the support of the gangs. We have obtained enough stuff on politicians, which if published, would turn the whole government of Chicago upside down. We also have much discreditable information on state and national politicians. The whole city political situation is unspeakably corrupt—it is impossible to exaggerate it. (Thrasher, quoted in Knox, 1994, quoted in Dimitriadis, 2006: 349)

Indeed, according to Dimitriadis (2006) Thrasher was rumoured to have had to leave Chicago because of his inside knowledge of political corruption. In a radical criminological version of C. Wright Mills's (1956) *The Power Elite*, Chambliss interpreted organised crime as a form of quintessentially capitalist activity, elements of which were protected from police intervention by the very fact of links with other powerful social interests. This is long-standing, he suggests, for 'The first President of the United States, George Washington, used the office of the presidency to enhance his personal fortune. A precedent was established that one way or another has characterized every administration since' (1978: 201). In the conclusion (1978: 209) the influence of Marxism on Chambliss's radical criminology is clear:

> Criminal behaviour is generated because of the contradictions that inevitably arise in the course of the working out of the particular form of social, political, and economic structures. The types of crime, the amount of crime, and the distribution of crime in a particular historical period and society depend on the nature of existing contradictions, and conflicts that develop as people respond to the contradictions, and the mechanisms institutionalized for handling the conflicts and dilemmas produced by the contradictions.

From Conflict to Peacemaking

In addition to Turk and Chambliss, the third important figure in American radical criminology in this period is Richard Quinney. Quinney's work has undergone a number of mutations over the years, beginning as a form of conflict theory not unlike that of Turk and Chambliss, subsequently radicalising under the influence of the Frankfurt School, latterly transforming into his more recent advocacy of what he terms 'peacemaking criminology'—influenced as much by theological writings as Marxist political economy. In his early work Quinney, like other conflict theorists, was preoccupied with the social construction of crime and how this related to the distribution of power in contemporary society. Thus, for Quinney (1970: 16) 'criminal definitions describe behaviours that conflict with the interests of segments of society that have the power to shape public policy'. By the mid-1970s Quinney's position had become even more straightforwardly Marxist, as summarised in the following six propositions (1974: 16):

1. American society is based on an advanced capitalist economy.
2. The state is organised to serve the interests of the dominant economic class, the capitalist ruling class.
3. Criminal law is an instrument of the state and ruling class to maintain and perpetuate the existing social and economic order.
4. Crime control in capitalist society is accomplished through a variety of institutions and agencies established and administered by a governmental elite, representing ruling class interests, for the purpose of establishing domestic order.
5. The contradictions of advanced capitalism—the disjunction between existence and essence—require that the subordinate classes remain oppressed by whatever means necessary, especially through the coercion and violence of the legal system.
6. Only with the collapse of capitalist society and the creation of a new society, based on socialist principles, will there be a solution to the crime problem.

He summarised his position in the following way:

> The reality of crime that is constructed for all of us by those in a position of power is the reality we tend to accept as our own. By doing so, we grant those in power the authority to carry out the actions that best promote their interests. This is the politics of reality. The social reality of crime in a politically organised society is constructed as a political act.

In *Class, State and Crime* Quinney (1977) outlined a typology of crime in which he distinguished between:

- *Crimes of domination* which included:
  - *crimes of control* such as crimes committed by the police;
  - *crimes of government*;
  - *crimes of economic domination* such as white-collar or organised corporate crime.
- *Crimes of accommodation and resistance* which included:
  - *predatory crimes* such as burglary and theft;
  - *personal crimes* such as robbery and homicide.
- *Crimes of resistance* such as political crimes and terrorism.

Chambliss on the Laws of Vagrancy

Chambliss's paper concerns the introduction of vagrancy laws in England and America. The laws in England compelled people to work, imposed a standard wage and limited the movement of workers.

[T]here has been a severe shortage of sociologically relevant analyses of the relationship between particular laws and the social setting in which these laws emerge, are interpreted, and take form...

There is general agreement among legal scholars that the first full fledged vagrancy statute was passed in England in 1349.... The prime-mover for this legislative innovation was the Black Death which struck England about 1348. Among the many disastrous consequences this had upon the social structure was the fact that it decimated the labour force. It is estimated that by the time the pestilence had run its course at last 50% of the population of England had died from the plague.... Even before the pestilence, however, the availability of an adequate supply of cheap labour was becoming a problem for the landowners...

The immediate result of these events was of course no surprise: wages for the 'free' man rose considerably and this increased, on the one hand, the landowners' problems and, on the other hand, the plight of the unfree tenant. For although wages increased for the personally free labourers, it of course did not necessarily add to the standard of living of the serf, if anything it made his position worse because the landowner would be hard pressed to pay for the personally free labour which he needed and would thus find it more and more difficult to maintain the standard of living for the serf which he had therefore supplied. Thus the serf had no alternative but flight if he chose to better his position. Furthermore, flight generally meant both freedom and better conditions since the possibility of work in the new weaving industry was great and the chance of being caught small.

It was under these conditions that we find the first vagrancy statutes emerging. There is little question but that these statutes were designed for one express purpose: to force labourers (whether personally free or unfree) to accept employment at a low wage in order to insure the landowner an adequate supply of labour at a price he could afford to pay...

... these laws were a legislative innovation which reflected the socially perceived necessity of providing an abundance of cheap labour to landowners during a period when serfdom was breaking down and when the pool of available labour was depleted...

This analysis of the vagrancy statutes... has demonstrated the importance of 'vested interest groups in the emergence and/or alteration of laws. The vagrancy laws emerged in order to provide the powerful landowners with a ready supply of cheap labour. When this was no longer seen as necessary and particularly when the landowners were no longer dependent upon cheap labour nor were they a powerful interest group in the society, the laws became dormant.

Source: Chambliss (1964: 67–77).

By the time of the second edition of the book, although Quinney continued to advocate responses that would be identified as socialist, he also 'increasingly emphasised the *religious* nature of the goal, going so far as to reject Marxist materialism' (Lilly *et al.*, 2002: 152) arguing that political consciousness in late capitalism 'is increasingly accompanied by a consciousness about matters of ultimate concern' (Quinney, 1980: 112). Within a short period Quinney's approach had shifted significantly away from his earlier Marxist position and gradually coalesced, in part through his work with Hal Pepinsky, into what he came to refer to as 'peacemaking criminology'. Though continuing from the baseline assumption that conflict is a root cause of crime, peacemaking criminology seeks solutions that do not involve the further infliction of violence and pain and, rather, stresses conflict resolution, mediation and conciliation. Thus, the traditional approach of the criminal justice system, according to Quinney, is to impose a form of 'negative peace' through the use of threats and sanctions. Peacemaking criminology involves a search for means of establishing 'positive peace' (1997: 117):

> There can be no peace—no positive peace—without social justice. Without social justice and without peace (personal and social), there is crime. And there is, as well, the violence of criminal justice.... Criminal justice keeps things as they are. Social policies and programs that are positive in nature–that focus on positive peacemaking—create something new. They eliminate the structural sources of violence and crime. A critical, peacemaking criminologist is engaged in the work of positive peace.

Quinney's later peacemaking criminology was, in his words, more influenced by socialist humanism than Marxism and took as its objective being 'kind to one another, to transcend the barriers that separate us from one another, and to live everyday life with a sense of interdependence' (Quinney, 2000: 26). It took much of the language of pacifism, and elements of Buddhism, to mount a critique of the violence that was perceived to lie both at the heart of our responses to crime as well as framing the way we talk about crime. It rejected retributive forms of punishment and sought to direct attention to the need to improve social and individual relationships as the basis for solving conflict. More recently, Fuller (2003) has outlined what he calls a 'peacemaking pyramid paradigm' in an attempt to use the perspective as the basis for constructing practical programmes to address the problem of crime. The paradigm has six major characteristics:

- *Non-violence*—Peacemaking attempts to eschew violence and is, therefore, against capital punishment.
- *Social justice*—It aims to be anti-discriminatory.
- *Inclusion*—Involving those from the most affected communities, and including victims and others in criminal justice processes.
- *Correct means*—Protecting due process and ensuring that coercion isn't used.
- *Ascertainable criteria*—Everyone involved in criminal justice processes should understand and be aware of rules, regulations and procedures.
- *Categorical imperative*—Everyone should be treated with respect and dignity.

Similar practical and normative features can be found in much conflict resolution and restorative justice theory and practice and, indeed, peacemaking criminology has strong links with both the alternative dispute resolution movement and with restorative justice.

Radical Criminology in Britain

Somewhat later than it had appeared in the United States, radical criminology began to emerge in the UK. Once again, though, this development was very much a child of the times, reflecting the emergent radical political developments of the period; developments that sought to challenge established ways of thinking and behaving and, not least, that sought to challenge the established forms of authority.

According to Jock Young (1988: 159) 'British criminology in the late 1960s was at a cross-roads. The social democratic positivism which had been dominant in the post-war period entered into a period of prolonged crisis, out of which emerged the two major contending paradigms: radical criminology and administrative criminology.' By administrative criminology, Young meant a form of inquiry that was largely empiricist and narrowly policy-oriented in its focus. By contrast, radical criminology was 'that part of the discipline which sees the causes of crime as being at core the class and patriarchal relations endemic to our social order and which sees fundamental changes as necessary to reduce criminality' (1988: 160).

In the UK the organisational home of radical criminology was the National Deviancy Conference which was established in the late 1960s and disappeared in the late 1970s. Jock Young describes its thrust as follows:

> Positivism was perhaps the main enemy: its ontology was seen to take human creativity out of deviant action, its sociology erected a consensual edifice from which deviants were bereft of culture and meaning, its methodology elevated experts to the role of fake scientists discovering the 'laws' of social action and its policy, whether in mental hospitals, social work agencies or drug clinics, was self-fulfilling and mystifying. (Young, 1998: 17)

Crucial to this development was the 'impact of the West Coast labelling theory centring around Howard Becker which set the creaking chariot of radical criminology off on its course' (Young, 1988: 163) and also to the social movements and politics of the 1960s (Scraton and Chadwick, 1991). Labelling theory had identified the source of deviance in social reaction and pointed to the importance of understanding the way in which the power to label was utilised. Out of an amalgam of Durkheimian sociology, interactionism, labelling theory and Marxism there emerged a new criminology in Britain that was intent on achieving a radical break with previous theoretical approaches.

The New Criminology

In 1973, Ian Taylor, Paul Walton and Jock Young published their manifesto for a critically engaged criminology: *The New Criminology*. In the book and through their critique of existing criminological theories, they suggested that what they wished to develop was a fully 'social theory of deviance'. Although forewords to books are probably slightly unreliable guides to the import of what follows—the author of the foreword is naturally positively inclined toward the merits of the work—Alvin Gouldner's assessment of *The New Criminology* is nevertheless worth repeating:

> If any single book can succeed in making 'criminology' intellectually serious, as distinct from professionally respectable, then this study, remarkable for its combination of the analytical with the historical,

will do it... . What this important study does then, is this: it redirects the total structure of technical discourse concerning 'crime' and 'deviance'. (Gouldner, 1973: ix)

Not only did *The New Criminology* seek to make a radical break with what it took to be positivist criminology, it also sought to develop a highly politicised position, taking the view that 'any criminology which is not normatively committed to the abolition of inequalities of wealth and power, and in particular of inequalities in property and life-chances, is inevitably bound to fall into correctionalism' (1973: 281). The task, according to the authors, was 'to create a society in which the facts of human diversity, whether personal, organic or social, are not subject to the power to criminalize' (*ibid.*).

By contrast, a fully social theory, such as that they were attempting to construct must, they said, break entirely with correctionalism, in which they included even the social reform efforts advocated and engaged in by the Chicago School theorists. Lanier and Henry (1998) summarise the radical theory offered in *The New Criminology*, and by other radical criminologists such as Spitzer, Quinney (in his earlier guise) and Chambliss, in the following six statements:

1. *Capitalism shapes social institutions, social identities, and social action*—The mode of production shapes the nature of social institutions and the behaviour and activities of individuals within those institutions.
2. *Capitalism creates class conflict and contradictions*—The nature of contemporary capitalism impoverishes the working class and restricts their ability to resist or change the system.
3. *Crime is a response to capitalism and its contradictions*—Crime is a logical or rational response to the structural position people find themselves in under capitalism and, in some cases, a form of resistance or rebellion.
4. *Capitalist law facilitates and conceals crimes of domination and repression*—The focus on the behaviour of the subordinated class deflects attention from the crimes of the powerful (including by the state itself).
5. *Crime is functional to capitalism*—Crime provides work (for those in criminal justice) and legitimises the operation of the system of law and justice.
6. *Capitalism shapes society's response to crime by shaping law*—The content of the criminal law reflects the need to control subordinated social classes and protect the property of the powerful; the law enables the continuation of the capitalist system of production, in part by protecting the interests of the powerful and by shaping the behaviour of the powerless. As Scraton and Chadwick (1991: 181) put it, 'The criminal justice process and the rule of law assist in the management of structural contradictions and the process of criminalization is central to such management.'

Taylor *et al.*, (1973) rejected the passive view of the offender that appeared in much criminology—what Gouldner referred to as 'man on his back'—and started out from the view of the deviant as 'a decision-maker who actively violates the moral and legal codes of society' (1973: 163). Building on Marxist foundations, they examined and developed a critique of the criminogenic consequences of capitalism. They argued explicitly that 'much deviance is in itself political' (as, indeed, was their project in response: see below). However, as Tierney (1996: 157) notes, two years later 'by 1975, with the publication of a follow-up collection of readings, *Critical Criminology* (Taylor *et al.*, 1975), Jock Young was already starting to review his position'. Tierney (1996: 183) suggests that the position adopted by Taylor, Walton and Young in *The New Criminology* can be summarised in five main points:

- They adopted and espoused a commitment to a *normative* criminology–their work was part of a larger political project. This project was to 'argue for a criminology which is normatively committed to the abolition of inequalities of wealth and power [and]...to attempt to create the kind of society in which the facts of human diversity are not subject to the power to criminalise' (Taylor *et al.*, 1975: 44).
- They envisaged a socialist future in which crime as we currently understand it, would be absent.
- They sought to create a sociological criminology that was simultaneously anti-positivist yet avoided the relativism that some of the more subjectivist accounts of crime fall into.
- Great emphasis was placed upon the structural constraints and determinants of human action, not least the impact of class society.
- A central feature of their explanation was the role of the state and the main powerful institutions of society—in this explanation crime was a rational response to the social arrangements of a capitalist political economy.

The New Criminology was both normative and highly idealistic. Its authors argued that 'close reading of the classical social theorists reveals a basic agreement; the abolition of crime is possible under certain social arrangements' (Taylor *et al.*, 1973: 281). The task for *The New Criminology*, they argued, 'is to create a society in which the facts of human diversity, whether personal, organic or social, are not subject to the power to criminalize' (1973: 282).

Contemporary Radical Criminology

Although there has been a marked turn away from Marxist theory in contemporary criminology, elements of such thinking can still regularly be found. In particular, the work of Antonio Gramsci (see box) and his notion of 'hegemony' remains of considerable importance. Building on Marx's notions of class conflict, Gramsci sought to explain how ruling classes maintain their position of dominance without relying on force. His argument, in brief, was that the consent and cooperation of the masses was secured through *hegemonic strategies*. These strategies—which are cultural and ideological—generate and maintain popular support for existing relations. Subordinate groups are, in effect, persuaded of, rather than forced to accept, the normality and legitimacy of current social arrangements. The means by which hegemony is achieved, and consequences of challenges to hegemony, have been important tools in elements of radical criminology.

As one example, Beckett and Sasson (2000) use elements of Gramsci's theory as the basis for analysing changes in the nature of American crime control policy from the New Deal in the 1930s to the present day. From the 1930s, they argue, the USA used social policies focused on poverty-reduction and tackling related social problems, together with a partially welfarist criminal justice policy in which rehabilitation was an important facet, as its primary means of governing the population and maintaining order and stability. However, the upheavals of the late 1960s/1970s brought various challenges to the established order—not least via the civil rights movement, the campaign against the war in Vietnam and the rise of

Antonio Gramsci (1891–1937)

Born in Sardinia in 1891, one of seven children, Antonio Gramsci initially left school at 11 in order to work to help support his impoverished family (his father had been imprisoned after being accused of embezzlement). He continued to study and eventually was able to return to school and in 1911 won a scholarship to the University of Turin. He studied linguistics, humanities and courses in the social sciences, also joining the Italian Communist Party and becoming involved in radical politics. By 1915 he was working as a journalist and became an important radical voice on both the local and national political scene. In the early 1920s he spent 18 months living in Russia as an Italian delegate to the Communist International (also known as Comintern, an organisation set up in 1919 to support international communism). Gramsci met his future wife whilst working as a delegate to Comintern. In November 1926

Antonio Gramsci (1891–1937). Italian journalist and political philosopher, imprisoned by Mussolini's fascists, his *Prison Notebooks* had a huge impact on twentieth-century radical thought.

Copyright in the Public Domain.

he was arrested and imprisoned by Mussolini's fascists. He remained in hospital until 1933, his poor health leading to his transfer to a clinic and then hospital subsequently—though always under guard. He died in 1937 from a cerebral haemorrhage. It is his *Prison Notebooks* and the idea of 'cultural hegemony' for which he is now chiefly remembered.

the youth counter-culture. Together, 'these protest movements constituted a serious "counter-hegemonic" challenge to prevailing social and economic arrangements' (2000: 66).

The consequence, Beckett and Sasson (2000) argue, was a political reaction which sought to re-establish hegemony by abandoning the 'inclusionary' social policies that had developed since the 1930s and, instead, sought to discredit the socially marginal. The new model of governing shrank the welfare state and expanded what one might think of as the 'security state'. At the core of this new strategy were the 'war on drugs' and the 'war on crime' and the shift toward the use of incarceration as a standard means of dealing with offending. This, together with the introduction of mandatory minimum ('three strikes') sentences, the scaling back of parole and the revival of the death penalty was, Beckett and Sasson (2000: 68) suggest, 'a hegemonic project of the ruling class, speatheaded by political conservatives (neoliberals and social conservatives) in response to the various challenges of the late 1960s and early 1970s'.

Zemiology

More recently a number of radical criminologists have also begun once again to question the entire criminological enterprise. Given that one of the fundamentals of much radical scholarship is to treat categories such as *crime* as being deeply problematic, this raises awkward issues for the criminologist and, they suggest, should make one ask 'what is the theoretical rationale and political utility of retaining a commitment to the analysis of crime, (criminal) law and the criminal justice system?' (Hillyard *et al.*, 2004b: 1).

Their response is to offer an alternative focus for such scholarship: social harm. The intention is to broaden the focus of inquiry beyond crime to various social phenomena that cause harm (irrespective of whether or not they are currently defined as criminal). At one stage such an approach was known by the label *zemiology,* though in recent times the terminology appears to have been dropped. A recent important collection (Hillyard *et al.*, 2004) designed to illustrate the breadth and strengths of such an approach, includes a range of thoughtful and provocative articles on topics such as state harms, migration, workplace injury and death, and poverty. It is perhaps particularly in the area of corporate (mis)conduct that the potential strength of an approach that is not limited by a concern with 'crime' is clearest.

Zemiology, or whatever the study of social harms comes to be called, is unlikely to displace criminology, at least not in the short term. Nevertheless, it presents a healthy reminder to criminologists of one of the more obvious limitations of their subject as well, potentially, as being a focus for what will likely stimulate important and provocative research.

Assessing Radical Criminology

The influence of Marx and Engels runs through criminology just as it does through sociology. Though they had relatively little to say about crime—particularly Marx—their analysis of social organisation, power and exploitation had a powerful impact upon much twentieth-century criminology, particularly in the post-war period. More particularly, the idea of *criminalisation* has been a hugely important organising idea in both radical/critical and what are sometimes referred to as social constructionist theories of crime. And, yet, despite this influence, radical criminology is, currently at least, somewhat marginalised within contemporary scholarship.

In part this is a reflection of the times; the political context in which criminology is practised. However, it is also because, intellectually, elements of radical criminology have been subjected to sustained and substantive criticism, sometimes from within. Three criticisms have been voiced most frequently, those of teleology; determinism; and idealism.

Teleology

First, in certain versions of critical criminology there is a teleological, almost conspiratorially functionalist quality. Put in simpler language, it appears that some radical theories view crime or deviance as a straightforward product of capitalism and the operation of the criminal justice system as seamlessly meeting the needs of capitalism. Working-class resistance is criminalised—the process of criminalisation being an important part of the maintenance of the capitalist system. At its worst the argument is entirely circular. Criminal law as currently constituted is vital in sustaining class domination. Crime is therefore *functional* so far as capitalism is concerned. But showing that something has a social function is not the same as explaining why it occurs or exists (as Durkheim observed). The historian E.P. Thompson was particularly critical of some Marxist theory which he felt overlooked the 'difference between arbitrary power and the rule of law. We ought to expose the shams and inequities which may be concealed beneath this law. But the rule of law itself…seems to me to be an unqualified human good' (1975: 266).

Determinism

Second, some critics have argued that the new criminology suffered from just the sort of determinism for which its authors had criticised others. In particular, the structural features of capitalism appear to produce effects that allow for little human agency or resistance. In some radical theorising the contradictions of capitalism, or the structural imbalance between social classes, appears to be the crucial determinant of criminal conduct, overriding all other considerations and in which the individual actor, as Taylor *et al.* (1975: 108) said of Mertonian anomie theory, 'boxed into a fixed social position—is rarely seen to evolve a solution to his problem in his own terms'.

One of the most trenchant critics of *The New Criminology* was Paul Hirst (1975a, 1975b), who argued that crime and deviance were not proper objects of study. He was also critical of the 'crime as resistance and rebellion' thesis that appeared to lie at the heart of much conflict theory: 'The romanticisation of crime, the recognition in the criminal of a rebel "alienated" from society, is, for Marxism, a dangerous political ideology. It leads *inevitably*…to the estimation of the lumpenprole-tariat as a revolutionary force' (1975a: 218).

Some critics have also argued that there is little empirical support for radical criminological ideas. Klockars (1979) suggested that Marxist criminologists appeared like 'true believers' in a 'new religion' and argued that such ideas were able to explain neither the relatively low crime rates in some capitalist societies nor the problems that existed in communist societies. Klockars (1979: 506) accuses such theorists of utopianism and critical irresponsibility:

> By presenting itself as an ideal and as inevitable, of inexorably moving toward a crime-free, unexploitive, unrepressive, unoppressive future, Marxist theory relieves itself of all responsibility for the exploitation, crime and human abuse which has been and continues to be perpetuated in its name.

Though less a criticism of critical criminology than simply a reflection upon the state of affairs in British criminology in the early 1980s, Stan Cohen (1981: 236) noted its lack of impact:

> There are more corners and cavities than ten years ago, but for the most part the institutional foundations of British criminology remain intact and unaltered, for the establishment saw the new theories as simply fashion which eventually pass over or as a few interesting ideas which could be swallowed up without changing the existing paradigm at all.

Idealism

As was implied in the earlier discussion, some Marxist treatments of crime appear somewhat idealistic, not least in their portrayal of the possibility of a crime-free society. Similarly, the tendency in elements of critical criminology to view criminal activity as a form of resistance—as a political or quasi-political act—arguably led to the underestimation of the impact of crime on the working classes. Indeed, this observation was one of the stimuli for the development of left realism. Jock Young, one of the most impor tant figures in radical criminology in Britain, also became one of its most vocal critics. In outlining the case for a realist criminology, he and Roger Matthews (Matthews and Young, 1986: 1) were highly critical of its failures:

> The tide is turning for radical criminology. For over two decades it has neglected the effect of crime upon the victim and concentrated on the impact of the state—through the process of labelling–on the criminal. There was nothing wrong with this *per se*. It was a necessary antidote to orthodox criminology.... But radical analysis also lost touch with the most obvious focus of criminology—crime itself. It became an advocate for the indefensible: the criminal became the victim, the state the solitary focus of attention, while the real victim remained off-stage.

DISCUSSION QUESTIONS
By John M. Stogner

1. Do radical and critical criminological theories present an inaccurate depiction of capitalism and/or socialism?
2. What is peacemaking criminology?
3. Are radical and critical criminological theories testable and falsifiable?
4. Does equality eliminate crime? If everyone has the same resources, would some individuals still choose to steal or victimize others?
5. Do you see this perspective gaining greater attention in the next two decades? Why or why not?

CPSIA information can be obtained
at www.ICGtesting.com
Printed in the USA
LVHW050523160920
666097LV00003B/8

9 781634 873963